Public Management in Korea

Many books on performance management or evaluation are about the public sector in general or specifically about some programs or organizations. Only a few of them target the public institutions. This book addresses what types of challenges that performance evaluations of public institutions actually face and how to overcome them through the analysis of Korea's three-decade long experiences.

This book provides detailed descriptions on how performance evaluations of public institutions have been implemented in Korea. At the same time, it provides comprehensive analyses on theoretical issues such as validity analysis performance measure, the dynamic change of efficiency of public institution, impact of price regulation on profits, and qualitative approaches for evaluating governance.

Each chapter contains vivid theoretical debates and diverse views on performance evaluation and practical challenges, making the book a useful reference on managing and evaluating public institutions.

Soonae Park is Professor at the Graduate School of Public Administration, Seoul National University.

T0371630

Routledge Advances in Korean Studies

Modern Korea and its Others
Perceptions of the Neighbouring Countries and Korean Modernity
Vladimir Tikhonov

Samsung, Media Empire and Family
A Power Web
Chunhyo Kim

The Korean Tradition of Religion, Society and Ethics
A Comparative and Historical Self-understanding and Looking Beyond
Chai-sik Chung

Change and Continuity in North Korean Politics
*Edited by Adam Cathcart, Robert Winstanley-Chesters and
Christopher Green*

The Personalist Ethic and the Rise of Urban Korea
Chang Yun-Shik

Strategic, Policy and Social Innovation for a Post-Industrial Korea
Beyond the Miracle
Joon Nak Choi, Yong Suk Lee and Gi-Wook Shin

North Korea's Foreign Policy
The DPRK Part on the International Scene and Its Audiences
Lenka Caisova

Public Management in Korea
Performance Evaluation and Public Institutions
Edited by Soonae Park

For more information about this series, please visit: www.routledge.com/asian studies/series/SE0505

Public Management in Korea

Performance Evaluation and
Public Institutions

Edited by Soonae Park

Routledge
Taylor & Francis Group

LONDON AND NEW YORK

First published 2019
by Routledge
2 Park Square, Milton Park, Abingdon, Oxon OX14 4RN

and by Routledge
605 Third Avenue, New York, NY 10017

First issued in paperback 2020

Routledge is an imprint of the Taylor & Francis Group, an informa business

British Library Cataloguing-in-Publication Data
A catalogue record for this book is available from the British Library

Library of Congress Cataloging-in-Publication Data
A catalog record for this book has been requested

ISBN 13: 978-0-367-50409-0 (pbk)
ISBN 13: 978-1-138-48094-0 (hbk)

Typeset in Times New Roman
by Apex CoVantage, LLC

Contents

Figures

Tables

Preface

It was in the year 2003 that I first participated in an evaluation team for the performance evaluation of Korean government-invested institutions. At that time, the team consisting of five–six members evaluating about ten government-invested institutions and evaluation indicators of individual institutions were assigned to each member. The Korea Trade-Investment Promotion Agency and the Korea Agricultural and Rural Infrastructure Corporation (current Korea Rural Community Corporation) were categorized as government-invested institutions in the early 2000s. Afterwards, the performance evaluation system has been evolving and developing further as the evaluations of government-invested institutions and government-affiliated organizations were integrated by the Act on the Management of Public Institutions. The role of the performance evaluation system has become increasingly important, as the public have more concerned themselves with the performance of public institutions.

Ever since the Korean War, regardless of the government's political positions through time, there have been nation-wide hopes with which the people anticipate the public institutions to properly function. The public institutions were the core entities responsible for the production and provision of necessities of life in the times when the people were unable to even feed and house themselves, not to mention the absence of social infrastructure. The responsibilities of the public institutions have continuously broadened during and after the era of economic growth to building social infrastructure, supplying housing nationwide, developing overseas resources, and bridging for the reunification of Korea. Even now in the era of the 4th industrial revolution based on artificial intelligence (AI) and the internet of things (IoT), the government encourages public institutions to realize government's policy agenda such as job creation and social responsibilities. The performance evaluation system has continuously tried to improve the performance of public institutions under the banners of innovation, advancement, rationalization, and normalization.

Ironically, the public institutions are repeatedly considered as targets of reformation, even after the ceaseless efforts for performance improvement and innovation. As a scholar as well as an experienced expert, I am on the way to finding answers for the irony. The first attempt was publishing a book – *Public Corporation Reforms* – in which 16 issues related to the performance of public corporations were introduced and analyzed. Specifically, the book studied such issues as corporate governance, labor-management relations, privatization policy, public debt and utility fees, and the performance evaluation system. While the aforementioned book put an effort to seek measures to overcome the agency problems such as sloppy management and to maintain balance between publicness and efficiency, this present book takes a step further and focuses particularly on how to measure the performance more objectively.

Looking back at the history of the evolution of the performance evaluation system in countries such as the United States and the United Kingdom, much of the effort is concentrated on the development of performance indicators. While the targets of the evaluation and the follow-up measures, i.e. who participates in the evaluation process and what measures will be taken, were of constant interest, there have been controversies over what performance means in case of public institutions that run on the taxes of the people. In order to look for the answers for "how and what to measure," a series of seminars with the topic "Performance Measurement and Management in Public Sector" was conducted from September to December 2016 by the Public Performance Management Center at the Graduate School of Public Administration, Seoul National University. Many established scholars in the area of performance evaluation of public institutions were invited, and various topics were discussed in depth. This book is the result of the seminar work, covering the following topics: the historical transitions of the social values and publicness pursued by public institutions, the development of performance indicators, and issues related to the governance of performance evaluation.

Part I 'Overview' consists of four chapters. Chapter 1 "Performance evaluation of public institutions in Korea: historical evolution and challenges for the future" reviews the historical background of performance evaluation systems in Korea, focusing on legal and institutional frameworks as well as evaluation models. In addition, this chapter discusses various issues, including the current state and challenges of performance evaluation in Korea by analyzing longitudinal data related to evaluation results. Finally, lessons learned from the Korea case and policy implications for the future are suggested.

Chapter 2 "Achievements of the performance evaluation of public institutions: financial efficiency vs. publicness" analyzes the development of indicators based on the review of performance evaluation manuals from the past 20 years. Financial performances were analyzed by the indicators, such as the ROA and the ROS of the public corporations in the energy and social infrastructure sectors. Moreover, the indicators related to the publicness in both common management and main business activities were reviewed in order to identify the nation-wide public expectations toward the realization of public values.

Chapter 3 "Proper understanding of developing performance indicators and performance management in the public sector" studies appropriate performance indicators of public institutions, considering different characteristics of performance of the public sector from the private sector. The public sector requires us to focus on responsiveness to the demand of citizens. This responsiveness measures have an important meaning for the society in the sense that they reflect situational validation and societal vindication. This chapter discusses what should be considered to do right things right, using proper performance indicators in the public sector.

The last chapter in Part II, Chapter 4, "Improvements of management and the performance evaluation system of public institutions in the view of strategic performance management," reviews the current state and problems of the performance management in both national and individual institutional management aspects based on the strategic performance management model suggested by BearingPoint (2004). The author points out the problems of a dual system and suggests the fundamental reform of the performance evaluation system that has abnormally strengthened the evaluation and compensation function. He also emphasizes the strategic linkage function through reviewing and periodically updating the performance plans.

Part III "Performance evaluation and governance" consists of 4 chapters and covers issues related to core stakeholders of the performance evaluation, including main business activities of the institution, corporate governance, and labor-management relations.

First, in Chapter 5 "The views and measures of main business activities evaluation of public institutions revisited: focusing on the evolutionary logic model and evaluability assessment," the author criticizes that the current evaluation may involve fallacy of over-simplification in a complex atmosphere due to its limitation as a simple logic model, focusing on the cycle of Plan-Do-See-Act. This may lead to discordance between evaluation result and public opinion and degrading its result onto mere tools of classifying rankings for redistributing performance incentives. In the conclusion, he suggests possible remedies for better performance evaluation based on the theory of change and the complicated-complex logic model that could be applied to other developing countries.

Chapter 6 "Evaluation system for the heads of public institutions: current status and issues" reviews the chief executive performance evaluation system in public institutions. It is inevitable to evaluate the performance of the heads of public institutions, to check whether they have been simultaneously pursuing publicness and efficiency, because such institutions are funded by taxes. The evaluation system for the heads of public institutions in Korea is recognized as being very well established. This chapter intends to take a closer look at the evaluation system and its criteria in order to improve and enhance the system.

Chapter 7 "Analysis of the standing auditors' evaluation system and the performance indicators: with a focus on expertise" introduces the system for the performance evaluation of standing auditors of public institutions and its indicators, and then empirically analyzes the relationship between standing auditors' expertise level and evaluation results. The author emphasizes the importance of political implications surrounding the expertise of executive auditors. The expertise of the executive auditors was conceptualized separately into essential and supplementary expertise in order to determine whether the executive auditors who received performance fulfillment evaluations based on their career in years 2011–2012 and 2014–2015 possessed expected expertise.

The last chapter in Part II, Chapter 8 "Industrial relations and the performance evaluation of public institutions," proposes lessons that the following factors are necessary to improve the industrial relations: trust and cooperation between the labor and management, sharing of management information, active communication, investment in education and training, fair compensation and treatment, guarantee of worker participation, and the establishment of a productive bargaining culture. At the same time, the labor and management in public institutions should take joint responsibility and work together to establish industrial relations that could create sustainable values that contribute to social integration and development.

Part III 'Performance measurement and indicators' consists of seven chapters and analyzes the current state and problems related to the performance indicators under the performance evaluation system.

Chapter 9 "Target-setting in performance evaluation and public institutions' incentives" observes a ratchet effect on performance targets of public institutions through empirical work and then investigates what makes this happen under the current performance evaluation system. The author provides a variety of empirical findings such as target ratcheting phenomena, a negative association between ratcheting intensity and target achievability, serial correlation in target achievability, performance management, and effort reduction. Based on these empirical findings, he suggests that the qualitative evaluation should be incorporated into the quantitative analysis, and the qualitative levels should be considered not only in the target-setting stage but also in the final evaluation stage.

Chapter 10 "Issues in quantitative evaluation" reviews performance indicators on work efficiency under the current performance evaluation system and discuss related issues such as weights on the indicators and a link between evaluation results and payoffs. The author suggests evaluating the governance system rather than the performance itself in order to keep the performance indicator formula simple and to reduce evaluation costs. Further suggestions include lowering weights on productivity and efficiency to help institutions focus on primary goals. While a secure connection between performance and performance-related pay makes employees in public institutions work for the performance indicators, it creates incentives for the manipulation of indicators and results.

Chapter 11 "Investigation of theoretical foundation for quantitative indicator target assignment (deviation) evaluation method in performance evaluation of public institutions" aims to clarify the theoretical foundation of target assignment evaluation method which basically calculates a five-year standard deviation of a given quantitative indicator and grants full score for performance improvement in excess of one or two standard deviations above last year's performance. Instead of pointing out the problems of target assignment (deviation) evaluation method, the author shows that the perspectives of the post-evaluation and pre-incentives were separately analyzed to observe what purposes could be achieved in exploring the legitimacy of the evaluation method.

Chapter 12 "Empirical analysis of efficiency improvement in public corporations using data envelopment analysis (DEA)" tries to analyze how the economic efficiency of 27 public corporations has been changed between 2007 and 2015, using the semi-oriented radial model of data envelopment analysis. The results of analyses suggest that DEA can produce fairly robust results on the trend of efficiency and suggest the possibility of using DEA for the performance evaluation of public corporations. In particular, the efficiency trends were classified into 4 types: monotonic increase, U-shaped, inversed-U shape, and monotonic decrease. Such classification suggests the heterogeneous trends in efficiency of public corporations and calls for more individualized performance evaluation strategies according to the efficiency level of each public corporation.

Chapter 13 "Collaboration and performance evaluation: context and indicators" introduces the role of quasi-governmental institutions focusing on the cooperation. Quasi-governmental institutions in Korea have been established in the policy area of industry, employment, public health, safety, and environment. They have played a key role in developing policy implementation networks and facilitating collaboration between the public and private sectors. Although the practice of collaboration gains popularity and legitimacy in these days, there is the paucity of appropriate quantitative performance indicators to measure the performance by collaboration. The author analyzes performance indicators from the perspective of how much they reflect the performance through collaboration with other actors, and suggest practical implications for designing performance indicators to facilitate collaboration.

Chapter 14 "Public utility performance indicators under price regulation" investigates the hypothesis that the price regulation of public utilities leads to public institution's overinvestment. Especially the author verifies empirically that the rate-of-return regulations incur excessive investment from the public institutions through the example case of the Korea Water Resources Corporation. He also reviews the necessary conditions for the performance indicators influenced by the charges regulations and discusses appropriate performance indicators under the price regulation. The author concludes that the evaluation indicators under the current evaluation system contribute to some extent to mitigate the side-effects of the rate-of-return regulations.

The last chapter of this book, Chapter 15 "Plan for constructing performance governance of public corporations," studies performance indicators of Korea Electric Power Corporation (KEPCO) and makes suggestions for better indicators. The author evaluates the performance management of the Korean electric power industry using a model of Bouckaert and Halligan (2008). He emphasizes that individual performance management needs to be converted into performance governance model system by applying the concept of social governance that is linked to the overall performance management system.

The performance evaluation system tends to exert influence over public institution's goals and priorities in forceful ways. Although this characteristic is often criticized, the importance of the performance evaluation system cannot be emphasized more. The performance evaluation system is like a compass with which public institutions can actively modify their visions to fulfill the hopes of the public in the changing socio-economic environments and to contemplate what should be prepared for future generations. I expect that this book would contribute to the improvement of the performance evaluation system by giving insights into critical issues such as the primary objectives for public institutions, the design of performance indicators, corporate governance, and labor-management relations. I hope that our discussions and results would be valuable sources for the establishment of performance evaluation systems in many developing countries. This book was published with supports and efforts of many people including the co-authors. I would like to thank all the family of Routledge, especially for Ms. Samantha Phua and Ms. Yongling Lam, and special thanks to Prof. Kilkon Ko, Dr. Jinsub Choi who carefully reviewed every chapter, Hyeyeon Lee, Ahyoung Cho, and Doyeon Hwang, Ami Kim, and Jaeseon Lee, who spared no pains to publish this book.

Contributors

Daesik Choi is Certified Public Labor Attorney and Visiting Professor at the Graduate School of Business, Konkuk University.

Taehyon Choi is Associate Professor at the Graduate School of Public Administration, Seoul National University.

Youn Sik Choi is Associate Professor at School of Management, Kyung Hee University.

Tae Ho Eom is Professor at the Department of Public Administration, Yonsei University.

Kil Pyo Hong is Professor of Business Management at Baekseok University.

Sounman Hong is Associate Professor at the Department of Public Administration, Yonsei University.

Bong Hwan Kim is Associate Professor at the Graduate School of Public Administration, Seoul National University.

Kil Kon Ko is Associate Professor at the Graduate School of Public Administration, Seoul National University.

Illoong Kwon is Professor at the Graduate School of Public Administration, Seoul National University.

Seok-Hwan Lee is Professor of Public Administration, Kookmin University.

Soo Young Lee is Associate Professor at the Graduate School of Public Administration, Seoul National University.

Youngmi Lee is Budget Analyst at the National Assembly Budget Office.

Soonae Park is Professor at the Graduate School of Public Administration, Seoul National University.

Jieun Son is Senior Research Fellow at the Evaluation Institute of Regional Public Corporation, Seoul National University

Gu Hwan Won is Professor at the Department of Public Administration, Hannam University.

Yoon Seuk Woo is Professor at the Department of Public Administration, Soong-sil University.

Acknowledgements

This book was supported by research grant from Seoul National University.

The book is part of the Research Series of Public Performance Research Center, Graduate School of Public Administration, Seoul National University.

Part I
Overview

1 Performance evaluation of public institutions in Korea

Historical evolution and challenges for the future

Soonae Park

I Introduction

The Performance Evaluation of Public Institutions (PEPI) is conducted every year in Korea, and its results are of the people's great interest. The media covers the entire process from formation of the evaluation team to announcement of the results in special feature series, and politicians and academia criticize the validity and fairness of the process. Moreover, employees in the public sector as well as civic groups participate in continuous discussions about the relevance of the evaluated materials and enhancement of democracy in the evaluation process. Considering the roles and performance of the public institutions in the Korean society, such attention is likely to sustain in the future. The former administrations tended to exert authority to make public institutions to cooperate with their policy agenda, and such a practice seems to be difficult to change due to path dependency. From 'Fatherland Modernization, Economic Independence' of the Park Chung-hee administration, Gaesong Industrial Complex Project of the Kim Dae-Jung administration, and Construction of Innovative Cities of the Roh Moo-Hyun to the Overseas Resource Development and 4 Major Rivers Restoration Projects of the Lee Myung-Bak administration, the government has been cooperating with public institutions to attain major government projects. Thereby the public sector has performed roles in various areas ranging from economic development, social stability, welfare, unification, and regional development (Park and Lee, 2014). It is indisputable that Korea would not have secured a space in the list of top ten largest economies without the efforts of the government and public institutions, provided that there were times when essential infrastructure for national development and lives of the people were absolutely in shortage after the war and division of Korea.

In the era of economic development, the first priority of public institutions was to achieve its original goals such as building infrastructure and providing housing. Therefore, performance evaluation functioned as a management procedure to check execution rate. However, questions were raised about the inefficiency of the bloated public sector after the achievement of economic development. Eventually, a series of innovative measures in accordance with the 'new public management' approach was executed as the Kim Dae-Jung administration set a political slogan of small government and strong market as a solution to overcome the economic crisis. Such demands of the times have generated the development of PEPI into a core system for maximizing the efficiency in business administration and project implementation. The economic crisis that occurred in the late 1990s has changed the role of PEPI from preliminary examination for budget allocation and project execution status to a management system for checking the functionality and improving performances. As the people were considered as clients, their satisfaction in addition to the cost and efficiency became important.

Has the PEPI system evolved responding to the demands of the age? It can be said that the system has changed to facilitate preemptive responses of public institutions to the political demands and environmental change. For example, the Moon Jae-in administration highlights the function of PEPI in the emphasized role of public institutions to solve critical social problems such as low birth rate and high youth unemployment rate. Moreover, the role of public institutions is redirected from the past public service provision paradigm focused on provision of visible goods toward responding to various public value-oriented political demands in areas including welfare, labor, education, and housing. In order to incorporate such values into the performance evaluation process, the system has been modified to include indicators for job creation, work-life balance, etc. Individual researchers on this topic (Park, 2009; Kwak and Lee, 2010) have a general consensus that the PEPI system can function as a measure to effectively control the behavior of public institutions in the context of the principal-agent problem to further provide responsibility and motivation to workers for management innovation, improving performance, and enhancing management transparency.

This chapter reviews the transition of the performance management paradigm in the public sector in general and then examines the evolution of the PEPI system in Korea and characteristics of its evaluation models and indicators. Moreover, further directions for the system should follow and political implications are suggested.

II Transition of the performance management paradigm in the public sector

Experts provide different indices for classifying the performance evaluation in the public sector by time. For example, Van Dooren et al. (2010) explains how the performance-oriented social atmosphere was created and evolved by dividing the entire paradigm into 1900–1940, which is before World War II, 1950–1970 when the size and the role of the government widened following the transition to a welfare state, and after 1980 when new public management was introduced. On the other hand, whereas Heinrich (2002) defines the 1960s, when management techniques such as planning, programming, and budgeting began to be regularly utilized, as the start of the history of performance management, Verbeeten (2008) regards the era of governmental innovation around new public management when the term 'performance management' appeared directly in the management of the public organizations as the beginning of the

Table 1.1 Classification of public sector performance management history

	1900s–1950s	*1960s–1970s*	*1980s–1990s*	*2000s–present*
Core Management Techniques	– Scientific management and science of administration – Cost accounting	– Performance budget – Social indicators	– New Public Management – Evidence-based policies	– New Public Governance – New Public Services
Performance Management Paradigm	Management-oriented	Output-oriented	Client-oriented	Value-oriented and balanced
Characteristics of the Performance Management System	– Traditional accounting management system – Short-term performances, focusing on financial profitability – Functional performance measurement – One-time performance evaluation – Lack of performance information usage	– Financial, political management system – Short-term performances, focusing on economic feasibility and efficiency – Performance measurement for individuals – One-time performance evaluation – Use of performance information for specific management purposes	– Strategic planning system – Client satisfaction, focusing on short– and mid– and long-term performances – Performance measurement for organizations – Sustained performance evaluation – Use of performance information for performance improvements	– Total management system – Focusing on various values and mid- and long-term performances – Performance measurement for cooperation – Cyclical, integrative performance evaluation – Use of performance information for performance improvements and learning

Source: reconstituted from Pun and Whilte (2005: 53) and Van Dooren et al. (2010: 45)

paradigm. Here, I will discuss the historical evolution of the global paradigm of public performance management by classifying it into four stages over the time. The core contents and institutional characteristics of each of the four stages will be discussed. The four stages are: management-oriented era (1900s–1950s), output-oriented era (1960s–1970s), client-oriented era (1980s–1900s), and value-oriented, balanced era (2000s–present) (refer to Table 1.1).

1 Global performance management paradigm

The performance-oriented paradigm in the public sector was formed and highlighted in the early 20th century before World War II. Theories of scientific management and science of administration were introduced as scientific management techniques to enhance transparency and efficiency of corrupt government organizations that were insufficiently institutionalized (Henry, 1975; Williams, 2003). Also, in order to evaluate the financial performances of public organizations, that became increasingly complicated, cost accounting method was introduced (Rivenbark, 2005; Williams, 2002). The introduction of such techniques for organizational management has created the basis for performance-oriented paradigm in the public sector and facilitated the creation of performance management system (Van Dooren et al., 2010).

However, the techniques and the system introduced and operated during this time period seem to have been on the level of 'performance administration', which Bouckaert and Halligan (2007) called the most basic form of performance management. It was a half-fledged system in which only objective information about input and process could be utilized within own organization. Such an early form of the system was short-term based and focused mainly on financial performances. Furthermore, the results of performance evaluation were little fed back to organizations without a link between the results and the incentive system as the major focus of performance management was on functional performance evaluation (Pun and White, 2005; Williams, 2004).

The performance management paradigm became more common after mid-1960s as the idea of performance was more directly and more frequently mentioned in the public sector with the introduction of performance budgeting. As performance budgeting was settled and the relationship between budget appropriation and performances was clarified by systematic categorization of the government budget, management methods for financial performances such as planning programming budgeting system, management by objectives, and zero-based budgeting were widely utilized in the public sector (Bouckaert, 1990; Novick, 1973). Moreover, as developed countries which confronted with a slowdown in economic growth became interested in social indicators such as public health, crimes, and education to transition into a welfare state, such indicators were considered as indirect indicators of political performance of the governments, and consecutively the view that the performance management of public policies became available was widespread (Bulmer, 2001). Based on the social atmosphere, the performance management system evolved from the basic forms into more sophisticated and systemized ones. However, it is criticized that the system was not sufficiently sophisticated in that the focus on financial aspect and efficiency is not helpful for a more general performance management of individuals or the entire organization.

The emphasis on new public management and evidence-based policy after the 1980s is acknowledged to have significantly changed the performance-oriented paradigm in the public sector (Van Dooren et al., 2010). New public management put an emphasis on introduction of competition principles of the private sector and outcome-oriented values to improve efficiency in the public sector (Hood, 1991; Kettl, 2005; Terry, 1998), and the worldwide popularity of new public management led to establishments of Government Performance and Results Act of the United States, Public Service Agreements of England, and Loi Organique relatives aux Lois de Finances of France, providing a legal and systematic foundation for performance management(Kong et al., 2013b). The emphasis on establishment and implementation of evidence-based policies highlighted the importance of utilizing the performance evaluation results and feedbacks, based on the argument that the information about the results and performance of the previous policies must be utilized in selection of the following policies (Nutley et al., 2000; Solesbury, 2001). The client-based, cyclical performance management system constitutes basis for the current integrative performance management system. It was emphasized to aim for accomplishing the organization's vision and mission in a strategic point of view rather than just focusing on financial performance; it was also to measure the mid- and long-term performance from the client's point of view, who consumes public goods and services. The core purpose of performance management was to not only evaluate the performance but also to create an organizational atmosphere to learn about and be responsible for the results. It was intended to enthusiastically utilize the performance information to continuously improve the performance (Pun and White, 2005; Wilcox and Bourne, 2002).

The most recent performance management paradigm, arisen after the 2000s, encompasses the entire organization more comprehensively, is more integrative, and possess learning-oriented and value-oriented characteristics. The transition of the paradigm occurred with the rise of new public governance and new public service as a government reformation as an improvement or an alternative for new public management in the early 21st century. New public governance highlighted the importance of cooperative network in the provision of public services (Alford and Hughes, 2008; Osborne, 2006, 2010), and new public service provided various democratic values other than efficiency and productivity (Denhardt and Denhardt, 2000; Light, 2001), which emphasizes the universality and publicness of public services. With the rise of the two paradigms, there was in increased demand for measurement and evaluation of cooperative and invisible performances attained in the process of achieving the goals.

The current performance management system takes account of multi-dimensional and multi-layered performance objectives and pursues realization of various values including not only efficiency and effectiveness, which are important factors in management activities, but also equity and fairness of the public services. Thus, performance evaluation is conducted by using both qualitative and quantitative measures at the individual level as well as the organizational level in the aspect of both short and long periods of time. It is emphasized to construct a comprehensive system that encompasses strategic objectives and crisis management to provide the necessary public services to the people at all times. Moreover, the performance evaluation results are utilized for providing economic incentives and penalties to encourage organizations to enthusiastically improve the performance.

2 Transition of the performance evaluation of the public institutions system in Korea

The performance management system of public institutions in Korea follows the global performance management paradigm and can be described as the history of the PEPI system. Ever since its first introduction in 1962, the PEPI system has evolved along with the situations of the times. In more detail, as the performance management paradigm evolved from the past management- and output-oriented paradigm to client- and outcome-oriented paradigm after the economic crisis and eventually to the current administration's value-oriented paradigm focused on the publicness of the public sector, the systematic structure has advanced in more detailed aspects including selection of institutions to be evaluated, evaluation models and indicators, and a link between evaluation results and incentives. Depending on individual perspectives and criteria, there are different opinions on how to classify the periods of the PEPI system in Korea. For example, Yoon (2010) classified the periods according to enactment of different laws: phase 1 (1983–2003) when the Framework Act on the Management of Government-invested Institutions was applied to public institutions, phase 2 (2004–2006) when the Framework Act on the Management of Government-affiliated Institutions was implemented, and phase 3 (2007–) when the Act on the Management of Public Institutions was implemented. Hong (2015) segmented the division further by including more phases: phase 1 (1962–1984) when the Budget and Accounts Act on Government-invested Institutions and the Act on the Management of Government-invested Institutions were implemented, phase 2 (1984–1999) when the Framework Act on the Management of Government-invested Institutions was implemented, phase 3 (1999–2007) when the Framework Act on the Management of Government-invested Institutions and the Framework Act on Government-affiliated Institutions were implemented, phase 4 (2007–2011) when the Act on the Management of Public Institutions was implemented, and phase 5 (2011–) when a new system with new policies such as Evaluation of the Head of Institutions Performance Agreement was implemented. Jang et al. (2013) categorized the history into four divisions based on the operational characteristics of the performance evaluation system: the era of introduction and settlement (1983–1998), the era of expansion and application (1999–2006), the era of advancement (2007–2010), and the era of efficiency and characterization (2011–).

In this chapter the history is divided into three divisions based on major legal and systematic changes along the development history of the PEPI system, considering the evaluation criteria and methods and the operational characteristics of the system (refer to Table 1.2). The first division, 'the Introduction of performance evaluation System', refers to the years 1962–1983 when the government operated the system focusing on financial management. The second division, 'Implementation and Settlement', refers to the years 1984–2007 when the more modern concept of the PEPI system was introduced and became widespread with the enactment of the Framework Act on the Management of Government-invested Institutions. The last division, 'Development and Advancement', refers to the years 2008–present when the Act on the Management of Public Institutions was implemented.

1 The introduction of performance evaluation system: 1962–1983

The initial model of the current PEPI system in Korea can be identified as the performance evaluation system of government-invested institutions in 1984,

Table 1.2 Transition and characteristics of the PEPI system

	Introduction	*Implementation and Settlement*	*Development and Advancement*
Years	*1962–1983*	*1984–2007*	*2008–present*
Legal Framework	Budget and Accounts Act on Government-invested Institutions (1962) Act on the Management of Government-invested Institutions (1973)	Framework Act on the Management of Government-invested Institutions (1983) Framework Act on the Management of Government-affiliated Institutions (2003)	Act on the Management of Public Institutions (2007)
Major Change	– Implementation of the PEPI system by relevant government bodies – First implementation of performance bonus	– Full Implementation of the PEPI system – Installation of Public Corporations performance evaluation team – Dual system for management contract execution performance evaluation and PEPI – First execution of government-affiliated institution performance evaluation (2005)	– Reducing the number of target institutions – Separating operation of evaluation on the performances of the head of institutions – Implementation of autonomous performance evaluation (2010) – Implementation of 'Evaluation of the Performance Agreement of the Head of Institutions'(2014) – Implementation of performance evaluation of non-classified public institutions (2014)

Data: reconstituted from Park (2014: 13), Yoon (2011: 37), and Hong (2015: 4)

which originated from the first operation of performance evaluation in 1968. The original system is known to have been influenced by the case of the French government of the time, which operated an evaluation system to manage the performance of management contract system of public corporations, and operated control-based methods under the Budget and Accounts Act on Government-invested Institutions (Jang et al., 2013). However, the performance evaluation system of the time could not avoid the criticism that it digressed from its original purpose and operated superficially (Yoo, 1997; Song, 1983). Although the core purpose of the evaluation system is to enable government-invested institutions to construct an independently responsible management system, it can be said that the limitations were destined due to the government control-based management system. Moreover, rather than functioning as a comprehensive evaluation system for management performances, the system merely evaluated the profits and losses in the budget and lacked a separate incentive system, which otherwise could have enabled feedback and learning of evaluation results.

Taking such criticism into account, efforts were put to enhance the effectiveness of the evaluation system with the implementation of the Act on the Management of Government-Invested Institutions in 1973. There was not much change until 1976 as the evaluations were still operated by the relevant government bodies. In 1977, a more systemized evaluation system was constructed as the multiple evaluation institutions were unified into the Economic Planning Board and performance merits were provided for the first time (Yoo, 1997). However, the improved system in the 1970s could not avoid criticism that the evaluation indicators had technological limitations and that the operation was still superficial (Song, 1983; Song et al., 1987). The indicators were criticized for redundancy, focus on financial analyses, and short-term based and control-based characteristics and the operation of the newly imposed incentive system was so perfunctory that almost all government-invested institutions received incentives of 200% of monthly wages. Moreover, the system was recognized as unable to secure government-invested institutions' discretion on management.

2 Implementation and settlement: 1984–2007

The Framework Act on the Management of Government-invested Institutions implemented in 1983, as an alternative measure for existing the Budget and Accounts Act and the Act on the Management of Government-invested Institutions, is recognized for founding the basis of systematic management and the current structure of the PEPI system (Park, 2003; Yoon, 2011). By implementing the act, the government intended to transition the conventional system under pre-control by the relevant government bodies to a post-evaluation system, professionalize the executive function of the government-invested institutions, and construct an autonomous, responsible management system of the public institutions. In the previous structure, the government-invested institutions were under exhaustive pre-control measures by the relevant government bodies and influenced by multiple departments at the central government, such as the Economic Planning Board and the Ministry of Finance. As the Framework Act on the Management of Government-invested Institutions was implemented, the post-evaluation system was introduced, while the control power of relevant government bodies was moderated and the autonomy and responsibility within the government-invested institutions expanded (Yoon, 2010; Song, 2015; KDI, 1981).

The Framework Act on the Management of Government-affiliated Institutions in 2003 was implemented to construct a new management system for government-affiliated institutions which were not covered by the Framework Act on the

Management of Government-invested Institutions as they were criticized for lack of efficiency and transparency and reckless management. Whereas in the years 1984–2003, about 20 government-invested institutions received performance evaluations according to the Framework Act on the Management of Government-invested Institutions, both government-invested and government-affiliated institutions became subject to the management evaluation system during 2004–2007 as a result of the implementation of the Framework Act on the Management of Government-affiliated Institutions. The Committee for the Management of Government-affiliated Institutions which is responsible for deliberation and resolution of the evaluation system was installed under the Ministry of Planning and Budget, and the process and operational system of the evaluation were prepared similarly to those for the government-invested institutions. Moreover, in this period, new programs such as open recruitment of chief managers, public disclosure of performance data, and client satisfaction surveys were introduced (Song, 2004; Jang et al., 2013).

Even after the PEPI system was reformed as described above, the limitations of the system and inefficiency of public institution management were criticized (Cho, 2008; KDI, 2008). Critiques suggested that demarcation between government-invested and government-affiliated institutions were not clear, so there were blind spots in the management, and that there were cases of dual- scale evaluation systems for the same institution. Moreover, it was found out that there were still excessive influences from the central government, hindering the management autonomy of the public institutions. Especially, the organizations installed for internal checks such as boards of directors and auditors were criticized for superficial operation.

3 Development and advancement: 2008–present

As the solution for the aforementioned drawbacks, the government sought to reform the governance structure of the public institution through the implementation the Act on the Management of Public Institutions (AMPI) in 2007. The act has a focus on integrating the performance evaluation systems for government-invested institutions and government-affiliated institutions into a single system. With references to international standards, the public institutions were categorized more clearly into public corporations, quasi-government institutions, and non-classified public institutions, and additional public institutions became subject to the evaluation system. Supervisory functions were strengthened by introducing the obligatory public announcement of management information of all target institutions and by integrating the evaluation systems into one. Furthermore, the job performance evaluation system was established for individual board members such as non-executive directors and auditors to enhance executive responsibility (Sonu and Kwak, 2006; Hong, 2015).

The PEPI system was fundamentally changed in this period. The major changes include the introduction of the Cycle Model, the separation of CEO evaluation to an independent evaluation team, and the construction of the database system for public announcement of management information. First, the Malcom Baldrige (MB) model, widely known internationally as a standard for management quality evaluation, was applied to the performance evaluation system to more accurately measure management performance.[1] Moreover, to enhance the connectivity of high performance of the pertinent year to long-term empowerment, a sustainability focused approach was proposed as an alternative for the initial short-term focused approach. While the initial evaluation system had a focus on *execution* in planning-execution-outcome process, the MB model emphasized improvement acts for the inadequate stages to generate learning and innovation (Ministry of Planning and Budget, 2007; Korea Management Association Consulting, 2007). Second, the separate CEO evaluation system was developed to create the environment for the head of institutions to enhance management innovation and leadership.[2] The evaluation system was focused on an integrative evaluation of the chief manager's capability in the aspects of leadership, management performances, and major projects and the evaluation results were actively used for rewards such as provision of performance pay and re-appointments. Third, the All Public Information In-One (ALIO) system was constructed to systemize the accumulation and management of evaluation data by computerizing the process of the PEPI system and creating a database of evaluation information. The ALIO system is recognized for significantly enhancing public institution transparency through the online integrative provision of major information about public institution management evaluation (Kwak, 2007). The ultimate purpose of the system was to keep procedural records of evaluation and enhance fairness of the evaluations by having the evaluation team members personally input the management evaluation results. However, it remains a drawback that the utilization within the scope of the purpose was limited and the data recording ceased eventually.

Toward the end of 2013, there was another major change in the PEPI system due to the implementation of the 'public institution normalization policy'. In order to account for the drastic increase in the public debt caused by such as the overseas resources development project, the 2014 performance evaluation had its focus on evaluation criteria related to debt reduction and sloppy management. The CEO evaluation changed to *execution performance evaluation* due to the implementation of *the management performance agreement* (Ministry of Strategy and Finance, 2013). In addition, performance evaluations were utilized enthusiastically in measures, such as public institution functional adjustments, the wage-peak policy, the adoption of annual performance salary system, and the setting of 2-Sigma level target for major projects,[3] for enhancing the management efficiency of public institutions. However, the new system failed to settle due to an early downfall of the administration. Though not very salient, public institution's social responsibility (e.g. job creation) was considered one of the important indicators for performance evaluation in this period. (Ministry of Strategy and Finance, 2016).

While the implementation of AMPI seems to have positive effects from the development of legal basis of the performance evaluation system and the evolution of evaluation models, it is true that there is still room for improvements. The problems of sustained debts and sloppy management of public institutions persist, and issues such as the design of valid indicators to measure social responsibilities of public institutions remain. Furthermore, there still exist such issues as the classification of public institutions, the impartiality and the professionalism of the evaluation team, and objective indicators to measure performance.

III Historical transition of evaluation models and methods

As the PEPI system has evolved, so has performance evaluation model and measuring indicators. In the years 1962–1983 when the evaluation model was introduced and implemented for the first time, a performance evaluation model was not very sophisticated as the focus was on business administration, prime costs, and input resources (Jang et al., 2013). It was in 1984 when the first form of performance evaluation model appeared which in the early 2000s was improved and systemized. After the implementation of AMPI, the world-renowned PDCA (Plan-Do-Check-Act) model of Malcolm Baldrige was applied and has been used in the system of common management and core business activities until nowadays (refer to Table 1.3). In the following sections, I will review the characteristics of PEPI's evaluation models from 1984 to present.

1 Implementation and settlement: 1984–2007

1 Implementation: 1984–2000

According to the manual for the performance evaluation of government-invested institutions, the evaluation model was expanded during 1993–2000 as the management efficiency sector was added to the previous criteria utilized during 1986–1992[4] with three sectors of comprehensive management, common management activities, and achievement of establishment purposes (core business activities). The model can be described as the first form of performance evaluation and composes of up to 58 evaluation indicators, including both quantitative and qualitative indicators. For example, the comprehensive management criterion composed of qualitative indicators such as creativity of institutions, adaptability to environmental changes, and morale of employees and quantitative indicators such as productivity of fixed capital and balance management. The common management activities criterion was graded based on indicators of long-term business management, management system improvements, internalization of inner evaluation system, and effort for research and development, and the achievement of establishment purposes was evaluated according to indicators of execution of national projects and achievement of institutions' establishment purposes (Figure 1.1).

The initial model gave higher weights to quantitative indicators than qualitative indicators (6 to 4) overall.[5] Efforts were made to increase the objectivity and fairness of the evaluations and acceptance from the institutions by weighing the quantitative indicators higher than qualitative indicators which may be affected by individual subjectivity of the evaluators.[6]

Table 1.3 Historical transition of public institution performance evaluation model

	Introduction	Implementation and Settlement		Development and Advancement	
		Implementation	Settlement	Development	Advancement
Years	1962–1983	1984–2000	2001–2007	2008–2010	2011–now
Evaluation Criteria	Management efficiency (Financial evaluation of profits and losses)	Comprehensive management, Common management activities, (Management efficiency), Main(Core) business activities	Comprehensive management, Common management activities, Main business activities	Leadership/Strategy, Management system, Management performance	(Leadership/ Responsible management) Management efficiency, Main business activities
Weight	–	Quantitative evaluation: 40–70% Qualitative evaluation: 30–75%	Quantitative evaluation: 32–45% Qualitative evaluation: 60–70%	Quantitative evaluation: 45–55% Qualitative evaluation: 45–60%	Quantitative evaluation: 55–65% Qualitative evaluation: 35–45%

Source: reconstituted from Jang et al. (2013: 374) and Yoon (2010: 127–144)

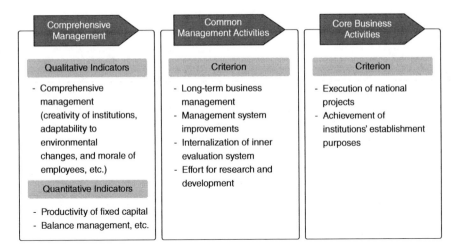

Figure 1.1 Evaluation model in the implementation period (1986)

Source: constituted with reference to the Government-invested Institution Management Evaluation Team (1986)

2 Settlement: 2001–2007

The evaluation model in this time period was reduced to three fields of comprehensive management, main business activities, and common business activities (including previous fields of management efficiency) and consisted of maximum 37 sub-indicators. As shown in Figure 1.2, the comprehensive management sector in the 2nd generation model composes of four common qualitative indicators of responsible management and public interests, restructuring and management innovation, operation of the board, and client satisfaction enhancement and two–four quantitative indicators including labor productivity, fixed capital productivity, and operation cost management, selective for individual institutions. The common business activities sector was divided into human resources management, financial and budget management, and other business administration measures. The human resources management was further segmented into indicators including organization and personnel management, wage and labor management, and operation of internal evaluation system. The main business activities sector had individual institutions select three–five major projects relevant with their establishment purposes and evaluate the performance utilizing appropriate quantitative and qualitative indicators. According to the annual manuals for the performance evaluation of government-invested institutions and government-affiliated institutions during 2001–2006, weights on qualitative indicators increased in the total score unlike in the initial model.

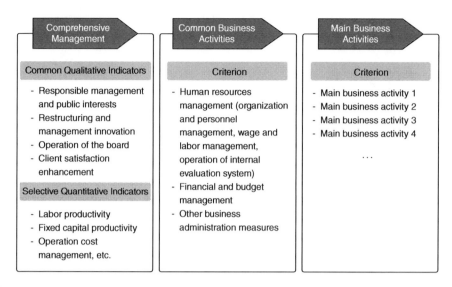

Figure 1.2 Performance evaluation model in the settlement period (2001)

Source: constituted with reference to the Ministry of Strategy and Finance (2001)

2 Development and advancement: 2008–present

1 Development: 2008–2010

The performance evaluation model and indicators changed significantly in this time period due to the application of Malcolm Baldrige (MB)'s PDCA (Plan-Do-Check-Act) model in 2007. The MB model categorized the evaluation criteria into sectors of leadership/strategy, management system, and management performance and guided the evaluation process to follow the PDCA approach. In detail, the leadership/strategy sector was divided into the Plan stage, the management system sector into the Do stage, and the management performance sector into the Check stage, with the basic premise that the sectors were not independent but sequential and connected. Moreover, procedural evaluations and consequential evaluations were distinguished by constituting the leadership/strategy and management system sectors with qualitative indicators and the management performance sector with quantitative indicators.

The evaluation model in 2008 shows that the leadership/strategy sector is composed of indicators of executive leadership, operation of board of directors and auditors, customer satisfaction-oriented management, ethical and transparent management, and vision and strategy development. The management system sector was divided into main business activities and management efficiency. The efficient implementation of main business activities was evaluated for each institution, and the common management efficiency was measured through indicators including

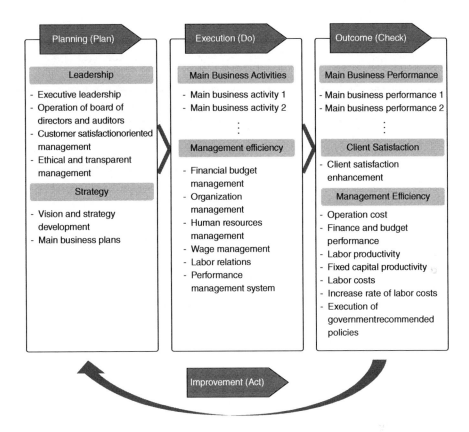

Figure 1.3 Example of performance evaluation model in the development period (2008)

Source: constituted with reference to the Ministry of Strategy and Finance (2008) and Korea Management Association (2007)

financial budget management, organization management, human resources management, wage management, labor relations, and performance management system. The management performance sector was divided into performances in main business activities, client satisfaction, and management efficiency and each sector was evaluated by the degrees of performance goal achievement, improvement, and efficiency enhancement. In this period, the average number of indicators has remained at around 30, with the quantitative indicator of 45 to 55 percent and the qualitative indicator of 45 to 60 percent respectively.

2 Advancement: 2011–present

The PDCA approach introduced after the implementation of AMPI 2007 was transformed into a simpler version in 2011. Especially with the separation of the Evaluation team on performances of the Head of Institutions since 2014, the original division into three sectors of leadership/responsible management, management efficiency, and main business activities was reconstructed into two sectors of common business and main business activities. Moreover, vigorous efforts were put into reorganizing the complicated structure of the evaluation model with more efficiency, including the reduction of the evaluation indicator to less than 20, which is the smallest number of indicators in the performance evaluation history.

As shown in Figure 1.4, the common management activities sector in the 2014 evaluation model is divided into 5 sub-sectors of business strategy and corporate social responsibility, business process efficiency, management of organization and human resources, management of finance & budget and its accomplishments, management of remuneration and employee welfare benefits and evaluates each stage with quantitative and qualitative indicators based on the PDCA model. The main business activities sector evaluates overall planning, execution, and outcome of performance goals of major projects assigned according to the establishment purposes of individual institutions and composes mainly of quantitative indicators. As a whole, quantitative indicators accounted for 55–65 percent of the total, so that weights on quantitative indicators increased as in the initial model.

3 Evaluation on the performances of heads of institutions

Evaluation on the performances of the heads of institutions was operated independently from the evaluations on institutions since 2009.[7] The 2009 evaluation utilized a model with detailed indicators under two major categories: progress in major pending projects described by the management plan (50 points) and progress in the task of public institutions reform and management efficiency enhancement (50 points). Each stage of the planning (25 percent), execution (25 percent), and output (50 percent) was evaluated for the major pending project sector and the reform and efficiency enhancement sector was evaluated based on seven indicators of privatization, rearrangement and function adjustment, employee quota reduction, wage adjustment, labor relations advancement, investment company restricting, and recruitment of youth interns. The evaluation results were graded into four levels of 'excellent, good, average, and insufficient'.

The evaluation model in 2011 composed of three sectors of leadership and responsible management (20 points), management efficiency (40 points), and major projects (40 points) and was based on the institution evaluation model except the major projects sector which was evaluated separately according to management plans proposed by individual head of institution. The leadership and responsible management sector composed of four indicators of leadership, responsible management, public evaluation, and social contribution, the management efficiency sector of three indicators of organization and human resources management, wage and performance management, and labor relations management, and the major projects sector of two indicators of major projects (30 points) and sustainable development projects (10 points). The final integrative scores

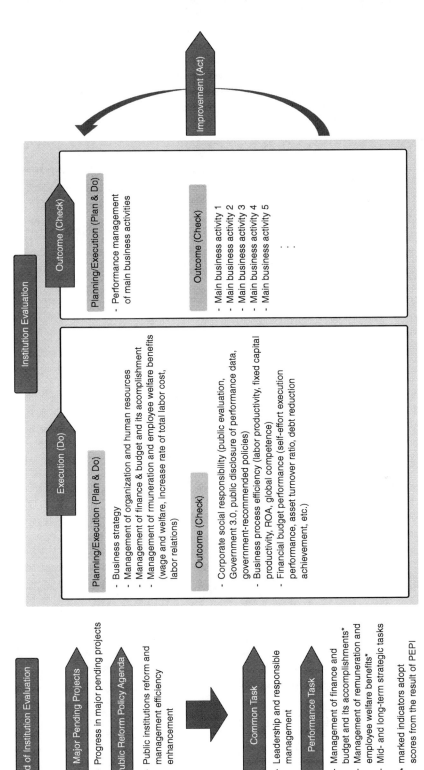

Figure 1.4 Example of performance evaluation model in the advancement period (2014)

Source: constituted with reference to the Ministry of Strategy and Finance (2014)

were divided into six levels (outstanding, good, satisfactory, average, insufficient, and very insufficient) and were publicly announced.

The institution evaluation and the head of institution evaluation models were separated again since the evaluation in 2015, and the evaluation was conducted under the new major categories composed of the common task (30 points) and the performance task (70 points). The common task composed of indicators for evaluating the level of leadership and responsible management of the head of institution and the performance task composed of management of finance and budget and its accomplishments (15–20 points), management of remuneration and employee welfare benefits (15–20 points), and mid- and long-term strategic tasks (30–40 points). The institution evaluation and the head of institution evaluation models were separated except that the indicators of management of finance and budget and its accomplishments and remuneration and employee welfare benefits in the performance task were graded based on the institution evaluation results. The final weighted scores were divided into three levels (good, average, and insufficient) and were utilized as references for personnel administrations of the head of institution.

Compared to the institution evaluation model, the head of institution evaluation model was relatively simple, and the evaluation of the head of institution in 2016 was conducted by a separate committee composing of five members. While the problems of separation and integration with the institution evaluation and evaluation cycles are continuously raised, a more fundamental issue is that the head of institution with unsatisfactory evaluation results might partly lose control of own organization, leading to weaker leadership for performance improvement. One of the possible solutions is to give grace periods to the heads of institutions with low performance and keeping the evaluation results and reports closed.

IV Current state and challenges: performance evaluation committee and indicators

The PEPI system has consistently been modified to enhance the validity and reliability of the evaluation process and results. However, many scholars and the people concerned point out that the performance evaluation system has its innate limitations that need to be revised. Particular aspects for revision can be summarized as the composition of the performance evaluation team, the validity of the evaluation, the relevance of the categorization of public institutions, and the utilization of the evaluation results. In the following sections, the problems and measures for improvement of the current evaluation system will be discussed by analyzing empirical data from mainly the Development and Advancement period when the system was operated with stability.

1 Composition of the performance evaluation team

According to the sixth clause of Article 48 of AMPI, the performance evaluation team may be organized and operated 'to ensure professional and technical research or consultation concerning the evaluation of management performance'.

The Enforcement Decree of the Act exemplifies the qualification conditions for the evaluation team members as follows.

- A professor of a college or a university who has expertise in operation and business administration of public institutions
- A person working for a government-funded research institute with a doctorate degree or deemed to have an equivalent qualification
- A certified public accountant, a lawyer, or a specialist in management consulting with an experience of practice for at least five years
- A person recognized otherwise as having good expertise and experience in operation and business administration of public institutions

As the evaluation team have great influence on the validity and credibility of the evaluation results, there have been endless disputes about the relevant size and composition of the team. It was particularly pointed out that the gradual expansion of the team was inappropriate with the necessity and the qualification and capability of the members in terms of professionalism and fairness were upon continuous discussions.

As shown in Table 1.4, the evaluation team composed of about 130 members in 2008–2009 and slightly increased in size to hold 169 members in 2010. After the reduction to 149 members in 2011, the team composed of around 160 members during 2012–2015 without significant fluctuations.[8] In comparison to the years 2004 (129 members), 2005 (259 members), and 2006 (155 members) when the evaluations for government-invested institutions and government-affiliated institutions were separated, it is difficult to say that the size was conspicuously expanded.[9] Per person count of evaluated institutions is calculated to be around 0.7 until the team size was sharply reduced to 109 members in 2016 and the count increased to more than one institution per person.

As illustrated in Table 1.4 and Figure 1.5, a college or a university professor is the most dominant group during 2008–2015, constituting more than 65 percent in all of the years.[10] The performance evaluation team also comprises of consulting and accounting experts (around 20 percent), researchers (around 10 percent), and members in other occupation fields such as lawyers and certified labor consultants (around 5 percent).

Reflecting on the high proportion of professors, it is criticized that the practical and realistic circumstances of the evaluated institutions may not be considered enough and that fairness issues may be raised if the professors received benefits from the evaluated institutions such as research project contracts. However, the conflicts of interests may be observed more seriously among experts from consulting companies or accounting firms whose clients are mainly public institutions. In order to calm such disputes, the government has recently strengthened the ethical regulations and conducts strict verification of interest conflict, research project contracts and consultations in selection of evaluation team members. In the case of the professors, the disputes about the professionalism could be moderated by selecting the members from diverse fields evenly and positioning them in the team so that experts from various occupation fields can create synergy, and by

Table 1.4 Transition of size and composition of the management evaluation team (2008–2016)

	2008		2009		2010		2011		2012		2013		2014		2015		2016	
	members	%	members	%	Members	%	members	%	members	%	members	%	members	%	members	%	members	%
College/University Professor	105	75.5	86	66.2	111	65.7	102	65.7	107	68.5	102	67.3	111	65.0	103	68.5	71	65.1
Accountant/Expert	24	17.3	30	23.1	34	23.1	29	20.1	32	19.5	43	20.1	42	27.2	46	25.9	31	28.4
Government-employed Researcher	9	6.47	11	8.46	17	8.46	11	10.1	8	7.38	12	5.03	8	7.6	10	4.9	6	5.5
Other	1	0.72	3	2.31	7	2.31	7	4.14	12	4.7	1	7.55	1	0.6	2	0.6	1	0.9
Total	139	100	130	100	169	100	149	100	159	100	158	100	162	100	161	100	109	100
Per Person Count of Evaluated Institutions	100	0.72	96	0.72	112	0.74	109	0.66	109	0.73	117	0.69	117	0.74	116	0.72	119	1.09

Source: The division of the years is based on performance evaluation reports

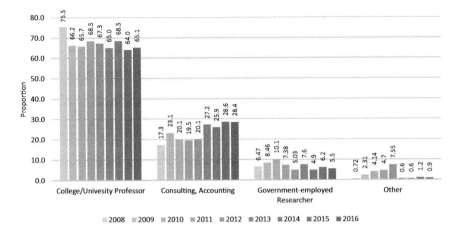

Figure 1.5 Occupational proportions of the performance evaluation team (2008–2016)

maintaining the rate of replacement of previous members with new members to secure professionalism and consistency. Moreover, the professionalism of the evaluation team members could be enhanced by simplifying the manuals on the vast business fields of the public institutions and dozens of evaluation sub-indicators and by providing internal workshops and systemized education.

Meanwhile, in order to overcome the criticism that there is the gap between the results of PEPI and public's expectations, the evaluation process could be announced transparently and the team could select a certain proportion of its members from candidates recommended by civic groups.

2 Evaluation system and indicators

Ever since the PEPI system was implemented and operated, the validity of measuring indicators and weight settings has been continuously questioned. As observed in the previous sections, evaluation criteria and sub-indicators as well as the weights on quantitative and qualitative indicators have been repeatedly modified over the years.

As shown in Table 1.5 and Figure 1.6, the evaluation criteria composed of 3 categories of leadership/strategy, management activities, and main business activities until 2013 and were reduced to 2 categories of common management activities and main business activities since 2014 by combining the leadership and common management activities categories. The weights of the main business activities which were only 30 percent in 2008 have increased gradually, and starting in 2013, the weights of the two sectors remain the same.

The chronological changes of the political demands of the public and the demands of the institutions have been incorporated into the composition of

Table 1.5 Indicator composition and weight transition (2008–2017) (unit: %)

Category		2008	2009	2010	2011	2012	2013	2014	2015	2016	2017
Leadership	Quantitative	–	–	–	10	10	10	–	–	–	–
	Qualitative	20	18	13	10	10	10	–	–	–	–
	Subtotal	20	18	13	20	20	20	–	–	–	–
Common	Quantitative	30	30	30	20	20	17	28	28	28	23
Management	Qualitative	20	17	17	15	15	13	22	22	22	27
Activities	Subtotal	50	47	47	35	35	30	50	50	50	50
Main	Quantitative	15	20	25	30	30	28	37	37	37	32
Business	Qualitative	15	15	15	15	15	22	13	13	13	18
Activities	Subtotal	30	35	40	45	45	50	50	50	50	50
Total		100	100	100	100	100	100	100	100	100	100

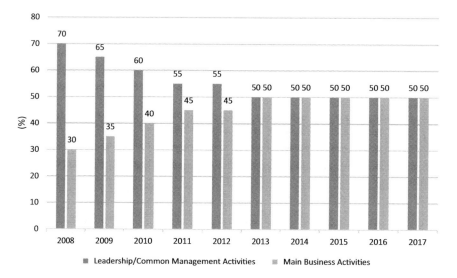

Figure 1.6 Weight transition of leadership/common management activities and main business activities sectors (2008–2017)

evaluation criteria, the setting of indicators, and the distribution of weights. Considering the ultimate goal of the performance evaluation as the improvement of public services quality, the system needs to play a role in signaling what kind of goal and strategy public institutions should have so as to respond to the public demands. During the earlier periods of the evaluation system, the focus was on the common management activities which is relatively easily quantifiable, in order to enhance the settlement of the system and the acceptance of the institutions. As the evaluation system settled and operated more stably, relatively more focus has been put on core business performances of the individual institution, i.e. publicness.[11]

As shown in Figure 1.7, a weight on qualitative indicators decreased gradually from 55 percent in 2008 to below 45 percent after 2010. The sharp reduction in the weight in 2014 occurred because a large number of qualitative indicators in the category of common management activities was abolished or integrated and because qualitative indicators such as responsible management and social contribution originally utilized for performance evaluation of the head of institutions were replaced by the Evaluation of the Head of Institutions Performance Agreement (Ministry of Strategy and Finance, 2013). Figure 1.8 illustrates that the weight on qualitative indicators is similar to or greater than that of quantitative

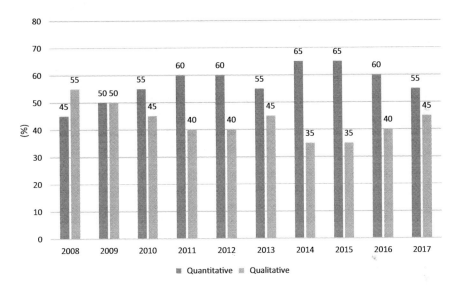

Figure 1.7 Weight transition of metric and non-metric indicators (2008–2017)

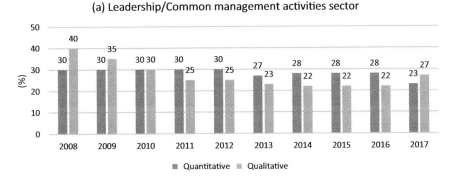

Figure 1.8 Weight transition of quantitative and qualitative indicators by evaluation sector (2008–2017)

indicators in the leadership/common management activities category. On the other hand, the weight on quantitative indicators is consistently greater in the main business activities category.

Generally, qualitative indicators are considered to be less reliable due to the potential intervention of evaluator's subjectivity in the evaluation process. On the other hand, quantitative indicators are widely considered appropriate for evaluation as they are thought to be based on objective standards and exclusive of arbitrary judgments of the evaluator. As a result, some argue that the weight on qualitative indicators should be reduced and that of the quantitative indicators be increased. However, quantitative indicators are not perfectly objective as it is difficult to separate influences of uncontrollable exogenous factors such as exchange rates and oil price fluctuations on the performance of the institution. In the evaluation of qualitative indicators, objectivity can be maintained by specifying evaluation items and considerations in detail to enhance validity and credibility of the evaluation. Moreover, qualitative indicators have the advantage of flexibility that could account for institution's own characteristics and policy environments.

3 Evaluation target institutions and categorization

While the target institutions for performance evaluations are currently categorized as public corporations, commissioned-service-type quasi-governmental, fund-management-type quasi-governmental, and small but strong quasi-governmental institutions, concerns about the possible impartiality problems are raised for applying uniform standards since there are differences in the establishment purposes, characteristics of the main business, and the size of the institutions. It may be a reasonable criticism to describe the current system as *rank ordering* with little specifications in setting the indicators and weights that does not take the institutional differences into account, as the major goal of public corporations is to pursue profitability and that of quasi-government institutions is to execute government-entrusted projects. If that is the case, is the current evaluation system actually in favor of particular types of institutions?

Authority were removed from the public corporation group I (Busan Port Authority and Incheon Port Authority were transferred to group II). Every year, more target institutions were added to the public corporation group II including Korea Hydro and Nuclear Power Corporation and 5 Power Corporations (2011) and Yeosu Port Authority (2012). Refer to the footnote for yearly record of target public corporation counts.

Based on the 2016 manual for public institution categorization,[12] Table 1.6 and Figure 1.9 analyze trends in the evaluation results for market-type public corporations (public corporation group I) and quasi-market-type public corporations (public corporation group II). On average, group II shows slightly greater scores in quantitative indicators and group I in qualitative indicators.

If the results for each leadership/common management activities and main business activities categories are viewed closely, we can clearly observe sub-score differences between the group I and II by indicator type as well as evaluation

Table 1.6 Evaluation result trends of public corporation groups I and II (2008–2016)

Category			2008	2009	2010	2011	2012	2013	2014	2015	2016
Market-type Public Corporations (Group I)	Quantitative	Average (points)	81.92	85.65	88.86	87.87	86.14	86.31	78.64	77.80	78.80
		Standard deviation	7.37	8.24	5.67	6.84	8.68	7.03	8.25	9.37	8.37
	Qualitative	Average (points)	71.55	77.49	81.30	79.76	78.49	69.31	68.17	67.94	70.59
		Standard deviation	5.93	6.13	2.89	4.35	5.75	3.84	5.61	4.64	4.78
Quasi-market-type Public Corporations (Group II)	Quantitative	Average (points)	85.91	85.28	89.80	90.33	89.69	87.61	77.63	80.09	81.69
		Standard deviation	8.42	9.13	4.80	3.66	8.13	5.67	9.71	9.95	9.68
	Qualitative	Average (points)	67.40	71.86	72.79	71.98	71.13	67.33	63.84	63.84	63.27
		Standard deviation	5.13	4.07	5.12	6.52	7.48	6.06	5.62	4.80	4.64

Notes
1 The standard deviations are based on a 100-point scale conversion
2 In 2010, the Busan Port Authority, Incheon Port Authority, and Korea Container Terminal

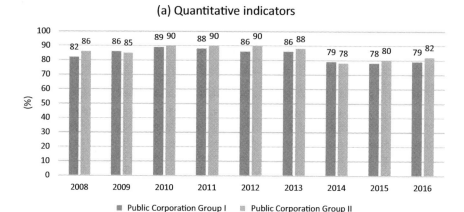

(a) Quantitative indicators

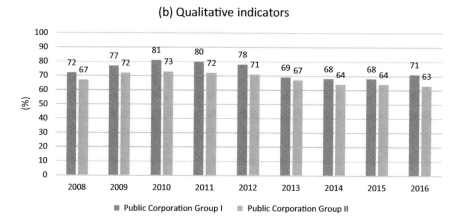

(b) Qualitative indicators

Figure 1.9 Average score trends of public corporation groups I and II (2008–2016)

category. From the figures, it can be conjectured that the group differences in a total score might largely come from the difference in the main business activities score. The figures also show that group II has generally higher quantitative scores than group I has, but the score gap is reversed by qualitative scores. Considering that the reversion occurs even within the relatively homogenous group of public corporations, it might be controversial to apply the same evaluation model to the heterogeneous group of quasi-government institutions which greatly differ from each other in size and goal. It cannot be generalized that score differences exist among all of the institution types and are caused by negligence of individual institution characteristics. Also, it cannot be concluded that the score

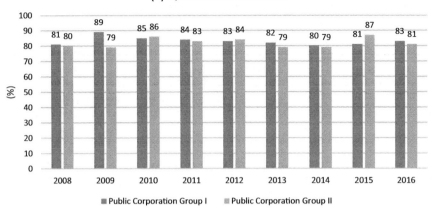

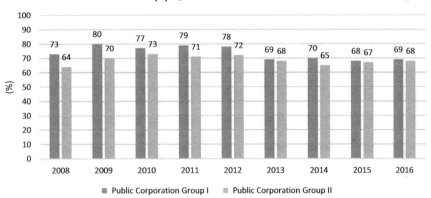

Figure 1.10 Leadership/common management activities category: average score trends of public corporation groups I and II. Ministry of Strategy and Finance (2008–2016).

differences among the institution types hinder validity and fairness of the entire performance evaluation system. However, since performance evaluation is conducted on hundreds of diverse public institutions, the detailed indicators should be constructed and operated cautiously to prevent discriminations among and within the individual institution types due to standardized criteria or evaluation system in favor of large public corporations.[13] Moreover, efforts should be made to achieve the original purpose of performance evaluation by focusing more on comparative improvements from the previous year within the framework of absolute scales instead of ranking institutions.

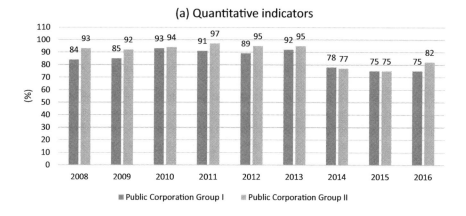

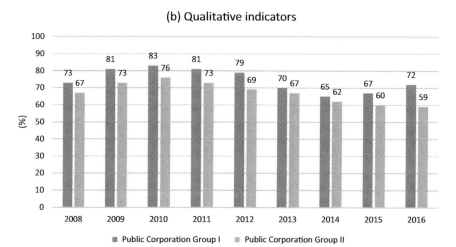

Figure 1.11 Main business activities category: average score trends of public corporation groups I and II. Ministry of Strategy and Finance (2008–2016).

V Lessons learned and conclusion

1 Lessons learned

The PEPI system in Korea is acknowledged by the IMF (International Monetary Fund) and the World Bank as an outstanding system and has attracted much attention as a benchmarking target in many developing countries. Even though there would be differences in national definitions of public institutions and objectives of performance evaluation, the case of Korea is expected to provide valuable lessons in three key aspects for countries that are seeking to further develop and settle the

PEPI system. First, the case of Korea, which has firmly established the performance evaluation system through its continuous evolution for over half a century, might be able to provide ideas for the future direction of institutional development for countries that have temporary and incipient stages of the system. According to OECD (2016), formalized performance evaluation systems in countries such as Myanmar and Pakistan do not exist; although there are certain types of systems in countries like Singapore, Bhutan, and Kazakhstan, they are still in the early stages. Likewise, based on the case of Korea, such countries with inadequate or nascent systems could establish plans for design and development of the system. In particular, it would be possible to benchmark strategies to devise and jointly operate other systems that can further formalize the PEPI system – e.g. the head of institutions performance agreement and annual performance salary system of Korea. Second, ideas for devising desirable performance evaluation tools can be attained by considering the evolutionary process of the performance evaluation model in Korea as well as the changes in the composition of financial/non-financial and quantitative/qualitative indicators. Unlike Western developed countries such as the United Kingdom, France, New Zealand, and Sweden, developing countries in other continents – including Asia – mainly focus on financial performance of public institutions and conduct quantitative evaluations (Park, 2013; Ra and Yun, 2013). Acknowledging that non-financial and qualitative performance such as the realization of publicness are important goals to be achieved by the public institutions, developing countries can benchmark the performance evaluation model of Korea – i.e., main business activities-related quantitative/qualitative indicators – in order to design and operate more comprehensive evaluation models. Third, the PEPI system in Korea, having an enormous power as the results of performance evaluation not only influence the payment of financial incentives but also the appointment of top executives, is an unprecedented case in other countries. Developing countries could thus benchmark the Korean system when devising incentives and sanctions based on the results of performance evaluation. In most countries, the ripple effects of the results of performance evaluation are insignificant as having influences only on performance-based pay, whereas in some countries like Korea and China, the performance evaluation is considered important to practitioners considering its impacts on executive reappointment or dismissal decisions (OECD, 2016). Therefore, the case of Korea can be a good paradigm for countries that are seeking to strengthen the fields of incentives and sanctions of the performance evaluation system.

2 Conclusion

While the PEPI system in Korea has continuously been developed as one of the world's best systems, it is true that there are fundamental challenges related to the evaluation system on the inside ranging from the governance structure to the expertise of the evaluation team and validity of evaluation indicators. The concerns about the governance structure relates to the level of independence from the government and the Ministry of Strategy and Finance with which the evaluation team can participate in the process and produce objective results. Although it was suggested that the committee for the management of public institutions and the PEPI system be transferred to the Prime Minister's Office, the suggestion cannot be viewed as relevant, considering the ineffectiveness of the government performance evaluation currently operated under the Prime Minister's Office. The expertise of the evaluation team is directly related to the capabilities of individual members and encompasses the level of understanding of the businesses of evaluated institutions and the professional knowledge of performance measurements. As most of candidate experts seem to have a conflict of interests in some ways, however, the selected experts have assignments in the consideration of a conflict of interests, as the second best way. Lastly, the design of indicators to measure performance is the most fundamental basis of the evaluation system and therefore requires not only professionalism but also fairness.[14] Until 2007, the names and responsible areas of the participant experts were listed in the manual for the performance evaluation, clearly indicating who were responsible for the design of indicators. However, the list of names seems to have been removed in the manual after the evaluation system for government-invested institutions was integrated with the system for government-affiliated institutions. An independent indicator design team was active after the evaluation in 2014, but it was considered to have not functioned effectively. In 2017, the actual responsibility for the design of the indicators was transferred to public officials in relevant government bodies as the team was discontinued in the evaluation system.

Although it is indisputable that the government has enthusiastically utilized the performance evaluation system to improve performance, the current public institution governance has its limitations in opening and preparing for a new era in Korea. The current organizational structure of public institutions, which has existed for more than 30 years, might be outdated, so that it might become an obstacle to the realization of the current government's national agenda for job creation and employment-friendly evaluation system. In the present structure, the major task of the public institution that started as an executive agency are replaced by outsourcing and subcontracts and the majority of the employees are composed of clerical officers who execute the functions of preparation and approval of official documents. Whether this structure is an ideal organizational form to timely provide public services needs to be thoroughly reviewed. Also, PEPI should not be considered as an almighty measure for performance improvement. Specifically, the system has limitations in taking overlapped functions resultant of the functional expansion and diversification of the government into account, or in providing incentives for active exploration of government-led projects. Therefore, the future PEPI system should evolve, so that the performance of overlapped functions and cooperative tasks would be more systemically managed. In case of major national projects, indicators and output data need to be clarified in order to accurately measure performances and contributions of each institution.[15] Furthermore, the future PEPI system should also play a role in encouraging public institutions to pioneer the new business model that contributes to the economic growth of the country; public institution's redundant functions should be updated and replaced by new functions that meet the changing demand of the people. The future performance evaluation team should therefore settle the unbiased evaluation criteria and establish relevant professionalism in order to strictly examine the role and the performance of the public institutions.

Notes

1 The initial evaluation model categorized the operation of institutions by their functions and was based on the process of *leadership, strategy (planning) – management system (execution) – management performance (outcome)*. Therefore, the input-output or process-outcome was ambiguous and a clear classification of performances in aspects of business administration and projects was difficult.
2 Evaluations on the institutions and the head of institutions were operated separately in the years 2008–2010 until the two evaluation systems were unified again in 2011. The two systems were separated again in 2014 and the annual head of institutions evaluation was reformed to Evaluation of the Head of Institutions Performance Agreement.
3 By the modification of the manual in 2013, the institutions are required to set score targets for major projects higher than before (e.g., an increase in a score by twice as much as a standard deviation of scores last five years) in order to enhance the qualities of public services.
4 In the years 1983–1984, evaluations were based on quantitative and qualitative indicators without specific categories, and in 1985 a total of six evaluation categories of comprehensive, management goal, business management, efficiency, service, and research and development and relevant sub-indicators were introduced. However, since 1986 a stable evaluation model was developed and utilized continuously, in this chapter the model used in 1986 is considered as the initial performance evaluation model.
5 Before 1990, higher weights (60 percent) were given to quantitative indicators for institution's performance except for institutions whose performance was difficult to be quantified (e.g., Korea Trade-Investment Promotion Agency, Korea Stock Exchange, Korea Petroleum development Corporation, Korea Gas Corporation, and Korea Tourism Organization). From 1990 until the economic crisis in 1997, quantitative and qualitative indicators have similar weights. Weights on qualitative indicators rose to about 60 percent during 1998–2007. After the implementation of the Act on the Management of Public Institutions in 2008, weights on quantitative indicators began to rise until they reached 65 percent during 2014–2015 and started to decline again.
6 According to Song (2015) who actively participated in the development of the initial model, weights on quantitative indicators were higher than those on qualitative indicators not only because the indicators were designed mainly by accountants, but more in order to enhance the objectivity and fairness of the evaluation.
7 While evaluations on the performances of the head of institutions were conducted separately from evaluations on the performance of institutions since 1999, the evaluation model on the head of institutions of the time was greatly similar to the institution model in various aspects including the distribution of weights (Cho, 2009). The evaluation model on the head of institutions became modified and different from the institution model in 2009. The detailed description of the evaluation model on the performances of the head of institutions is presented in Chapter 2.
8 There was a sharp reduction in the size to 109 members in 2016 due to 'management evaluation team efficiency enhancement' demand of the Ministry of Strategy and Finance.
9 From perspectives of the people or outside, the team may still be considered a grand scale as it is a rare occasion that a group of more than 100 experts gather for the evaluation for several months.

10 Recently, retired public officials and those who retired from public institutions are increasingly participating in the performance evaluation team with titles such as adjunct or visiting professors.

11 Since 2007, the author has insisted that the common management activities be weighted less and the main business activities be weighted more in the evaluation indicators to find balance. Provided that the common management activities is weighted excessively greater, if the heads of institutions are interested mainly in the evaluation results and incentives, it is highly probable that the they will focus on the common management activities sector, i.e. profit creation through enhancing productivity and efficiency, rather than on the main business activities for public service quality enhancement.

12 The numbers of evaluation target institutions are as follows.

Categorization	2008	2009	2010	2011	2012	2013	2014	2015	2016
Public corporation Group I	14	13	10	10	10	10	10	10	10
Public corporation Group II	10	10	11	17	18	20	20	20	20
Total	24	23	21	27	28	30	30	30	30

Public corporation group I composes of market-based public corporations with asset sizes greater than two trillion won and the proportion of self-revenue in the total revenue greater than 85 percent: Incheon International Airport Corporation, Korea Gas Corporation, Korea Airports Corporation, Korea Expressway Corporation, Korea National Oil Corporation, Korea Water Resources Corporation, Korea Electric Power Corporation (KEPCO), Korea District Heating Corporation, Korea Railroad Corporation, and Korea Land and Housing Corporation (ten institutions). Public corporation group II composes of quasi-market-based public corporations: Korea Coal Corporation, Busan Port Authority, Yeosu Gwangyang Port Authority, Ulsan Port Authority, Incheon Port Authority, Jeju Free International City Development Center, Korea Housing and Urban Guarantee Corporation, Korea Appraisal Board, Korea Tourism Organization, Korea Resources Corporation, Korea South-East Power Co. Ltd., Korea Southern Power Co. Ltd., Korea East-West Power Co. Ltd., Korean Racing Authority, Korea Broadcast Advertising Corporation (KOBACO), Korea Western Power Co. Ltd., Korea Hydro and Nuclear Power Co. Ltd., Korea Minting & Security Printing Corporation, Korea Midland Power Co. Ltd., and Korea Marine Environment Management Corporation (20 institutions).

13 In order to overcome such drawbacks, the previous division in which public corporations and commissioned-service-type/fund-management-type quasi-government institutions were categorized as one group, was modified in the evaluation in 2016 and the ranks of public corporations and quasi-government institutions have been separately calculated.

14 Especially in the case of quantitative indicators, about 70 percent of the evaluation score is already decided when the indicators and the formulas are created.

15 According to the 2016 manual, indicators related to job creation are included in the evaluation of 14 institutions and in 21 indicators. It may seem the indicators are considered with great importance but there is a possibility that job creation results were double-counted from the Worknet system and employment insurance database records.

References

Alford, J., and Hughes, O. (2008). Public Value Pragmatism as the Next Phase of Public Management. *The American Review of Public Administration*, 38(2), 130–148.

Bouckaert, G. (1990). The History of the Productivity Movement. *Public Productivity & Management Review*, 14, 53–89.

Bouckaert, G., and Halligan, J. (2007). *Managing Performance: International Comparisons*. New York, NY: Routledge.

Bulmer, M. (2001). Social Measurement: What Stands in Its Way? *Social Research, 68*, 455–480.

Cho, T. (2008). A Study on Performance Evaluation System of Quasi-Governmental Bodies – Its Change and Reform Proposal. *Korean Journal of Governance, 15*(3), 155–178.

Cho, T. (2009). *Issues and Challenges of Public Institution Chief Manager Evaluation*. Presented at the 2009 Winter Conference of Korean Association for Public Administration, Wonju, South Korea, December 2009.

Cho, T., and Song, S. (2010). The Effects of the Management Performance Evaluation System on Management Efficiencies of Quasi-Governmental Agencies. *Korea Governance Review, 17*(3), 85–108.

Committee of Planning and Budget. (1998–1999). *Manual for Performance Evaluation of Government-Invested Institutions*. Ministry of Planning and Budget.

Denhardt, R. B., and Denhardt, J. V. (2000). The New Public Service: Serving Rather Than Steering. *Public Administration Review, 60*(6), 549–559.

Gong et al. (2013). *Performance Management: Foreign Example*. Seoul: Daeyoung Co.

Government-Invested Institutions Performance Evaluation Committee. (1986). *Manual for Performance Evaluation of Government-Invested Institutions 1986*. Ministry of Planning and Budget.

Heinrich, C. J. (2002). Outcomes – Based Performance Management in the Public Sector: Implications for Government Accountability and Effectiveness. *Public Administration Review, 62*(6), 712–725.

Henry, N. (1975). Paradigms of Public Administration. *Public Administration Review, 35*(4), 378–386.

Hong, G. (2015). *Study on Improvement Measures for Public Institution Management Performance Evaluation System*. Public Institution Management Research Institute.

Hood, C. (1991). A Public Management for All Seasons? *Public Administration, 69*(1), 3–19.

Jang, J., Kwak, C., Shin, W., and Oh, C. (2013). *Study on Transition Process of Public Institution Management Evaluation System (II)*. Korea Institute of Public Finance.

Kettl, D. F. (2005). *The Global Revolution in Public Management*. Washington, DC: Brookings Institution Press.

Korea Development Institute. (1981). *Improvement Measures for Government-Invested Institutions Management System*. Korea Development Institute.

Korea Development Institute. (2008). *Study on Improvement Measures for Public Institution Management Structure*. Korea Development Institute.

Korea Management Association Consulting. (2007). *Study on Reconstruction of Public Institution Management Evaluation System*. Ministry of Strategy and Finance.

Kwak, C. (2007). The Power of Information Announcement. *Seoul Daily News*, October 31.

Kwak, C., and Lee, C. (2010). *Directions for the Development of the Public Institution Management Evaluation System*. Public Institution Trends.

Light, P. C. (2001). *The New Public Service*. Washington, DC: Brookings Institution Press.

Ministry of Planning and Budget. (2000–2007). *Manual for Performance Evaluation of Government-Invested Institutions*. Ministry of Strategy and Finance.

Ministry of Planning and Budget. (2007). *Opening of Public Hearing for Derections for the Innovation in Public Institution Management Evaluation System*, November 28. Ministry of Planning and Budget.

Ministry of Strategy and Finance. (2008–2017). *Manual for Performance Evaluation of Public Corporations and Quasi-Government Institutions.* Ministry of Strategy and Finance.

Ministry of Strategy and Finance. (2013). *Improvements of the Performance Evaluation of Public Institutes System*, December. Ministry of Strategy and Finance.

Novick, D. (1973). *Current Practice in Program Budgeting (PPBS): Analysis and Case Studies Covering Government and Business.* London: Heinemann.

Nutley, S. M., Davies, H. T., and Smith, P. C. (2000). *What Works? Evidence-Based Policy and Practice in Public Services.* Cambridge, MA: MIT Press.

OECD. (2016). *State-Owned Enterprises in Asia: National Practices for Performance Evaluation and Management.* OECD and Korea Institute of Public Finance.

Osborne, S. P. (2006). The New Public Governance? *Public Management Review, 8*(3), 377–387.

Osborne, S. P. (2010). *The New Public Governance: Emerging Perspectives on the Theory and Practice of Public Governance.* London: Routledge.

Park, H. (2013). *Comparative Legislative Analysis on the Management System for Public Institutions.* Seoul: Korea Institute of Public Finance.

Park, S. (2005). 20 Years Outlook of Performance Evaluation of Public Corporation System and Transition Analysis, *15*(1), 11–47.

Park, S. (2009). Issues and Future Tasks of Pevaluation System of Public Institutions in Korea. *Korea Public Administration Winter Forum*, 1–18.

Park, S. (2014). History and Transition of Public Corporations: Focusing on Publicness. In *Public Corporations Reformation: Issues and Examples* (pp. 3–27). Seoul: Pakyoungsa.

Park, S., and Lee, H. (2014). National Projects and the Role of Public Corporations. In *Public* Corporations *Reformation: Issues and Example* (pp. 29–59). Seoul: Pakyoungsa.

Pesch, U. (2008). The Publicness of Public Administration. *Administration & Society, 40*(2), 140–193.

Pun, K. F., and White, A. S. (2005). A Performance Measurement Paradigm for Integrating Strategy Formulation: A Review of Systems and Frameworks. *International Journal of Management Reviews, 7*(1), 49–71.

Ra, Y., and Yoon, T. (2013). *An Analysis and a Proposal for Restructring the Performance Evaluation of Public Institutions System in Korea.* Seoul: Korea Institute of Public Finance.

Rivenbark, W. C. (2005). A Historical Overview of Cost Accounting in Local Government. *State and Local Government Review, 37*(3), 217–227.

Solesbury, W. (2001). *Evidence Based Policy: Whence It Came and Where It's Going.* ESRC UK Centre for Evidence Based Policy and Practice, Working Paper 1. London: ESRC UK Centre.

Song, D. (1983). A New Methodological Approach to Public Corporations Performance Evaluation. *KDI Journal of Economic Policy, 3122*, 106–123.

Song, D. (2015). Implementation Process of Korea's Public Corporation Evaluation System and Experiences During Early Operation. In *30 Years of Public Institution Performance Evaluation, Recollection and Outlook* (pp. 73–90). Korea Institute of Public Finance.

Song, D., Lee, J., Kim, S., and Yoo, H. (1987). *Theoretical Background and Methods of Public Corporation Performance Evaluation.* Seoul: Korea Development Institute.

Song, H. (2004). Analysis on the Systemization of Government-Affiliated Institution Management Evaluation. *Journal of Korea Association for Policy Studies, 13*(5), 73–93.

Sonu, W., and Kwak, C. (2006). *Study on Operation of Public Institution Board Performance Evaluation System.* Korea Corporate Governance Service.

Terry, L. D. (1998). Administrative Leadership, Neo-Managerialism, and the Public Management Movement. *Public Administration Review*, *58*(3), 194–200.

Van Dooren, W., Bouckaert, G., and Halligan, J. (2010). *Performance Management in the Public Sector.* New York, NY: Routledge.

Verbeeten, F. H. (2008). Performance Management Practices in Public Sector Organizations: Impact on Performance. *Accounting, Auditing & Accountability Journal*, *21*(3), 427–454.

Wilcox, M., and Bourne, M. (2002). *Performance Measurement and Management: Research and Action.* Paper presented at the Performance Management Association Conference, Centre for Business Performance, Boston, MA.

Williams, D. W. (2002). Before Performance Measurement. *Administrative Theory and Praxis*, *24*(6), 457–486.

Williams, D. W. (2003). Measuring Government in the Early Twentieth Century. *Public Administration Review*, *63*(6), 643–659.

Williams, D. W. (2004). Evolution of Performance Measurement Until 1930. *Administration & Society*, *36*(2), 131–165.

Yoo, H. (1997). Transformation of Control Over Government-Invested Institutions in Korea. *Korean Journal of Public Administration*, *35*(2), 205–219.

Yoon, H. (2011). Evaluation of Public Institution Management Evaluation System and Directions for Future Development. In *Public Institution Advancement, the Past, Present, and the Future* (pp. 25–51). Korea Institute of Public Finance.

Yoon, T. (2010). *Study on Transition Process of Public Institution Management Evaluation System.* Korea Institute of Public Finance.

2 Achievements of the performance evaluation of public institutions

Financial efficiency vs. publicness

Soonae Park, Jieun Son and Youngmi Lee

I Introduction

Recently, *social values* have become a rising topic in the Korea. The civil society as well as the legislature and the government are competitively taking measures for the realization of social values. The Framework Act on the Social Values Realization of Public Institutions (proposal) (hereafter Social Values Act) was proposed in 2014 and was incorporated into the PEPI as criteria for the efforts and performances for the realization of social values in 2018. Social values are not a newly introduced concept in the academic domain and can be interpreted as the previous roles of the government and as values described as publicness or public values. On the other hand, the Social Values Act suggests the detailed definition and concept of social values realization in order to facilitate the achievement of publicness.[1] The Social Values Act lists 11 items that the government should carry out, including protection of human rights, maintenance of safe environment from disasters and accidents, provision of health and welfare, assurance of labor rights, provision of opportunities for the socially disadvantaged and social integration, coexistence of large and smaller companies, and creation of high quality job opportunities. The post-democratization administrations have put endless efforts to realize such values and considerably utilized the PEPI system in order to motivate public institutions to participate in achieving public and social values. However, some critiques argue that the public institutions incline to focus on maximizing financial efficiency rather than strengthening publicness due to the biased PEPI system toward financial efficiency.

Why has the PEPI system been stigmatized in such ways? In order to find an answer, this chapter discusses the role and achievement of the PEPI system. On the one hand, based on a theoretical review, we analyze the trends of performance indicators for the management of finance and budget – such as the profitability of public corporations – to understand the system's contribution to the improvement of financial efficiency of public corporations. Although the trends may be different from those of the entire public institutions because the analysis is limited to public corporations, we believe meaningful findings can be suggested. On the other hand, we analyze how the PEPI system contributes to the realization of public values of public corporations. The PEPI system is composed of numerous indicators related to compliance with the government policies and the realization of public values in order for the public institutions to enthusiastically materialize publicness and social values. Therefore, we have examined closely how the PEPI system contributed to the financial performance and the realization of publicness

II Theoretical backgrounds and previous studies

1 Definition of financial performance and publicness

The two prominent values – financial efficiency and publicness that public institutions should fundamentally pursue – are defined in various ways due to the multidimensionality of the values and the ambiguity of the performance objectives in the public sector. Likewise, the two values are measured by diverse variables.

In the private sector, financial efficiency refers to a combination of different aspects including profitability, productivity, and financial condition and is measured usually with values such as the return on assets (ROA), the return on equity (ROE), the return on sales (ROS), and the return on investment (ROI). However, financial efficiency in the public sector does not solely mean calculations through profit maximization measures. Sun and Tong (2003) and Park and Hong (2010) state that the management performance of the public sector can be defined in various dimensions such as productivity, profitability, and efficiency and that the indicators of value added, labor productivity, sales to total assets ratio, labor efficiency, and capital efficiency. Cho and Song (2010) suggests that a reduction in debt ratio can be utilized as an indicator for increases in financial management efficiency of public institutions, considering the current situation in which the sloppy management and excessive business expansion of public institutions become social issues. Moreover, the indicators widely utilized for profitability measurements in the private sector such as ROA, ROE, and ROS can be applied to the evaluation of financial efficiency in the public sector and Dewenter and Malatesta (2001), Ahn and Yoon (2009), and Yoo and Park (2013) measure the profitability of public institutions with the indicators mentioned. In all, the financial efficiency of public institutions can be evaluated by indicators for monetary profitability as well as by indicators that reflect specific financial environments surrounding public institutions such as the debt ratio.

On the other hand, there is little consensus on a definition of publicness due to its relatively greater multidimensionality and ambiguity.[2] While the definition can vary in accordance with the theoretical backgrounds and public-private classification approaches taken into account, the mainstream considers government's actions for pursuing public interest as publicness. In this approach, publicness is defined as the involvement of the government in the production of public goods and services and the activities regarding public interests. In other words, publicness refers to the production and the provision of public goods and services that the market is incompetent for (publicness of public goods) and the realization of public interest of the social community (publicness of public interest) (Pesch, 2008: 175–177). Based on this viewpoint, publicness composes of core values such as accessibility, public interest, publicly sharedness, and fairness (Park and Lee, 2014: 33). This chapter borrows the definition by Yoo and Park (2013) defining the publicness of public institutions as 'the level of public value achievement from public services provided by public institutions under the government's control'.

In the previous studies on the public value realization of public organizations, publicness is measured through various measures. Bozeman (2002, 2007) and Haque (2001) argue that the extent of how much public institutions consider public values important and how much public values are realized through the provision of public goods and services should be measured. Moulton (2009) suggests the concept of 'realized publicness' and states that publicness could be measured with the achievement level of project objectives for public values realization. Meanwhile, Kim (2014) utilizes the concept of *social satisfaction* suggested by Geyskens and Steenkamp (2000) and measured publicness with the level of resident satisfaction from goods and services provided by public institutions. Overall, publicness could be measured with the common management activities of the public institutions and the level of considerations for public interest, fairness, and social equity in the provision of public services and with the level of people's satisfaction from the services provided by public institutions.

2 Previous studies on the contributions of the PEPI system

Previous studies on the PEPI system can be distinguished as normative studies focused on theoretical aspects and empirical studies based on analyzing surveys and statistical data. The normative studies conducted by Kim (2001), Oh (1996), Song (1987), and Shim (2001) view the system positively and anticipate that the PEPI system will generate management innovation in the public institutions not only to enhance the efficiency, responsibility, and autonomy, but also to strengthen public benefits to ultimately heighten the credibility and satisfaction of the people.

The empirical studies are conducted in order to systematically conceptualize and objectively measure the effectiveness of the PEPI system. It is reported that the PEPI system has contributed to various dimensions of performance including management efficiency, profitability, responsibility, and improvements in service qualities (Kwak, 2003; Kim, 2010; Nam and Choi, 2011; Ra and Yoon, 2013; Park, 2006; Lee, 2011; Cho and Song, 2010; Choi and Park, 2009). For example, Kwak (2003) conducts analyses on the manual for the performance evaluation of government-invested institutions and employee surveys. He finds that there are positive influences on the transparency, customer satisfaction, management efficiency, and productivity enhancement. However, Kwak (2003) concludes that there is relatively little success in strengthening the management autonomy. Park (2006) analyzes the long-term time series data during 1965–2004 focusing on each ratio of administrative expenses, labor expenses, personnel increase, financial expenses, and debt ratio of 13 public corporations. He finds that PEPI has positive influences on human resource administration efficiency but insignificant influences on financial structure improvement. In the survey conducted by Ra and Yoon (2013), a large number of public institution employees and related experts states that the current system contributes highly to enhancing management efficiency, responsibility, and publicness but is inadequate in enhancing profitability and autonomy. On the other hand, Kim (2010) states that the analyses on 1999–2009 public institution panel data shows improvements in profitability after the implementation of the management evaluation system. Moreover, Nam and Choi (2011) propose survey results that the PEPI system has positive contributions in increasing the profitability, publicness, and service qualities in case of local public corporations. Overall, the PEPI system appears to have relatively clear positive influences in the aspects of management efficiency enhancement and publicness realization but minor influences in the aspect of financial efficiency.

Evidence for better financial efficiency appears to be insufficient in the studies on the central government performance evaluation, as well (Park, 2002; Lee, 2003; Hwang and Cho, 2016). For example, Lee (2003) analyzes the survey for experts and public officers responsible for evaluation in the central government organizations. It is reported that there was a dominant recognition that the evaluation system was helpful for enhancing the efficiency and responsibility of civil services but contributes little to enhancing the efficiency of budget execution. Hwang and Cho (2016) also surveys public officers to investigate if the evaluation system boosts the effectiveness, efficiency, and responsibility of the government operation. They conclude that the system is most suitable for securing the responsibility for the results, rather than the effectiveness – which refers to the level of goal achievement or the efficiency – which refers to input-output ratio calculation.

Overall, first, the previous studies on the effectiveness of the PEPI system have been conducted mainly based on theoretical aspects or analyses of survey results, and it is only recent that empirical studies have been increasing. Although the expansion of empirical studies is desirable as the performance of the evaluation system is defined with greater detail and measured with higher precision, more studies and researches need to be conducted and accumulated since consensually acceptable variables related to the performance and measurement methods are yet to be suggested.

Second, empirical studies suggest conflicting results about the impact of the PEPI system on performance, especially for financial efficiency. Due to the inherent characteristics of the public sector, the concept of performance is multidimensional and composes of conflicting values. Therefore, it is difficult to set up relevant analysis models and interpret the results. However, as long as the PEPI system operates, continuous attempts should be made to collect more accurate data and construct more solid models to estimate its performance. In order to expand the base of empirical studies and explore the implications of the performance evaluation system, we analyze the effectiveness of the PEPI system in enhancing the profitability and publicness of public corporations based on statistical data and manuals for PEPI.

III Contributions to financial efficiency

One of the major purposes of PEPI is to objectively measure the management efficiency of public institutions and utilize the information to find and rectify the features in need of management improvement, in order to enhance the responsibility and responsiveness of the institutions as public organizations. Therefore, the PEPI system has been consistently developing the indicator framework to check the financial performance such as the efficiency and profitability of the public institutions. For example, in the 1999 manual for the performance evaluation of government-invested institutions, management efficiency is measured by the indicators of the productivity of fixed capital and labor productivity in the comprehensive management sector and by the indicators of administrative expenses, labor expenses, capital management and inventory management in the management efficiency sector. The indicators are further systematically developed and structured into fields such as management of remuneration and management of finance and budget and its accomplishments. Whereas the indicator for the labor productivity was measured with public benefits per employee until 2006, it is pointed out in the 2007 manual that the unclear concept of public benefits is eliminated in the productivity measurement and substituted with the concept of value added.[3] It seems that efforts were made to incorporate public interest into the quantitative indicators for financial efficiency.

The current indicators for financial efficiency of the public corporations are work efficiency (labor productivity, capital productivity, value added ratio),[4] finance and budget performance (debt ratio, interest coverage ratio, level of debt reduction achievement), administrative expenses, and total labor expense increase ratio. *Based on the evaluation materials*, the keywords for evaluation of the profitability of public corporations can be assets, profits, revenues, and efficiency. Profits and efficiency created by such factors are reflected in the PEPI system by utilizing measures such as the ROA.[5] The 'ROA global competence' indicator of the Incheon International Airport Corporation is a good example of the utilization of the net income to total assets ratio.

Figure 2.1 illustrates the trends in two indicators for profitability, ROA, and ROS[6] at 22 public corporations for the period 2003–2016 that submitted the balance sheet to the board of audit and inspection.[7] The trends of the both indicators show an overall decrease. The sharp decrease in 2015 is presumed to result from the realization of the debts of the institutions related to overseas resource development due to oil price fluctuations. In order to investigate whether the stagnation or decrease in the profitability is due to the nature of the business, the 22 public corporations are divided into institutions related to energy businesses and institutions related to social infrastructure, and then the individual ROA and ROS trends are observed. While the public corporations in the energy division are more likely to experience changes in the sales-related profit ratio as the prices are mostly set based on the prime cost, the assets-related profit ratio tends to be significantly lower due to the possession and operation of social infrastructure with characteristics of public goods.

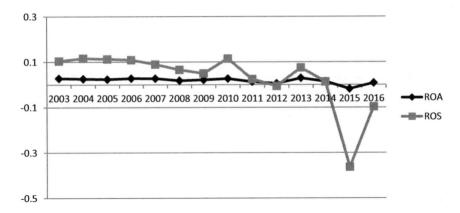

Figure 2.1 Profitability trends at 22 public corporations (2003–2016)

As shown in Figure 2.2, while the institutions in the social infrastructure field show slightly increasing trends, drastic decreases in some of the institutions affect the entire trends in both divisions. The Korea Railroad Corporation in the social infrastructure field and the Korea Coal Corporation in the energy field are consistently in the state of capital impairment and the Korea Resource Corporation, Korea National Oil Corporation, and Korea Water Resources Corporation are also observed to be experiencing financial difficulties.

Meanwhile, as the sloppy management and increased debt of public institutions have increasingly become a major social issue, PEPI has put more emphasis on indicators for debt reduction in the aspects of financial and budget management of the individual institutions. In order to examine the results of such efforts, the trends in indicators for the management of financial and budget at 22 public corporations that submitted the balance sheet to the board of audit and inspection for the period of 2003–2016 are presented in Table 2.1 and Figure 2.3.

In the fiscal year of 2016, the total debts amount to around 362 trillion won and the capital to around 196 trillion won, showing a decrease of approximately 10 percent in the debt ratio compared with the previous year. Whereas the debt ratio has been intensely rising since 2008, the decrease in the debt ratio is believed to have happened due to the ceaseless efforts including the reinforcement of finance and budget management and disposal of non-core assets as a part of the public institution normalization policy in 2013. The increase in the equity is comparably smaller than that of the debt and the revenue. The net profit maintains similar levels except in 2016. Overall, the financial soundness has been moderately recovered despite there are differences associated with the institution types and characteristics of the times. Although the rally is possible with to the national attention and self-efforts of the institutions, it is not difficult to believe that institution's efforts are caused by PEPI's carrot-and-stick features such as performance pay, chief manager dismissal, and other management improvement measures.

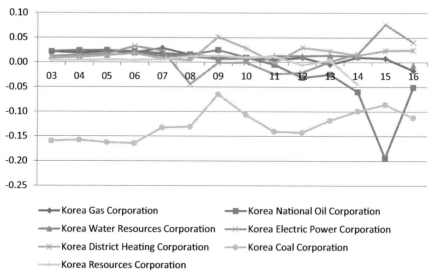

Energy field (ROA)[8]

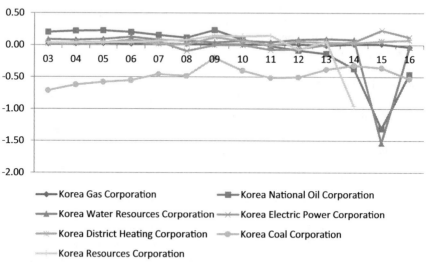

Energy field (ROS)[9]

Figure 2.2 Trends of the profitability of public corporations in the energy field and the social infrastructure field (2003–2016)

Social infrastructure field (ROA)

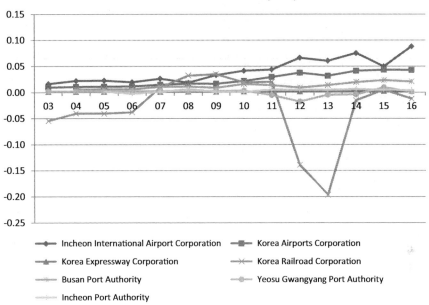

- Incheon International Airport Corporation
- Korea Expressway Corporation
- Busan Port Authority
- Incheon Port Authority
- Korea Airports Corporation
- Korea Railroad Corporation
- Yeosu Gwangyang Port Authority

Social infrastructure field (ROS)

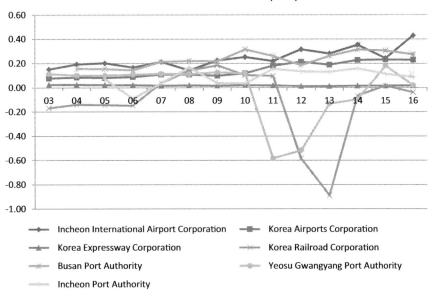

- Incheon International Airport Corporation
- Korea Expressway Corporation
- Busan Port Authority
- Incheon Port Authority
- Korea Airports Corporation
- Korea Railroad Corporation
- Yeosu Gwangyang Port Authority

Figure 2.2 (Continued)

Table 2.1 Trends in indicators for the management of finance and budget at 22 public corporations (2003–2016) (unit: hundred billion won)

Year	Total Debts (A)	Assets (B)	Equity (C)	Revenue (D)	Net Profit (E)	Debt Ratio (F = A/C)
2003	646.97	1,574.35	895.81	526.11	19.02	72.22%
2004	692.65	1,687.81	962.08	521.29	23.18	71.99%
2005	741.90	1,752.11	1,028.10	563.67	26.35	72.16%
2006	684.93	1,751.05	1,064.11	584.66	35.79	64.37%
2007	714.52	1,828.78	1,117.20	645.13	36.44	63.96%
2008	941.46	2,043.36	1,134.40	781.37	−9.56	82.99%
2009	2,129.70	3,516.15	1,390.09	832.17	21.38	153.21%
2010	2,457.14	3,908.02	1,454.05	983.90	29.35	168.99%
2011	3,286.94	4,988.25	1,701.30	1,285.37	−5.69	193.20%
2012	3,531.27	5,227.61	1,696.34	1,451.59	−34.13	208.17%
2013	3,736.76	5,475.42	1,738.66	1,479.65	−24.26	214.92%
2014	3,770.07	5,584.03	1,813.95	1,533.76	39.85	207.84%
2015	3,648.09	5,523.00	1,874.79	1,469.52	42.04	194.59%
2016	3,623.96	5,593.52	1,969.56	1,410.06	85.9764	184.00%

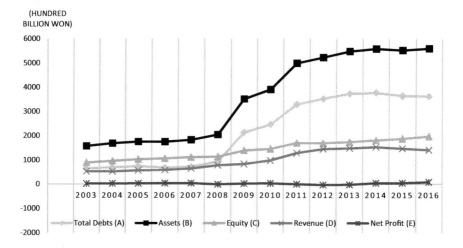

Figure 2.3 Trends in indicators for the management of finance and budget at 22 public
corporations (2003–2016)

IV Contributions to the realization of public values

As mentioned previously in the theoretical discussions, publicness can be conceptualized as the level of public value achievement of public services provided
by the government through public corporations. The PEPI system has been continuously constructing the indicator framework to check the degree of publicness
realization by public corporations along with the financial efficiency, and a variety

of indicators can be found in the manual for PEPI. In the following sections, the indicators related to publicness are categorized into common management activities and main business activities. In order to observe how publicness is considered in the process of evaluation, the transition of the indicators in the manuals for PEPI is reviewed.

1 Contribution to publicness in the aspect of common management activities

Apart from the individual businesses carried out by the public corporations, qualitative indicators related to the common management activities that are generally applied to all evaluation institutions include the efforts to evaluate the government's responsibility, responsiveness, and social responsibility implementation in overall management. While the bigger frame of reflecting publicness has remained, detailed criteria used for the evaluation have changed with time as the social responsibility of public institutions varies according to the economic, social, and political environments. In the following sections, the transition characteristics of indicators in individual sectors of comprehensive management (including leadership, strategy, and corporate social responsibility), organization and human resources, finance and budget, and labor-relations are reviewed with reference to the discussions of publicness in the aspects of government organizations and systems[10]

The performance indicators during the Kim Dae-Jung administration explicitly provided that the public interest and efficiency of government-invested institutions be objectively measured by weighing the 'executive efforts for responsible management and enhancement of public interest (weight 18/32)' in the comprehensive management sector. Moreover, the management philosophy of the CEO and efforts for management innovation in response to changes in the organization environment were evaluated to facilitate the achievement of visible long-term system and performance of the corporations in the aspects of efficiency and publicness. In particular, the efforts of the institutions for management innovation plans are reflected in quantitative indicators to emphasize the enhancement of fairness and rationality of the evaluation system and cost reduction for internal administration such as capital system improvements, restructuring, and evaluation of job performance. Moreover, the efficiency of the public sector was pursued to overcome the financial crisis with measures such as the execution and joint efforts of labor and management. Indicators for the efforts for client satisfaction enhancement, competence- and performance-oriented human resources management, and equal employment opportunity were added since 2001 to increase the public responsiveness of the institutions.

The Roh Moo-Hyun administration continued with the principles of the former administration. Weights for indicators such as realization of responsible management and public interest enhancement increased and the effort for ethical management was added as an indicator. Also, the term *social responsibility* was first introduced in the indicator to evaluate efforts for government policy compliance and performance. It was during this administration when the aspects of public interest and social value realization of the public institutions were greatly emphasized.[11] Since 2006, the socio-economic role of the government was emphasized by stipulating 'efforts for supporting small and medium sized enterprise (SME) and performance' as an evaluation factor. Moreover, socially balanced recruitment was more enthusiastically practiced by including the expansion of employment opportunities for women and the disabled and the employment equity according to majors (natural sciences and engineering) as evaluation factors. Furthermore, new indicators were added to concurrently pursue publicness and efficiency, including cooperative productivity enhancement efforts of the labor and management, cooperative social responsibility realization of the labor and management, and budget planning standards considering public interest and profitability and rationality of the process.

The Lee Myung-Bak administration emphasized the management philosophy, core values and the connectivity between them in the leadership and strategy sector and sought to increase the responsiveness of the public institutions by evaluating the strategies for the rapidly changing environment. The realization of social values and execution of duties were emphasized with the establishment of the corporate social responsibility indicator in 2011. Both the quality and quantity of newly created jobs in the private sector was considered, and the realization of the fair society, mutual growth with SME partners, and social service activities of public institutions were emphasized.[12] In particular, the social service activities of public institutions were evaluated based on whether they were responsible activities related to the major tasks of the institution for the community or the whole country in terms of social responsibility, not simply volunteer level activities. While the effort for fair contracts was included in the finance and budget management indicator, the socially balanced recruitment in the public sector was widened to academic backgrounds.

The Park Geun-hye administration stipulated the settlement and connectivity of vision, core values, and management goals and the efforts for government project execution and performance evaluation to facilitate the public institutions to actively execute government projects. Moreover, the corporate social responsibility of public institutions, guarantee of equal opportunities and establishment of fair trade order, support for strengthening competences of SME partners, and efforts for supporting women and social enterprises were evaluated. In the aspects of organization and human resources management, systematic management as well as transition to regular (indefinitely contracted) employment of non-regular employees and the appropriateness of indirectly employed workers were newly added as evaluation contents. From 2015, the evaluations for preparations for the future and efforts for establishment of new growth engine were implemented.[13]

In the current Moon Jae-in administration, it appears that efforts for pursuing the social responsibility and publicness will be further strengthened with measures such as job creation and regularization of non-regular employment as announced in the presidential pledge.

Table 2.2 Transition of qualitative indicators related to publicness in common management activities by government administrations

	Kim Dae-Jung Administration	Roh Moo-Hyun Administration	Lee Myung-Back Administration	Park Geun-hye Administration	Moon Jae-in Administration
Comprehensive Management (including leadership, strategy, and corporate social responsibility)	– Executive effort for responsible management and enhancement of public interest – detailed and shared vision within the organization, response to organizational environment change – Effort for customer satisfaction enhancement	– Strengthening social responsibility, execution of ethical management – Effort for government policy compliance and performance – Corporate social responsibility activities and performance – Support for SME	– Relevance, interconnectivity, responsiveness of management philosophy and core values – Corporate social responsibility, job creation – Emphasis on fair society, mutual growth – Emphasis on social services activities (major tasks related to social responsibility)	– Effort for government project execution and performance evaluation – Support for SME partners – Support for women and social enterprises	– Realization of social values, vitalization of social economy – Leading 4th industrial revolution – Establishment of fair market order

(Continued)

Table 2.2 (Continued)

	Kim Dae-Jung Administration	Roh Moo-Hyun Administration	Lee Myung-Back Administration	Park Geun-hye Administration	Moon Jae-in Administration
Organization and Human Resources	– Enhancement of fairness and rationality of internal performance evaluation system – Socially balanced recruitment: enhancement of equal employment	– Socially balanced recruitment: women, the disabled, major (natural sciences and engineering) and regions	– Socially balanced recruitment: expansion of academic backgrounds (inclusive of high school graduates)	– Management of non-regular employment and transition to regular (indefinitely contracted) employment and adequacy of indirectly employed workers – Preparations for the future and efforts for establishment of new growth engine	– Job creation in the public sector – Solution for the non-regular employment issue – Establishment of fair and competence-oriented recruitment environment
Finance and budget	– Effort for cost reduction	– Budget planning standards considering public interest and profitability – rationality of the process	– Effort for fair contracts	– Do.	– Balance between efficiency and publicness
Labor-management relations	– joint effort for productivity enhancement between labor and management	– Appropriateness of cooperative social responsibility realization of the labor and management	– Do.	– Do.	– Realization of laboristic society

Source: Committee of Planning and Budget, (1998-1999). Manual for Performance Evaluation of Government-Invested Institutions; Ministry of Planning and Budget. (2000–2007). Manual for Performance Evaluation of Government-Invested Institutions; Ministry of Strategy and Finance. (2008-2017). Manual for Performance Evaluation of Public Corporations and Quasi-Government Institutions. Ministry of Strategy and Finance.

Note: For the Moon Jae-in administration, the 100 government projects and 5-year government operation plans are reviewed.

Overall, PEPI indicators have been directed at strengthening the normative identity of public corporations as agents for public interest achievement. It can be observed that the public corporations have reinforced the responsibility and responsiveness of the institutions to fulfill the demands of the people according to the socio-economic changes.

2 Contribution to publicness in the aspect of main business activities

Whereas the indicators in the common management activities are applied to all of the institutions, the indicators in the main business activities that evaluate the appropriateness and contents of the main business are inevitably distinguished for individual institutions. The indicators for the main business activities of individual institutions since the 1999 government-invested institution evaluation to the 2016 PEPI have been focused on evaluating values such as public interest, fairness, and social equity of services that the people need but are insufficiently provided by the market. While the main business to accomplish such values are varied for the individual institutions, this chapter aims to analyze how public interest was considered in the area of safety and environment which are thought to be the role of the government. In the following sections, we investigate safety-environment related public corporations that were established initially as government-invested institutions, which include the Korea Water Resources Corporation, Korea Mint-ing and Security Printing Corporation, Korea Coal Corporation, Incheon Interna-tional Airport Corporation, also including institutions that were classified later as a public corporation such as the Korea Hydro and Nuclear Power Co. Ltd. and other 5 power corporations and the Incheon Port Authority.

The indicators related to the safety and environment have been continuously expanded and strengthened in the aspects of evaluation scope and importance after the 2000s. During the Kim Dae-Jung administration, the Korea Water Resources Corporation focused generally on the facility maintenance and quantity management of water resources, and flood control. For example, in the indica-tor for 'water resources facility maintenance and safety management,' the pub-lic corporation was encouraged to enthusiastically make efforts to prevent ages from natural disasters and protect the people and their properties by evaluating the appropriateness of the safety diagnosis of dams and the activities of maintenance inspections.[14] The appropriateness and performance of water quality management for both the raw water and purified water were evaluated for water quality man-agement along with the quantity management. The Roh Moo-Hyun administra-tion continued efforts for the water quality and quantity management. In addition, the effort for water resource development and environmental conservation were newly added for a balance of conflicting values of development and conserva-tion. The Lee Myung-Bak administration introduced the indicator for the level of achievement of the global water quality standard and applied the strictest qualifi-cation for the drinking water by comparing with those of the developed countries. Also, new environmentally friendly growth projects were promoted including the development of environmentally friendly water resources and energy, and

expansion of new renewable energy development. The Park Geun-hye administration increased the weights for the flood damage reduction and drinking water
quality and safety enhancement. Furthermore, the indicators for the construction
and soundness enhancement of waterfront spaces were newly implemented to
evaluate the efforts to improve the waterfront environments that the people can
directly experience.

In cases of the Korea Railroad Corporation and Incheon International Airport
Corporation that were evaluated since the Roh Moo-Hyun administration, safety
was considered as the most important indicator. The indicators for the railroad
service were designed to consider both operation and human accidents to facilitate the diligent involvement of service providers including the locomotive engi-
neers and anticipatory prevention of potential hazards including the carelessness
of the users.[15] Also, the emphasis was on the quality management and reduction of
breakdown for the railroad facilities including the track safety and vehicle inspection. Similarly, the Incheon International Airport Corporation was evaluated on
the facility management for the airport safety and safe operation of aircrafts and
the security screening and counter-terrorism activities were strengthened. The Lee
Myung-Bak administration introduced the indicator for 'global competence for
railroad accidents' and compared the number of railroad accidents with those of
the global top 5 countries announced by the International Union of Railways.
Moreover, the safety management system and employee capability enhancement
for railroad safety management were also incorporated in the aspect of safety management. For the airport services, efforts were made not only to ensure facility-
based safety, but also to improve the level of safety to the international level. The
Park Geun-hye administration increased the weights for the safety-related indicators and continuously the importance of safety has been strengthened.

The Korea Hydro & Nuclear Power Co. Ltd. (converted to a market-type public
corporation in 2011) was incorporated into the PEPI system with the subsidiary
companies of KEPCO during the Lee Myung-Bak administration.[16] Weights for
nuclear safety management (17 points) were lower than that of power generation
business in the earlier manuals. The weights were increased in 2012 by 22 points
and became a core element of the main business activities. During the early stage,
the stability of the facility operation and employee safety management (employee
radiation dosage and industrial accidents) were the focus of the evaluation. In
2013, the 'appropriateness of emergency response' was added to the indicator for
'nuclear safety'. In the Park Geun-hye administration, weights for safety-related
indicators were significantly increased and emphasized the importance of nuclear
safety by adding safety to all of the indicator titles.

Overall, while indicators for some of the institutions including the Korea Coal
Co., Korea Expressway Co., Korea Water Resources Co., and Korea Electric
Power Co. were found to be related to safety during the Kim Dae-Jung administration, the safety-related indicators were expanded during the Roh Moo-Hyun
administration and focused mainly on the safety of the facilities. The Lee Myung-
Bak administration aimed for qualitative improvements in the safety indicators
and reflected the efforts for enhancing the public safety by facilitating preventive

safety responses through comparisons with the safety standards of the developed countries. Moreover, the Park Geun-hye administration increased weights for the national safety-related indicators, influenced by crises including the Sewol ferry accident. The Moon Jae-in administration inaugurated in 2017 emphasizes the role of the government for safety accidents and disasters. Sustainable supply of safe energy and enhancement of the public safety to protect the health of the people are proposed as major policy task with the anti-nuclear policies. An overall summary of the characteristics of safety indicators for the individual administrations is illustrated in Table 2.3.

Environment-related indicators have been less emphasized, compared to safety-related indicators. The Korea Coal Corporation had developed indicators related to environmental improvement during the Kim Dae-Jung administration and evaluated the prevention measures for environmental pollution and natural landscape destruction. The Korea Minting and Security Printing Corporation has been monitoring the BOD (Biological Oxygen Demand) and COD (Chemical Oxygen Demand) levels to maintain the drain water produced during the manufacturing process. It appears that the prevention of environmental pollution was strengthened as weights for the environmental improvement of the Korea Coal Co. and the water quality management of the Korea Minting and Security Printing Co. were increased in the latter half of the Kim Dae-Jung administration. The environment-related indicators of the Roh Moo-Hyun administration were structured similarly to those of the Kim Dae-Jung administration. The Korea Coal Corporation was evaluated based on the pollution prevention due to mining and technological development for the prevention measures. Korea Minting & Security Printing Co. was evaluated based on the drain water management as in the Kim Dae-Jung administration.

A significant characteristic of the environment-related indicators during the Lee Myung-Bak administration was the addition of the new renewable energy project. All of the five power generation companies included the renewable energy business. The Korea Hydro and Nuclear Power Co. also established an indicator such as future growth energy development, and encouraged to participate in the development of environmentally friendly energy. The environment-related indicators were relatively simplified during the Park Geun-hye administration compared with the former administrations. For the Korea Coal Corporation, power generation corporations, Korea Hydro and Nuclear Power Co. and Korea Minting & Security Printing Co., indicators related to environmental conservation were integrated or replaced with other indicators. However, in case of the Incheon Port Authority, a new indicator for reduction of environmental pollution was established for environmentally friendly port operation which was previously managed with the clean cargo indicator during the Lee Myung-Bak administration. The new indicator emphasized the reduction of dust scattering.

The environment-related government projects of the Moon Jae-in administration focus mainly on the prevention and reduction of air pollution directly affecting the lives of the people, energy development and welfare. It has been announced that the coal power generation will be reduced through measures such

Table 2.3 Example of safety-related indicators by administration

	Kim Dae Jung administration	Roh Moo-Hyun administration	Lee Myung-Bak administration	Park Geun-hye administration	Moon Jae-in administration
	Focus on facility safety		*Focus on safety quality*		*Focus on the people*
Incheon Intl. Airport Corporation	–	– Airport security management: Safety management: safe operation, airport facility safety, emergency management	– Airport safety management – Airport security system enhancement, security system maintenance – Global competence of airport operation: comparison with the ACI (Airport Council International) standards	– Airport safety, security management – Appropriateness for safe airport performance management	– Prevention of safety accidents and construction of national responsibility system for disaster – Competence for timely response to disaster and construction of integrative system – Reduction in nuclear power plants based on the anti-nuclear roadmap – Public safety enhancement for health of the people
Korea Railroad Corporation	–	– Facility maintenance and car inspection – Facility quality management, breakdown reduction	– Railroad accident global competence – Railroad safety management competence enhancement – Policy improvement for railroad safety – Mid– and long-term railroad security	– Train operation safety service – Appropriateness of performance management for comfortable and safe railroad services	

Korea Water Resources Corporation	– Water resources facility maintenance, safety inspection, maintenance check – Dam management: flood control, safety management	– Water supply plant management and appropriateness of operation – Dam management and appropriateness of operation, flood control	– Water quality global competence – Flood control securement	– Enhancement of drinking water quality and safety – Appropriateness of performance management for healthy tap water provision – Reduction of flood damage
Korea Hydro & Nuclear Power Co. Ltd.	–	– Facility operation security – Nuclear safety and emergency management – Employee safety management: radiation dosage and industrial accidents		– Integrative safety performance index of nuclear facility – Appropriateness of performance management for nuclear safety management – Active nuclear power plant safety management index

as the temporary shutdown of old coal power plants. Furthermore, strategies for the energy new industry and a transfer to a low carbon and high efficiency structure are likely to be incorporated as PEPI indicators.

V Lessons learned and conclusion

1 Lessons learned

It is evident that public corporations have played significant roles in Korea's economic development; however the expansion of the public sector in response to the economic growth has been condemned as another issue. After experiencing a foreign exchange crisis in the 1990s, South Korea has enforced a New Public Management (NPM) reform in order to maximize the efficiency of the public sector and, in consequence, it is considered as an exemplary case to successfully overcome the foreign exchange crisis. It is, thus, ironic that the topic of publicness or a realization of social value' is hotly debated than that of efficiency. What does this phenomenon imply? A conclusion is that the role of public institutions varies with the stage of economic growth and changes in social environment and it is imperative to develop a performance evaluation tool that can not only manage such changes effectively but can also cope with the situation proactively. From the 1950s, when the infrastructures were nonexistent until now, South Korea has achieved a rapid economic growth and experienced various problems accompanying it. The PEPI system in Korea, integrated with experiences and know-hows to solve these problems, can be an excellent guideline for establishing the role and vision of public corporations in developing countries.

In general, the most distinguished feature of public corporations is the separation of ownership and enforcement rights. The PEPI system may be the most effective way to solve the agency problems arising from separation of ownership and enforcement. More importantly, the PEPI system is a powerful tool that can have profound influence on the establishment of long-term vision and goals for public corporations. Therefore, in order to enable public corporations to actively cope with changes in public demand and level of expectation for public services according to the stages of economic development, it is essential to contemplate how to reflect various values that people wish to realize as well as financial efficiency.

In recent years, the role of public corporations in many developing countries in Asia has been worthy of close attention. According to the OECD (2010), public corporations comprise about 30 percent of GDP in China,[17] about 38 percent of GDP in Vietnam, about 25 percent in India and Thailand, and about 15 percent in Malaysia and Singapore (ADBI, 2017: 1). The PEPI system in Korea can provide meaningful implications for the management of public corporations in developing countries. As a sophisticated tool for evaluating and managing performance and building a monitoring system, it can be a useful reference. In particular, the notion of 'publicness' is worthy of notice. In most developing countries which currently operate public corporations, performance management is mostly focus on the financial aspect. For instance, net interest margin, revenue, total profit, economic value added, and debt ratio are considered as indicators to quantitatively evaluate financial efficiency while qualitative aspects including strategic planning, cooperate responsibility, vision setting, and risk management are also considered in some countries. However, customer satisfaction is the only indicator that evaluates the public function of public corporations. Although India exceptionally considers aspects of 'corporate social responsibility,' there are limitations that it is approaching through restricted viewpoint such as support for only underdeveloped regions and creation of employment opportunities.

Publicness (social values) can be defined differently according to the historical context and situation of each country as well as public demand for service. The PEPI system has reflected both the financial efficiency and public values which the government should realize according to the stages of economic growth and development. This allowed them to specify the role that the public sector should play and to faithfully carry out the monitoring function that can enhance the level of publicness at a national level rather than realizing gains of each public corporation. The transition of publicness indicators as shown in the PEPI system can be a guideline for the developing countries in setting the public values and the role of the state.

2 Conclusion

The PEPI system has played a role of encouraging the public institutions to achieve their original establishment purposes by evaluating not only the financial efficiency in the aspect of common management activities but also performances in the main business activities. The PEPI system has been continuously modified to facilitate the public institutions to satisfy the demands for public services. The evaluation structure and indicators as well as the weights for the indicators have been revised according to the economic and social changes. It is generally acknowledged that the PEPI system has the positive effect on the performance of the public sector. Although the scope of this chapter's analysis is limited, the results show that the financial soundness of public corporations has been improved and that the public corporations are implementing self-measures to improve their financial efficiency. In addition, the PEPI system has contributed to ultimately realizing the social values by facilitating the public corporations to enthusiastically participate in the aspects of publicness that are directly related to the lives of the people and are vulnerable to market failure such as safety, disasters, welfare, and environment.

While it has proven the positive influence and performance, the PEPI system will be encountering a substantial, forthcoming reformation. As the system ultimately evaluates how the people are efficiently and sufficiently provided with the demanded public services, the evaluation system should be improved according to the changing expectations of the people or the social environment around the public sector. However, in order for the public corporations to achieve the values of both the financial efficiency and publicness, the reformation ought to be implemented in a balanced perspective. The legitimacy of the existence of the public corporations would not be supported if the emphasis was limited to the financial efficiency. If the emphasis is only on the realization of publicness, then public corporations will be no different from social enterprises. In the similar context, if the focus of the performance evaluation was on the output, the initial purpose of the public corporations could be neglected. On the other hand, if extensive focus was on the outcome, the input resources and activities would be overlooked until the performance becomes visible or sufficient for measurement. Moreover, the evaluation system needs to adhere to a balanced viewpoint about the he organizational activities, as the performance of the institutions are closely related to the organization scale, project stability, and various types of know-hows established within the organization. It is obviously challenging to pursue the conflicting values of profitability and public interest at the same time. Particularly if the public institutions were considered as mere instruments for execution of government projects, it may become more difficult to decide how the financial efficiency, and publicness should be weighted differently.

While the center of focus may have varied according to the economic and social circumstances, it is clear that the PEPI system is a touchstone to establish an integrative vision and widely examine the profitability and publicness for a timely provision of public services in demand. Although the PEPI system of Korea that has been evolving for the past 30 years may not be perfect, we highly recognizes it as one of the most sophisticated systems even in the global standards. Nevertheless, it is a problem in a different dimension whether the PEPI has entirely achieved its intent in the process of actual operation. We need continuous efforts to improve the PEPI system as well as to properly operate it, like the proverb 'move like a cow, with the eyes of a tiger.'

Notes

1 The Social Values Act defines the purpose of the Act as: 1) considering economic values as well as the societal, environmental, and cultural values in establishing and executing the policies of public institutions; 2) constructing the framework for legitimate evaluation of public institutions' social values realization; and 3) achieving economic order and economic democratization that respect freedom and creativity.

2 Refer to "History and Transition of Public Corporations: Focusing on Publicness", pp. 3–14; "National Projects and the Role of Public Corporations: Focusing on Housing and Overseas Resource Development", pp. 33–37 (Park, 2014), 'Public Corporation Reformation: Issues and Examples') for detailed discussion of the different views on publicness and dimensions.

3 According to the definition in manual of the time, public benefit refers to the corporate profit before transfer expenditure such as taxes and interest expenses was subtracted. In principle, net sales must be calculated after deducting the material costs, labor costs, other costs (exclusive of depreciation, taxes, and dues), and the opportunity costs of the working capital and may be adjustable according to the individual characteristics of the institutions (Manual for the performance evaluation of government-invested institutions, 1999).

4 Sub-indicators for work efficiency measurements have value added as the numerator. The value added composes not only of net profit but also of labor expenses, net

financial expenses, rents, taxes and dues, and depreciation. In other words, as value added encompasses most of the expenses generated by the institutions in the execution of projects, it can be understood that value added measures the socially added value created by the institutions.

5 ROA can be used to evaluate the increase rate of the current net income compared to the total assets and is utilized in performance calculation of the indicators such as capital productivity and total assets turnover ratio.

6 ROS is calculated as the revenue to profit ratio.

7 The analysis is aimed at ten institutions from the public corporation group I (Incheon International Airport Corporation, Korea Electric Power Corporation (KEPCO), Korea Gas Corporation, Korea Airports Corporation, Korea National Oil Corporation, Korea District Heating Corporation, Korea Land and Housing corporation, Korea Expressway Corporation, Korea Water Resources Corporation, and Korea Railroad Corporation) and 12 institutions from the public corporation group II (Busan Port Authority, Incheon Port Authority, Korea Minting & Security Printing Corporation, Korea Tourism Organization, Korea Broadcast Advertising Corporation (KOBACO), Korean Racing Authority, Korea Resources Corporation, Korea Coal Corporation, Korea Housing & Urban Guarantee Corporation, Jeju Free International City Development Center, Korea Appraisal Board, and Yeosu Gwangyang Port Authority).

8 The extreme values of the ROA data of Korea Water Resources Corporation in 2015 and Korea Resources Corporation in 2015 and 2016 are excluded from the figure. The average ROA value of the other five institutions during 2013–2016 is −0.020. The ROA value of Korea Water Resources Corporation is 0.084 in 2015. The ROA values of Korea Resources Corporation are −0.440 and −0.226 in 2015 and 2016, respectively.

9 The extreme values of the ROS data of Korea Resources Corporation in 2015 and 2016 are excluded from the figure. The average ROS value of the other six institutions during 2013–2016 is 0.084. The ROS values of Korea Resources Corporation are −6.93 and −2.99 in 2015 and 2016, respectively.

10 Analyses of individual government administrations are based on the year of the performance evaluation manual. Therefore, the 1999–2003 manuals are reviewed for the Kim Dae-Jung administration; 2004–2008 for the Roh Moo-Hyun administration; 2009–2013 for the Lee Myung-Bak administration; 2013–2016 for the Park Geun-hye administration.

11 The social responsibility indicator was discontinued in 2006 but the evaluation items were added to the indicator for realization of responsible management and enhancement of public interest.

12 The efforts for the new job creation in the private sector include the outsourcing strategies, invested project orders, and partnership formation with the private sector, and it was specified that direct employment by public corporations (recruitment of new employees of public institutions, interns, etc.) was excluded. The quality of created jobs was judged based on whether they were regular or non-regular employment (2011 manual for the public performance of public institutions, pp. 12–13).

13 The future growth projects have been evaluated in the main business activities sector according to individual characteristics of the public institutions.

14 The term safety was removed since the 2001 manual and the safety management efforts of the dam have been evaluated from the detailed evaluation of 'appropriateness of dam management and operation.'

15 Operation accidents refer to the accidents that happened during the train service and are calculated by the sum of the number of train accidents and railroad crossing accidents. Human accidents refer to the sum of the number of the users or pedestrians killed within the railroad boundaries due to own carelessness or other reasons.

16 In the Kim Dae-jung government, Korea Hydro and Nuclear Power Co. was evaluated with the indicator for safety of nuclear power generation and formation of foundation

for electricity business (1 point/40 points) as one of the indicators of KEPCO's main business, and it has been removed since the 2001 manual.

17 In 2014, there are 38,000 legal entities affiliated to the 110 central public corporations with total assets, sales revenues and profits before tax accounting for 38.7 trillion RMB (210 billion USD) (OECD, 2016: 23).

References

Ahn, K., and Yoon, M. (2009). The Relationship Between Direction of Innovative Activities in Public Institutions and Organizational Performance. *Korean Political Science Review*, *13*(1), 51–74.

Asian Development Bank Institute. (2017). Efficient Management of State-Owned Enterprises: Challenges and Opportunities. *ADBI Policy Brief*. No. 2017-4, December.

Bozeman, B. (2002). Public-Value Failure: When Efficient Markets May Not Do. *Public Administration Review*, *62*(2), 145–161.

Bozeman, B. (2007). *Public Values and Public Interest: Counterbalancing Economic Individualism*. Georgetown University Press.

Cho, T., and Song, S. (2010). The Effects of the Management Performance Evaluation System on Management Efficiencies of Quasi-Governmental Agencies. *Korea Governance Review*, *17*(3), 85–108.

Choi, S., and Park, M. (2009). Performance Analysis of the Public Enterprise Evaluation System. *Collection of Treatises on Administration*, *47*(1), 183–208.

Committee of Planning and Budget. (1998–1999). *Manual for Performance Evaluation of Government-Invested Institutions*. Ministry of Planning and Budget.

Dewenter, K. L., and Malatesta, P. H. (2001). State-Owned and Privately Owned Firms: An Empirical Analysis of Profitability, Leverage, and Labor Intensity. *American Economic Review*, *91*(1), 320–334.

Geyskens, I., and Steenkamp, J. B. E. (2000). Economic and Social Satisfaction: Measurement and Relevance to Marketing Channel Relationships. *Journal of Retailing*, *76*(1), 11–32.

Haque, M. S. (2001). The Diminishing Publicness of Public Service Under the Current Mode of Governance. *Public Administration Review*, *61*(1), 65–82.

Hwang, H., and Cho, M. (2016). *Study on the Operation Effect of the Public Service Evaluation System*. Korea Instituted of Public Administration.

Kim, J. (2001). Special Research Forum: Policy, Performance and Evaluation of Public Enterprise Evaluation System in Korea: Current Issues and Future Agenda. *Korea Administration Research*, *10*(1), 97–123.

Kim, J. (2010). The Performance Evaluation System and Profitability of Public Corporations. *Korea Institute of Public Finance Monthly Finance Forum*, *10*, 26–47.

Kim, J. (2014). Analysis on the Influencing Factors of the Publicness and Profitability of the Local Public Enterprise: Focusing on the Environmental Factors. *Korea Governance Review*, *21*(1), 189–215.

Kwak, C. (2003). The Role and Operation Performance of the Performance Evaluation System for Controlling the Inefficiency of Government-invested Institutions. *Collection of Treatises on Public Corporations*, *15*(1), 49–91.

Lee, K. (2003). *A Study on Reforming the System for Government Performance Evaluation of Korea*. Korea Institute of Public Administration.

Lee, S. (2011). Study on the Political Effect of Systematic Change for Reinforcement of Regional Public Corporation Performance Management. *Korean Journal of Policy Analysis and Evaluation*, *21*, 27–50.

Megginson, W. L., and Netter, J. M. (2001). From State to Market: A Survey of Empirical Studies on Privatization. *Journal of Economic Literature*, *39*(2), 321–389.

Ministry of Planning and Budget. (2000–2007). *Manual for Performance Evaluation of Government-Invested Institutions*. Ministry of Planning and Budget.

Ministry of Strategy and Finance. (2008–2017). *Manual for Performance Evaluation of Public Corporations and Quasi-Government Institutions*. Ministry of Strategy and Finance.

Moulton, S. (2009). Putting Together the Publicness Puzzle: A Framework for Realized Publicness. *Public Administration Review*, *69*(5), 889–900.

Nam, C., and Choi, H. (2011). A Study on the Performance Evaluation System and Management Outcome of Local Enterprises: Focusing on the Cognition of the Staffs of the Subway Transportation Corporations. *Korean Public Administration Quarterly*, *23*(1), 1–23.

Oh, Y. (1996). Review of Evaluation System for Public Enterprise Performances and the System's Future. *Korean Journal of Public Administration*, *34*(1), 1217–1239.

Park, J. (2002). *A Study on the System for Government Performance Evaluation of Korea: With Focus of Institutional Evaluation*. Korea Institute of Public Administration.

Park, J., and Hong, Y. (2010). Comparative Analysis on Management Performance According to Listing of Public Corporations and Various Government Stake Ratio. *Public Institutions and National Policies*, 121–142.

Park, S. (2006). Performance Evaluation Systems and Organizational Competence in the Public Sector: An Empirical Analysis of 13 Korean State-Owned Enterprises. *Korean Public Administration Review*, *40*(3), 219–244.

Park, S. (2014). History and Transition of Public Enterprises: Focusing on Publicness. In *Public Enterprise Reformation: Issues and Examples* (pp. 3–27). Seoul: Pakyoungsa.

Park, S., and Lee, H. (2014). National Projects and the Role of Public Enterprises. In *Public Enterprise Reformation: Issues and Example* (pp. 29–59). Seoul: Pakyoungsa.

Pesch, U. (2008). The Publicness of Public Administration. *Administration & Society*, *40*(2), 170–193.

Ra, Y., and Yoon, T. (2013). *An Analysis and a Proposal for Restructring the Performance Evaluation of Public Institutions System in Korea*. Seoul: Korea Institute of Public Finance.

Shim, O. (2001). The Necessity and Anticipated Effects of the Establishment of the [Framework Act on Public Service Evaluation]. *Korea Administration Research*, *10*(1), 5–18.

Song, D., Lee, J., Kim, S., and Yoo, H. (1987). *Theoretical Background and Methods of Public Enterprise Performance Evaluation*. Seoul: Korea Development Institute.

Sun, Q., and Tong, W. H. (2003). China Share Issue Privatization: The Extent of Its Success. *Journal of Financial Economics*, *70*(2), 183–222.

Yoo, M., and Park, S. (2013). Dilemma of Public Corporation Performance Management: Publicness and Profitability. *Korea Public Administration Summer Forum Proceedings*, 1106–1138.

3 Proper understanding of developing performance indicators and performance management in the public sector

Seok-Hwan Lee

I Performance capacity and performance management in the public sector

1 Composition elements of performance capacity

The importance of performance management is highlighted recently as various issues related to the performance enhancement in the public sector received the attention of scholars and practitioners. The major difference from the performance enhancement in the private sector is that the performance enhancement in the public sector should be considered in both the political aspect and the managerial aspect. Holzer and Lee (2004) argued that performance enhancement is an integrative as well as a complicated concept.

Previous studies support that the performance enhancement is influenced by various factors including the support of the chief management staff, level of involvement of the organization members encompassing all of the classes, performance measurement system, education for the organization members, merit system, budget management based on the performance, and civic participation (Holzer and Lee, 2004; Lee, 2000; Greiner, 1986; Holzer and Callahan, 1998; Halachmi and Holzer, 1986; Werther et al., 1986). The most important factor is the will of the members to enhance the performance of the organization. In other words, people are the core element for the performance enhancement. Therefore, in order to construct an effective performance management system, performance and the concepts related to performance should be clearly understood and a continuous improvement that regularly measures and improves the development of detailed psychological indicators that the organization members can directly acknowledge and experience is necessary.

It is not a simple question what performance capacity composes of and how it can be measured. The important idea is that an infrastructure for creating and enhancing the performance or how effectively the precedent processes are executed ought to be the core factor. In order to understand the precedent processes of the performance capacity, the 10-step model suggested by Holzer (1995) can be utilized. The model was suggested with the idea that any organization would experience the following steps:

1 Obtaining top-management support,
2 Locating models,
3 Identifying promising areas,
4 Building a team,
5 Planning the project,
6 Collecting program Source,
7 Modifying project plans,
8 Expecting problems,
9 Implementing improvement actions, and
10 Evaluating and publicizing results.

While some of the steps may be skipped or reduced according to the conditions or scale of the organization, it was suggested that the performance enhancement is achieved usually through such a process.

McGowan (1984) stated that performance enhancement could be achieved provided that measures such as the partnership between the private and public sectors and public service marketing in the environmental domain, the structural changes, labor relations, and computer information technologies in the organizational domain, and the performance incentives, career professionalism, and development and education of management technologies in the individual domain were implemented.

Meanwhile, Buntz (1981) emphasized the importance of the environmental domain for the performance enhancement, encompassing the technology and staff ability, motivation, policy shifts, and the public recognition of the government. Moreover, Holzer and Callahan (1998) stated that performance enhancement could be achieved by the five dimensions comprehensively interrelated and emphasized the importance of the connectivity of the five dimensions divided as managing for quality, developing human resources, adapting technologies, building partnerships, and measuring performance.

2 Definition of concepts related to performance management

The essence of performance management can be defined as the "series of integrative processes of setting the aim of the organization to be provided with accurate information for future decision making in the uncertain environment whether the organization is private or public, and of constructing various cause and effect measures and regularly measuring the relationships between them to formulate accurate information". The core logic behind this definition is the idea that the ultimate purpose of performance management is to make decisions and that accurate decisions are made based on setting a proper aim reflecting the values of the members and the people (Lee, 2008: 25–26).

In other words, it can be summarized that a proper performance management system should define the mission of the organization and establish the necessary achievement strategies to provide meaningful information for the organization to make proper decisions.

II Definition of performance in the public sector: efficiency, effectiveness, and responsiveness

While the concepts efficiency and effectiveness have existed for a long time, scholars and practitioners have yet reached consensual definitions. Many scholars define effectiveness as the 'level of goal achievement', use efficiency as another term for proficiency and define it as the 'input to output ratio' (Bennewitz, 1980; Keane, 1980; Hatry and Fisk, 1994). Meanwhile, Drucker (1967) defined effectiveness as 'doing the right things' and efficiency as 'doing things right' and stated that the former corresponds to leadership and the latter to management. As effectiveness and efficiency are defined differently by scholars and the concepts are unclear, there are difficulties in understanding them in reality.

First, if effectiveness was defined simply as the level of goal achievement, it would be defined based on whether the goal was achieved regardless of the different types of indicators such as the input indicator, process indicator, or output indicator. The level of goal achievement would be identically conceptualized if the distinction between output and outcome indicators were to be discussed.

Usilaner and Soniet (1980) stated that effectiveness means the achievement level of the goals that the central and local government and local communities should pursue and includes the quality (responsiveness, priority, rationality, satisfaction, unexpected effects, number of service users, etc.), final outcome, and influence of the services. In other words, the output indicators are viewed as the numerical expressions of the government activity and services, and the outcome indicators as the dimension of effectiveness in which the quality and final outcome of the services are evaluated based on the output indicators. Moreover, the output indicators are evaluated also for efficiency and refer to the type of indicators in which the mission of the organization is directly reflected and the structure is maintained and managed. Therefore, it is not a specific policy or service but the resultant output of such service that becomes an output indicator.

Hence, the indicators for effectiveness are difficult to evaluate quantitatively or with one indicator and need to be decided by establishing multidimensional standards and by considering the quality and final outcome of the services in accordance with the goal of the local community.

The performance management has been unsatisfactory for the people and neglected by public officials not only because it was difficult to acknowledge what has been achieved or improved as the output indicators and outcome indicators were utilized without distinction due to the ambiguity or ignorance of the differences in the concepts, but also because the fundamentally important democratic values were not included in the effectiveness evaluation due to the focus on quantitative indicators.

Whereas there is considerable negative perception toward the performance management in the public sector and the perspective of the performance management was recognized as problematic, it can be acknowledged that the insensitivity to the inclusion of the political dimension in the dimension of effectiveness was the greater problem if the meaning of effectiveness was properly understood and applied. The dimension of effectiveness should possess the political values in evaluating the performance (Yang and Holzer, 2006), considering that a productive government cannot exist without the responsiveness for the people (Schachter, 1997) and that unproductive values are equivalently important (Waldo, 1980).[1]

Meanwhile, efficiency is the measure for how the available resources are utilized to efficiently create the services. Therefore, the input, process, and output indicators should not be considered individually. Instead, the three indicators should be combined and to measure the efficiency indicator (for example by the input to output ratio).

In reality, however, the relationship between the input, process, and output indicators within the efficiency indicator are not complexly considered even if the concepts of effectiveness and efficiency are separated. Rather, the input, process, and output indicators have been utilized and evaluated individually. Therefore, the indicator for the input to output ratio, i.e. goal achievement per working hour, labor expense, or business expense, is not measured. While the level of goal achievement from the input of capital and labor ought to be measured (despite great difficulties), the input, process, and output indicators are individually utilized under the pretext for measuring the efficiency indicator that the information cannot be utilized in any way (Epstein, 1992).

A summary of the discussion on the definition of the performance in the public sector is provided in Figure 3.1.

As shown in Figure 3.1, effectiveness and efficiency can be calculated with a 50:50 ratio, and the dimension of responsiveness holds a coefficient value between 0 and 1. In other words, if the responsiveness coefficient is 0.5, the total score is 50 even if the sum of effectiveness and efficiency is 100. This means that a practical and sustainable performance is difficult to achieve if the values of the public are not included in the achievement of efficiency and effectiveness. As a result, the performance evaluation in the public sector cannot entirely follow that in the private sector.

III Specialty of the public sector (management of "ε")

The core purpose of the performance management is to clarify the cause and effect relationship among the goals (indicators) ultimately for the decision making and it would not be wrong to say that the performance management system was created to facilitate the process. The cause and effect relationship in the private sector has been sufficiently established without particular obstacles and the corporations were able to strategically execute management activities through relevant performance management. Problems arose as the various performance

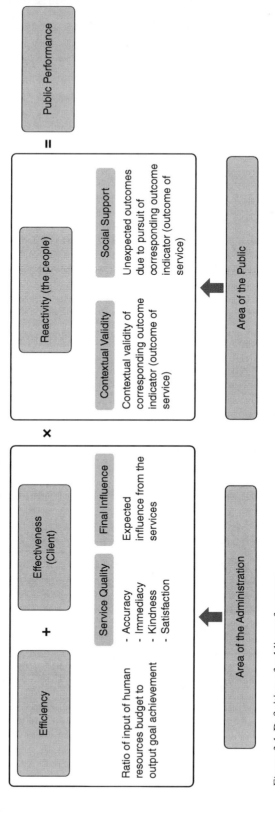

Figure 3.1 Definition of public performance

Source: Lee (2017, scheduled for publication), UOFO II: Strategic Performance Management for Sustainable Government and Society'. Seok-Hwan Lee (2019, forthcoming), UOFOII, Strategic Performance Management for Sustainable Government and Society.

management tools (including BSC) were transferred to the public sector without any adjustment.

The construction methodologies and operation and evaluation framework for the performance management system developed in the private sector were a tailored audiovisual system for the private sector and needed to be significantly modified for application in the public sector.

The cause and effect relationships in the public sector are mostly uncontrollable and it was overlooked that the controllability of the relationships in the private sector was not appropriate for the public sector. It is undoubtedly certain that the cause and effect relationships in the public sector are difficult to control. This is the reason that the market failed and the public sector had to exist. Though understandably difficult, the public sector was created with the aspiration to control the cause and effect relationships by the power of man.[2]

The present writer believes that the constant failures were caused by the ignorance of the characteristics of the public sector and application of identical methodologies and operation methods developed in the private sector in the government and public institutions.

While some scholars argue that private institutions possess little difference compared with public institutions, it must be remembered that these institutions operate in greatly different environments. The success or failure in the public sector is more integrative and complicated, possesses higher uncertainty, and is decided by the reaction or response of the people not as customers but as the owners.

The core element of the public sector performance management can be found in the management of "ε" in the regression analysis equation. The "ε" refers to the group of any and all obstacles that hinder the explanation of "Y" by the equation "$aX + b$". In order for the "$aX + b$" to function in the public sector, the components of the "ε" should be understood and regularly measured to be used for the discovery of appropriate $X1, X2, \ldots$, ultimately for the achievement the preferable "Y". This implies that the assumptions behind the cause and effect relationship are different in the respective private and public sectors.

The present writer believes that the most important reason for the cases developed in the private sector failing in the public sector is that it was not admitted that the assumptions were different for the two sectors. Both the private and public sectors establish the goals in the uncertain environments and design and realize the cause and effect relationships in the process of devising the methods for the achievement of those goals. However, in the private sector, the logic is relatively clearer, and there are smaller chances of outer variable interventions in the process of goal achievement.

In all, while uncertainty and complicatedness are characteristics for both of the sectors, the extent of the characteristics is much greater in the public sector.[3]

In the following sections, specific characteristics of the public sector are observed in comparison with the private sector. These are the major components that construct the "ε" of the public sector. It can be understood that the problems in the area of the "ε" cannot be solved entirely by specific projects of particular institutions, and that there should be cooperation or shared governance with the members of the society or other institutions.

1 Controllability: the probability of outer variable intervention in the process of goal achievement and the cause and effect relationship

Unlike in the private sector, the cause and effect relationships between the goal and the measures are much more complicated and there are greater chances for the outer variables to intervene.

For example, suppose that an outcome indicator Y (goal) of "maintenance of the fine dust concentration in the air below the environmental standards" was created. If the indicators chosen for the goal achievement were indicators (measure) such as the projects to "implement 1,000 natural gas busses" and to "oblige the installation of emission reduction device up to 10,000 busses", there would not be much probability for the government departments actually responsible for the environment to control the outcome indicator. There would be even higher probability for failure if there were several cases of the Chinese yellow dust or the grand scale new town development constructions continue.

This is when the public sector comes into play. It would be inappropriate to argue that the government can control only 5 percent of the indicators related to the dust in the atmosphere and the indicator cannot be achieved because of the Chinese yellow dust. The role of the public sector is to seek for the measures to enhance that 5 percent to 6 percent.

It can be argued that the outcome indicators should be utilized, as any indicator should be controllable. If the "emission level of the cars with emission reduction device installed" was considered as an indicator, it would be a relevant outcome indicator for the private bus company to manage as a social responsibility. Also, if the outcome indicator of "increase rate of users of public transportations" was observed in order to create a comfortable traffic system, the increase rate in the perspectives of the bus company and the government relates to different projects, and thus, different indicators. In other words, the "increase rate of users of public transportations" viewed in the public sector must be understood within a larger frame in which the cause and effect relationships are more complicated and more probably intervened by outer variables. The settlement of the cause and effect relationships is not simple in the public sector as described.

Therefore, in order to overcome the difficulties, the public sector should present the outcome indicators and operate the performance management and evaluation systems to enhance the morale by analyzing the events and conditions that are uncontrollable with human power and qualitatively evaluating the circumstances. The public officials will then be able to present proper outcome indicators and accomplish meaningful jobs with verification.

The two standards considered most importantly in deducing the performance indicators provided in the management strategies of the private sector are the measurability and controllability. Whereas the measurability is a standard that was automatically included, the logic of controllability was followed overly faithfully in the public sector. Therefore, the focus was on action indicators related to the tasks and the core purpose of the public sector was not examined. As a result, the people were not able to feel or experience what the government had achieved and the public officials were not able to prove or acknowledge themselves how the society had improved.[4]

It can be concluded that the view toward the cause and effect relationship should be changed. In other words, the focus of the public sector performance management should be redirected to include the management of uncontrollable areas from the initial focus mainly on the controllable cause and effect relationships. While the approach in the private sector executed the performance management based on the simplified equation of $Y = aX + b$ and the public sector followed the method without any alterations in the past, it is now the "ε" in the equation $Y = aX + b + \varepsilon$ that should be managed with greater weight. In social sciences, the value of the explainability of the independent variable X for the dependent variable Y is difficult to exceed 20–30 percent. However, it is as meaningless to state that performance was achieved with only the 20–30 percent of the Source without the management of the 70–80 percent portion.

Therefore, the uncontrollable 70–80 percent portion should be included in the performance management. The future discussion on the capability of the public sector should be focused on how to reduce the 70–80 percent portion.

Another misunderstanding about the uncontrollability is the confusion with the environmental threat factors that should definitely be managed in the process of the accomplishment of the original mission of the organization. This should not be considered an uncontrollable factor but considered an obstacle factor that the organization should sincerely be concerned with and try to overcome.[5]

Therefore, in addition to the measurement of the level of the simple, controllable task indicator achievement, the previously uncontrollable factors in the process of achieving the outcome indicators should be identified. Moreover, the information should be utilized to simultaneously mange other factors such as whether the goal was properly directed by the public officials and the cause and effect relationships for the execution and settlement of the projects and policies were agreed by the people.

It would be then sufficient for the public officials to present proper outcome indicators, pursue the challenges with more freedom, and seek reasonably the causes should there be any problem.

2 Legitimacy of the outcome (goal) aimed by the policy: conflict among the outcomes, social desirability

Sometimes in the public sector, the complicated question of whether the goal defined as the desirable state that we should reach in the future is one that is socially "correct"s. Such questions are not raised at least in the private sector, i.e. there are no concerns about the correctness of the goal (Lindblom, 1959). Basically, the values and world view of the top manager are reflected already in the process of setting the strategic goal and it is difficult to establish clear standards for whether the setting of the strategic goal today will be relevant also in the future considering that the environment is significantly changing. While some may argue that there are no significant differences between private organizations and public organizations, it should not be forgotten that these organizations operate in distinct environments.[6]

The question of correctness appears frequently in the conflicts among the policy goals and is influenced also by the specific social atmospheres and value systems of the time. For example, the goal of strengthening environmental regulations constricts the investor sentiment of the corporations for the economic development and the goal of stabilizing the real estate prices constricts the construction business and eventually slows down the economic growth. It is difficult to decide which goal is the correct goal with the dilemma. However, the public sector should endeavor to manage the balance in such challenging environment. In the aspect of public interest values, both goals should be considered as correct goals and be achieved with balance. Since every policy involves both the parties that receive benefits and losses, efforts should be made to persuade the people to minimize the conflicts and discord among the different parties, involve them, and design detailed execution strategies. The rationality of the policies in the uncertainty is created through this process.

3 Rationality of the policy: conflict among the policies, responsiveness of the people to the policy

There are cases in which policies designed to achieve certain goals interrupt with the execution with other policies. For example, the efforts made to resolve civil complaints related to the construction business may hinder the construction process and corporation activities. In such case, the problem of rationality of the policy (project) is raised and efforts should be made to resolve the problem. Meanwhile, these policies are different from product types created by private corporations that, even if the policies are realized, the goal of the policies is not achieved if the people do not express their reactions to the created policies. It can be more easily understood by looking at the cases in which numerous policies result in failures regardless of how many preliminary evaluations were executed.

4 Intangibility of the policy: difficulty of service quality examination (difficulty of communication)

The people cannot feel or experience the values of the policies as much as those of tangible products from private corporations, as policies are intangible services. Therefore, it is difficult to prove the efforts and the outcomes produced by the government. The only way to enable this is to publicly announce the indicators, especially to simultaneously announce the outcome indicators and the project indicators (or the preliminary indicators). These indicators should be defined with easily understandable language for the people, unlike the performance indicators of private corporations. The titles of the indicators should be easy and intuitive enough for the people to instantly understand that the people would not have to understand the indicators after viewing the calculation equations. Therefore, the government should try to create obvious titles as well as to find the proper indicators, as the indicators are the only method of communication between the people and the government. Through such process, the people can understand the established goals and the progress and ultimately build the trust in the government.

IV Conditions for preferable public performance indicators and operational definition of the goal

1 Definition and importance of the Unreasonable Objectives (UO)

A relevant checklist for the public sector should be utilized to find the preferable public performance indicators. As illustrated in Table 3.1, it is desirable for the performance indicators to be deduced from the outcome indicators and preliminary indicators to achieve this include the calculation indicators. In other words, the outcome indicators (strategy) and project indicators (tactic) should be separately deduced. Also, it should be emphasized that controllability should be excluded from the conditions for the preferable indicators in the case of outcome indicators. There are more uncontrollable indicators that are more important than controllable indicators in the public sector due to its purpose of existence. As discussed previously, the management of the "ε" in the '$Y = aX + b + \varepsilon$' equation is particularly important in the public sector. The indicators arising from this aspect

Table 3.1 Categorization of performance indicators

Driver Measures			Outcome Measures
Inputs	*Processes*	*Outputs*	*Outcomes*
Invested resources or capital to achieve the goal	(Future) Activities to achieve the goal	Output elements from the activities for goal achievement	Resultant social influences or final effects of the activities for goal achievement
– Number of input human resources – Input cost – Amount of used resources, etc. – Number of bus drivers – Number of busses	– Effective plan establishment – Efficient execution – Lead-time, per capita performance, etc. – Establishment of public transportation system reconstruction	– Number of reports – Number of consultations – Number of applications – Scale of organization fund – Securement of exclusive bus lanes	– Increase rate of transportation usage – Proportion of the people who answered with "safe and comfortable" in satisfaction survey

Source: Lee (2008), UOFO: Strategic Performance Management for Trusted Government and Corporations

are the UO (Unreasonable Objectives) and this is where the cooperation between the institutions appears. It should be remembered that the performance indicator pool for the public organizations would be filled with meaningless, simple task indicators if only the controllable indicators were deduced with the identical standards utilized in the private sector (refer to Table 3.2).

The definition of performance goals is based not on the process of problem solving but on the process of problem defining. The relevant departments, outer experts, and the people – including the stakeholders should collectively define the problem.

As shown in the figure below, the process of finding performance indicators based on the concept of performance in the public sector may produce preferable indicators and it is through such indicators that relevant performance goals are defined.

It is important to learn how to construct the operational definition about the performance goal. Let us look at the phrase 'maintenance of law and order' that Peter Drucker exemplified in explaining the MBO (Management By Objectives). How specific and detailed does this phrase seem? It is a highly abstract and ambiguous phrase. Suppose that the phrase was concretized more to 'prevention of crime'. Then, does this phrase have a specific and clear meaning? Although it may seem explicit as it is written, the phrase is not yet precise or obvious. It is difficult to find the accurate interpretation if what the prevention of crime means for the people.

Table 3.2 Checklist for deduction of performance indicators

No.	Condition for Preferable Indicator
1	Is the indicator measurable?
2	Does the indicator enhance the responsibility of the public sector for the people (customer)?
3	Does the indicator enhance the responsibility of the public officials for the organization?
4	Does the indicator enhance the responsibility between the positions of the public officials?
5	Does the indicator enhance the efficiency of the distribution of physical resources?
6	Does the indicator enhance the efficiency of analysis, planning, and operation?
7	Does the indicator positively motivate the public officials to improve the performance?
8	Does the indicator provide relevant information to the organization to produce new improvement strategies?

Source: Lee (2008), UOFO: Strategic Performance Management for Trusted Government and Corporations

Notes
1 A newly developed performance indicator needs to meet all of the standards provided above to be considered preferable.
2 The conditions related to the controllability or whether conflicts are absent are irrelevant for the public sector.
3 Indicators in the public sector may be more important with greater uncontrollability and conflicts among the indicators are unavoidable.
4 It is important to find conflicting indicators to achieve the goal with balance.

Does the prevention of crime mean how safely the ordinary people walking on the streets at night return to their homes? Does it mean that the people can rest peacefully at home in the evening without robbers breaking into their homes? Does it refer to the police patrol expanding to the dark, grim streets in the evening? Or are the foreign workers wandering and the disordered regional environment of the residential neighborhoods the problem? According to Drucker, the internal surveys of the policemen show that the most urgent issue is to stop the corruption of the policemen. This means that in order to realize the performance goal of 'prevention of crime', the first priority indicator as a detailed strategic performance indicator would be to reduce the corruption within the policemen. While the final outcome indicator under the performance goal of 'prevention of crime' would be the 'reduction in the crime rate' and 'increase in the awareness for safety', it would be necessary for the people, public officials, and relevant persons involved need to gather to find the problem in order for these indicators to be improved simultaneously in the process of constructing the operational definition. The crime rate and the fear for crimes are actually independent and individual social existences (Kim, 2014). Also, the perceived safety is defined as a function influenced by the capabilities of the policemen, the messages from the press, and the demographical characteristics (Kim, 2014). Therefore, it is necessary to identify such factors and create relevant performance indicators to ultimately reduce the crime rate as well as improve the perception toward safety. As explained, the real problems need to be deduced but the identification of such real problems does not end here. The potential negative influences on the persons involved or on other groups of people need to be considered in the process of preventing the crimes or reducing the crime rate, as mentioned previously. Otherwise, if the unexpected negative influences were not considered, the vicious cycle of the targets of the control or regulation returning to cause crimes, the level of perceived safety decreasing, and the crime rate increasing will be repeated.

Defining the 'prevention of crime' in greater detail produces several operational definitions and the real problem is defined. Figure 3.2 provides a template for the operational definition of the performance goals and creation of relevant indicators. The real problems identified through the process are highly likely to be considered as UO (Unreasonable Objectives) in the perspective of the organization, as such indicators are achievable not based on the inherent missions of the organization itself but through cooperation with outer institutions or other departments. The organizations focused mainly on the unreasonable objectives are called the UOFOs (Unreasonable Objectives-focused Organizations).

The UOFO is the organization responsible for finding the real problem in the division of the public to achieve the value of efficiency. It is with the UOFO that the real problem can be identified and sustainable growth and inclusive society. By answering to the questions from the nine divisions illustrated in Figure 3.2, the indicators exceeding the boundaries of the previous missions and the indicators conflicting with one another can be identified. Through this process, the organization can innovate itself as well as execute limitless, traversal administration across the boundaries. It is believed that the identification of the UO will

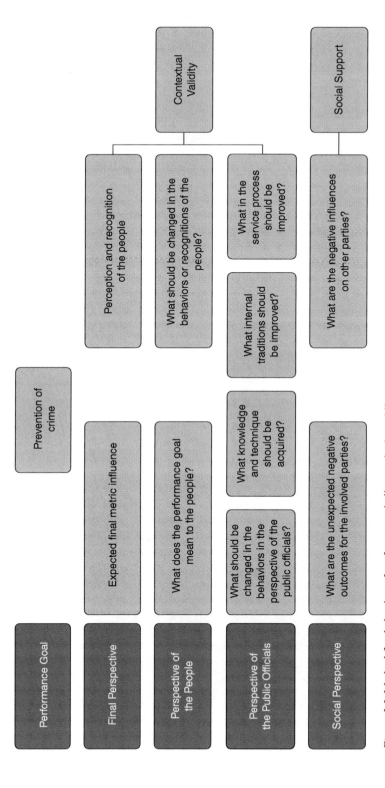

Figure 3.2 Method for deduction of performance indicators in the public sector

Source: Lee (2017, scheduled for publication), UOFO II: Strategic Performance Management for Sustainable Government and Society

definitely contribute as the significant rudder for establishing the direction for the ultimate creation of sustainable society.

While the UO can intentionally create conflicting indicators through the application of the social perspective from the template above to facilitate the organization innovation, in case of the corporations, the market acts as a constraint condition that constantly functions as a conflicting indicator in the process of innovation that if the goal of certain indicators were internally set unreasonably high, the indicators are caused to be in conflicting relationships automatically.

In order to facilitate innovation in public organizations, however, the conflicting indicators need to be established even more intentionally as the market is absent unlike for the corporations. For example, the case of the performance goal of 'construction of preferable environment for corporations' can be considered. If the indicator for the 'level of corporation installation within the jurisdiction' was identified and the indicator for the 'reduction of burden ratio in relation to the increase in environmental development charges' was established in the perspective of the social acceptance, the two indicators would be conflicting with each other. The two indicators can be combined that the organization can cooperate with the relevant government bodies to achieve both of the indicators. Through such processes, innovations such as the development of environmental technologies can be achieved. This is an example of the UO. The UO are difficult to achieve and cannot be created by setting only one of the goals as extensive. Therefore, the UO can facilitate the members of the entire organization to acknowledge their importance. Identifying the UO under one performance goal points out disparate and variously conflicting situations. There have been numerous success cases of public organization innovation through implicit but intentional positioning of the concept of the UO in the process.

From now on, all organizations (regardless of private or public organizations) should endeavor to find their own UO. Resolving the UO means that the organization is taking a step further, that the organization is taking the shortcut to becoming a strong, productive organization. As mentioned previously, the UO are found rather through systematically well-structured performance management system than by inspiration or intuition of the head of institution. It should be pointed out that the organizations that survived in the changing environment have succeeded in identifying the UO and become UOFOs (Unreasonable Objectives-focused Organizations).

2 Establishment of execution plans for the achievement of performance indicators

After the performance indicators corresponding to the UO are identified, detailed execution plans or tasks need to be identified as well. Combining the conflicting indicators results in innovation and identifying the individual UO creates the situation where the organization needs to cooperate with other departments or institutions.

When the UO are identified, the execution plans through which the resources are directly distributed need to be constructed. The execution plans need to be in an instrumental cause and effect relationship with the UO (practically the KPI). In other words, the logical cause and effect relationship should be established, in which the achievement of the UO follows the execution plans (refer to Figure 3.3, Figure 3.4, Figure 3.5).

This model refers to the dual structure of strategies and tactics and illustrates the two elements for the realization of the strategy-focused organization. It is through this process that the innovation of the organization is facilitated and the goals exceeding the boundaries or in conflicting relationships are achieved. The members would be encouraged to gather for discussions, be less constricted by routine tasks, and enthusiastically create the relevant tasks. Also, this model is closely connected to the budget system of individual projects. In order to establish and manage the vision which is the system of the most significant goals in the strategic performance management system, the projects and challenges should be managed. This means that the strategic units should be reorganized with the focus on the goal or unit projects rather than on the structure of the organization.

As illustrated in the following figures, the previous performance management was operated previously by establishing the execution plans first and listing the various performance indicators based on the plans. However, this method decreased the efficiency of the distribution of the resources by hindering the organization in focusing on the strategies. A proper strategic performance management system should be structured so that diverse execution plans and projects can be identified around one outcome indicator.

VI Lessons learned and conclusion

1 Lessons learned

Public performance management must start from switching abstract and vague goals to right performance indicators. Outcome indicators always matter. That does not necessarily mean one goal has to have one performance indicator from a final result perspective. Public managers should develop multiple measures under one goal. One must realize that one performance indicator so often comes into conflict with another indicator under the same goal. This means that public managers should be able to prioritize the indicators according to the importance. Many public organizations in Korea still fail to find multiple performance measures under the same goal and thereby fail to make performance management meaningful. Public organizations need performance capacity so that they identify meaningful performance measures and allocate resources to the right problems.

2 Conclusion

As observed above, performance management functions to manage the empty area of the organizational map. The existing management with the focus on the

Cooperation for Achieving Organization's Goal
Beyond Boundaries (UOFO)

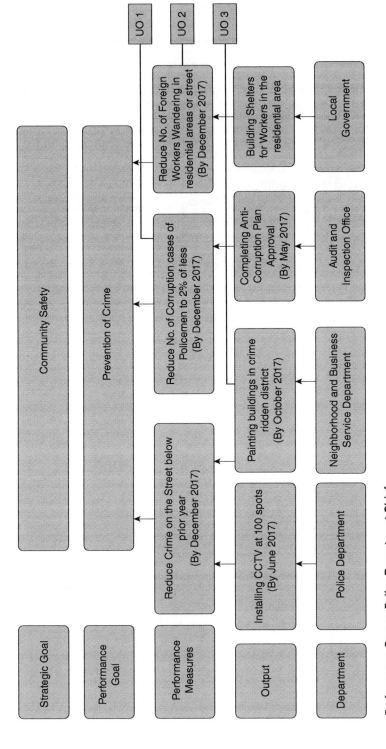

Performance Owner: Police Department Chief

Figure 3.3 Example of formation of cooperation through the UOFO and performance responsibility system

Source: Lee (2017, forthcoming), UOFO II: Strategic Performance Management for Sustainable Government and Society

Figure 3.4 Structure of a proper strategic performance management system

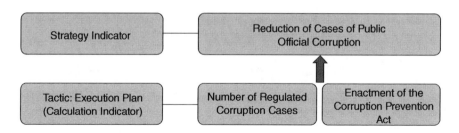

Figure 3.5 Proper relationship between indicators and execution plans

Source: Lee (2017, scheduled for publication), UOFO II: Strategic Performance Management for Sustainable Government and Society

organizational map is limited to the considerations focused on the professional function and thus is limited to partial management instead of an integrative management. The real purpose of the organization is to draw the employees working within the box of the organizational map out of the box through management. The construction and operation of an organization that enables horizontal or cross-functional working environment for the achievement of the higher goals of the organization are possible only when a proper performance management system is installed. Unlike our expectation or common sense, all of the goals including the vision which is a mid- and long-term goal that exists in the uppermost area of strategic performance management, the core strategic goal, performance goals, and performance indicators need to be unreasonable. The vision is a dream and a dream cannot be replaced with a reasonable goal establishment that is seemingly achievable. The vision ought to be a big, hairy, and audacious goal and the final performance indicators deduced accordingly should not deviate from these characteristics. Therefore, a desirable organization with a well-operating performance management should be in the form of an UOFO (Unreasonable Objectives-focused Organization). This applies to all of the central government, public institutions, and local governments.

Notes

1 From this perspective, the policy evaluation integrative model of Fischer (1997) suggests a suitable framework. Fischer proposed an evaluation model with 4 stages in which he stated that, apart from measuring and analyzing the quantitative indicators in the viewpoint of efficiency, the contextual relevance of the goal, social acceptance, and correspondence with the social values related to the policy and program need to be discussed and evaluated. The factors mentioned are the important values in the dimension of effectiveness.

2 As stated in the market failure theory, the area in which the "give and take relationship" between people does not function refers to the area in which the cause and effect relationships in the market function fail. It is suggested that the public sector take the responsibility for that area.

3 The statement that the public sector possesses greater uncertainty and complicatedness can be explained multidimensionally, through the clarity of the goal (Dahl and Lindblom, 1953; Lan and Rainey, 1992), the multidimensionality of the goal (Banfield, 1975; Rainey, Backoff and Levine, 1976), the limitations of the free hand in the decision making (Rainey et al., 1976; Pugh et al., 1969), and the service and sacrifice characteristics of the motivation (Banfield, 1975; Cacioppe and Mock, 1984).

4 In the past, the indicator for the "maintenance of the fine dust concentration in the air below the environmental standards" was not selected as a performance indicator due to the lack of controllability. On the other hand, the indicators for tasks and projects, which were easier to control, such as "to implement 1,000 natural gas busses" and "to oblige the installation of emission reduction device up to 10,000 busses" were selected and managed. Therefore, the members of the organization did not know how to apply the information from such project indicators to the decision making and there was not much significance even if the information was applied. For example, could it be considered a decision-making process if the goal of implementing 1,000 natural gas busses was reclaimed after the initial deadline due to an insufficient achievement of the goal? The decision-making process discussed here refers to the process for the achievement of the goal (for the achievement of the outcome indicators). It is difficult to make a meaningful decision as long as the outcome indicators are not measured.

5 Due to the recent MERS outbreak, the management evaluations of public institutions were affected in various directions. Whereas the number of customers and travelers decreased for KORAIL and the Korea Tourism Organization, the number of cars utilizing the roads increased for the Korea Highway Corporation and the usage rate indicator was positively influenced. It should be recognized that such uncontrollable environmental variable arises almost every year. The 2015 management evaluation team for the Ministry of Strategy and Finance decided to disregard such circumstances. While this shows that the interpretation of the uncontrollability is strictly managed, it can be acknowledged that the evaluation is reasonable if the Source from the relevance sector

in the performance management of the main business activities that considers such circumstances qualitatively is reflected.

6 Although it is repeatedly mentioned in this manuscript, the environments in which the private and the public sectors operate are becoming more similar, and the trend is expected to continue in the future.

References

Banfield, E. (1975). Corruption as a Feature of Governmental Organization. *Journal of Law and Economics*, *20*, 587–605.

Bennewitz, E. (1980). Evolution of Budgeting and Control Systems. In G. Washnis (ed.), *Productivity Improvement Handbook for State & Local Government* (pp. 115–132). New York, NY: A Wiley-Interscience Publication.

Buntz, C. G. (1981). Problems and Issues in Human Service Productivity Improvement. *Public Productivity & Management Review*, *5*, 299–320.

Cacioppe, R., and Mock, P. (1984). A Comparison of the Quality of Work Experience in Government and Private Organizations. *Human Relations*, *37*(11), 923–940.

Dahl, R. A., and Lindblom, C. E. (1953). *Politics, Economics and Welfare: Planning and Politico-Economic Systems, Resolved into Basic Processes*. New York, NY: Harper & Brothers.

Drucker, P. (1967). *The Effective Executive*. New York, NY: HarperCollins.

Epstein, P. (1992). Measuring the Performance of Public Services. In M. Holzer (ed.), *Public Productivity Handbook* (pp. 161–193). New York, NY: Marcel Dekker.

Fischer. (1997). *Evaluating Public Policy*. Chicago, IL: Nelson-Hall Publishers.

Greiner, J. M. (1986). Motivational Programs and Productivity Improvement in Times of Limited Resources. *Public Productivity Review*, 81–101.

Halachmi, A., and Holzer, M. (1986). Introduction: Toward Strategic Perspectives on Public Productivity. In A. Halachmi and M. Holzer (eds.), *Strategic Issues in Public Sector Productivity: The Best of Public Productivity Review* (pp. 5–16, 1975–1985). San Francisco, CA: Jossey-Bass.

Hatry, H., and Fisk, D. M. (1994). Measuring Productivity in the Public Sector. In M. Holzer (ed.), *Public Productivity Handbook* (pp. 139–160). New York, NY: Marcel Dekker.

Holzer, M., and Callahan, K. (1998). *Government at Work*. Thousand Oaks, CA: Sage.

Holzer, M., and Lee, S-H. (2004). Mastering Public Productivity and Performance from a Productive Management Perspective. In M. Holzer and S-H Lee (eds.), *Public Productivity Handbook* (pp. 1–16). New York, NY: Marcel Dekker.

Keane, M. E. (1980). Why Productivity Improvement? In G. Washnis (ed.), *Productivity Improvement Handbook for State & Local Government* (pp. 7–15). New York, NY: A Wiley-Interscience Publication.

Kim, Jisun. (2014). *Factors That Affect the Perception of the People, Public Security Activities with the Focus on the 4 Major Social Hazards – Academic Symposium on the Connectivity of Perceived Safety*, pp. 3–26.

Kim, Taeyoung. (2014). *Influence of Press Reports on Perceived Safety, Public Security Activities with the Focus on the 4 Major Social Hazards – Academic Symposium on the Connectivity of Perceived Safety*, pp. 27–52.

Lan, Z., and Rainey, H. G. (1992). Goals, Rules, and Effectiveness in Public, Private, and Hybrid Organizations: More Evidence on Frequent Assertions About Differences. *Journal of Public Administration Research and Theory*, *2*(1), 5–28.

Lee, Seok-Hwan. (2008). *UOFO: Strategic Performance Management for Trusted Government and Corporations*. Paju: Bobmunsa.

Lee, Seok-Hwan. (2019, forthcoming). *UOFO II: Strategic Performance Management for Sustainable Government and Society*. Paju: Bobmunsa.

Lee, S. H. (2000). Understanding Productivity Improvement in a Turbulent Environment: A Symposium Introduction. *Public Productivity & Management Review*, 423–427.

Lindblom, C. E. (1959). The Science of Muddling Through. *Public Administration Review*, 79–88.

McGowan, R. P. (1984). Improving Efficiency in Public Management: The Torment of Sisyphus. *Public Productivity Review*, 162–178.

Pugh, D. S., Hickson, D. J., and Hinings, C. R. (1969). An Empirical Taxonomy of Structures of Work Organizations. *Administrative Science Quarterly*, 115–126.

Rainey, H. G., Backoff, R. W., and Levine, C. H. (1976). Comparing Public and Private Organizations. *Public Administration Review*, *36*(2), 233–244.

Schachter, H. L. (1997). *Reinventing Government or Reinventing Ourselves: The Role of Citizen Owners in Making a Better Government*. New York, NY: SUNY Press.

Usilaner, B., and Soniat, E. (1980). Productivity Measurement. In G. Washnis (ed.), *Productivity Improvement Handbook for State & Local Government* (pp. 91–114). New York, NY: A Wiley-Interscience Publication.

Waldo, D. (1980). *The Enterprise of Public Administration*. Novato, CA: Chandler & Sharp Publishers.

Werther, W. B., Ruch, W. A., and McClure, L. (1986). *Productivity Through People*. New York, NY: West Publishing Co.

Yang, K., and Holzer, M. (2006). The Performance Trust Link: Implications for Performance Measurement. *Public Administration Review*, *66*(1), 114–126.

4 Improvement of management and the performance evaluation system of public institutions in the view of strategic performance management

Kil Pyo Hong

I Introduction

In general, performance management refers to the processes and system such as the performance plan, performance measurement, performance pays, and performance reports and the utilization of the reports on the individual or organization levels for the achievement of the goal of the organization (Yoon and Lim, 2009). Presently, the private sector as well as the government and the public sector utilize the performance management. The performance management system in the public sector composes of the following steps. First, the administrative institutions establish strategic plans related to the mission of the institutions including the goal of the institutions. The strategic plans are utilized to set the goal and purpose of the yearly operation. Second, in order to measure the performance level based on the realization of the goal, performance indicators are established to measure the performance and report and publicly announce the performance information (GAO, 1996; Park and Han, 2004).

In order for the performance management to be successfully operated, determined and proper utilization of the Key Performance Index (KPI) as a type of performance measurement is emphasized. The KPI refers to the core, important performance indicators among the indicators for the measurement of the level of goal achievement of the organization. The performance measures that the organizations should utilize need to meet the following conditions. First, the performance measurement indicators need to be connected with the strategies of the organization. Second, the individual performance measurement indicators of smaller units need to be integrated with the performance measurement indicators of the entire organization. Third, the measurement should be executed systematically according to the performance measurement system. Fourth, the measurement should have influence on the performance. Lastly, the measurement indicators have to be trustworthy (Parker, 2000). It is necessary for the KPI to possess the characteristics mentioned above since it is considered the representative performance measure.

Lee (2012) raised the problem that the following requirements for successful operation are not working properly in Korean public institutions. The following requirements are; the top management who properly understand and provide strong support; the entire organization goal which is established and measured with relevant indicators focused on the outcome; the performance indicators for the individuals and departments to be connected for the goal achievement of the organization; the different departments within the organization to cooperate or execute adjustments or organizational alignments; and the measured performance information which is utilized in the decision-making for resource distribution. However, these conditions have not been satisfied in the reality (Lee, 2012). This study generally agrees with this point. This study will be discussing the issues in more detail in the aspect of the process of performance management.

In order to accurately understand the characteristics of the performance management of Korean public institutions, the specific structural environment of Korea surrounding the performance management system should be analyzed. Ra (2011) suggested the following to describe the overall performance management system of Korean public institutions.

As illustrated in Figure 4.1, in order to understand the characteristics of the performance management system for Korean public institutions, the multi-layered structure is presupposed for the performance management for the individual

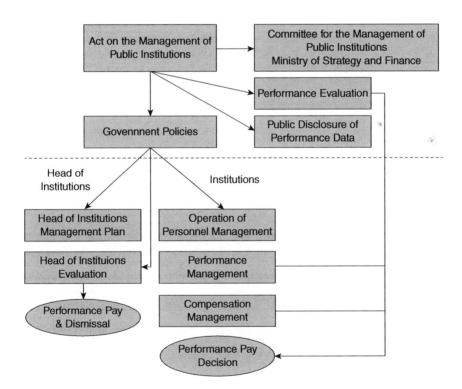

Figure 4.1 Overall performance system of Korean public institutions

Source: Ra(2011)

institutions and for various public institutions on the level of national management. Therefore, in case of Korea, the performance management of individual public institutions as well as the performance management system in the aspect of the management of the public institutions (public corporations, quasi-governmental institutions, other public institutions) under the Act on the Management of Public Institutions. Hence, this study aims to simultaneously analyze the performance management of public institutions on the national management level and the internal performance management on the level of individual institutions.

This study will focus on the exploration of the following issues. (1) Is systematic performance management needed on the level of national management besides internal performance management on the level of individual institutions? (2) What are the differences and the desirable correlation between the performance management of public institutions on the level of national management and the strategic performance management on the level of institution management? (3) From a strategic performance management process and KPI perspective, what are the characteristics and problems observed in the performance management of public institutions on the level of national management and the internal performance management on the level of institution management, and what are the desirable future improvements?

II The current state and the multi-layered structure of performance management of public institutions

1 Strategic performance management and the utilization in the public sector

It is important to observe the relation between the performance management based on the KPI and the strategies of the company. The performance management in the private sector has been developing into a strategic performance management focused on the linkage with corporate strategies. This development trend is expanding into the public sector. Strategic performance management refers to the system in which the performance management is connected with the strategic management process and operated with the series of processes from the selection of performance indicators to the evaluation of the outcome and compensation (BearingPoint, 2004). As shown in Figure 4.2, the strategic planning and performance management processes operate under a mutual linkage. Above all, the selection of the Key Performance Index (KPI) connected with the strategic plans and the establishment of the goal based on the KPI are emphasized in the perspective of strategic performance management. While the evaluation and compensation based on the KPI are considered importantly, the evaluation and compensation hold the significance as a feedback factor to enhance the achievement of the goal connected to the strategic plans.

The strategic performance management applied on the level of the management of individual public institutions has been accepted after Kaplan (2001) suggested the importance of the connectivity between strategies and performance evaluation

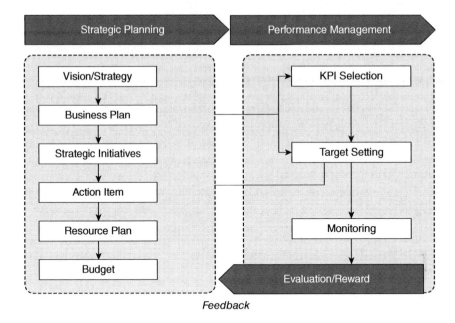

Figure 4.2 Structure and process of strategic performance management

Source: BearingPoint (2004)

in the non-profit sector through the Balanced Scorecard (BSC). Many Korean public institutions have implemented a similar structure.

Meanwhile, it is important to reexamine whether it is necessary and effective for the integrative management authority (institutions with ownership) to execute strategic performance management for the public institutions on the level of national management in the case of Korea. Although the current government of Korea possesses the system for an integrative management of the public institutions with the Act on the Management of Public Institutions, the strategic performance management structure for these public institutions has not been established. While the performance is evaluated and relevant compensation is provided through performance evaluation, the connectivity between the strategies on the national management level and the performance evaluation is observed to be insufficient. Regardless of the importance of the strategic management, the performance management system in public institutions tends to weigh in the performance measurement and compensation rather than the strategic management for pursuing long-term goals. In doing so, they are inclined to focus on high evaluation scores (Yoo and Yoon, 2009).

The importance of strategic performance management that functions to distribute the resources – evaluation and compensation – with the connection to the strategies for the public institutions can be acknowledged with the performance management system in developed countries such as the GPRA (GPRAMA after 2010) of the United States. The GPRA composes three sectors of the strategic planning, performance planning, and performance reports. The strategic planning refers to the activities for checking and constructing the long-term goals and mission of the organization, the performance planning refers to the establishment of action plans to set-up and achieve detailed goals, and the performance reports refer to the process of evaluating and reporting the outcome of the activities (Lee and Lee, 2012).

The OECD Guidelines on Corporate Governance of State-Owned Enterprises (OECD, 2015) suggests the necessity of the goal assignment and monitoring and evaluation which are the bases for strategic performance management. The articles 3 – "Setting and monitoring the implementation of broad mandates and objectives for SOEs, including financial targets, capital structure objectives and risk tolerance levels" – and 4 – "Setting up reporting systems that allow the ownership entity to regularly monitor, audit and assess SOE performance, and oversee and monitor their compliance with applicable corporate governance standards" – provide the related information about the role of the government. Another guideline from the OECD (OECD, 2010) emphasizes the importance of the performance reports and integrative public announcement process for the enhancement of responsibility and transparency of public corporations in addition to the goal set-up and evaluation process.

Reflecting on the examples of the developed countries and the OECD guidelines, the performance management for public institutions on the level of national management is structured as a strategic performance management that emphasizes both the connectivity between the performance evaluation and compensation and the connectivity between the strategy and performance management. In comparison, whereas the evaluation and compensation function is greatly implemented with the performance evaluation system under the current system with the Act on the Management of Public Institutions (with some side-effects), the connectivity with higher strategies and the resources distribution function are observed to be significantly insufficient. As a result, the problem of insufficiency is derived for the strategic connectivity and the ordering of the performance management on the level of national management and the performance management on the level of management of the public institutions.

2 Characteristics of the multi-layered structure of performance management in Korea and challenges

Table 4.1 summarizes the current state and characteristics of the components of the performance management on the level of national management and of the internal performance management for the management of individual public institutions.

From the outside, the internal performance management practices for the management of individual institutions as well as the public institution performance management system on the national management level are observed to possess the necessary components. In the 2015 performance evaluation in which

Table 4.1 Current state of the public institution operation system and the performance management system in the view of strategic performance management

Category	Performance Management of Public Institutions on the National Management Level		Internal Performance Management on the Institutional Management Level
Operation Basis	Act on the Management of Public Institutions		Articles of association and performance management regulations, regulations related to the Act on the Management of Public Institutions, etc.
Goal	Enhancement of efficiency and responsibility of public institutions		Achievement of the mission and strategic goal of the institution
Participants	Committee for the Management of Public Institutions, Public Policy Bureau of the Ministry of Strategy and Finance (responsible department), Performance evaluation Team, separate special examination committee, etc.		Board of directors, performance evaluation team (Committee for the Management of Public Institutions), head of institutions, performance management bureau, etc.
Connectivity System with Higher Strategies	For Institutions Public institution policies of the Ministry of Strategy and Finance (Committee for the Management of Public Institutions) and Operation Guidelines Operation of report and approval system of mid- and long-term financial plans with the Ministry of Strategy and Finance	For Head of Institutions Performance contracts (3 years) between the relevant government bodies and head of institutions, implicit management practices	Selective acceptance of outer demands through mid- and long-term strategies Operation of internal strategic management system
Evaluation Function	Institution performance evaluation system One-year basis/ performance evaluation team (institution)	Head of institutions execution performance evaluation Three-year basis/ performance evaluation team (head of institutions)	Board of directors (formal), internal performance evaluation

(Continued)

Table 4.1 (Continued)

Category	Performance Management of Public Institutions on the National Management Level		Internal Performance Management on the Institutional Management Level
KPI Utilization	Qualitative indicators + Quantitative indicators (partially resembling the KPI characteristics)	Focus on qualitative indicators + Assignment of partial performance goal	Performance evaluation indicators reflected as the institution KPI Hierarchal KPI system by outstanding institution
Compensation Function	Connectivity between evaluation outcome and financial merit ratio for employee	Connectivity between evaluation outcome and the term of office and financial merit for chief manager	Decision of compensation resource according to the performance evaluation outcome Integration with the internal evaluation outcome for compensation distribution for individual/by department
Resources Distribution Function	Implicit management practices (budget/ employment quota adjustments)	Implicit management practices (participation in the projects of government bodies, etc.)	Resources distribution according to the project policies of relevant government bodies instead of the performance evaluation outcome

Source: Reconstructed by the author based on Hong et al. (2015)

I participated, it can be observed that the internal performance management system for the management of individual public institutions attempts to acquire the conditions for the strategic performance management, focusing on the conditions of the performance evaluation indicators and detailed evaluation contents. The problem arises in the performance management of public institutions on the national management level. While the management and evaluation of the public institutions are observed to be somewhat complicated and multi-layered under the system of the Act on the Management of Public Institutions, the actual practices of evaluation and compensation function observed through the operational process are activated through the performance evaluation system (with some side-effects). The connectivity with the higher strategies and the resource distribution function are discovered to be significantly insufficient.

The insufficiency in the performance management on the national management level is derived from the segmentation of the functional management system.

Whereas the Committee for the Management of Public Institutions is theoretically responsible for the performance management, the individual functions are managed segmentally by the Ministry of Strategy and Finance, the ministries responsible for their institutions, the Evaluation Committee of Public Institutions (ECPI), and the board of directors of each institution. While, in reality, the higher strategies for the main business of the public institutions are established mainly by the ministries responsible for their institutions, the quantitative performance indicators and level of the goal of the main business for the performance evaluation are decided by the performance evaluation team (indicator improvement division). Meanwhile, the Ministry of Strategy and Finance that represents the government ownership shows its limitation by reflecting mainly the national projects related to finance or human resources and labor relations in the common management activities sector. In spite of the segmentation of the higher strategies for the public institutions and the distortion in the performance evaluation due to the segmentation, public institutions have been making efforts to reflect the outer political demands to the establishment of mid- and long-term strategies and to include theses in the internal performance management and the KPI. Although it may seem rational on the individual institution level, the outer irrationality is projected and passed on to the internal performance management due to the unfiltered reflection of the segmented demands of the outer policies on the mid- and long-term strategies.

In order for the strategic performance management to be applied to the performance management of public institutions on the national management level, the current distorted performance evaluation system with abnormally strengthened

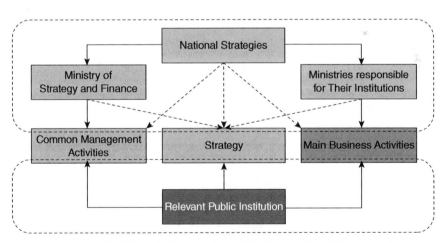

Accomplishment of Strategic Purpose through the Strategy Establishment and own Performance Management by Individual Institutions

Figure 4.3 Segmentation of the higher strategies for the public institutions and distortion of the performance evaluation

Source: Created by author

evaluation and compensation function should be fundamentally reformed. Also, the current governance system under the Act on the Management of Public Institutions needs a fundamental reformation. Possible measures for the reformation include reviewing and periodically updating the performance plans for strategic connectivity and appointing an integrative management system to activate the functions such as adjustment of resource distribution reflecting the monitoring and evaluation outcomes.

3 The problem of connectivity between the performance management on the national management level and the performance management of individual institutions

What are the problems in the connectivity between the performance management on the national management level and the performance management of individual institutions, and what measures could be implemented to improve the situation? The problem of insufficient strategic connectivity and ordering of the performance management on the national management level and for the management of individual institutions derives from the previously mentioned problems of the performance management on the national management level (segmental higher strategies, insufficient connectivity between the higher strategies and performance goals, abnormal emphasis on the evaluation and compensation function).

In the current system of the Act on the Management of Public Institutions, the establishment of strategic goals by the individual institutions and the performance management are absolutely influenced by the detailed evaluation indicators and the level of goals demanded by outer evaluations (performance evaluation, etc.). In reality, the public institutions reflect the outer demands, regardless of their rationality or validity, on the internal strategic goals and performance indicators almost completely, in order to receive outstanding scores in outer evaluations which are directly connected to the compensation of the executives and employees. If the demands of the outer evaluations not verified of the rationality and validity are reflected almost identically on the strategic goals and performance indicators, there is a threat that the underlying irrationality and incongruity in the goals and indicators may affect the entire management and project management.

Therefore, the proper and adverse functions of performance evaluation should be considered more profoundly. The measures to minimize the adverse functions of performance evaluation in the perspective of the recipient (institution) should be sought before the proper and adverse functions of the performance evaluation system were evaluated in the perspective of the provider (relevant government bodies), especially the Ministry of Strategy and Finance that represents the government ownership. In particular, it is important to arrange relevant measures to stop the potential distortions of the strategic goals and performance indicators caused by the performance evaluation system. Hence, it should be seriously contemplated that the establishment of the level of the goals and the performance indicators be transferred from the initial solitary execution by the performance evaluation team (with consultation with the Ministry of Strategy and Finance) to cooperative establishment with relevant government bodies (main business sector) and the board of directors of the institutions (common management activities sector). Simultaneously, in case of the main business, the decision-making methods for the selection of quantitative indicators and the level of the goals should be modified and, in case of the common management activities, the period of evaluation indicator improvement and modification should be extended to a minimum of three-year unit basis.

III Analysis and evaluation of the current operation of the strategic performance management

While many companies implement performance management, the consulting firm BearingPoint (2004) suggests that companies may fall into the traps and problems of the performance management. First, many companies lacked or possessed unclear strategies, which are the presumption for the performance management. One of the reasons may be that the companies misunderstand the strategies as the project plans or consider the establishment of strategies and performance management as separate processes. Second, the indicators utilized in many companies were either absent for the measurement of performance or irrelevant with the strategies. Third, there were frequent cases in which the infrastructure for a proper performance management was not arranged. Generally, in order to execute a systematic performance management, institutional basis need to be founded and additional infrastructure to assist the process such as an information system should be prepared. Fourth, the individuals and organizations related to the

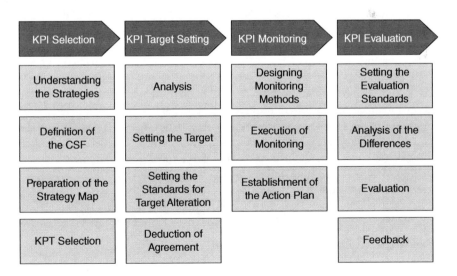

Figure 4.4 Process of strategic performance management based on the KPI

Source: BearingPoint (2004)

performance management lack an accurate understanding of their roles in the performance management process. Fifth, performance management is considered only as an evaluation tool for the outcome. However, performance management begins with the establishment of performance plans connected with the strategic plans and continues until ultimately the feedback for the outcome of the performance management is reflected in the plans and goals of the following year. The traps and problems that private corporations may fall into pointed out by Bearing-Point (2004) are observed in similar aspects in the performance management of Korean public institutions.

This study aims to highlight the problems in the performance management of public institutions including both the national management level and the individual institution level in the aspect of the process and operational conditions of strategic performance management. BearingPoint (2004) suggested that the process of strategic performance management encompasses the process and execution of each stage of the process from the selection of the KPI to the evaluation. Therefore, the current state and problems of the performance management of Korean public institutions are observed based on the model suggested by BearingPoint (2004).

1 Step 1: KPI selection

The selection of the KPI in private corporations is based on the strategic plans as companies with greater appropriateness of the strategic plans and the KPI show relatively higher management performance (Park and Kim, 2006). The first step of the strategic performance management is the selection of the KPI. In the KPI selection step, the following aspects are important: the connectivity between the strategy establishment and the KPI, the management of the hierarchy of the strategies and the KPI, the systematic selection of the KPI, and the practicality examination of the KPI.

Based on the 4 factors of the KPI selection, Table 4.2 describes the problems of the performance management practices of Korean public institutions in the 2 dimensions. The KPI selection activities in the performance management on the national management level are observed to be generally unsystematic and have not improved the sporadic and arbitrary characteristics. The KPI selection on the national management level ultimately governs the rationality of the KPI selection on the institutional management level. Therefore, it is urgent to improve the irrationality of the KPI selection on the national management level.

In order to enhance the efficiency of the KPI selection that is the first step of performance management of public institutions, various improvements are needed. One of the core issues to be reviewed in seeking the improvement measures is 'whether the KPI should be focused on the final outcomes or on the critical success factors (CSF) for final performance enhancement'. Both the quantitative indicators and the KPI for performance evaluation implemented autonomously by the institutions are focused on the final outcome instead of on the CSF. Whereas the CSF emphasizes controllable factors, the final outcomes usually reflect the

Table 4.2 Evaluation and issues of the current KPI selection

Category	Performance Management of Public Institutions on the National Management Level	Internal Performance Management on the Institutional Management Level
Connectivity between Strategy Establishment and the KPI	– Establishment of mid-term strategies by department (yet, significant fluctuations on a five-year basis and unsystematic fluctuations emerge) – Connectivity between the public institution management strategies from the Ministry of Strategy and Finance and the performance evaluation indicators (yet, insufficient predictability) – Insufficient connectivity between the relevant strategies and the project indicators in case of other departments	– Establishment of mid-term strategies on institutional level (yet, influenced by fluctuations in the government or head of institutions, etc.) – Attempt to connect the mid- and long-term strategies and the KPI (yet, focusing on the final outcome instead of on the CSF) – Low consistency between the KPI reflecting the demands from the outside and the KPI reflecting the demands of the institution project strategies
Management of Hierarchy of the Strategies and the KPI	– Management focused on the institutional indicators included in the KPI – Lack of higher KPI through sectional integration of the institutional indicators -> despite the indicators and the level of the goal are assigned according to the political goal, the integration logic for the performance of the higher indicators is lacked	– Different level of hierarchy management by institution – For outstanding institutions in this section, construction of hierarchal structure such as the KPI for the entire corporation – the KPI for the sectors/projects – the KPI for the departments – Partial attempt to connect the KPI for the departments and the KPI for individuals (yet, insufficient ordering of the level of the goals)
Systematic Selection of the KPI	– In case of main business, effort to establish customized indicators according to the characteristics of the projects (yet, focusing on the final outcome instead of on the CSF) – In case of common management activities, uniform indicators are established, not considering the individual characteristics of the institutions (yet, fine control to reflect type characteristics)	– Passive acceptance of the KPI and the level of the goals according to the performance evaluation demands from the outside (the suggestions from the institutions are partially accepted in the stage of selection and setting of main business indicators, but the external evaluation team has the final authority) – Establishment of necessary internal KPI apart from the performance evaluation indicators

(Continued)

Table 4.2 (Continued)

Category	Performance Management of Public Institutions on the National Management Level	Internal Performance Management on the Institutional Management Level
Practicality Examination of the KPI	– In case of main business, unsystemized selective examination in the processes of indicator construction and evaluation team review through consultation between the institution and the evaluation team – In case of common management activities, indicator construction based on the qualitative judgment of the evaluation team without separate examination as a standardized system	– Passive acceptance of the KPI and the level of the goals (due to problems of evaluation and compensation, institutions will almost accept them) – In case of the own KPI, the selection is based on standards such as the SMART (yet, the focus as a formal requirement)

Source: Reconstructed by the author based on Hong et al. (2015)

influences of uncontrollable factors. If the purpose of the performance management is to decide the compensation, it is inevitable to put an emphasis on the final outcomes. However, if monitoring the performance enhancement is also a goal, the CSF should as well be emphasized. Therefore, in the strategic performance management view, the final outcomes as well as the CSF should both be considered importantly with the main business in the center.

For qualitative indicators in the performance evaluation, institutions set and manage the ratings of the indicators as the KPI. It is an abnormal practice. Due to the conditions of the performance evaluation, the ratings of the qualitative evaluation are often decided by other political factors rather than by the improvement effort or level of the relevant sector. In reality, the qualitative evaluation indicators rated and announced reflecting the qualitative evaluation of the evaluators cannot function as the KPI. In order for the qualitative indicators to function as practical performance indicators, the way they operate should be changed to assigning measurable, detailed improvement goals for the following year. If it seems unrealistic, another way would be to transfer to the evaluation methods utilized by various certification systems. In the common management activities fields (organization/personnel, finance/budget, wage/labor relations, etc.), the introduction of the certification system is observed to stabilize the levels of the system and competence after reaching a certain stage (Hong et al., 2015).

2 Step 2: KPI target setting

In the second step of the strategic performance management, the activities related to the target setting of the KPI are involved. In this step, the following aspects are important: distinction between the short-term and long-term KPI, target setting for the short-term KPI, modification plans for the KPI according to the changes in the environment, and the target agreement method. This is the step where the performance management of Korean public institutions is most vulnerable. Table 4.3 describes the overall current state and problems.

In order to enhance the effectiveness of the target set that is the second step of performance management of public institutions, more improvements need to be sought compared with the previous KPI selection step. One of the core issues

Table 4.3 Evaluation and issues of the current KPI target setting

Category	Performance Management of Public Institutions on the National Management Level	Internal Performance Management on the Institutional Management Level
Distinction between the Short-term and Long-term KPI	– [Performance evaluation] Qualitative evaluation for the short-term/long-term strategic (performance) indicators and goals – [Quantitative] Interest in the short-term goals based on the analysis of the past data of the selected indicators * submission of the mid-term financial plan (debt, etc.)	– [Performance evaluation indicator] Traditional complete acceptance of the demands of the evaluation team – [Internal indicator] Distinguished management of the short-term and long-term KPI in outstanding institutions, insufficient distinction between the short-/long-term in plenty institutions
Target Setting for the Short-term KPI	– [Qualitative] Suggestion of general comments – [Quantitative] Standardized goal setting and challenge for +2 sigmas based on the past data	– [Performance evaluation indicator] Traditional complete acceptance of the demands of the evaluation team * Management of increased goal in outstanding institutions – [Internal indicator] Suggestion of various basis for the setting such as trend analysis and comparison with the previous year
Modification Plans for the KPI according to the changes in the environment	– In principle, uniform maintenance of the methods selected two years ago for setting the indicators and goals * Partial modification annually for the mid-term financial plans (caused by policy changes, unsystemized modification)	– [Performance evaluation indicator] Traditional complete acceptance of the demands of the evaluation team – [Internal indicator] Modification of the goals possible in some institutions through half-yearly examination, lack of guidelines for previous modification in most institutions
Target Agreement Method	– While considering the opinions of the institutions, the priority emphasis on the qualitative decisions of the performance evaluation team	– [Internal indicator] Insufficient functioning of systematic examination and revision about the level of the goals

Source: Reconstructed by the author based on Hong et al. (2015)

to be reviewed in seeking the improvement measures is 'whether, in case of the main business sector in the performance evaluation, the methods selected two years ago for setting the indicators and level of the goals should be maintained'. As the global economic environment as well as the domestic circumstances are changing dramatically, the fundamental question whether the indicators and level of the goals set two years ago is appropriate for the context at the time of the performance calculation and the influences from outer variables on the achievement of the goal must be considered. The current excessive deviations among the performance of some public corporations are generated rather by outside factors such as the outside economy (oil prices, exchange rates, etc.) and policies (price determination, etc.) than by internal efforts of the institutions. Therefore, it should be seriously considered that new methods for the target setting and performance measurement be implemented for some of the quantitative indicators that are significantly influenced by outside factors. A possible way is to apply the adjusted performance measures (APM) method for the target setting and performance measurement of the performance indicators considerably influenced by outside variables. The APM is a method utilized to produce valid performance indicators by eliminating the influences from the uncontrollable factors through statistical adjustments using regression equations. Lee (2005) applied the APM method to analyze the outcomes of the 2003 performance evaluation of government-invested institutions and observed that there were significant differences between the analyzed outcomes and the accumulated outcomes from the raw scores. He stated that results imply that the factors uncontrollable by the evaluated entities in the measurement of the performance indicators are considerably reflected in the performance evaluation. The burden of adjusting the performance levels through qualitative evaluations would be significantly reduced if the APM (measurement) methodology could be applied. Also, the institutions would be able to create systematic responses with predictability if they possessed an APM (measurement) simulation model.

Another issue is 'deciding which direction would be more desirable if the demands of the outside evaluations (evaluation indicators and level of the goal) including the performance evaluation and the autonomous management demands of the institutions were distinct'. A possible situation the public institutions may confront can be illustrated as below. Notwithstanding each situation requires a different type of adjustment, public institutions tend to be obedient to the superior authorities unofficially and apply evaluation with a one-size-fit-all approach.

Instead of emphasizing the uniform selection of indicators and target setting, the measures such as the outside and internal demands matrix should be utilized to apply differentiated methods for the selection of indicators and target setting for different indicator groups. It is believed that the method for customized indicators and adjusted goals is recommendable for most of the institutions (mainly public corporations) in case of the main business. The current methods can be maintained in case of the indicators appropriate for the demand of the superior authorities such as the wage increase rate. The conflicting cases such as the debt

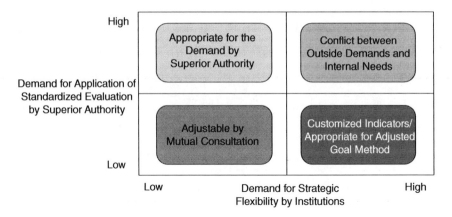

High

Demand for Application of
Standardized Evaluation
by Superior Authority

Low

	Appropriate for the Demand by Superior Authority	Conflict between Outside Demands and Internal Needs
	Adjustable by Mutual Consultation	Customized Indicators/ Appropriate for Adjusted Goal Method

Low   Demand for Strategic   High
Flexibility by Institutions

Figure 4.5 Possible situations of demands from outside evaluations and internal demands for management of the institutions

Source: Created by author

ratio can be adjusted differently for individual institutions through methods such as operating a council.

3 Step 3: KPI monitoring and execution

In the third step of the strategic performance management, the activities related to monitoring and executing the KPI are involved. In this step, the following aspects are important: the monitoring function (existence and level of activation), the Early Warning function (existence and actual utilization), and monitoring and improvement feedbacks. Based on the three factors of the KPI monitoring and execution, Table 4.4 describes the problems of the performance management practices of Korean public institutions in the two dimensions. In particular, as there is almost a lack of the KPI monitoring and execution in the performance management on the national management level, urgent improvements are needed.

It is in this step in which the performance management activities on the national management level completely lacks the function. While the performance evaluation system is involved in the target setting and evaluation processes, there is almost a lack of the monitoring function, the Early Warning function, and the improvement feedbacks reflecting the monitoring outcome. In order to implement the strategic performance management for the public institutions on the national management level, systematic monitoring and improvement feedback functions should be strengthened.

It could be recommended that the relatively activated autonomous monitoring activities of the public institutions be utilized. The applicable autonomous monitoring system in public institutions will allow the superior authorities to monitor on a regular basis. The worldwide renowned ALIO system (www.alio.go.kr/) for public disclosure of performance data can be utilized to strengthen

Table 4.4 Evaluation and issues of the current KPI monitoring and execution

Category	Performance Management of Public Institutions on the National Management Level	Internal Performance Management on the Institutional Management Level
Monitoring Function	– [Performance evaluation] Emphasis limited to the outcome evaluation with a lack of the monitoring function in the process – [Ministry of Strategy and Finance/Committee for the Management of Public Institutions] Examination of the progress related to specific political guidelines (indicators) (yet, evaluation is difficult as a systematic monitoring)	– [Performance evaluation indicator] Active monitoring through measures such as operating separate committees or quarterly reports – [Internal indicator] Though not as active as for performance evaluation indicator, monitoring for individual indicators is constructed (yet, it is unclear if it is actually operated)
Early Warning Function	– [Performance evaluation] Lack of monitoring in the process – [Ministry of Strategy and Finance/Committee for the Management of Public Institutions] Selective examination and involvement related to specific political guidelines (indicators)	– Compared to the relatively active monitoring activities, selective utilization of the systematic Early Warning function limited for the finance and core projects fields
Monitoring and Improvement Feedbacks	– [Performance evaluation] Lack of monitoring in the process – [Ministry of Strategy and Finance/Committee for the Management of Public Institutions] Selective examination and involvement related to specific political guidelines (indicators)	– Selective application of feedback improvement activities in the process reflecting the monitoring outcome in relation to the importance of the indicators

Source: Reconstructed by the author based on Hong et al. (2015)

the monitoring functions (Hong et al., 2015). Whereas currently the performance evaluation supporting information system is operational, the system is limited to accumulating the data and outcomes of the evaluation and the actual utilization in the evaluation team is significantly low. Moreover, the current performance evaluation supporting information system lacks the monitoring function. Therefore, instead of completely reforming the system for utilization, the system could be connected with the ALIO public disclosure system to strengthen the monitoring function. Both the efficiency of the evaluation and the transparency of the public institutions could be heightened by reflecting the execution progress and project performances of the government policies announced publicly through the ALIO system in the mid-process monitoring and evaluations of management and execution performances.

4 Step 4: KPI evaluation and feedback

In the fourth step of the strategic performance management, the activities related to the evaluation and feedback of the KPI are involved. In this step, the following aspects are important: the establishment of evaluation criteria and execution of the evaluation, the application of the adjusted target, and the connectivity between the evaluation outcomes and the feedback and the compensation. Based on the 3 factors of the KPI evaluation and feedback, the performance management practices of Korean public institutions in the two dimensions are

Table 4.5 Evaluation and issues of the current KPI evaluation and feedback

Category	Performance Management of Public Institutions on the National Management Level	Internal Performance Management on the Institutional Management Level
Establishment of Evaluation Criteria and Execution of the Evaluation	– [Performance evaluation] Systematic establishment of evaluation criteria and execution of evaluation -> evaluation advancement stage – [Ministry of Strategy and Finance/Committee for the Management of Public Institutions] Selective evaluation (examination) related to specific political guidelines (indicators)	– [Performance evaluation] Acceptance of the evaluation and evaluation outcomes dependent on the outside performance evaluation team (yet, significantly insufficient evaluation function for the board of directors) – [Internal evaluation] Regular execution of performance evaluation
Application of the Adjusted Target	– [Performance evaluation] Lack of application of quantitative indicators, unofficial adjustment of outcome scores through qualitative evaluation – [Ministry of Strategy and Finance/Committee for the Management of Public Institutions] Lack of the concept of the adjusted target	– [Performance evaluation] Complete acceptance of the performance evaluation outcomes – [Internal evaluation] Rare cases of the application of the adjusted target, unofficial adjustment of outcome scores through internal qualitative evaluation methods
Connectivity between the Evaluation Outcomes and the Feedback and the Compensation	– [Performance evaluation] Tolerance for monetary compensation based on the systematic feedback and standards (yet, problems of late feedback and uniformity arise) – [Ministry of Strategy and Finance/Committee for the Management of Public Institutions] Indirect ways for compensation through reflecting the selective feedback for the institutions in the performance evaluation	– [Performance evaluation] Direct reflection in the internal evaluation and execution of formal compensation on similar level to the performance evaluation compensation – [Internal evaluation] Internal evaluation system separated in the operation stage with connectivity with the performance evaluation scores -> Reflection of the feedback and compensation

Source: Reconstructed by the author based on Hong et al. (2015)

evaluated to generally possess the relevant characteristics except for the application of the adjusted target. The performance management on the national management level, especially the connectivity between the evaluation outcomes and the feedback and the compensation, is observed to be excessive through the performance evaluation system.

Unlike the other steps (processes) of the performance management, the last step involving the KPI evaluation and feedback is observed to be the most advanced and developed step. However, the contextual appropriateness of the feedback and the compensation related to the evaluation outcomes is observed to be relatively insufficient due to the construction and application of stiff evaluation criteria. While the incentives desired by the institutions and members of the institutions are decided based on the final evaluation ratings announced as the performance evaluation outcomes, the authentic strategic functions of the performance management should be considered more importantly than the evaluation ratings.

IV Lessons learned and conclusion

The Korean government has made great use of performance management tools to improve the outcomes of public institutions. In this way, we have developed sophisticated and complex performance management of public institutions system and method that cannot be found in other countries. However, we have developed a performance management system targeting more than 200 public institutions, and unexpected side effects have also appeared in addition to the advantages. In this research, I tried to investigate the problems of the performance management system of the public institution in Korea which we have applied so far and to explore the improvement measures.

The lessons learned by this are as follows. First, it is necessary to convert the existing performance management system, which focuses on evaluation and compensation, to a strategic performance management system focusing on setting goals and achieving goals at the national level. Second, from the viewpoint of strategic performance management, the Korean performance management of public institutions system has the future task of overcoming the problems of the multi-layered structure where national level and institutional level are included together. Third, in order to implement strategic performance management at national level, it is important to set goals and systematically monitor using KPIs as performance evaluation indicators. Fourth, we must recognize the difference between national-level strategic performance management and institutional performance management, and develop a performance management system tailored to each characteristic. Also, we must make efforts to ensure that both parties operate in close interlinkage. Fifth, in order for operation in close interlinkage between the national level strategic performance management and the institutional performance management, we must seek an alternative reform plan of governance structure for public institutions.

References

BearingPoint. (2004). *Strategic Performance Management, Lecture Material*. www.kmis. or.kr/3_sig/sem_data/sem(dec04).pdf.

GAO. (1996). *Executive Guide Effectively Implementing the Government Performance Results Act*, GAO/GGD-96–118.

Hong, K.P. et al. (2015). *Study on Improvement Measures for Public Institution Performance Evaluation System*. Ministry of Strategy and Finance Service Research Report.

Kaplan, R. S. (2001). Strategic Performance Measurement and Management in Non-Profit Organizations. *Nonprofit Management & Leadership*, *11*(3), 353–370.

Lee, S. W. (2005). Measuring the Performance Using Adjusted Performance Measure: Application to the Performance Assessment of Public Enterprises in Korea. *Korean Public Administration Review*, *39*(4), 81–104.

Lee, G. and Lee, K. (2012). *Study on the Construction Measures for Mid- and Long-Term Management System for Performance of the Central Administrative Agencies*. Korean Institute of Public Administration, KIPA Research Report 2012–18.

Lee, S. H. (2012). 7 Deadly Sins in Performance Management in the Public Sector: Implications for Linking Theory to Practice. *The Korea Local Administration Review*, *16*(1), 353–380.

OECD. (2010). *Policy Brief on Corporate Governance of State-Owned Enterprises in Asia: Recommendations for Reform, Network on Corporate Governance of State-Owned Enterprises in Asia*. OECD.

OECD. (2015). *OECD Guidelines on Corporate Governance of State-Owned Enterprises: 2015 Edition*. OECD.

Park, J. and Han, H. (2004). *Analysis and Improvement Measures for the Performance Evaluation System and Its Operation: Exploration of an Integrative Performance Management*. Korean Institute of Public Administration.

Park, S. and Kim, B. (2006). The Effect of the Fitness Between Strategic Tasks and KPI on the Business Performance in BSC. *Korean Academic Society of Accounting*, *11*(3), 247–275.

Parker, C. (2000). Performance Measurement. *Work Study*, *49*(2), 64–66.

Ra, Y. (2011). *Current State and Issues Related to the Performance Management of Public Institutions*. Seoul Association for Public Administration Conference Proceeding, 77–91.

Yoo, S., and Yoon, K. (2009). Success Factors for Implementing a Performance Management System in the Public Sector: Focusing on the Principles of the Strategy-Focused Organization. *Korea Administration Research*, *18*(4), 117–143.

Yoon, S. and Lim, D. (2009). *A Study on the Operation and Improvement of the Performance Management System in the Korean Central Government*. Korean Institute of Public Administration, KIPA Research Report 2009–05.

Part II

Performance evaluation and governance

5 The views and measures of main business activities evaluation of public institutions revisited

Focusing on the evolutionary logic model and evaluability assessment

Yoon Seuk Woo

I Introduction: the potential and limitations of the performance evaluation of public institution

The performance evaluation of main business actives of the performance evaluation of public institutions (PEPI) aims to examine whether the relevant institutions achieved the expected performance of the projects during the period of evaluation. However, performance in the public sector is difficult to understand and can be interpreted differently according to how the concept, the measurement target, and the measurement methods are defined. The PEPI in Korea implements the qualitative evaluation based on the traditional logic model centered at the Plan-Do-See-Act cycle and the quantitative evaluation based on the predefined performance indicators. Qualitative evaluation can be considered as a form of evaluation by performance indicators as well since the PDCA model is included in the evaluation criteria and the performance is evaluated using different set of quantitative and qualitative indicators. Whereas the evaluation based on the performance indicators has the advantages of the securement of objectivity and comfortability of evaluation, it also has the disadvantages of the insufficient representability of the proxy variables, the possibility of distorted judgment due to simplified logic, and the threshold effects for the relevant performance in the target setting. Therefore, the construction of the performance indicators is the most important prerequisite for the performance evaluation, as the outcomes may be significantly diversified according to how the performance indicators are defined, composed, and measured.

The current performance evaluation of the main business activities is based on the traditional program theory and simple logic model. Therefore, it has a high probability of creating the error of simplicity in complicated and complex environments. Moreover, it can be inappropriate for the utilization in the change management through which the competence could be strengthened based on the performance evaluation. Ultimately, the performance evaluation outcomes may deviate from the cognition and expectation of the people and fall into a tool for the provision of 'their own compensation'. In order to assess whether the current performance evaluation is properly functioning, this study aims to reexamine the evaluability[1] of the current performance evaluation based on the problems mentioned above. First, the potential and limitations of the public sector performance evaluation in the theoretical dimension will be reviewed and the Theory of Change and the complicated/complex logic model for the evolution to a new perspective will be introduced. And next, the evaluability of the current performance evaluation will be assessed in the dimensions of perspective and methods focusing on the examples from the public corporation group I.

II Necessity and direction of change in the perspective

1 Limitations of performance evaluation of public sector

The 4 dimensions of problematics pointed out by Talbot (2010) (analysis unit, concept, technique, and politics and value) related to the performance in the public sector provide various implications about the current performance evaluation. First, the problem of analysis unit arises due to the difficulty of defining the range of the public sector. As Bozeman (1987) pointed out, all organizations are essentially public to some extent as they receive a uniform section from the government. With the advent of the governance era, various stakeholders are involved in the public policies and programs. Therefore, the boundaries become so blurred that it is quite difficult to decide who shall be included in the target to be analyzed. For example, the increase in the inbound volume of travel may have been influenced more significantly by the efforts of institutions related to the Korean Wave (Korea Tourism Organization or entertainment companies, etc.) than by the performance of the Incheon International Airport Corporation or the Korea Airports Corporation, but it is impossible to include Korean Wave institutions in the performance evaluation of the Incheon International Airport Corporation or the Korea Airports Corporation. Second, the problem of the concept arises due to the difficulties of deciding what should and what should not be considered as performance in defining the input, output, and outcome. In particular, the input, output, and outcome can be divided into 3 factors of quantity, quality, and satisfaction. Therefore, the evaluation becomes even more difficult with the 9 dimensions created. For example, although the construction of the highways or pavement ratio improvements are mere output indicators for the Korea Highway Corporation, these are considered as representative performance indicators since the mid- and long-term outcomes (real performance) such as regional development or increase in traffic safety are difficult to be estimated and identified in the short-term period.

The technical problem refers to the impossibility of completely evaluating all of the performance due to the practical problem related with the costs involved and the theoretical problem that the accuracy of measurement cannot be promised due to inevitable errors. For example, if significant amounts of resources (data collection, proof expenses, etc.) are consumed in the measurement process, institutions with greater performance for the core tasks may be evaluated more poorly than institutions with lower performance. In other words, public institutions that can relatively easily prove the performance numerically may be evaluated highly than other institutions. Moreover, the difference between subjective judgment and objective measurement may provoke another problem. For example, the evaluators shall be constrained to the frame created by media or personal bias which leads to the false rating of the real performance of institutions.

Last, the political and value-related problem means that the objectives of the performance evaluation become fuzzy due to the multi-layered values and politics. In case of the public institutions in the public corporation group I, the problem of conflicting values may expand even more greatly because they possess a twofold position in which they must pursue the publicness and commerciality at the same time. Also, the dual relationship with the relevant ministries can be problematic since the performance evaluation is led by the Ministry of Strategy and Finance and performance evaluation team, while general monitoring is implemented by ministries to which they are affiliated. As illustrated in Figure 5.1, Waterman and Meier (1998) expanded the traditional Principal-Agent theory to match the conflicting interests of the two parties.

According to Waterman and Meier (1998), apart from the traditional situation of the Principal-Agent theory in quadrant 2, the quadrants 6–8 are possible in which the goals of the two parties match. In the performance evaluation operated by the Ministry of Strategy and Finance and the evaluation team, the responsible authorities that each of the institutions belongs to are excluded. Moreover, in the relationship between the Ministry of Strategy and Finance/evaluation team and the public institutions, the former possesses unilateral information about the evaluation system whereas the latter possesses more information about the actual performances or for the proposal of changing quantitative indicators. Therefore, the Ministry of Strategy and Finance/evaluation team and the public institutions belong to the patronage system in quadrant 4 that the former acquires a relatively

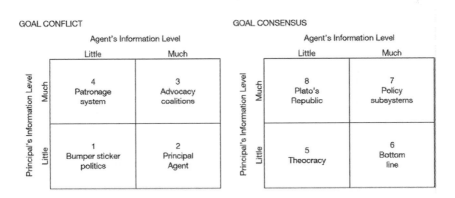

Figure 5.1 Expanded principal-agent model (integration of conflicts and information asymmetry)

Source: Waterman and Meier (1998: 188)

superior position during the evaluation stage. On the other hand, during the stage of proposing change or setting indicators, the two form the traditional Principal-Agent relationship in quadrant 2. Whereas the institutions and the ministries to which the institution is affiliated are in a relationship in which the interests of the two match, the relationship is situated in the bottom line model in quadrant 6 in which the responsible authorities possess relatively inadequate information during the implementation stage and in the policy subsystems model in quadrant 7 during the evaluation stage. The values and political dynamics of individual entities will proceed differently in each of the cases that the goal of the performance evaluation become fuzzy and thus various conflicts arise.

2 *Importance of logic model evolution for project evaluation: program theory and theory of change, simple logic model, and complicated/complex logic model*

Current evaluations of the main business activities are based on the program theory and logic model. The problem is that, as the results of main business activities evaluation are used in rating or ranking the evaluated institutions, the evaluation may be limited to simply quantifiable achievements. The project evaluation can be defined as the measurement of the level of project goal achievements (Suvedi, 1998). However, in accordance with Wotthen and Sanders (1987), who pointed out that the project evaluation is a political activity of deciding the values of the projects, it is necessary to concern the fundamental values that the evaluation must pursue rather than simply applying evaluation technique. As it is important to provide public services to the people without discontinuity, the aim of project evaluation for public corporations should be changed to strengthen the competence of the service providers to secure the provision of public services. Hence, it is important to consider the Theory of Change for evaluation to contribute to identifying real value considering its environmental context which is complicated and complex. In the following sections, the logic models based on the Program Theory and the Theory of Change and the complicated/complex logic model are discussed in more detail.

1) *Logic models based on the program theory and the theory of change*

The Program Theory refers to 'systematically arranging the normative hypotheses for what activities are necessary to solve the social problems and the descriptive hypotheses for whether such activities will solve the social problems', while the logic models visualize the Program Theory that attempts to explain the logical cause and effect relationships among the stages involved in the project activities by defining the stages of the input, transfer, output, and outcome (Kim, 2005: 101). Therefore, the logic model is sometimes called the Program Theory or the Program's Theory of Action.[2]

It is assumed that the input resources, project activities, outputs, individual purposes, and long-term goal are arranged in a vertical logic system in the logic model. Park (2009) exemplified a development project and stated that the following assumptions would be fulfilled in order for each step and that the vertical logic system is in a mutual cause and effect relationship as seen in the Figure 5.2.

The logic model can be helpful for the construction and improvement of the program by understanding the issues related to the evaluation and identifying the projects related to the achievement of the goal of the program. Moreover, it enables the stakeholders to share the value by systemizing the planning, managing, and evaluating functions of the program and linking the various activities and relevant expected outcomes (National Assembly Budget Office, 2016). On the other hand, the interpretation in the logic model possesses the limitation of over-simplifying the reality by putting the complicated cause and effect relations and various interactions among the stakeholders into simple terms and unidirectional relationships. Also, it is liable to lose adaptability of actual activities as the focus is given to measuring and achieving the result of performance indicators arranged in the planning process in advance without appreciating the efforts of adapting to the changing environment. Furthermore, the achievement of quantitative performance indicators may mistakenly be considered as real achievements of the goal of the project even when it shows only the numbers of quantifiable output (Park and Kim, 2015).

Unlike the logic model which was initiated during the 1970s, the Theory of Change was initiated in the United States during the 1990s when it was applied to the evaluation of programs in the local communities and was more widely applied to international development assistance with an aim to improve the limitations of the project evaluations based on the logic model (Stein and Valters, 2012). The Theory of Change pays attention to the fact that the programs for the development of the local communities or assistance programs for the less-developed countries did not have sustained influences in spite of the huge investment. The water pumps provided in African regions can be exemplified. Whereas the water pumps were provided to solve the problem of water scarcity, the sense

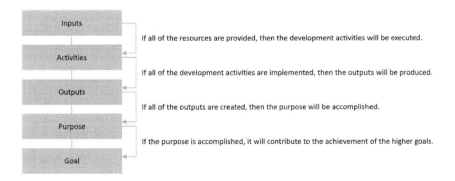

Figure 5.2 Vertical logic relationships of the logic model

Source: Park (2009: 28)

of hygiene of people did not improve and the water pumps were out of order within several years as there was not anyone who had the ability to fix broken water pumps. This is an example where the problem of water scarcity was solved temporarily but it failed to secure the relevant competence to maintain the change (IBR, 2014). Therefore, the holistic perspective should be emphasized to strengthen the competence and pursue sustainable changes instead of the traditional program business model that focuses on financial investments for purpose-oriented projects.

Weiss (1995) stated that the Theory of Change is a theory that tells 'how and why a project will work' and a method to describe a series of assumptions to explain the relationships between the small changes and activities that develop into the achievement of the long-term goals of the program and the outcomes. The focus of it is to investigate the relations between the activities and outcomes with an assumption that there are implicit or explicit theories explaining how the programs will work. As Stein and Valters (2012) argued that the Theory of Change belongs to a wider ranged of the Program Theory or the logic model. Rogers (2008) argued that the Program Theory, intervention logic, influence evaluation, theory-based evaluation, and the Theory of Change are essentially identical, and there is not yet an agreed upon definition of the Theory of Change. However, the Theory of Change is different[3] from the traditional logic model in the following aspects as seen in the Table 5.1.

Table 5.1 Comparison between the logic model and the theory of change

	Logic Model	Theory of Change
History	30 years	Utilized since the 1990s
Usage	– Used to identify and visualize the components of the program – Simplified complicated theories	– Planning/Evaluation of complex initiatives through the causal model – Critical insights about the program (strict evaluation, identification of reasons for game failure)
Composition	List of components	Pathway of change
Characteristic	Descriptive arrangement of the program components	Connection between the activities and outcomes, explanation of how and why changes will occur
Starting Point	What you are doing	What you want to achieve
Considerations	– Identification of the program components – Indicators (not always utilized)	– Rationalization of the game necessary for every stage (causal model) – Indicators (always necessary) –> identification of the meaning of the game
Limitations	Lack of explanations for the reasons for the outcomes	Need for considerable amounts of effort and time

Source: IBR (2014) (http://ibr.kr/2976)

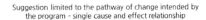

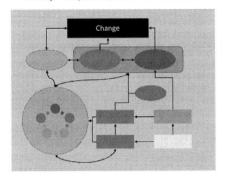
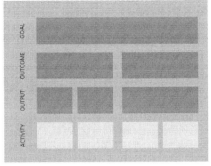

Figure 5.3 Pathway comparison for the theory of change and the logic model

Source: Park, and Kim. (2015: 106 Quoted)

Clark and Anderson (2004) stated that, whereas the logic model clarifies the input and activities and the output and outcomes by schematizing the program components, the Theory of Change connects the outcomes and activities to explain how and why the intended changes occur. Therefore, while the former initiates by schematizing the programs and their components and does not explain why the activities are linked to the outcomes, the Theory of Change initiates by clarifying what the purpose of the changes is before deciding what programs are needed and forms a causal model by verifying the links between the causes and outcomes. In all, it can be summarized that the logic model is a descriptive representation of the list of components and that the Theory of Change is an explanatory method for the pathway of change based on critical thinking (Clark and Anderson, 2004).

While the traditional logic model assumes a single cause and effect relationship among the intervention-output-purpose-long-term goal, the Theory of Change admits various complicated cause and effect relationships and thus helps the understanding of the missing middle that explains how the instant outcomes of individual projects influence the outcomes in the other dimensions and the hidden situations behind the arrow as seen in the Figure 5.3 (Park and Kim, 2015).

2) Simple logic model and complicated/complex logic model

In spite of the usefulness, logic models have been criticized that they are based on the assumption that the complicated variables and interactions of the projects work without problems in complex and confusing situations (Pinnegar, 2006; Stufflebeam, 2004). The criticism is based on the fact that most logic models show a single, linear cause and effect pathway as illustrated in Figure 5.4.

Although this structure is suitable to show the overall process and intent of the policies, the causal contribution of the policies can be overestimated due to the

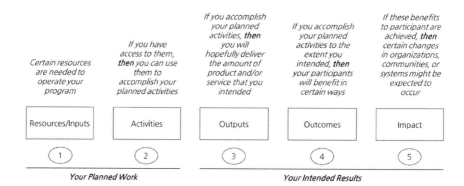

Figure 5.4 Structure of simple logic model

Source: WkK.Kellogg Foundation (2004: 3)

lack of considerations for the environment in which the execution takes place, the characteristics of the stakeholders, and the other projects simultaneously in progress. Also, the assumption for a stable environment instead of a complicated environment in which uncontrollable situations emerge is problematic (Eoyang et al., 1998; Perrin, 2003). The environment in which the projects are operated possess complicated and complex characteristics due to the variety of participants and a high degree of uncertainty. Glouberman and Zimmerman (2002) categorized the simple, complicated, and complex problems in Table 5.2 and stated that, unlike the simple problems, the complicated problems have lots of parts for consideration and the complex problems have uncertain and emergent characteristics.

Rogers (2008) referred to the traditional logic model as the simple logic model based on the categorization above and stated that a separate logic model was necessary for complicated and complex interventions. He compared and categorized the situations of complicated interventions and complex interventions with the situations of simple interventions as described in the Table 5.3 and suggested the complementary measures for the simple logic model.

If the projects are proceeded in multiple spaces by multiple organizations, it is necessary to integrate the individual logic models composed of individual projects to evaluate the overall intervention effects. Also, if multiple changes in the outcome according to the changes in the causes occur simultaneously, individual flows of the causes and effects should be comprehensively reflected in the logic model. In case of the alternative flows of cause and effect, serial analysis considering the environmental factors or comparative review about various cases should be executed. Due to the context dependency, the changes in the causes do not simultaneously induce the changes in the results. Instead, the changes in the outcomes appear selectively according to the conditions. If the cause and effect relationship is based on the causal cycle, the tipping point should be accurately

Table 5.2 Simple/complicated/complex problems

Simple	Complicated	Complex
– example: following a recipe – the recipe is crucial-the recipe is easily repeatable – professionalism is not needed but increases the success probability – the recipe can be standardized – good recipes induce good outcome every time	– example: sending a rocket to the moon – the equations are important – a successful case increases the success probability of the following cases – a high level of professionalism is crucial – rockets are similar in important aspects – high certainty of performance inducement	– example: raising a child – the equations have limits – a successful case cannot promise the success of the following cases – professionalism is helpful but not crucial and insufficient for promised success – every child is unique – the uncertainty of performance inducement

Source: Glouberman and Zimmerman (2002: 2)

Table 5.3 Situation types of complicated and complex interventions

Type	Conditions	Simple Form	Non-Simple Form	Threat Factors for Evaluation
Complicated	Multiple Spaces and Organizations	Single Organization	Multiple Organizations, Interdisciplinary, Mixed Jurisdiction	Establishment of evaluation indicators and efforts for consultation for effective collection and analysis of the data
	Simultaneous Flow of Cause and Effect	Single Flow of Cause and Effect	Multiple Simultaneous Flows of Cause and Effect	Optimization for various flows of cause and effect necessary
	Alternative Flow of Cause and Effect	Universal Structure	Different Causal Structure for Different Situations	Necessary to understand the situation
Complex	Non-linear, Unbalanced Outcome	Linear, Balanced Influence	Influence of Causal Cycle and Tipping Point	Necessary to identify the early influences that can expand
	Emergent Outcome	Outcomes Identified Beforehand	Emergentness	Difficult to compare the before and the after due to the impossibility of predevelopment of evaluation measures

Source: Rogers (2008: 32)

identified as the cycle is not unidirectional but has the characteristic of a virtuous circle. Lastly, in case of emergent outcomes, an elastic variant of the Theory of Change should be applied to continuously upgrade and evolve the initial logic model since wicked problems[4] that are difficult to identify and solve may arise.

Most of the main business activities proceeded by the public institutions in the public institution group 1 are complicated and complex. For example, the Korea Airports Corporation deals with the problem of multiple spaces and organizations as it manages 14 airports, the LH implements lots of projects simultaneously, and the Korea Electric Power Corporation has multiple choices for profits came from decreased oil price to either reduce the electricity price or invest on new renewable energy projects. A non-linear, cyclical loop was created for the Korea National Oil Corporation due to the mistakes in the early set-up for the overseas resources development project and the flood control project of the Korea Water Resources Corporation is confronted with an unexpected, emergent situation of the regime change. Therefore, the traditional project evaluation based on the simple logic model should evolve into an integrative project evaluation system to manage the complicated and complex situational changes.

III Evaluability assessment for evaluation of main business activities

1 Are the weights of the performance indicators balanced with the resource distribution?

The weights of the quantitative indicators should be balanced with the input budget and human resources and the importance which refers to the political priority. High inputs of budget and human resources imply that the task is primarily related with the mission of the institution and a high priority implies that the relative value of the task is high in relation with the vision of the institution. However, from the perspective of the institution, even if the task is primary and the relative value of the task is high, the weights may not be set high enough if it is difficult to set challenging goals or to achieve the goals, or when its achievement may be considered as granted. As a result, the institutions may assign higher weights for projects that are easier to receive desirable ratings or advertise. Based on the data reported by the institutions (Performance Evaluation of Public Institution Team, 2016b), the weights of the performance indicators and proportions of the relevant resources are illustrated in Table 5.4 in order to examine the aspects mentioned above.

In the analysis of the correlations between the quantitative weights and proportions of the relevant sectors, there were no statistically significant correlations observed for all of the institutions except for the Korea Railroad Corporation. The quantitative weights and the proportions of human resources and importance were found to have significant correlations for the Korea Railroad Corporation. In case of the Korea Highway Corporation and Korea Water Resources Corporation, the quantitative weights and the proportion of budget showed even negative

Table 5.4 Weights and proportions of relevant sectors of individual main business activities by institution (%)

Institution	Main business activities	Proportion of Quantitative Weights	Proportion of Budget	Proportion of Human Resources	Proportion of Importance
Korea Gas Corp.	• Implementation and Sales • Production & Provision • Overseas	44 44 13	85 12 3	3 91 6	25 54 22
Korea Highway Corp.	• Construction Management • Traffic Management • Maintenance Management • Business Management	16 44 25 16	68 11 14 8	17 19 44 20	30 40 20 10
Korea Water Resources Corp.	• Water Resources Securement • Tap Water Provision • New Growth	43 57–	19 38 42	33 54 13	26 48 26
Korea Electric Power Corp.	• Electric Supply • Transmission and Transformation • Power Distribution • Future Growth	19 25 41 16	11 32 36 22	21 32 38 10	20 30 35 15
Korea District Heating Corp.	• Development and Construction • Production and Operation • Transport and Distribution	28 47 25	8 83 9	17 58 25	30 40 30
Korea Railroad Corp.	• Passenger Trains • Logistics Trains • Safety Management • Non-Transport	41 13 34 13	65 13 22 0.3	49 15 34 1.5	40 15 30 15
LH Corp.	• Housing Welfare • Public Housing • Economic Infrastructure Construction • Urban Environment Construction	31 31 16 22	21 32 11 36	31 23 11 31	35 30 15 20

Source: Performance Evaluation of Public Institution Team (2016b)

correlations (no statistical significance). Table 5.5 summarizes the comparative analysis of the quantitative evaluation scores and the proportions of relevant sectors of the Korea Highway Corporation, Korea Water Resources Corporation, and Korea District Heating Corporation.

In case of the Korea Highway Corporation, the proportion of weight for the project with the greatest proportion of budget is equivalent to that of the business management project that has the lowest proportions of budget and importance. The average quantitative evaluation score of the project with the third highest proportion of importance was observed to be greater than those of the projects with the first and second highest proportions of importance. Similarly, the average quantitative evaluation score was greater for the project with a lower proportion of importance for the Korea Water Resources Corporation and the new growth project with the greatest proportion of budget even lacked quantitative projects for evaluation. In case of the Korea District Heating Corporation, the average evaluation score of the project with lower proportions of importance, budget, and human resources is observed to be greater than that of the project with the highest proportion of importance, budget, and human resources. Although these examples may be inappropriate to be considered as objective evidence, there is a possibility

Table 5.5 Proportions of weights, relevant sectors, and evaluation scores (%) of main business activities

Institution	Major Projects	Proportion of Metric Weights	Proportion of Budget	Proportion of Human Resources	Proportion of Importance	Total Evaluation Score (Weight/ Average)
Korea Highway Corp.	Construction Management	16	68	17	30	91(17/91)
	Traffic Management	44	11	19	40	272(50/91)
	Maintenance Management	25	14	44	20	100(18/100)
	Business Management	16	8	20	10	84(15/84)
Korea Water Resources Corp.	Water Resources Securement	43	19	33	26	188(42/94)
	Tap Water Provision	57	38	54	48	260(58/87)
	New Growth	–	42	13	26	–
Korea District Heating Corp.	Developments Construction	28	8	17	30	65(22/65)
	Production and Operation	47	83	58	40	130(44/65)
	Transports and Distribution	25	9	25	30	100(34/100)

that the institutions may increase the weights of the projects that are easier to receive scores for more than the weights of projects with greater proportions of importance, budget, and human resources. While it may be impossible to always perfectly match the weights of the performance indicators for the main business activities with the proportions of the relevant sectors, the two elements need to be properly balanced in order for the performance for the tasks with significant importance can be acknowledged.

2 Are the criteria for the qualitative ratings rational and clear?

Unlike the quantitative indicators qualitative evaluation is based on the PDCA perspective and the rating range from A^+ to E^0. According to the evaluation manual, the ratings are set considering both the overall level of performance of the year and the overall improvement level of performance compared to previous year as seen in the Table 5.6.

Theoretically, it may be appropriate to simultaneously consider the performance of the year as well as the level of improvement compared to the performance of the previous year. However, institutions with the outstanding rating in the pertinent year are highly likely to have received the same in the previous year and thus, the performance of the pertinent year is less likely to be significantly greater than that of the previous year. Similarly, institutions with poor ratings in the pertinent year would rarely have performed better compared with the previous year. Meanwhile, in the perspective of the evaluators, it is quite natural for them to feel burdensome to give ratings above A or below D since they have to prove the result and persuade executive committee members. Therefore, there is a great probability that the final ratings will be limited to B and C. In reality, according to the outcomes of the 2015 main business activities performance evaluation, the ratings for the individual main business activities of most institutions were limited to B^0 and C, except for some project that received B^+ rating.

The bigger problem exists in the indicator of 'desirability in composition of quantitative indicators and relevance of them with the target'. Since the weight proportion of it is so high to overwhelm the other ratings of main business

Table 5.6 Criteria for evaluation ratings

		Overall Level of Performance			
		Outstanding	*Good*	*Average*	*Insufficient*
Overall	Outstanding	A+	A0	B+	B0
Improvement	Good	A0	B+	B0	C
Level of	Satisfactory	B+	B0	C	D+
Performance	Average	B0	C	D+	D0
compared to	Insufficient	C	D+	D0	E+
previous year	Very insufficient	D+	D0	E+	E0

Source: Performance Evaluation of Public Institution Team (2016a: 23)

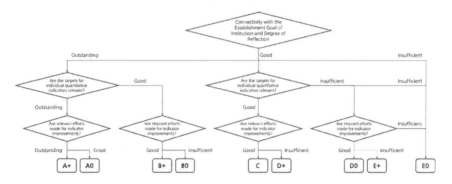

Figure 5.5 Evaluation criteria for the relevance of quantitative indicators

Source: Internal data of the Performance Evaluation of Public Institution Team

activities in spite of its ambiguity or possibility to be locked onto the evaluation results of previous year. The criteria for the rating are composed of 3 parts: connectivity with the purpose of establishment of the institution, relevance of the target goal, and the relevance of efforts for indicator improvements. As illustrated in Figure 5.5, the ratings are given based on the sequential flow.

The first factor is supposed to be identical with the previous year unless the indicators are changed and the second factor is difficult to control for institutions as most of the goals are set by the rule of increasement by two-standard deviation method. For the third factor, the efforts made for the improvements are difficult to examine under the circumstances that the indicators should be maintained at least for three years. The final rating result of the 2015 qualitative evaluation of main business activities shows that it was significantly influenced by the rating of this indicator. The purpose of this assessment is to adjust the imbalance of the evaluation ratings between the quantitative and qualitative indicators since the evaluation result is dominated by quantitative indicators with higher points of weights. Such problems of possibility of subjective judgments, insufficient differentiation in the ratings, and the weight imbalances need to be improved.

3 Is the division of roles between the qualitative and quantitative evaluations relevant?

The sum of weights for qualitative and quantitative indicators are 13 points and 37 points respectively (with an exception of 15 points and 35 points for the Korea Airports Corporation). The weight of the quantitative range is almost a triple that of the qualitative range. Provided that the proposition of P. Drucker that the inability to measure means the inability to manage is admitted, the higher proportion of quantitative evaluation based on the level of achievement of rationally established quantitative indicators can positively affect the enhancement of objectivity, fairness, and accuracy of the evaluation. However, the quantitative indicators might be changed in favor of the institutions by including beneficiary equations of better

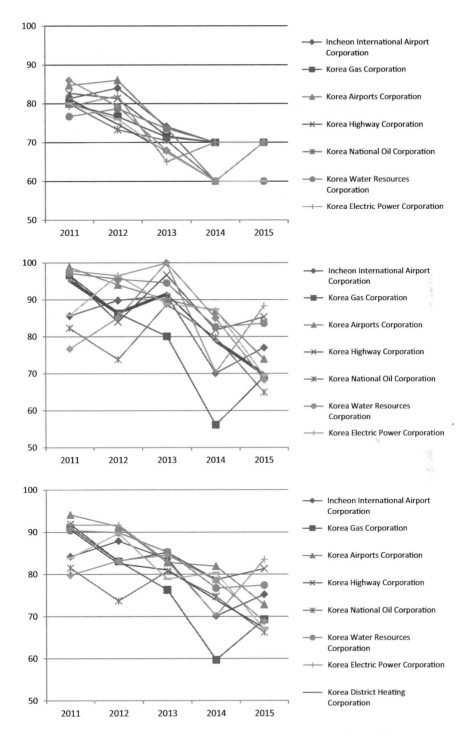

Figure 5.6 Trends of the qualitative, quantitative, and total scores of the public institution group I main business activities (past five years)

Table 5.7 Trend of qualitative score rankings

	2011		2012		2013		2014		2015
86	Korea Land and Housing Corporation	86	Incheon International Airport Corporation	74.1	Incheon International Airport Corporation	70	Incheon International Airport Corporation	70	Incheon International Airport Corporation
84.7	Korea Airports Corporation	84	Incheon International Airport Corporation	73.6	Korea Airports Corporation	70	Korea Gas Corporation	70	Korea Gas Corporation
82.7	Korea Highway Corporation	82	Korea Electric Power Corporation	73.6	Korea Water Resources Corporation	70	Korea Airports Corporation	70	Korea Airports Corporation
81.3	Incheon International Airport Corporation	81.3	Korea Highway Corporation	71.7	Korea Highway Corporation	70	Korea Highway Corporation	70	Korea Highway Corporation
81.3	Korea District Heating Corporation	79.3	Korea Land and Housing Corporation	71.4	Korea Gas Corporation	70	Korea Electric Power Corporation	70	Korea National Oil Corporation
80	Korea Gas Corporation	78.7	Korea Water Resources Corporation	70.5	Korea National Oil Corporation	60	Korea National Oil Corporation	70	Korea Electric Power Corporation
80	Korea National Oil Corporation	76.7	Korea Gas Corporation	67.9	Korea Land and Housing Corporation	60	Korea Water Rescurces Corporation	70	Korea Land and Housing Corporation
80	Korea Railroad Corporation	76	Korea Railroad Corporation	67.7	Korea District Heating Corporation	60	Korea District Heating Corporation	60	Korea Water Resources Corporation
79.3	Korea Electric Power Corporation	74.7	Korea District Heating Corporation	67.4	Korea Railroad Corporation	60	Korea Railroad Corporation	60	Korea District Heating Corporation
76.7	Korea Water Resources Corporation	73.3	Korea National Oil Corporation	65	Korea Electric Power Corporation	60	Korea Land and Housing Corporation	60	Korea Railroad Corporation

Table 5.8 Trend of quantitative score rankings

2011		2012		2013		2014		2015	
Korea Airports Corporation	98.8	Korea Electric Power Corporation	96.5	Korea Land and Housing Corporation	100	Korea Railroad Corporation	87.4	Korea Electric Power Corporation	88.3
Korea Electric Power Corporation	97.9	Korea Railroad Corporation	96.5	Korea Electric Power Corporation	99.9	Korea Airports Corporation	86.9	Korea Highway Corporation	85.3
Korea Water Resources Corporation	97.2	Korea Water Resources Corporation	95.6	Korea Highway Corporation	96.7	Korea Land and Housing Corporation	85	Korea Water Resources Corporation	83.6
Korea Gas Corporation	96.7	Korea Airports Corporation	94	Korea Water Resources Corporation	94.5	Korea Water Resources Corporation	82.6	Incheon International Airport Corporation	77
Korea Highway Corporation	96.5	Incheon International Airport Corporation	89.8	Korea District Heating Corporation	91.5	Korea Highway Corporation	81.8	Korea Airports Corporation	73.9
Korea District Heating Corporation	95.2	Korea District Heating Corporation	86.4	Incheon International Airport Corporation	91.1	Korea National Oil Corporation	79.8	Korea District Heating Corporation	69.8
Korea Railroad Corporation	85.8	Korea Gas Corporation	86.3	Korea Airports Corporation	90	Korea District Heating Corporation	78.8	Korea Railroad Corporation	69.4
Incheon International Airport Corporation	85.6	Korea Land and Housing Corporation	85.1	Korea Railroad Corporation	88.8	Korea Electric Power Corporation	70.3	Korea Gas Corporation	69.1
Korea National Oil Corporation	82.3	Korea Highway Corporation	84	Korea National Oil Corporation	88.7	Incheon International Airport Corporation	70.1	Korea Land and Housing Corporation	68.3
Korea Land and Housing Corporation	76.7	Korea National Oil Corporation	73.8	Korea Gas Corporation	80.1	Korea Gas Corporation	56.1	Korea National Oil Corporation	64.9

Table 5.9 Trend of total score rankings

2011		2012		2013		2014		2015	
Korea Airports Corporation	94.1	Korea Electric Power Corporation	91.7	Korea Water Resources Corporation	85.3	Korea Airports Corporation	81.9	Korea Electric Power Corporation	83.5
Korea Highway Corporation	91.9	Korea Airports Corporation	91.3	Korea Highway Corporation	85.2	Korea Railroad Corporation	80.3	Korea Highway Corporation	81.3
Korea Electric Power Corporation	91.7	Korea Water Resources Corporation	89.9	Korea Land and Housing Corporation	84.6	Korea Highway Corporation	78.7	Korea Water Resources Corporation	77.4
Korea Gas Corporation	91.1	Korea Railroad Corporation	89.7	Incheon International Airport Corporation	83.6	Korea Land and Housing Corporation	78.5	Incheon International Airport Corporation	75.2
Korea District Heating Corporation	90.6	Incheon International Airport Corporation	87.9	Korea Electric Power Corporation	83.1	Korea Water Resources Corporation	76.7	Korea Airports Corporation	72.8
Korea Water Resources	90.4	Korea Land and Housing Corporation	83.2	Korea Airports Corporation	82.8	Korea National Oil Corporation	74.7	Korea Gas Corporation	69.3
Incheon International Airport Corporation	84.2	Korea Gas Corporation	83.1	Korea District Heating Corporation	81	Korea District Heating Corporation	73.9	Korea Land and Housing Corporation	68.8
Korea Railroad Corporation	83.9	Korea Highway Corporation	83.1	Korea National Oil Corporation	80.7	Korea Electric Power Corporation	70.2	Korea District Heating Corporation	67.2
Korea National Oil Corporation	81.5	Korea District Heating Corporation	82.5	Korea Railroad Corporation	78.9	Incheon International Airport Corporation	70.1	Korea Railroad Corporation	67
Korea Land and Housing Corporation	79.8	Korea National Oil Corporation	73.7	Korea Gas Corporation	76.3	Korea Gas Corporation	59.7	Korea National Oil Corporation	66.2

results arbitrarily for their own interest. The focus on the quantitative aspect may make the evaluation of qualitative efforts difficult and the level of achievement may fluctuate due to the changes of outside environment that are uncontrollable by the institutions. Whereas these issues need to be redeemed or controlled through the evaluation of the qualitative range, it is arguable that the division of the roles is appropriate in terms of the balance between their values of weight. The graphs in Figure 5.6 illustrate the trends of the qualitative, quantitative, and total scores for the main business activities of the institutions in the public corporation group I within the past five years. It can be observed that the trend of the total score is dissimilar to the trend of the qualitative scores but similar to the trend of the quantitative scores.

The changes in the ranking of the qualitative, quantitative, and total scores in the past five years are illustrated in Tables 5.7, 5.8 and 5.9. Though not completely matching, the changes in the ranking of the total scores is more similar to the changes in the ranking of the quantitative range, as the weight of the quantitative range is much greater. The institutions and ranks are completely identical for the rankings of the quantitative and total scores in 2015. In 2014, two institutions of the top three institutions match in the rankings of the quantitative and total scores.

The similarity emerges more obviously if the trends of the top three institutions were observed. Table 5.10 summarizes the number of times the institutions were included in the top three of the ranking. It can be observed that the Korea Airports Corporation, Korea Highway Corporation, Korea Water Resources Corporation, and Korea Electric Power Corporation have been included in the top three of the ranking for three–four times and that the data is similar to the trend of the ranking of the metric scores.

In case of the qualitative range, the Incheon International Airport Corporation and Korea Gas Corporation that were not in the upper ranks are observed to have ranked in the upper ranks for two–four times. A few institutions are taking turns in the upper ranks in the ranking of the total scores and the trend is similar to that of the ranking of the quantitative scores. This implies that institutions with advantages in acquiring quantitative scores receive higher evaluations as a whole more easily. On the other hand, the fact that institutions with high scores in the qualitative range experience difficulties in increasing the ranks in the ranking of the total

Table 5.10 Comparison of the number of times of selection in the top three

Institution	Qualitative	Quantitative	Total
Incheon Intl. Airport Corp.	4		
Korea Gas Corp.	2		
Korea Airports Corp.		2	3
Korea Highway Corp.	1	2	4
Korea Water Resources Corp.	1	3	3
Korea Electric Power Corp.	1	4	3
Korea Railroad Corp.		2	2
Korea Land & Housing Corp.	1	2	2

scores implies that the qualitative evaluation outcomes have little contribution to the fluctuations in the overall ranking.

Even when we admit the validity of higher weight of the quantitative range, for example, in terms of objectivity and measurability,, the following problems still remain. First, as most of the quantitative targets are set by 2-standard deviation method (target of next year should be set by higher than previous year by 2-standard deviation of the last five years), the scoring trends may fluctuate regardless of the efforts institutions made. If an institution receives a high score in one year, the much higher goal is given in the following year which may lead to lower score in next year, and vice versa. In Table 5.11, the scoring trends show that institutions such as the Korea Highway Corporation, Korea National Oil Corporation, Korea Electric Power Corporation, Korea District Heating Corporation, and Korea Railroad Corporation have cyclical patterns in the score trends. The Korea Highway Corporation and Korea Electric Power Corporation have been ranked in the top three most frequently.

Another problem is that the partial modifications in the equations for the quantitative indicators may result in big change of the score. The examples of three institutions that modified the equations partially in the 2015 evaluation are illustrated in Table 5.12, and all of them experienced increases in the scores. In Table 5.13, it can be observed that the ranks changed significantly as well. Whereas the three institutions were in the lowest ranks for the quantitative and total scores in 2014, the Korea Electric Power Corporation dramatically increased to the top rank and the Incheon International Airport Corporation from rank 9 to 4 in 2015.

Therefore, measures are needed to establish balance between the weights of the quantitative and qualitative sectors to prevent excessive influence of the quantitative score on the evaluation outcomes.

4 Other issues

A fallacy of generalization may emerge if the institutions in the public institution group I were evaluated with uniform criteria where each of them has their unique characteristics. For example, applying same criteria for evaluating achievements of the Incheon International Airport Corporation who has lucrative cash cow and the Korea Airports Corporation who has not could be problematic. Whereas the former that manages one hub airport for international flights can take measures to enhance its profitability, the latter that manages 14 international and domestic airports cannot.

Moreover, if the ministry to which each institution affiliated decides the goal of the performance indicators, e.g. the target number of rental housing supply for the Korea Land and Housing Corporation, the application of the 2-standard deviation method would be meaningless. Furthermore, it should be pointed out that, if the spatial range for business activities is limited by the government as for the Korea District Heating Corporation, setting challenging targets would be impossible.

Table 5.11 Scoring ratio trends in the quantitative sector

Institution	2011			2012			2013			2014			2015		
	Weight	Score	Scoring Ratio	Weight	Score	Scoring Ratio	Weight	Score	Scoring Ratio	Weight	Score	Scoring Ratio	Weight	Score	Scoring Ratio
Incheon International Airport Corporation	30	25.668	85.560	30	26.940	89.800	28	25.502	91.079	37	25.938	70.103	37	28.502	77.032
Korea Gas Corporation	30	29.007	96.690	30	25.903	86.343	28	22.431	80.111	37	20.771	56.138	37	25.554	69.065
Korea Airports Corporation	30	29.646	98.820	30	28.207	94.023	28	25.210	90.036	35	30.430	86.943	35	25.881	73.946
Korea Highway Corporation	30	28.950	96.500	30	25.194	83.980	27	26.121	96.744	37	30.254	81.768	37	31.550	85.270
Korea National Oil Corporation	30	24.692	82.307	30	22.148	73.827	28	24.846	88.736	37	29.544	79.849	37	24.017	64.911
Korea Water Resources Corporation	30	29.158	97.193	30	28.670	95.567	28	26.473	94.546	37	30.560	82.595	37	30.924	83.578
Korea Electric Power Corporation	30	29.361	97.870	30	28.959	96.530	26	25.973	99.896	37	26.016	70.314	37	32.672	88.303
Korea District Heating Corporation	30	28.568	95.227	30	25.913	86.377	28	25.613	91.475	37	29.167	78.830	37	25.815	69.770
Korea Railroad Corporation	30	25.750	85.833	30	28.943	96.477	27	23.974	88.793	37	32.334	87.389	37	25.691	69.435
Korea Land and Housing Corporation	30	23.006	76.687	30	25.534	85.113	26	26.000	100.000	37	31.454	85.011	37	25.277	68.316

Table 5.12 Score fluctuations after modifications in the equations

		2014 Equation	2015 Equation	Fluctuation
Incheon Intl. Airport Corp.	Global Competence Index for Airport Operation	5.015	5.377	0.362 ↑
	Global Competence Index for Facility Effectiveness	4.942	5.447	0.506 ↑
Korea Electric Power Corp.	Management of Global Load Factor	4.968	6.390	1.422 ↑
	Management of Loss Factor for Global Transmission and Transformation	1.560	3.968	2.408 ↑
Korea Gas Corp.	Competence Enhancement for Unit Price of LNG Implementation	5.621	6.576	0.955 ↑

Table 5.13 Rank fluctuations after the score fluctuations (2014 -> 2015)

Rank	Quanti-tative scores	Rank	Quali-tative scores	Rank	Sum	Rank	Quanti-tative scores	Rank	Quali-tative scores	Rank	Sum
KRC	32.334	KAC	10.500	KAC	40.930	KEPC	32.672	KAC	10.500	KEPC	42.472
KLHC	31.454	IIAC	9.100	KRC	40.134	KHC	31.550	KEPC	9.600	KHC	41.050
KWRC	30.560	KGC	9.100	KHC	39.354	KWRC	30.324	KGC	9.601	KWRC	39.924
KAC	30.430	KHC	9.100	KLHC	39.254	IIAC	28.502	KHC	9.500	IIAC	37.702
KHC	30.254	KEPC	9.100	KWRC	38.360	KAC	25.281	IIAC	9.200	KAC	36.381
KNOC	29.544	KNOC	7.800	KNOC	37.344	KDHC	25.840	KNOC	9.100	KGC	35.155
KDHC	29.167	KWRC	7.800	KDHC	36.967	KRC	25.691	KWRC	9.630	KDHC	34.416
KEPC	26.016	KDHC	7.800	KEPC	35.116	KGC	25.554	KLHC	8.800	KRC	34.091
IIAC	25.938	KRC	7.800	IIAC	35.038	KLHC	25.277	KDHC	8.601	KLHC	34.077
KGC	20.771	KLHC	7.800	KGC	29.871	KNOC	24.017	KRC	8.400	KNOC	33.117

IIAC :   Incheon International Airport Corporation
KGC :   Korea Gas Corporation
KAC :   Korea Airports Corporation
KHC :   Korea Highway Corporation
KNOC :   Korea National Oil Corporation
KWRC :   Korea Water Resources Corporation
KEPC :   Korea Electric Power Corporation
KDHC :   Korea District Heating Corporation
KRC :   Korea Railroad Corporation
KLHC :   Korea Land and Housing Corporation

IV Lessons learned and conclusion

1 Lessons learned

The performance evaluation for the main business activities of public institutions is appraised that it contributed significantly in preventing the moral laxity by regularly examining the performances achieved by the public institutions and in facilitating the smooth provision of the public services. In Korea, performance evaluation of public institutions has contributed profoundly to enhancing the level of integrity, reducing principal-agent problems, increasing effectiveness and efficiency of public sector management. Such tradition shall be applied to other developing countries for better public management of not only public institutions but also government ministries related to of public institutions. However, some caveats are to be addressed to diagnose practical pros and cons.

The limitations of evaluation indicators have diminished the acceptance of the evaluation results and the results were even used to justify providing more performance-based merit to public corporations. Moreover, the insufficiency in the procedural rationality for collecting the evidence for the actual execution of the main business activities evaluation needs to be improved. Case et al. (1988) stated that performance evaluation is a process of deciding the acceptable standards (criteria) by collecting the evidence to clearly understand entire or some of the values of a program. Two core conceptual factors are included in this definition. The standards or the criteria refer to the desirable conditions or qualitative states for measurement with a comparison to the real goal. The evidence refers to the necessary information provided to examine whether the uniformly applied standards or criteria are fulfilled by specific projects (programs). However, the rationality to collect the evidence is largely absent according to the process of main business activities evaluation. Time for briefing sessions given by each institution to enhance the understanding of the main business activities of them toward evaluators is only about 30, minutes which is too short to give adequate information. While there are opportunities for listening to the opinions of the responsible persons from the ministries for the institutions, the opportunities are distorted as measures for defending the positions of the institutions. On the other hand, the headquarter of the evaluation team distributes the comments of the board of audit and inspection and the national inspection and the press reports from the previous year. However, the comments from the board of audit and inspection and the national inspection are most of the time about aspects that have already been desalted and finalized already which give no more insights. The press reports are often biased for the evaluators to be trapped in the frame of the reported data. Moreover, if unfavorable reports are released in the media at the time of the evaluation, the subjective judgments of the evaluators may be negatively influenced even if it was not the case in evaluation period. Whereas a checklist is sent to institutions in advance as a kind of pre-questionnaire by 48 hours before the audit the answers are prepared by the day of audit, which means the evaluators have no time to review the answers. Furthermore, as the audit takes place in meeting rooms at the headquarters of the institutions instead of on the site where the main business activities are executed, evaluators have to assess the performance by the report only written by institutions.

2 Conclusion

This study aimed to analyze the limitations of the main business activities evaluation and suggest improvement measures based on new perspectives. It was pointed out that the transition from the traditional program logic model view that assumes a linear and stable business environment to the perspective of the Theory of Change in which the complicated and complex factors can be addressed. Also, the improvement measures for the performance indicators and the enhancement measures for the procedural rationality in the execution process were suggested. It is unfortunate that detailed theoretical consideration and precise analysis were insufficient due to the limited availability of previous studies and difficulty of collecting objective data.

In order to secure the evaluability of performance evaluation, the following improvement measures could be sought. First, the audit and field inspection should be an opportunity to examine the actual site of the main business activities. A tour of the site for the entire group of evaluators should be operated in advance. If conflicts arise with combining the schedules of the evaluators, weekend tours should also be available. The tours should be operated as group activities instead of as individual contacts. The fact that the previous evaluations consisted of 100% documentary evaluation is a procedural limitation that must be improved. On the other hand, the field inspection previously held at the institutions should be transferred to designated conference spaces where the representatives of the institutions can participate and conduct a question and answer session. In some cases, institutions implemented the 'human-wave strategy' by which a large group of attendants participate in the event or performed excessive protocol presumably with an aim to overwhelm the mentality of the evaluators. Moreover, the answers for checklist should be distributed earlier than field audit for the evaluator to have a look before the hearing session. The information provided by the headquarter of the evaluation team should not be limited to the press reports or national inspection data but incorporate various measures to explain the performance of the institutions or the progress of the main business activities. The data related to the topics such as the market flow, evaluation in the private sector, and international trends should be provided to the evaluators in order for them to carefully examine whether the main business activities performances boasted by the institutions are genuine and what the weak points that the institutions try to hide. Provided that the performances of the institutions in the public institution group I are based on the mid- and long-term, it can be considered that the evaluation is executed on a two-year or three-year basis instead of on an annual basis and that the performance is more strictly analyzed. It is hoped that theoretical studies based on evidence will continue.

Notes

1 It can be considered as an exploratory meta evaluation, as the performance indicators utilized as the evaluation criteria are reviewed based on the evidence.
2 Rogers (2008: 30) assumed that the logic model and the Program Theory were another name for the cause and effect model that connects the chain processes involving the input and activities of the program and the expected outcomes. Therefore, the logic model was considered a summarized theory that explained how interventions worked

through schematic methods and the Program Theory was considered as the procedure for the development of the logic model or as the application to the evaluation.

3 While this manuscript views that the Theory of Change belongs to the wider definition of the logic model, the traditional logic model is considered to be based on the traditional Program Theory and the Theory of Change is considered to be a logic model as an attempt to exceed the Program Theory. Park, K. (2015) stated that the Theory of Change has been utilized as a variant of the logic model.

4 Unlike for the tame problem, the problem is difficult or even impossible to define and understand for the wicked problem until it is solved. Also, the problem cannot be solved completely due to the lack of precedence examples or alternative solutions. Moreover, the solution is not concluded as a right or wrong answer but a preferable or undesirable answer (Rittel and Weber, 1973).

References

Anderson, A. (2009). *The Community Builder's Approach to Theory of Change: A Practical Guide to Theory Development*. New York, NY: The Aspen Institute.

Bozeman, B. (1987). *All Organizations Are Public: Bridging Public and Private Organizational Theories*. San Francisco, CA: Jossey-Bass.

Case, R., Andrews, M., and Werner, W. (1988). *How Can We Do It?: An Evaluation Training Package for Development Educators*. Interaction.

Clark, H., and Anderson, A. (2004). *Theories of Change and Logic Models: Telling Them Apart*. PPT presented at American Evaluation Association, Atlanta, November.

Eoyang, G., Yellowthunder, L., and Ward, V. (1998). *A Complex Adaptive Systems Approach to Public Policy Decision Making*. Paper presented to the Society for Chaos Theory in Psychology in the Life Sciences, August.

European Commission. (1997). *Evaluating EU Expenditure Programmes: A Guide*. http://www-esd.worldbank.org/popstoolkit/POPsToolkit/EC_EUR/BUDGET/LIBRARY/PUBLICATIONS/FINANCIAL_PUB/GUIDE_EVAL_EN.PDF.

Glouberman, S., and Zimmerman, B. (2002). *Complicated and Complex Systems: What Would Successful Reform of Medicare Look Like?* Discussion Paper 8. Commission on the Future of Health Care in Canada.

HM Treasury, Cabinet Office, National Audit Office, Audit Commission, Office for National Statistics. (2001). *Choosing the Right Fabric: A Framework for Performance Information*. https://www.nao.org.uk/wp-content/uploads/2013/02/fabric.pdf

Impact Business Review. (2014). *If You Dream Change, Pick up the Pen: Knowing the Change Theory*. http://ibr.kr/2976

Japan International Cooperation Agency. (2004). *JICA Guideline of Project Evaluation: Practical Methods for Project Evaluation*. Planning and Coordination Department, Japan.

Kim. (2005). *A Study on the Development and Utilization of Performance Indicators Based on the Program Theory*. The Board of Audit and Inspection Dissertation Collection, 99–135.

National Assembly Budget Office. (2016). *Financial Projects Evaluation and Examples*. www.nabo.go.kr

Office of Management and Budget. (2003). *Performance Measurement Challenges and Strategies*. https://georgewbush-whitehouse.archives.gov/omb/performance/challenges_strategies.html

Organization of Economic Cooperation and Development. (1998). *Towards Sustainable Development Environmental Indicators*. Paris: OECD.

Organization of Economic Cooperation and Development. (2010). *Glossary of Key Terms in Evaluation and Results-based Management*. Paris: OECD.

Park, K. (2009). *Project Planning, Monitoring and Evaluation Handbook*. Seongnam: Korea International Cooperation Agency.

Park, K. (2015). Theory of Change and Consideration for Performance Management of Development Cooperation Projects. *Korea International Cooperation Agency International Development Cooperation, 2005*(2), 91–110.

Performance Evaluation of Public Institution Team. (2016a). *Workshop Materials for the Evaluators of the Performance Evaluation of Public Institution Team*. Unpublished internal document prepared by PEPIT and Ministry of Strategy and Finance.

Performance Evaluation of Public Institution Team. (2016b). *2017 Performance Evaluation Manual Improvement Suggestions (Proposal) for Evaluation Indicators*. Unpublished internal document prepared by PEPIT and Ministry of Strategy and Finance.

Perrin, B. (2003). *Implementing the Vision: Addressing the Challenges of Result-Based Management*. OECD.

Pinnegar, S. (2006). *Are Complex Programs the Best Response to Complex Policy Issues? City Future Research Centre Issues Paper*. Kensington: UNSW.

Rittel, H., and Webber, M. (1973). Dilemmas in a General Theory of Planning. *Policy Sciences, 4*, 155–169.

Rogers, P. (2008). Using Programme Theory to Evaluate Complicated and Complex Aspects of Interventions. *Evaluation, 14*(1), 29–48.

Rogers, P. (2014). Theory of Change. *Methodological Briefs Impact Evaluation*, No. 2, UNICEF.

Roh. (2015). *Policy Evaluation*. Seoul: Bobmunsa.

Stein, D., and Valters, C. (2012). *Understanding Theory of Change in International Development*. JSRP, The Asia Foundation.

Stufflebeam, D. L. (2004). The 21st Century CIPP Model. In A. C. Alkin (ed.), *Evaluation Roots* (pp. 245–266). Thousand Oaks, CA: Sage.

Talbot, C. (2010). *Theories of Performance: Organizational and Service Improvement in the Public Domain*. New York, NY: Oxford University Press.

W. K. Kellogg Foundation. (2004). *Using Logic Models to Bring Together Planning, Evaluation, and Action: Logic Model Development Guide*. www.wkkf.org.

Waterman, R., and Meier, K. (1998). Principal-Agent Models: An Expansion? *Journal of Public Administration Research and Theory, 8*(2), 173–202.

Weiss, C. H. (1995). Nothing as Practical as Good Theory: Exploring Theory-based Evaluation for Comprehensive Community Initiatives for Children and Families. In J. Connell, A. Kubisch, L. Schorr, and C. Weiss (eds.), *New Approaches to Evaluating Community Initiatives: Concepts, Methods and Contexts* (pp. 65–92). New York, NY: The Aspen Institute.

Wilson, G., and Buller, H. (2001). The Use of Socio-Economic and Environmental Indicators in Assessing the Effectiveness of EU Agri-environmental Policy. *European Environment, 11*, 297–313.

6 Evaluation system for the heads of public institutions

Current status and issues

Soo Young Lee

I Outline of the evaluation on the performance of the heads of public institutions

Public institutions, which are operated with taxpayer's money, implement and run various institutional systems to prevent or solve the information asymmetry and moral hazard found in the multilevel agency relationship among the people, the government, which has been entrusted with the ownership from the people, and the agent, which is in charge of management. Internally, public institutions have institutional arrangements, such as the board of directors, auditors (or audit committees), the general meeting of stockholders (in the case of listed public corporations) and labor unions. Externally, there are instruments such as parliamentary inspections held by the National Assembly, performance evaluations by relevant government bodies and performance evaluation teams, inspections conducted by the Board of Audit and Inspection, and the notification system for management information. Among such instruments, the performance evaluation of public institutions, which is conducted in accordance with the Act on the Management of Public Institutions, is recognized as a powerful monitoring system which helps public institutions retain the two pivotal values of publicness and efficiency. This study focuses on the performance evaluation on the heads of institutions, rather than on the institutions, and examines its current status and issues.

The performance evaluation of public institutions is a fair and objective system for the evaluation on the management performance of public corporations and quasi-governmental institutions, in accordance with Articles 15 and 48 of the Act on the Management of Public Institutions. The performance evaluation is also a process of reflecting the evaluation results to future management plans for improved management efficiency (Seong, 2009: 279). The performance evaluation of government-invested institutions has been conducted since 1984. Performance evaluation on government-affiliated institutions began in 2005. The current performance evaluation, which evaluates both government-invested and government-affiliated institutions under the single category of public institutions, was established after the legislation of the Act on the Management of Public

Institutions in 2007 (Cho, 2007). The evaluation on the performance of the heads of institutions, on the other hand, began in 1999; 15 years after the performance evaluation of public institutions began in 1984 under the "Evaluation on the Performance of the Heads of Government-invested Institutions" system. The evaluation on the performance of the heads of institutions during this period, however, was a part of the performance evaluation of the institutions. The performance evaluation on the heads of institutions was separated from the performance evaluation of the institution in 2008 after the legislation of the Act on the Management of Public Institutions in 2007. The evaluation on the performance of the heads of institutions was later reintegrated into the evaluation on the institutions in 2001, but since 2015, there have been demands for the re-separation and independence of the two evaluation systems.

The purpose of the evaluation on the performance of the heads of public institutions could be understood as follows.[1] First, for the people, the evaluation on the performance of the heads of public institutions could help keep the responsibility, transparency, publicness and efficiency of public institutions in check, and prevent public institutions from reverting into an embodiment of inefficiency. Second, for the government, a regular evaluation on the objective performance of the heads of public institutions could serve as a systematic policy tool for efficient management. The government can also hold the heads of public institutions who were appointed for political reasons amid controversy accountable for their performance. Lastly, for the heads of institutions, the evaluation could be an opportunity to review and improve their management performance, and to get advice on how to improve their management skills and leadership.

II Analysis of the evaluation on the performance of the heads of public institutions

1 History of the evaluation system

The evaluation on the performance of the heads of public institutions was first conducted in 2009; ten years after the initial evaluation on the heads of public institutions began. This system has been implemented in accordance with Articles 15 and 48 of the Act on the Management of Public Institutions. While the weights of the categories and indicators of the previous evaluation system had been similar to the performance evaluation of institutions, the new evaluation system in 2009 was conducted via a newly created evaluation team with independent indicators (Cho, 2009). The evaluations on the institutions and their heads were reintegrated from 2011 to 2013 but the evaluation on the performance of the heads was separated again in 2015. Table 6.1 summarizes the changes made in the evaluation on the performance of heads of public institutions after the Act on the Management of Public Institutions was enacted in 2007.

Table 6.1 Changes in the evaluation on the performance of heads of public institutions

Year	2007	2008	2009	2010	2011
Relevant Act	Act on the Management of Public Institution (Enacted in April 2007)				
Changes in the Evaluation System	–	• Integrated as a single performance evaluation of public institutions	• Separation of the evaluation system for the heads of public institutions (evaluation on the performance of the heads)		• (Partial) Reintegration of the evaluation on the performance of heads and the evaluation on the institution
Specific Changes in the Evaluation System	–	• Reflected 50 percent of the results of the performance evaluation of institutions • Linked with performance pay of the heads	• 92 heads of institutions evaluated (12 others) (Heads who have been appointed for six months or longer) • Reflected 50 percent of the results of the performance evaluation of institutions • Rating system (four grades, absolute evaluation) • Performance pay based on the results of the evaluation on the performance of the heads of institutions and the performance evaluation of public institutions • Evaluation results used for dismissals and giving warnings	• 96 heads of institutions evaluated (12 others) • Rating system (six grades)	• 96 heads of institutions evaluated (12 others)

(*Continued*)

Table 6.1 (Continued)

Year	2012	2013	2014	2015	2016
Relevant Act	Act on the Management of Public Institution (Enacted in April 2007)				
Changes in the Evaluation System	• Complete integration		• No evaluation on the heads of institutions conducted in 2014	• The evaluation on institutions and on the heads (Evaluation of the heads of institutions performance agreement) re-separated	
Specific Changes in the Evaluation System	• 70 heads of institutions evaluated (6 others) • Reflected 90% of the institution evaluation results • six grades (partial relative evaluation)	• 96 heads of institutions evaluated (five others)	• Linked with the performance pay of the heads of institutions	• 21 heads of institutions evaluated (Heads who have been appointed for one year and six months or longer) • Three grades, absolute evaluation • Used as personnel information	• 49 heads of institutions (Heads who have been appointed for one year and six months or longer) • Three grades, absolute evaluation • Used as personnel information

Source: Based on Korea Institute of Public Finance (2013b) and the *Handbook of the Performance Evaluation of Public Institutions* published by the Ministry of Strategy and Finance

2 Issues concerning the evaluation system

1 The separation and integration of the evaluations on the heads of institutions and the institutions

The evaluation on the performance of heads of institutions was held separately from the performance evaluation of public institutions for three years since 2009, due to the concerns raised on the validity of the methodology and content of the evaluation on the performance of the heads as a part of the performance evaluation of public institutions. The composition and analysis of the indicators used in the former evaluation on the performance of heads were inadequate and the evaluation itself was not differentiated from the performance evaluation of the institution. The former evaluation was not sophisticated enough to provide meaningful information on the heads of the institutions or to have binding power to hold the heads accountable for their performance. Moreover, the evaluation was criticized for applying the performance of the entire institution to the performance evaluation of the individual head of institution, thereby ignoring the methodological error that could occur between different units of analysis. This called for a differentiated evaluation of the management capacity and the efforts made by the individual head of institution, which led to the separation of the evaluation on the performance of heads of institutions.

Nevertheless, other problems, such as the dualistic management of the evaluations on the institutions and their heads, as well as the issue of having too many evaluation indicators, arose after the separation. The inefficiency of the evaluation system also became an issue. Each institution had to separately yet simultaneously prepare for the performance evaluation of the institution and on its head. Not only were there overlaps in the evaluation indicators but a review on the representativeness and the exclusiveness of the indicators revealed that some of the specific indicators needed to be integrated. Fundamentally, while the evaluation results may differ due to the difference in the evaluation logic and the structures of the indicators, the system had a danger of producing dramatically different results in the performance evaluation of an institution and that on the performance of its head. To counter this, a task force for improving the performance evaluation of public institutions and the evaluation on the performance of the heads of institutions was launched in September 2010, and called for the reintegration of the two evaluation systems.

The evaluations on institutions and their heads, however, were once again separated (the evaluation team for the heads being a part of a single evaluation team) in 2015. The difference with the former separation was that the new evaluation would be conducted only once in every three-year term of the head of an institution as an evaluation of the head of the institution's performance agreement, rather than being conducted annually. There have been attempts to differentiate the evaluation on the performance of the heads of institutions from the performance evaluation of institutions, by removing the indicators on leadership and responsible management from the performance evaluation of institutions and adding them to the evaluation on the performance of the heads of the institutions. Yet the evaluation on the performance of the heads of the institutions still reflected the evaluation results from the performance evaluation of institutions for the indicators on "management of finance and budget and its accomplishments" and the "management of remuneration and employee welfare benefits," which might induce the two evaluation systems to overlap.

As a solution, more people have called for the reintegration of the two systems (Nam, 2012; Park, 2009; Lee and Yoo, 2010; Korea Institute of Public Finance, 2013b), the basis for this argument is that both the evaluation on the performance of the heads and the performance evaluation of the institutions have been implemented with the purpose to measure the performance made by the efforts of the members of the institutions. Moreover, conducting two evaluations on a single institution at the same time would be inefficient by causing redundant input. Not to mention that the grades between the performance evaluation of the institutions and the evaluation on the performance of the heads of institutions lack relevance and that the credibility of and receptiveness toward the evaluation results can be compromised.

2 Agents and targets of the evaluation on the performance of heads of institutions

After the Act on the Management of Public Institutions was enacted in 2007, relevant government bodies took turns in conducting the annual performance evaluations. However, since 2010, the evaluation system has been streamlined to have the Ministry of Strategy and Finance to take charge in all evaluations as the main ministry. Article 48 of the Act on the Management of Public Institutions, which serves as the legal basis for the evaluation of the head of institutions performance agreement, states that the performance agreement should be evaluated by the Minister of the Strategy and Finance and that the Minister has the authority to create and manage evaluation teams for the evaluations. However, it is worth considering that in private corporations, it is the board of directors who evaluates the performance of the head and provides her with appropriate compensation, and that the heads of public institutions are appointed either by the president or the minister of the relevant ministry. Whether it is appropriate to have the Minister of Strategy and Finance evaluate the performance of all the heads of public institutions remains questionable. There certainly have been some advantages to streamlining the evaluation system to the Ministry of Strategy and Finance for the integration of the evaluation on the performance of the head of institutions with the performance evaluation of public institutions for the efficiency of the evaluation. Moreover, concerns have been raised on the expertise and continuity of the evaluation teams which evaluate the performance of the heads. The evaluation teams have been launched as task forces to prevent the collusion and to capture that might take place between the evaluators and the institutions, and have enabled the evaluators to come from diverse backgrounds. This, however, has made it difficult to maintain the continuity in the evaluations and to utilize the compiled knowledge and experience of the previous evaluators. The evaluation system should be able to secure the stability of the evaluation teams and evaluators. The evaluation method should be improved to become multi-dimensional. In addition, the fact that the board of directors is at the apex of the governance structure in public corporations and quasi-governmental institutions and that the board makes collective decisions with the heads of institutions in important issues should also be considered. While the heads of public institutions may have signed the performance agreement, whether the individual head should take the sole responsibility for the management of the entire institution is debatable. Inviting directors from the outside or the officials from related government bodies in the evaluation process or conducting interviews with them would be helpful in securing the validity of the evaluation results.

3 The evaluation cycle

The existing evaluation on the performance of the heads of institutions included the annual management plan in the performance agreement signed between the head of institution and the minister of the relevant ministry under the performance agreement system. Specific plans for the implementation of the tasks were reflected and the heads whose terms had started less than six months before or the heads who were absent were excluded from the evaluation of the year. However, as the performance evaluation of the institution and the evaluation on the performance of the heads of institutions were separated again in 2015, the evaluation on the performance of the heads of institutions has been conducted only once in every head's three-year term, rather than every year, and changed into the evaluation on the implementation of the head of institution's performance agreement. Annual evaluations became a burden, not only for the evaluated institutions but to the evaluation teams. This also prevented the heads of institutions from managing the institution with a near-sighted perspective for short-term gains. In short, the head of a public institution is required to sign a three-year performance agreement with the minister of the relevant ministry within three months of her appointment, in accordance with the guidelines on the performance plan for the heads of public institutions set by the Ministry of Strategy and Finance. This performance agreement should include the head of institution's three-year performance goals, annual implementation plans for goal achievement, and the performance indicators for the evaluation on such goal achievement. The agreement should also include the head of institution's action plan for debt management and the prevention of sloppy management. Heads who have been in office for less than one and a half years or who are absent are excluded from the evaluation.

A survey on the evaluation cycle of the performance evaluation, conducted by the Korea Finance Research Institute (2013a), revealed a huge discrepancy between the perceptions of the evaluated institutions and the evaluators. A majority of the respondents from the evaluated institutions responded that the three-year cycle was the best option, while the evaluators considered the one-year cycle to be most desirable. The three-year cycle would be appropriate, considering that the evaluation on the performance of the heads of institutions is relatively different from the performance evaluation of public institutions and that the heads need more time to display their capability after taking office. Short-term goals induced by annual evaluations should be prevented and that the evaluation's connection with the mid- to long-term performance plan should also be considered. However, the evaluators should ascertain that no heads leave their offices without being evaluated during their terms, due to their time of appointment.

4 Utilization of the evaluation on the performance of the heads of institutions

The evaluation on the performance of the heads of institutions, which first began as evaluation of the head of institutions performance agreement after the Framework Act on the Management of Government-invested Institutions was amended in 1999, had limited use, since the results of the evaluation were only applied to the grades for the performance pay. As the evaluation on the performance of the heads of institutions was separated in 2009, its results were also utilized more widely. First, the results were linked to the appointment and dismissal of the heads of institutions, so that a head who received the "inadequate" grade in the evaluation could be dismissed. Furthermore, the results were reflected not only in the evaluation on the heads but also in the evaluation of the ministers of the relevant ministries.[2] Some of the heads of institutions were actually dismissed due to their evaluation results after 2009 (Cho, 2009). However, after the evaluation on the heads of the institutions was re-separated in 2015, the results of the evaluation have only affected the heads' performance pay, and the evaluation results have only been used as reference material for the heads' reappointment. Merely using the results of the evaluation as personnel information would likely decrease the interest toward the evaluation and weaken its importance and status. More effort is needed to utilize the evaluation on the performance of the heads of institutions by using the evaluation results as important reference materials for reappointments and dismissals or by increasing the ratio of performance pay and increasing the wage gap between each grade.

III Analysis of the evaluation indicators in the evaluation on the performance of the heads of institutions

1 Changes in the indicators

The evaluation indicators after the legislation of the Act on the Management of Public Institutions in 2007 and the separation of the performance evaluation of public institutions and the evaluation on the performance of the heads of institutions include leadership, tasks specific to each institution, and tasks for public institutions reform. The indicator on tasks for public institutions reform set by the Lee Myung-bak administration, in particular, measured the privatization, merger and adjustment of functions of public institutions, and has been included in the

Table 6.2 Changes in the evaluation indicators for the evaluation on the performance of the heads of institutions

Year	Evaluation Indicators	Notes
2000	• (Common Indicators) Comprehensive management: the Head's leadership and effort, quality of target indicators • (Individual Indicators) Consisted of indicators that varied by institutions, such as profitability, public interest, and customer satisfaction	Evaluation on the performance of the heads of institutions a part of the performance evaluation of public institutions
2001	• (Common Indicators) Comprehensive management, entrepreneurship, public interest, management innovation	
2002	• (Common Indicators) Comprehensive management, management goals, management innovation	
2005	• Comprehensive management, management goals, management innovation, practice of ethical management and activation of the board of directors	
2006	• Consisted of comprehensive management, main business activities, and management performance (1) Comprehensive Management: Leadership and performance of the top management for accomplishing institutional visions, practice of ethical management, activation of the board of directors, effort and performance for management innovation, customer satisfaction, indicators related to productivity (2) Major Projects: Performance evaluation on individual projects (3) Business Management: Evaluation on the management of human resources, organization and finance	
2008	• Responsible management, innovative management, ethical management, performance results of implementing government-recommended policies, performance of organizational management	
2009	• Pending (specific) tasks: Major pending task and the validity of setting the performance goals, the appropriateness of setting the performance indicators and the performance goals, the rationality in the implementation process, efficiency in the implementation process, the achievement rate of reaching performance goals • Common Tasks: Improving public institutions (privatization, merger/ adjustment of functions), enhancing the management efficiency (reducing the number of employees, adjusting wages, reforming labor relations, restructuring of mutual investment companies, employment of interns)	Separation of the evaluation on the performance of the heads of institutions

(Continued)

Table 6.2 (Continued)

Year	Evaluation Indicators	Notes
2010	• Leadership: Setting major pending tasks and the rationality of the established management plan, sustainability and communication effort • Pending (specific) tasks: Validity of performance indicators, appropriateness of performance goals, rationality of problem-solving, rationality of project implementation, accomplishment of performance goals • Reforms: Management efficiency, reforming labor relations	
2011	• Leadership: Rational setting of major pending tasks and establishing management plans, sustainability and communication effort • Institution-specific Tasks: Validity of performance indicators, appropriateness of performance goals, rationality of problem-solving, rationality of project implementation, accomplishment of performance goals • Reforming public institutions: Rationalization of the wages/ performance management system, efficiency in human resources/ adjustment of functions, reforming labor relations, rationality and improvement effort of collective agreements	
2012-2013	• Leadership and responsible management, management efficiency, major projects (1) Leadership and responsible management: Leadership and responsible management, social contribution (2) Management Efficiency: Management of organization and human resources, wages and performance management, labor management (3) Main Business Activities: Main business activities, sustainable projects	Reintegration of the evaluation on the performance of the heads of institutions and the performance evaluation of public institutions
2015-2016	• Common Tasks: Leadership, responsible management (1) Leadership: Evaluates the head of institution's effort and performance in setting the vision and key values of the institution, solving major tasks, and preparing for future tasks (2) Responsible Management: Measures the head's effort and performance in establishing an efficient management system for the board of directors and for activating the board • Performance Tasks: Management of finance and budget and its accomplishments, the management of remuneration and employee welfare benefits, mid- to long-term tasks (1) Management of finance and budget and of remuneration and employee welfare benefits (2) Mid- to Long-term Tasks: Evaluates the head's leadership, effort and performance in dealing with the mid- to long-term tasks within term	• Re-separation of the evaluation on the performance of the heads of institutions • Results of the performance evaluation applied to the management of finance and budget and its accomplishments and the management welfare of remuneration and employee welfare benefits

evaluation on the performance of the heads of institutions as an indicator. After the performance evaluation of public institutions and evaluation on the performance of the heads of institutions were reintegrated in 2012, the indicators consisted of leadership/responsible management, management efficiency, and main business activities. The indicator on leadership/responsible management measured the head of institution's leadership, responsible management, the national appraisal, and social contribution. The indicator of management efficiency evaluated the organizational and human resources management, wages and performance management and labor management; major projects included main business activities and sustainable projects. Since 2015, the re-separated evaluation on the performance on the heads of institutions consisted of indicators on common tasks and performance tasks. The common tasks indicator included leadership (which measures the head of institution's effort and performance in setting the vision and key values of the institution, solving impending tasks, and preparing for future tasks), responsible management (which measures the head's effort and performance in establishing an efficient management system for the board of directors and for activating the board). The performance tasks included the management of finance and budget and its accomplishment, the management of remuneration and employee welfare benefits, as well as the mid- to long-term tasks. The results of the performance evaluation of the institutions have been applied to the indicators on the management of finance and budget and its accomplishment and the management of remuneration and employee welfare benefits.

2 A comparison of leadership indicators in the public sector

The evaluation indicator most frequently found in the evaluation on the performance of the heads of public institutions is the leadership indicator, but theories on leadership provide little information on the leadership for the heads of public institutions. This study, therefore, examined the evaluation indicators for the heads of public institutions through the theory presented by Luther Gulick, a scholar who put emphasis on the administrative management perspective in organizational management. Gulick (1937) presented seven functions of the chief executive of an organization, which he called POSDCoRB. Gulick's administrative management theory understood administration as the "management of public affairs," and aimed to find the "general principles of public affairs" which could secure the overall efficiency of the organization. This study posits that this model could also be applied to the heads of public institutions. Under the premise that the evaluation indicators for the evaluation on the performance of the heads of public institutions should incorporate all such functions in order to make an overall judgment of the ability and effort of each head, this study compares the current evaluation indicators with Gulick's model.

Gulick (1937)'s POSDCoRB could be summarized as follows. First, planning entails that the chief of an organization should be able to present an outline of the organization's tasks as well as the specific methods to accomplish the tasks. Second, organizing is the ability to divide the tasks and to form a formal structure of

Table 6.3 Gulick's POSDCoRB model

Functions	Details
Planning	Presenting outline of tasks as well as the methods to reach the targets of such tasks
Organizing	Creating a formal structure of authority by division of labor
Staffing	All functions related to human resources management, from employing members of the organization to maintaining their optimal capacity for work
Directing	Making decisions and giving orders in a specific and general way
Coordinating	Integrating and adjusting tasks
Reporting	Having the people in charge keep records, research observe and to report the working progress
Budgeting	All tasks related to finance in the form of financial plans, accounting and control

authority. Third, staffing concerns the overall functions of human resources management and entails the ability to manage and maintain the capacity of the members for optimal task performance. Fourth, directing concerns the orders given as the chief executive. The chief executive should make decision for task performance and be able to give orders to the members of the organization in a specific yet general manner. Fifth, coordinating concerns all things related to tasks, and of integrating and adjusting the members' effort in reaching the shared targets. Sixth, reporting is to have the person in charge of tasks report on the progress of tasks. It is the chief executive's role to have their staff document, study and observe the working progress before reporting. Finally, budgeting concerns all tasks related to finance in the form of financial plans, accounting and control.

This study classified the evaluation indicators used in the evaluation on the performance of the heads of institutions after the legislation of the Act on the Management of Public Institutions, based on the seven functions in Gulick's model. The classification of the evaluation indicators since 2007 with the seven functions could be found in Table 6.4. The table shows that in 2012/2013 the evaluation was on the general tasks of the chief executive, but that in 2015/2016 the indicators were relatively scaled down.

Another characteristic of the evaluation on the performance of the heads is that the indicators include ethical factors aside from the tasks as the chief of an organization. For instance, the evaluation indicators of 2017 included ethical management and also evaluated the head's effort and performance in improving social responsibility. This was due to the characteristic of public institutions as they tend to focus more on the public sector than private enterprises. Public institutions also create public interest and serve as model employers in terms of organizational management.

The evaluation on the performance of the heads of public institutions also evaluated "the heads' actions." There was an indicator on the "implementation of government-recommended policies" and in 2010, the indicators "institution-specific

Table 6.4 Comparison of leadership indicators in the public sector

Year	Planning	Organizing	Staffing	Directing	Coordinating	Reporting	Budgeting
2009	Pending tasks	Reforming public institutions (privatization, merger/ adjustment of functions)	Promoting efficiency in management				
2010	Leadership (rational selecting major pending tasks and of establishing management plans)	Reforming public institutions (adjustment of personnel and functions and other efforts for enhanced efficiency)	Promoting efficiency in management, reforming labor relations		Leadership (Communication effort)		
2011	Leadership (rational selecting major pending tasks and of establishing management plans)	Reforming public institutions (adjustment of personnel and functions and other efforts for enhanced efficiency)	Reforming public institutions (rationalization of wages and performance management system, reforming labor relations, rationality in and improvement efforts for collective agreements)		Leadership (Communication effort)		
2012–2013	Leadership, sustainable development projects (The head of institution's effort)	Management efficiency (organizational management)	Management efficiency (management of human resources)	Sustainable development projects (performance)	Responsible management (establishment and implementation of autonomous and responsible management system)	Responsible management (transparency and ethicality of institution management)	Management efficiency (finance and budget management)
2015–2016	Leadership, mid- to long-term strategic tasks		Management of wages and welfare		Responsible management		Financial and budget management

task" and in the aftermath, "major projects" or "mid- to long-term strategic tasks" evaluated the details of the performance on mid- to long-term projects. These indicators may have benefits, as they not only evaluate the present status but also the future directions of the institutions, but whether evaluation of such projects could be conducted independently from other indicators is questionable. For instance, such indicators are similar to the indicators on sustainable development projects and leadership (the head's effort and performance in setting the vision and key values of the institution, dealing with main business activities, and preparing for future tasks) and there may be continuity or overlaps among such indicators. Moreover, when the organization or staffing needs to be adjusted for the implementation of "main business activities" or "mid- to long-term strategic tasks," this could not be separately evaluated with the implementation of general projects.

3 A comparison with the CEO evaluation in private corporations

In order to provide suggestions on the current evaluation on the performance of the heads of public institutions, this study referred to the corporate documents and studies on the evaluation indicators for CEOs of private corporations, and used the data from 6 corporations or scholars. This paper extracted ten common indicators from 6 data sets, which were 1) finance, 2) customer, 3) human resources, 4) strategy, 5) system, 6) leadership, 7) relationship, 8) law/regulations, 9) knowledge, and 10) others. The definitions of the indicators could be found in Table 6.5.

Table 6.6 shows the differences between the indicators for the CEO evaluation in the private sector, as shown in Table 6.5, and the indicators for the evaluation on the performance of the heads of institutions conducted in the public sector. First, the CEO evaluation in the private sector has separate indicators for "customers" and "relationships." Such indicators emphasize that the CEO should not only manage the organization internally but should also maintain good relations with external stakeholders, which is also valid for the heads in public institutions who are also expected to be sensitive toward the external environment and stakeholders. However, while there are indicators on "effort for management for customer satisfaction" in 2007 and items on "national evaluation" and "social contribution" in the "leadership and responsible management" indicator in the evaluation conducted in 2011 and 2012, the current evaluation, which has been used since 2015, does not have any indicators on customer satisfaction.

Second, "strategy" and "leadership" are separately evaluated in the evaluation on the performance of the CEOs in private organizations. More specifically, "strategy" concerns the CEO's ability to present future directions while "leadership" is on how the CEO manages the organization members for achieving strategic goals. The leadership indicator evaluates how the CEO presents measurable indicators for goal achievement as well as the CEO's ability to present specific directions for the organizations, such as presenting deadlines. The leadership indicator in the evaluation on the performance of the heads of Korean public institutions, on the

Table 6.5 Indicators in the CEO evaluation in private corporations

Indicator	Definition
Finance	Evaluates the financial management, financial plan and performance, financing, finance sustainability and business performance. Evaluates whether the CEO understands such items and whether the CEO is immediately aware of changes in such details
Customer	Evaluates the relationship and communication with the customer. Evaluates how much the CEO values the customer and the market
Human Resources	Indicator on human resources management. Evaluates training, motivation, employment and maintenance and support
Strategy	Evaluates whether the CEO is making decisions on strategies, missions, plans and goals, and on how appropriate such decisions have been and whether the CEO is delivering such plans with accuracy
System/ Management	Evaluates how efficiently the CEO is managing the regulations, system, process, organization and programs for the accomplishment of the organization's goals
Leadership	Evaluation on the overall leadership of the CEO. Evaluates whether the CEO presents measurable goals and rational due dates and whether the CEO is efficient in managing crisis the organization faces
Relationship	Evaluates how well the CEO is maintaining the relationship with the customers, suppliers, the board of directors and other stakeholders, that is, whether the CEO listens to the stakeholders' demands and has an accurate idea of the corporation's response. Whether the CEO represents and defends the corporation in such situations is considered as a critical evaluation item
Law/ Regulations	Evaluates whether the CEO observes related laws and regulations and has the ability to compile such information
Knowledge	Evaluates whether the CEO is managing the data and information related with the organization in a quick and safe (confidential) manner
Others	Evaluates the quality of the merchandise and service and the social influence

other hand, is more centered on "strategies," and the evaluated item, "the CEO's effort and performance in preparing for future tasks," was somewhat abstract.

Footnote 1: The indicators were classified as follows: leadership (leadership, strategy), responsible management (relationship – relationship with the board of directors), national evaluation (customer), social contribution (other – social influence), management of organization and human resources (human resources), management of wages and performance (system/management), labor relations (human resources), major projects (strategy), sustainable development projects (strategy).

Table 6.6 CEO evaluation indicators in private corporations

Researcher/Corporation	Finance	Customer	HR	Strategy	System/Management	Leadership	Relationship	Law/Regulations	Knowledge	Other
MARSH and McLENNAN Companies	○	○	○							○
Kaufman	○	○	○	○		○	○			
Simone	○		○	○		○	○			
Joyaux					○			○		
Saskatchewan School Boards Association		○	○	○		○	○		○	
MBNQA	○	○	○	○	○	○			○	
EFQM		○	○	○	○	○	○			○○○
Evaluation of CEOs in Public Institutions (2012, 2013)					○	○	○		○	
Evaluation of CEOs in Public Institutions (2015, 2016)[2]	○			○	○	○	○			

Footnote 2: The indicators were evaluated as follows: leadership (leadership, strategy), responsible management (relationship), management of finance and budget (finance), management of wages and welfare (system/management), strategic tasks (strategy).

Third, there also is a difference in the indicator on "law/regulations." This indicator concerns whether the CEOs have observed law and regulations. This indicator also evaluates whether the CEOs have collected the necessary information. While this indicator would not have direct influence in improving the performance, it is essential for the management of an organization. In public institutions, which are more regulated by law and regulations than private organizations, observing rules are considered to be much more important. Nevertheless, this indicator is missing in the evaluation on the performance of the heads of public institutions.

The final difference is found in the indicator of human resource management. The "human resources" indicator was evaluated by all six data sets provided by private corporations for this study, and is therefore considered very important. The indicator on human resources questions the motivation of the members of the organization as well as the training they received. It also evaluates whether the CEO was employing and maintaining the talented personnel. Although the maintenance of personnel is considered pivotal due to the relocation of public institutions and the downsizing of welfare benefits, evaluation on the human resources management performance of the heads in public institutions has been overlooked and instead, evaluation has been conducted on the management of wages and welfare.

4 Issues on the current evaluation indicators[3] and points for improvement

1 Leadership

The leadership indicator was added to the evaluation system in order to evaluate the head of public institutions' effort and performance in setting the vision and key values of the institutions. It measures the head of institutions' effort in solving pending tasks and their preparation for future tasks. More specifically, the indicator evaluates whether the head has placed appropriate effort in setting a fitting vision of the institution and key values. It also evaluates whether the head's effort in solving major pending tasks and in preparing for future tasks has been appropriate. The first limitation to this indicator is that the difference between pending tasks, future tasks and the mid- to long-term tasks, which would be touched upon later, was unclear. More effort on providing a clear definition of the three tasks is necessary so that the evaluated institutions would not be confused with the terms. Next, the details of this indicator seemingly have more emphasis on the bottom-up method of gathering the opinions of the organization's members in the process of setting its vision, strategies and key values, but the opposite case could work as well. That is, if a head of institution with an excellent vision could take lead in presenting strategies and the strategies have been well received by the members, the head's effort in this case should also be evaluated accordingly.

Moreover, the leadership indicator is the most important indicator in the evaluation on the performance of the heads of institution, since leadership is the key capacity as a head of an institution. There, however, is no difference in the weight placed on the leadership indicator with the weight placed on other indicators. If it is agreed that the leadership of the head is the key to the success or failure of an institution, evaluators should consider putting more weight on the leadership indicator. According to a survey conducted by the Korea Financial Research Institute (2013a), 38 percent of a total of 843 workers in public institutes replied that the head of institution's leadership and capacity should be central in the evaluation of the heads of public institutions, a result which could form a basis for putting weight on the indicator. Since the leadership and responsible management indicator uses 3 grades, while the mid- to long-term strategic tasks indicator uses nine, the option of unifying the grades should also be considered. Finally, more specific indicators (such as performance management, organizational culture, and human resources management), which could provide more details on the head of institution's leadership, should be developed. In addition, the evaluators should take caution so that the evaluation results would not be affected by the halo effect caused by the personal image of the head of the institution (National Assembly Research Service, 2010).

2 Responsible management

The indicator on responsible management was intended to measure the head of institution's effort and performance in establishing an effective management system to activate the board of directors. More specifically, the indicator has evaluated whether the head of institution has established an effective management system for the board of directors so that the board could be activated and its actual role could be expanded, and whether there have been appropriate effort and performance by the head in expanding and enhancing the role of strategic business consulting and in providing support so that the expertise of non-executive board members could be utilized. The responsible management indicator is linked with the issue of whether the head of the institution has the autonomy to manage, operate, and utilize the board of directors. More specifically, factors such as how much influence the head of the institution has over the appointment process of the board members, and the non-executive board members, and whether the non-executive members are experts in the field of the organizations, are important for this indicator. The low participation rate of ex officio (external) board members in board meetings and board members having their substitutes sit in the meetings cannot be changed by the effort of the head alone, yet has critical impact on the evaluation results. In addition, a large part of the evaluation indicators consists of conventional indicators such as the participation rate of board meetings, the ratio of amended decisions, and the rate of contribution to the meetings, the focus on the attainment of which could lead to the displacement of the objective and means.

Therefore, the option of lowering the weight of indicators on responsible management that cannot be changed by the head of institution's efforts alone should be considered. Adding indicators such as ethical management, anti-corruption management, corporate social responsibility, and shared growth should also be considered to diversify the indicators.

3 Mid- to long-term strategic tasks

The indicator on mid- to long-term strategic tasks was created to evaluate the head of institution's effort and performance on mid- to long-term strategies, which the head should take initiative to solve during their term. The indicator consists of detailed items on whether the implementation plan for the mid- to long-term strategic tasks has been appropriately established and whether the head of institution's effort and performance for their implementation have been appropriate. It also evaluates whether the qualitative achievement for each strategic task was appropriate and whether the head of institution's effort and performance for feedback for each mid- to long-term strategic plan have been adequate. The mid- to long-term strategic tasks are included in the performance agreements signed by the heads of public institutions and the minister of the relevant ministry when starting their terms. The indicator consists of annual implementation strategies and performance goals for two strategic tasks the heads of institutions would like to achieve within their three-year terms. The aforementioned argument that the leadership indicator should have a clear definition of pending tasks, future tasks and mid- to long-term tasks also applies to the indicator on mid- to long-term strategies. Moreover, the fact that leadership and responsible management are evaluated in three grades, whereas the mid- to long-term strategic tasks are evaluated in nine grades, also needs to be addressed, in order to streamline the indicators. There have been difficulties in objectively judging the head of institution's success in achieving the mid- to long-term strategic tasks, due to the mixed use of quantitative and qualitative indicators in the performance goals of mid- to long-term strategic tasks. For a more accurate judgment of whether the heads of institutions have accomplished their qualitative performance goals, the validity of the qualitative evaluation indicators, as well as a checklist for the points of consideration should be improved. Furthermore, standards for improving the evaluating method of evaluators should also be presented (Korea Financial Research Institute, 2013b). Finally, the correlation between the results of the evaluation on the performance of the heads of institutions and the performance evaluation of public institutions would be guaranteed if the heads of institutions' mid- to long-term strategic tasks are strongly related to the major projects of the institution.

4 The necessity of the customer indicator

As mentioned above, the evaluation indicators for the CEOs in private corporations include separate indicators on customers and relationship, which implies that the head of an institution should not only manage the institution but also manage external relationships outside the institution and be responsive toward the external environment. While the evaluation on the heads of public institutions had evaluation indicators on "effort and performance on management for customer satisfaction," "national evaluation," or "social contribution" in the past, the current evaluation does not have any indicators on such issues. The category of leadership and responsible management in the performance evaluation in 2014 included evaluation indicators of national evaluation and social contribution (social contribution and government-recommended policies) aside indicators on leadership and responsible management. However, as the indicator on leadership and responsible management was moved to the evaluation on the performance of the heads of public institutions, these two indicators were incorporated into the business management category in the performance evaluation of public institutions. Considering that the evaluation on the performance of the heads of institutions is more focused on management factors, such as strategies, the board of directors, and strategic tasks than in the past, indicators that could assess the customer or citizen satisfaction and evaluate the institution's effort to respond to the external environment should be added.

5 Standardizing the indicator system

The performance evaluation of public institutions has been most frequently criticized for "comparing apples with oranges." In other words, many critics have questioned whether one evaluation standard could be used to evaluate institutions which differ in character, size, capacity and characteristics, an issue which also applies to the evaluation on the performance of the heads of institutions. Table 6.2 showed that evaluation indicators were divided into the common indicators and the individual indicator in the evaluation on the performance of the heads of institutions conducted in 2000. The common indicators evaluated the head of institution's leadership and effort and the qualitative level of the goals in a comprehensive manner. The individual indicators were composed of indicators of profitability, public interest and customer satisfaction, and differed by institution. The individual indicators were designed so that each institution could choose various and differentiated indicator systems that fit their institutional characteristics. Unfortunately, the evaluation indicators that differed by institution led to a complex evaluation process which was difficult to manage, so that only the common indicators were maintained the next year in 2001. Starting with the evaluation on the performance of the heads of institutions in 2015, the evaluation system has allowed differentiation in the weight of indicators on finance and budget management and accomplishments and on the management of remuneration and employee welfare benefits for institutions with excessive debt or institutions which are suffering from sloppy management. A standardized evaluation indicator system could improve the comparability of the evaluation results, increase competition among institutions and could make the performance evaluation more transparent and efficient. It, however, could adversely affect the accuracy, validity, and fairness of the performance evaluation, which is why the implementation of indicators that differ by each institution should be reconsidered in various ways.

6 Stability of evaluation indicators

The evaluation indicators and the weight of the indicators for the evaluation on the performance of the heads in public institutions, presented in Table 6.2, have changed continuously on a one- to two-year cycle. There have been little changes in the evaluation categories, after the categories on comprehensive management, entrepreneurship, public interest and management innovation have been applied on all institutions since 2001 and the leadership category was added in 2010. The evaluation indicators and the weight on each indicator, on the other hand, have changed nearly every year. Frequent changes are likely to cause fatigue and transaction cost for both evaluators and evaluated institutions. It also weakens the stability and credibility of the evaluation system. While the changes in the indicators and their weight may be inevitable to reflect the social change and demands and to make the evaluation more responsive and rational, changes should not be made so often for the system's credibility and stability.

IV Lessons learned and conclusion

1 Lessons learned

The performance evaluation of public institutions is a process of including the evaluation results to future management plans for the efficient management of public institutions. In Korea, the evaluation on government-invested institutions has been conducted since 1984 and evaluation on government-affiliated institutions began in 2005. The evaluation on the performance of the heads of public institutions, on the other hand, began in 1999; 15 years after the first evaluation of public institutions began in 1984, under the "Evaluation on the Performance of the Heads of Government-invested Institutions" system. Yet, the evaluation of the heads during this period was a part of the evaluation on the institutions. The evaluation on the heads' performance was separated from the evaluation of the institution in 2008, after the Act on the Management of Public Institutions was legislated in 2007. It was, however, later reintegrated into the institution evaluation in 2001. Since 2015, there have been demands for the separation and independence of the 2 evaluation systems.

As mentioned earlier, the purpose of the evaluation on the performance of the heads of public institutions could be understood as follows. For the people, the evaluation of the heads of public institutions could serve as a tool that could secure the responsibility, transparency, public interest and efficiency of public institutions, which were once the symbol of inefficiency. For the government, regular evaluations on the objective performance of the heads of public institutions could be a systematic policy instrument for efficient management. In addition, the government could hold the heads, who have been appointed for political reasons amid controversy, accountable for their management performance. For the heads of institutions themselves, the evaluation could be an opportunity to review and improve their performance, and to get advice for improving management skills and policy leadership.

2 *Conclusion*

This study has so far examined the issues concerning the system and indicators of the evaluation on the performance of the heads of public institutions and presented improvement plans. Performance evaluations, which check whether public institutions running on tax money have pursued both publicness and efficiency, are inevitable for public institutions. Evaluations on the performance of the heads of such public institutions have been conducted, either as a part of or separately from the performance evaluation of the institutions since the Act on the Management of Public Institutions was legislated in 2007. South Korea's evaluation system on public institutions has been internationally recognized for its elaborate structure. Accordingly, more effort should be focused on putting the final finishing touches on the evaluation of the performance of the heads of the institutions and its indicators. This study, however, would like to point out that there have been cases where the heads' knowledge on the evaluation indicators (and the performance agreement they signed when taking office, in particular) was questionable. It is important for the heads of institutions to perform their everyday tasks based on an understanding on the evaluation system, rather than trying to find about the evaluation just before the evaluations begin, in order to be evaluated accurately based on their own performance.

Notes

1 Based on the argument presented in Cho (2009).
2 While it was not compulsory to reflect the results directly to the evaluation on the ministers, the results were shared with the Office of the Prime Minster so that they could be used as personnel information (Korea Finance Research Institute, 2013b).
3 The evaluation indicators used in 2016.

References

Bass, B. M., and Riggio, R. E. (2006). *Transformational Leadership*. Psychology Press.
Board of Audit and Inspection of Korea. (2011). *Request for Action on Auditing Results – Management Status of the Performance Evaluation System of Public Institutions*.
Cho, T. (2007). A Study on New Performance Indicators of Public Bodies. *Korean Governance Review*, *14*(3), 285–313.
Cho, T. (2009). *Issues and Tasks for the Evaluation of the Heads of Public Institutions*, Conference Program, The Korean Association for Public Administration Conference, 1532–1546.
EFQM, Model Criteria: What an Organization Does It and How It Does It. www.efqm.org/efqm-model/model-criteria

Gulick, L. (1937). Notes on the Theory of Organization. *Classics of Organization Theory*, *3*, 87–95.

Hersey, P., and Blanchard, K. H. (1974). So You Want to Know Your Leadership Style? *Training & Development Journal*, *28*(2), 22–37.

Joyaux Associates. (2008). *Performance Appraisal Process for the CEO.*

Kaufman, P. S. (2008). Evaluating the CEO: How I Got the Board to Give Me Real Feedback Once I Became CEO. *Harvard Business Review*, October.

Korea Institute of Public Finance. (2013a). *Analysis on the Performance Evaluation of Public Institutions and the Development of a New Model.*

Korea Institute of Public Finance. (2013b). *A Study on the Changes in the Performance Evaluation of Public Institutions (II).*

Lee, O., and Yoo, S. H. (2010). *A Study on the Issues and Improvement Plans for the Performance Evaluation of Public Institutions: With a Focus on the Management Performance Evaluation System of 2008.* Audit and Inspection Research Institute.

Lewin, K., and Lippitt, R. (1938). An Experimental Approach to the Study of Autocracy and Democracy: A Preliminary Note. *Sociometry*, *1*(3/4), 292–300.

MARSH and McLENNAN Companies. (2013). *Blueprint for a Better CEO Evaluation Process: Unlocking Real Value in Executive Rewards & Performance Effectiveness Perspective.*

Ministry of Strategy and Finance. (2013). *Evaluation Report on the 2012 Public Institution Heads' Implementation Performance of Management Agreement.*

Ministry of Strategy and Finance. (2015a). *Evaluation Report on the 2014 Public Institution Heads' Implementation Performance of Management Agreement.*

Ministry of Strategy and Finance. (2015b). *2015 Manual on the Performance Evaluation of Public Institutions.*

Ministry of Strategy and Finance. (2015c). *Research on Improving the Management Performance Evaluation System for Public Institutions.*

Ministry of Strategy and Finance. (2016). *2016 Manual on the Performance Evaluation of Public Institutions.*

Moon, G. W., Choi, S. B., and Moon, J. S. (2009). Effects of Leadership Style and Features of Organizational Culture on Innovative Behavior. *Journal of Industrial Economics and Business*, *22*(6), 3289–3320.

Nam, H. W. (2012). A Study on the Factors Affecting the Financial Characteristics and Organization Performance in Quasi-Governmental Agencies. *Korean International Accounting Review*, *41*.

National Assembly Research Service. (2010). *Current Status and Future Tasks for the Performance Evaluation of Public Institutions.*

National Institute of Standards and Technology. (2011). *Criteria for Performance Excellence in Baldrige Performance Excellence Program.*

Park, S. H. (2009). *Issues and Future Tasks of Business Performance Evaluation System on Public Entities in Korea*, Conference program for the Korean Association for Public Administration Conference.

Public Institution Management Research Institute. (2015). *Research on the Methods for the Improvement of the Management Performance Evaluation System for Public Institutions.*

Public Institution Performance Evaluation Team, Ministry of Strategy and Finance. (2012). *2011 Evaluation Report on the Implementation of the Performance Agreement by the Heads of Public Institutions.*

Robbins, P. S., and Coutler, M. (2012). *Management.* Pearson Education Limited.

Saskatchewan School Boards Association. (2006). *CEO Performance Review Practices.*

Steering Committee for the Management of Public Corporations. (2000). *Handbook on the Evaluation on the Performance of the Heads of Public Corporations.*

Steering Committee for the Management of Public Institutions. (2008). *2007 Performance Evaluation of Public Institutions and Quasi-Governmental Institutions.*

Sung, M. J. (2009). *Policy Directions for Reforming Public Institutions.* Center for Research on Public Institutions, Korea Institute of Public Finance.

Youn, D. H., and Jung, S. T. (2006). A Study on the Effect of Transformational Leadership on Organizational Citizenship Behaviors and the Innovative Behaviors of Organizational Members. *Journal of Human Resource Management Research, 13*(3), 139–169.

7 Analysis of the standing auditors evaluation system and the performance indicators

With a focus on expertise

Tae Ho Eom

I Introduction

The "Performance Evaluation of the Standing Auditors and Members of the Audit Committees in Public Corporations and Quasi-governmental institutions," hereafter standing auditors evaluation, was established in 2007. The Ministry of Strategy and Finance is in charge of managing this institution built according to the firm demand created by some standing auditors from public institutions took part in the overseas training sessions. Various ways to improve the expertise of auditors had been proposed in meetings held by the Ministry of Strategy and Finance and as a result, the advanced auditor program and performance evaluations of auditors were newly introduced. The Ministry of Strategy and Finance, which has the power to appoint and dismiss standing auditors or to recommend them, may have neglected to evaluate the standing auditors so far because the performance evaluation on the audit departments of public institutions had already been conducted by the Board of Audit and Inspection. The complex and political nature of the appointment of standing auditors themselves may also have made it difficult for the ministry to conduct the evaluation. However, due to the lack of an evaluation system, the position of the standing auditor, which requires a very high level of expertise, has so far been occupied by non-experts, and has especially been favored by politicians. This made it difficult to realize the very objective of the standing audit system, which is to regulate poor management in public institutions.

Standing auditors have been granted an extremely powerful authority within the management system of public institutions. Their actions, however, have often stopped in merely holding the management in check, since the standing auditors do not have direct responsibility from the management outcomes. However, considering the contradiction between efficiency and public interest inherent in the management of public institutions, such traditional outlook on auditing clearly has its limits. As a result, the standing auditor evaluation conducted by the Ministry of Strategy and Finance has emphasized improving the auditors' capacity sustainably, by stressing the importance of preventive auditing through the improvements made the internal control system. In such case, the auditor's role is to systemize the tasks of the audit department into policies and to provide systematic support.

However, since it is virtually impossible to separate the contribution of the standing auditor from the performance of the audit department, both aspects have been considered in the evaluation. Although this was also found in the evaluation on the performance of the heads of public institutions, whether to separate the evaluation on the standing auditors from the evaluation on the audit department remains a controversial issue, due to the systematic characteristic of auditing.

The difference between the evaluation of the audit department conducted by the Board of Audit and Inspection of Korea and the evaluation conducted by the Ministry has also aroused controversy. Nevertheless, while some items may overlap, the standing auditor evaluation conducted by the Ministry of Strategy and Finance has a distinctly different structure compared with the evaluation conducted by the Board of Audit and Inspection, the most critical difference being that the Ministry evaluation conducts interviews to evaluate the expertise of the standing auditors directly. In spite of the controversies, the standing auditor evaluation conducted by the Ministry of Strategy and Finance is meaningful in that it evaluates the expertise of individual standing auditors and their contribution to the performance of audit departments.

Research on auditing in the public sector in Korea has been somewhat lacking. Auditing in the public sector is largely divided into the external evaluation and internal evaluation (Public Audit Support Group, Board of Audit and Inspection of Korea, 2016) and the fields of research could also be classified into research on external audit (Goolsarran, 2007; Stapenhurst and Titsworth, 2001; Lonsdale, 2008; Gomes, 2001) and studies on internal audit (Baltaci and Yilmaz, 2006; Diamond, 2002; Sterck and Bouckaert, 2006). Research on external audits has focused on the audits conducted by the supreme audit institutions. In Korea, external audits conducted by the Board of Audit and Inspection have been the main subject of research (Kim, 2010; Park, 2010, 2013; Oh et al., 2009; Lee and Lee, 2009; Kim, 2012). Studies on internal audits have mainly focused on the central government and local governments (Kim et al., 2002; Ahn, 2005; Choi, 1998; Yoon, 1995; Yum, 2010; Lee, 2007; Ko, 2015), and public institutions (Yoon, 2016; Ra, 2015, Ahn and Jeong, 2009; Yu and Ahn, 2011).[1]

Previous studies on internal audits of public institutions mainly analyzed the effectiveness of the overall system or presented improvement plans (Jin and Oh, 2012; Lee and Lee, 2006; Yoo, 2009). Previous studies suggested that the autonomy of the auditors and the auditing body, as well as the expertise of the auditors, should be guaranteed (Ahn and Jeong, 2009; Yoo, 2009). Studies also suggested that a new system should be introduced so that the Board of Audit and Inspection could directly appoint auditors of each public institution (Ahn, 2009; Heo and Cha, 2010) and the auditing could be conducted electronically.

Aside macroscopic and normative studies on internal audits in public institutions (Ahn and Choi, 2010; Sung, 2013), empirical research on standing auditors has been limited to Ra (2015) and Ryu and Kim (2013). Ra (2015) presented an operational definition on the career of standing auditors in public institutions and verified the difference with the auditing performance. Ra (2015) had the most direct influence on this study. Moreover, Ryu and Kim (2013) discussed the concept and range of the expertise on auditing in public institutions before conducting a comparative analysis on the auditing career and auditing performance, which also had significant implications to this study.

As mentioned above, there has been a lack of research on standing auditors because the research on auditing focused on the external audits conducted in the private sector, while that on the public sector mainly dealt with the traditional and administrative audits conducted by the Board of Audit and Inspection. This may be so because the concepts of the auditing model and the role of standing auditors that corresponds to the distinctive character of public institutions have not been clearly defined. This study aims to introduce the standing auditor evaluation system in public institutions and its indicators, and further intends to analyze the correlation between the expertise of the auditors and the evaluation results. This study has its limits as an exploratory study but would be meaningful as a basis for future in-depth research.

II The standing auditor evaluation system in public institutions: a summary

The system of the public audit could be divided into the audit conducted by the Board of Audit and Inspection and self-audit (Public Audit Support Group, Board of Audit and Inspection of Korea, 2016). The self-audits take place in accordance with the "Act on the Management of Public Institutions," the "Act on Public Sector Audits," the "Commercial Act," the "Public Audit Standards," and the "Audit Standards for Public Corporations and Quasi-governmental Institutions." The types of audits in public institutions reflect the characteristics of public institutions and could be classified as the auditor and the audit committee (Ra, 2015). All public institutions are required to have either an auditor system or the audit committee, and the two systems cannot be implemented together or be mixed (Ministry of Strategy and Finance, 2010; Song, 2012). Currently, market-type public corporations (Public Corporation Type 1) and quasi-market-type public corporations with an asset size of two trillion won or more (Public Corporation Type 2) are each required to have audit committees in lieu of a single person auditor (Article 20 Clause 2, Act on the Management of Public Institutions). Quasi-market-type public corporations with the asset size of less than two trillion won and quasi-governmental institutions can have audit committees in accordance with other legal regulations (Article 20, Clause 3, Act on the Management of Public Institutions).

Auditors could be classified into standing auditors and non-standing auditors. There is no substantial difference between the two types of auditors in their authority, obligations and responsibility; the only difference existing in their working patterns (Song, 2013). The audit committee has the same authority as the auditor but unlike the appointed auditors, the committee is a part of the board of directors. The audit committee is involved in the board's decision-making process, including the decision made by the majority under a collegial decision-making system. Also, the audit committee consists members with expertise There, however, are

Table 7.1 Comparison between the auditor and the audit committee in public institutions

Type	Auditor	Audit Committee
Status	• Authority as an individual auditor	• Dual authority as a board director and a member of the audit committee
Appointment	• Appointed by the President (or the Minister of Strategy and Finance)	• Appointed by the board of directors
The range of auditing	• Audits accounting and general administration in accordance with the Act on Public Sector Audits and the Act on the Management of Public Institutions	• The equal range of audit and authority with auditors
Decision-making System	• Unitary	• Collegial
Authority within the Board of Directors	• Separate from directors • Authority to provide statements	• A part of the board of directors • Right to vote in the board of directors
Tasks	• In case of standing auditors, to check the internal organization	• Guaranteed expertise

Source: Based on Public Audit Support Group Board of Audit and Inspection of Korea (2016: 39) and Ra (2015: 29)

limitations to the audit committee, since the members of the audit committee have dual status as a member of the board of directors, which may compromise the autonomy of the audit committee (Ministry of Strategy and Finance, 2010).

The appointment and dismissal of auditors and the range and standards of audit activities in Korea should be examined for further discussions on the role and responsibilities of auditors in public institutions. There is a difference in the appointment and dismissal of auditors by the size of the institution and the characteristics of the institution's tasks. In case of public corporations, the auditors are recommended by the Committee of Recommendation and verified and determined by the management committee, then to be appointed by the president, in accordance with the formal request made by the Minister of Strategy and Finance. However, unlike the public corporation that meets the standards prescribed by Presidential Decree, the committee of recommendation has been appointed by the Ministry of Strategy and Finance is mandated to make recommendations to the small-sized public corporations. The committee of recommendation is composed of qualified members approved by the management committee. Committee of Recommendation (Article 25, Clause 4 of the Act on the Management of Public Institutions). The auditors of quasi-governmental institutions are also appointed by the minister among the candidates recommended by the Committee of Recommendation and are verified by the management committee. If the size of an institution is larger than the standard specified by the presidential decree or if the institution's tasks are special, the auditor is appointed by the president per the formal request of the Minister of Strategy and Finance after the recommending and verifying process is complete.

In regards to the qualification standard of auditors, two-thirds of the audit committee should be composed of non-executive board members and members of the audit committee who are not should be equipped with certain qualifications for market-type public corporations and quasi-market-type public corporations with the asset size of two trillion won or more (Article 20, Clause 2, 3, Act on the Management of Public Institutions; Article 415, Clause 2, Commercial Act; Article 26, Clause 2, Financial Investment Services and Capital Markets Act). One member of the audit committee should be an expert in accounting or finance (Article 542, Clause 11–2, Commercial Act). In addition, the Committee of Recommendation is required to recommend candidates who are equipped with the knowledge, experience and the capacity necessary for auditing (Clause 2, Article 30, Act on the Management of Public Institutions). However, criticism has been raised on the fact that the standards applied in reality are too generic and that too many auditors have been former government officials or were appointed through the spoils system (Ra, 2015; Ryu and Kim, 2013).

The tasks of the auditors in public institutions are to inspect the tasks and accounting of public corporations or quasi-governmental institutions and to submit their findings to the board of directors, in accordance with the audit standards set by the Minister of Strategy and Finance, which is stipulated in Article 32, Clause 5 in the Act on the Management of Public Institutions (Audit Standards for Public corporations and Quasi-governmental institutions). The exemption from liability for the institution, stated in part on the liability of auditors in Article 414 (Liability of Auditors) and Article 415 (Provisions Applicable Mutatis Mutandis), also applies mutatis mutandis to the auditors in public corporations and quasi-governmental institutions and the members of audit committees.

The administrative rule of the Ministry of Strategy and Finance, the "Audit Standards for Public corporations and Quasi-governmental institutions," serve as the basis for the discussion on the roles of auditors in public institutions. However, the "Audit Standards for Public corporations and Quasi-governmental institutions" only stipulates partial roles of the auditors. Many of its rules are also declaratory, thus falling short of becoming the standard for the actual evaluation of the auditors' performances in public institutions.

III The structure of the evaluation system of auditors in public institutions

The evaluation of standing auditors has changed since 2013 to have a standing auditor of a certain institution be evaluated once during their term, and no evaluation was conducted in 2013. As the annual evaluation was discontinued, the system of connecting the results of the standing auditor evaluation with the performance pay for the audit department also stopped. Instead, the performance

Table 7.2 Comparison of evaluation indicators from 2011 to 2012 and from 2014 to 2015

Evaluation Indicators from 2011 to 2012		Evaluation Indicators from 2014 to 2015	
Evaluation Indicator	*Weight*	*Evaluation Indicator*	*Weight*
Effort and accomplishments of professional, ethical and autonomous auditing	15	Expertise of auditor	10
Effort and accomplishments for reinforcing internal control	15	Ethicality and autonomy of auditor	10
Effort to prevent sloppy management, and recurrence prevention	10	Reinforcing internal control	15
Appropriateness of audit and post management on the institution's compliance with management guidelines	10	Preventing sloppy management and preventing the detection and recurrence of reckless management	25
Effort for transparent and ethical management	15	Performance of internal audit and appropriateness of post management (External audit: Board of Audit and Inspection)	25
Appropriateness of management performance of internal audit and post management (External audit: Board of Audit and Inspection)	25	The integrity of Institution (External audit: Anti-Corruption and Civil Rights Commission)	5
Results of Performance Evaluation on Institution	10	Results of Performance Evaluation on Institution	10
Total	100	Total	100

Source: Performance Evaluation Team of Public corporations and Quasi-governmental Institutions (2012, 2013, 2015, 2016)

Notes
a) Referred to the Performance Evaluation Report of Standing Auditors from 2011 to 2012 and from 2013 to 2014
b) All indicators other than the external audit and the performance evaluation of public institutions use the 9-level grading system.

pay for the audit department was connected to the outcome of the performance evaluation of public institutions.

The most noteworthy change in the indicator system in 2014 was that the "preventing sloppy management and preventing the detection and recurrence of sloppy management" (hereinafter preventing sloppy management) was newly added and that the disputed indicator, "appropriateness of audit and post management on the institution's compliance with management guidelines" was excluded. The indicator on preventing sloppy management was introduced to assuage the social distrust of the management efficiency of public agencies at that time. The indictor, however, is too comprehensive in its concept and the division of roles between the management and the auditor is vague and overlaps too much with other indicators, especially with the indicator on the internal control structure.

Table 7.3 Evaluation indicators of self-audit conducted by the Board of Audit and Inspection

Areas and Items of Evaluation	Specific Factors	Evaluation Indicators (Weight)
Management of Auditing Body and Human Resources		*20*
Self-Auditing Body	Autonomy	Installation of full-time auditing body (2)
	Adequacy	Number of personnel (4)
Head of Self-Auditing Body	Autonomy	Degree of open recruitment (3)
	Expertise	Effort to secure expertise by the head of auditing body (3)
Person in Charge of Auditing	Expertise	Average employment period of audit department (2)
		Implementation of training sessions on auditing (2)
		Effort to secure expertise by employees in charge of auditing (4)
Auditing Activities		*40*
Preventive Auditing	Adequacy	Effort in implementing pre-audits (8)
	Appropriateness	Number of offenses and problems raised by the external audit (4)
Actual Auditing	Adequacy	Number of audits conducted by year (4)
	Appropriateness	Appropriateness of auditing practice, e.g. the observance of auditing procedure (7)
Processing auditing results	Appropriateness	Appropriateness in processing auditing results (11)
Sharing and Using Auditing Resources	Cooperation	Degree of cooperation from related institutions (3)
		Usage of auditing information system (3)
Auditing Accomplishments		*30*
Accounting Inspection	Financial Measures	Accomplishments in compensation, collection, rectification, etc. (12)
Tasks Inspection	Status Measures	Accomplishments in taking disciplinary action, reprimanding, warning and making accusations, etc. (10)
Other areas	Other Accomplishments	Administrative measures and finding exemplary cases (8)
Post Management		*10*
Post Management	Adequacy	Execution rate of issues pointed out in self-audits (4)
		Execution rate of issues pointed out in external audits (4)
Disclosure of Auditing Results	Appropriateness	Degree of disclosing self-auditing results (2)

Source: Ra (2015: 42)

The expertise of auditors was separated in the indicator system in 2014. This was a sign of recognizing the importance of the expertise of auditors and was also a way to tackle the problem of ethicality and autonomy – two concepts with clearly different definitions – being evaluated under the same indicator.

Significant differences could be found between the evaluation conducted by the Board of Audit and Inspection and the evaluation conducted by the Ministry of Strategy and Finance. First, with regards to the subject of evaluation, while the Board has evaluated the audit department of public institutions, the Ministry has evaluated both individual auditors and audit departments. In fact, although the standing auditor evaluation should be conducted on the individuals, both entities have been reflected in the evaluation indicators, since it is difficult to evaluate the effort and accomplishments of the individual auditor from that of the audit department.

Moreover, the evaluation conducted by the Board placed more emphasis on the auditing performance, while the Ministry evaluation reflected the performance but focused more on preventive auditing. The Ministry, therefore, showed a tendency of focusing on reforming the system and putting effort to stop sloppy management from recurring by reforming the internal control structure and preventing reckless management.

As to the evaluation method, the Ministry evaluation used reports and a face-to-face evaluation through interviews, thereby focusing on the individual capacity of each auditor. Thus, the expertise and effort of each individual auditor had a larger direct and indirect effect on the overall evaluation, compared with the Board evaluation.

Lastly, the results of the evaluation conducted by the Board of Audit and Inspection were reflected in the evaluation indicators of the Ministry evaluation by 25 percent, so that the outcome of the Board evaluation could have a critical influence over the overall evaluation results.

IV Analysis of the standing auditors' evaluation results by type of public institutions

1 Outline

The data used in this analysis were retrieved from the Standing Auditors' Performance Report from 2011 to 2012 and 2014 to 2015 and the Standing Auditors Performance Evaluation Report. The analysis was conducted on the four years' data in total. The public institutions which received the standing auditors' performance evaluation report during this period have been classified by type in Table 7.4. Public institutions with more than 50 employees, with self-generated revenue accounting for more than half of the total revenue, were classified as public corporations. Among public corporations, public corporations Type 1 are large-scale institutions which mostly plan, build and manage social infrastructure, while Type 2 are public corporations which focus on promoting certain

Table 7.4 Public institutions subject to standing auditors' performance evaluation (unit: number of institutions)

Type \ Year	2011	2012	2014	2015	Total
Public Corporation Type 1	10	10	4	8	32
	(16.95)	(17.24)	(14.81)	(27.59)	(18.50)
Public Corporation Type 2	15	15	8	7	45
	(25.42)	(25.86)	(29.63)	(24.14)	(26.01)
Quasi-Governmental Institution	15	15	5	8	43
(Commissioned-Service-Type)	(25.42)	(25.86)	(18.52)	(27.59)	(24.86)
Quasi-Governmental Institution	13	12	7	4	36
(Fund-Management-Type)	(20.34)	(20.69)	(25.93)	(13.79)	(20.81)
Small but strong quasi-	6	6	3	2	17
governmental institutions	(12.86)	(10.34)	(11.11)	(6.90)	(9.83)
Total	59	58	27	29	173
	(100)	(100)	(100)	(100)	(100)

Note: The values inside the parentheses are the ratios to the total value.

industries. Quasi-governmental institutions are non-market-type public institutions and have been classified into fund-management-type quasi-government institutions (which are institutions that manage funds or have been commissioned to manage funds in accordance with the National Finance Act) and the commissioned-service-type quasi-government institutions (which are quasi-governmental institutions not classified as fund-management-type quasi-governmental institutions). Finally, small but strong quasi-governmental institutions are commissioned-service-type, quasi-governmental institutions with less than 500 employees and fund-management-type quasi-governmental institutions with the asset size of less than one trillion won and less than 500 employees.

There was a total of 173 public institutions which were subject to the performance evaluation of the standing auditors (or members of the auditing committee). More specifically, 77 were public corporations, 79 quasi-governmental institutions, and 17 small but strong quasi-governmental institutions, which showed that quasi-governmental institutions were most subject to the performance evaluations. All standing auditors of the evaluated institutions were evaluated in 2011 and 2012, but from 2013, the evaluation method was changed so that the standing auditors were evaluated only once during their terms. Due to such change, no evaluation was conducted in 2013. In 2014 and 2015, only about a half of the public institutions which have been previously evaluated were subject to the performance evaluation.

2 Results

Table 7.5 shows the scores of the standing auditors' performance evaluation indicators by the type of public institution. Because the indicators from 2011

Table 7.5 Indicators and results of the standing auditors' performance evaluation by type of public institution[2]

2011–2012

Type	Auditing Committee	N	Expertise, Ethicality, Autonomy	Internal Control	Prevention of Sloppy Management	Observance of Guidelines	Transparent and Ethical Management	External Indicators		Overall Rating
								Achievements of Internal Audit	Performance Evaluation	
Public Corporation Type 1	O	20 (100.0)	5.5	6.1	5.3	5.95	5.85	.	3.4	4.1
Public Corporation Type 2	O	13 (43.33)	4.84	4.92	4	4.76	5.38	.	3.69	3.15
	X	17 (56.67)	5.11	5	4.23	5.23	5.05	.	2.35	3.17
	Total	30 (100.0)	5	4.96	4.13	5.03	5.2	.	2.93	3.16
Quasi-Governmental Institution (Commissioned-Service-Type)	O	2 (6.66)	5.5	5.5	4.5	5.5	5	.	2.5	2.5
	X	28 (93.34)	5.53	5.53	4.35	5.32	5.03	.	3.03	3.39
	Total	30 (100.0)	5.53	5.53	4.36	5.33	5.03	.	3	3.33
Quasi-Governmental Institution (Fund-Management-Type)	X	25 (100.0)	5.68	5.68	3.8	5.92	5.68	.	3.4	3.72
Small but Strong Quasi-governmental Institutions	X	12 (100.0)	5.5	5.5	3.58	4.83	4.5	.	3.41	2.91
Total	O	35 (29.91)	5.25	5.25	4.77	5.48	5.62	.	3.45	3.65
	X	82 (70.09)	5.48	5.48	4.35	5.41	5.15	.	3.06	3.37
	Total	117 (100.0)	5.41	5.41	4.47	5.43	5.29	.	3.17	3.46

2014–2015

Type	Auditing Committee	N	Expertise	Ethicality, Autonomy	Internal Control	Prevention of Sloppy Management	External Indicators			Overall Rating
							Achievements of Internal Audit	Integrity	Performance Evaluation	
Public Corporation Type 1	O	12 (100.0)	5.66	5.75	5.58	5.5	19.01	4.03	3.41	2
Public Corporation Type 2	O	10 (66.66)	5.7	4.9	5	5.4	19.03	4.15	3.4	1.9
	X	5 (33.34)	5	4.4	4.4	4.8	18.64	4.24	4	1.8
	Total	15 (100.0)	5.46	4.73	4.8	5.2	18.9	4.1	3.6	1.86
Quasi-Governmental Institution (Commissioned-Service-Type)	O	13 (100.0)	5.3	5.07	5.15	5.15	19.57	4.09	4	1.92
Quasi-Governmental Institution (Fund-Management-Type)	X	11 (100.0)	5.63	5.09	5.36	4.72	19.48	4.15	4.27	2.09
Small but Strong Quasi-governmental Institutions	X	5 (100.0)	4.8	4.8	4.8	4.6	17.15	4.05	4.2	1.8
	O	22 (39.28)	5.68	5.31	5.31	5.45	19.02	4.08	3.4	1.95
	X	34 (60.72)	5.29	5.05	5.05	4.88	19.05	4.13	4.11	1.94
	Total	56 (100.0)	5.44	5.16	5.16	5.1	19.04	4.11	3.83	1.94

Note
a) The values inside the parentheses are the ratios to the total value.
b) Specific scores of the internal auditing management indicator from 2011 to 2012 were not released.

to 2012 and from 2014 to 2015 were different, the two periods were analyzed separately.

The performance indicators from 2011 to 2012 showed that the Type 1 public corporations received higher ratings in a majority of indicators, including internal control (6.1), the prevention of sloppy management (5.3), observance of guidelines (5.95), transparent and ethical management (5.85) and in performance evaluation (3.4). The same phenomenon was found in the period from 2014 to 2015, as Type 1 public corporations received higher ratings in expertise (5.66), ethicality and autonomy (5.75), internal control (5.58), and prevention of sloppy management (5.5). Even in the overall ratings with weight calculation showed that the Type 1 public corporations received the highest ratings in 2011–2012 (4.1) and were second to the fund-management-type quasi-governmental institutions (2.09) but higher than other institutions (2.0) from 2014 to 2015. Small but strong quasi-governmental institutions, on the other hand, generally received lower scores than other institutions; in 2011–2012 they received lower scores in prevention of the sloppy management (3.58), observance of guidelines (4.83), transparent and in ethical management (4.5). In 2014–2015, small but strong quasi-governmental institutions received the lowest ratings excluding the indicators of management evaluation and ethicality and autonomy.

The results suggest that the standards (of asset size, number of employees, and type of business) and characteristics (fund-management type, etc.) which are used to classify the institutions subject to management evaluations could have a systematic effect on the results of the standing auditors' performance evaluation. For instance, fund-management-type institutions are relatively well equipped with the preventive internal control structure required in the financial business, which would likely have a positive effect on the scores of overall indicators. Such distribution may also be perceived to be natural, as the structure of the evaluation indicators for standing auditors consists of the joint efforts of the individual standing auditors and the audit departments.

The evaluation results by the existence of auditing committees clearly differed by the period.[3] Whereas the Type 2 public corporations which did not have auditing committees received higher scores in all other indicators aside transparent and ethical management, when compared to Type 2 institutions with no auditing committees, the results were completely different in 2014–2015. While it may be difficult to generalize such results, concerns have been raised that auditing committees may experience difficulties in producing predictable and positive effects due to the characteristics of such committees in Korea. That is, since auditing committees are a part of the board of directors, they are more likely to lack autonomy (Ministry of Strategy and Finance, 2010). Moreover, the auditing member takes part in the decision-making process as a member of the board, which may cause conflicts of interest between auditing and making decisions as a board member (Ra, 2015).

V Analysis of evaluation results by characteristics of standing auditors

1 Outline

The affiliations and careers of standing auditors (or members of audit committees), which serves as the preliminary data for the analysis on the standing officer's expertise were retrieved from the career information submitted from each institution to the evaluating board when evaluating the performance of standing auditors. Auditors' career information registered in news corporations (The JoongAng Ilbo and The Chosun Ilbo) and found in online portal websites (Daum and Naver) was used for classification. In most cases, standing auditors had multiple working experiences, which is why this study focused on their representative careers. In order to avoid overlaps with other categories, the analysis on the auditors with political careers was conducted in twofold, in accordance with the narrow definition of politicians and with the extended definition.

That is, standing auditors who have spent most of their careers as executives of political parties and who have actively participated in party activities by working as the regional chairs of political parties, and all in all, who could clearly be classified as politicians were classified as politicians in the narrow sense. On the other hand, standing auditors who have work experience in organizations, such as the government, corporations or NGOs, and were either elected as officials (member of the National Assembly or the head of local governments) or took part in political party activities were classified as politicians in the wider sense. For other major careers, government officials were classified as general government officials who worked for the central or local government or as former officials from the Board of Audit and Inspection, while there were also categories for high-ranking executives in corporations (board members, etc.) and managers in private corporations (department heads, section heads, team managers, etc.). This paper also categorized the major career paths of standing officers into former professors, former military or police officers, auditors who worked in the media industry, and lastly, other careers (celebrities, NGOs, etc.). The major careers of standing officers in public institutions by year are shown in Table 7.6.

Among the major careers of 171 standing auditors who were evaluated for their performance during the 4 years, in terms of the extended definition of politicians, the most common career was politicians with 60 auditors (35.09 percent), followed by general officials with 30 auditors (17.54 percent). On the other hand, the least common careers of auditors were media (four auditors, 2.34 percent) and the managers in private corporations (seven auditors, 4.09 percent). Even when adopting the narrow definition of politicians, politicians, with 45 auditors (26.32 percent) out of 171 had the highest percentage, followed by general officials with 33 auditors (19.3 percent). The least common career was media (four auditors, 2.34 percent) and academics (eight auditors, 4.68 percent).

Table 7.6 Major careers of standing officers by year (unit: person)

	2011		2012		2014		2015		Total	
	(1)	(2)	(1)	(2)	(1)	(2)	(1)	(2)	(1)	(2)
Politicians	28 (47.46)	23 (38.98)	15 (26.32)	12 (21.05)	9 (33.33)	6 (22.22)	8 (27.59)	4 (13.79)	60 (35.09)	45 (26.32)
General Officials	9 (15.25)	11 (18.64)	12 (21.05)	13 (22.81)	7 (25.93)	7 (25.93)	3 (10.34)	3 (10.34)	30 (17.54)	33 (19.30)
Board of Audit and Inspection Officials	4 (6.78)	4 (6.78)	9 (15.79)	9 (15.79)	3 (11.11)	3 (11.11)	1 (3.45)	2 (6.90)	17 (9.94)	18 (10.53)
Academics	1 (1.69)	1 (1.69)	2 (3.51)	2 (3.51)	0 (0.00)	0 (0.00)	5 (17.24)	5 (17.24)	8 (4.68)	8 (4.68)
Executives in Private Corporations	7 (11.86)	7 (11.86)	6 (10.53)	6 (10.53)	3 (11.11)	4 (14.81)	7 (24.14)	8 (27.59)	24 (14.04)	26 (15.20)
Managers in Private Corporations	2 (3.39)	3 (5.08)	4 (7.02)	5 (8.77)	0 (0.00)	0 (0.00)	1 (3.45)	1 (3.45)	7 (4.09)	9 (5.26)
Military/Police	4 (6.78)	5 (8.47)	5 (8.77)	5 (8.77)	1 (3.70)	1 (3.70)	1 (3.45)	1 (3.45)	10 (5.85)	11 (6.43)
Media	2 (3.39)	2 (3.39)	2 (3.51)	2 (3.51)	0 (0.00)	0 (0.00)	0 (0.00)	0 (0.00)	4 (2.34)	4 (2.34)
Others	2 (3.39)	3 (5.08)	2 (3.51)	3 (5.26)	4 (14.81)	6 (22.22)	3 (10.34)	5 (17.24)	11 (6.43)	17 (9.94)
Total	59 (100.0)		57 (100.0)		27 (100.0)		29 (100.0)		172 (100.0)	

Notes
a) (1) for politicians in the narrow sense, (2) for politicians in the wider sense
b) The values inside the parentheses are the ratios to the total sum.

In regard to the main careers of standing auditors by year, there were 28 standing auditors (47.46 percent) who were politicians in the wider sense out of 59 standing auditors in 2011, but the rate decreased in 2012 as 15 were politicians (26.32 percent) out of 57. On the contrary, there were only four standing auditors who were officials at the Board of Audit and Inspection (15.25 percent) in 2011 but this increased to 12 (15.25 percent) in 2012. There was only one standing auditor from academia in 2011 (1.69 percent), but in 2015 the number increased to five (17.24 percent) out of 29.

The major careers of standing officer by the type of public institution could be found in Table 7.7.

There were 76 standing auditors in public corporations (Public Corporation Type 1 and 2) during the four years and there were 79 in quasi-governmental institutions (commissioned-service-type and fund-management-type) and 17 in small but strong quasi-governmental institutions. All in all, 172 standing auditors worked in public institutions. In terms of the wider definition of politicians, politicians had the largest ratio in all types of public institutions. In Type 2 public corporations, in particular, 21 standing auditors out of 45 (46.67 percent) were politicians, during the 4 years. Even when applying the narrow definition of politicians, there were 16 standing officers who had been politicians (35.56 percent), which made Type 2 public corporations the public institution type with the largest number of politicians as standing auditors. Former general officials and officials from the Board of Audit and Inspection worked as standing auditors mostly at service-commissioned-type quasi-governmental institutions. More specifically, there were 12 auditors who had been general officials in service-commissioned-type quasi-governmental institutions (28.91 percent), and six who worked at the Board of Audit and Inspection (13.95 percent). In addition, five out of eight standing officers from academia during the 4 years worked at service-commissioned-type quasi-governmental institutions. For standing auditors who used to be chief executives at private corporations, nine out of 24 worked in Type 2 public corporations, which comprise of 20 percent of all standing auditors who worked in Type 2 public corporations. In case of standing auditors who had been managers in private corporations, four out of seven auditors worked in fund-management-type quasi-governmental institutions. These auditors had mostly worked in the finance sector before becoming auditors. In case of 11 standing auditors who were former military officials or police officers, seven worked in Type 1 public corporations and among them three worked as standing officers at the Incheon International Airport Corporation. Lastly, three out of four standing officers from the media industry worked at funding-management-type quasi-governmental institutions.

2 Results

1) Evaluation results of standing auditors by career

The results of the comparative analysis of the standing auditors' performance based on the major careers of standing auditors are as follows.[4] The indicators

Table 7.7 Major careers of standing auditors by type of public institution (unit: person)

	Public Corporation Type 1		Public Corporation Type 2		Commissioned-Service-Type		Fund-Management-Type		Small-Scale	
	(1)	(2)	(1)	(2)	(1)	(2)	(1)	(2)	(1)	(2)
Politicians	9 (29.03)	6 (19.35)	21 (46.67)	16 (35.56)	14 (32.56)	11 (25.58)	14 (38.89)	11 (30.56)	2 (11.76)	1 (5.88)
General Officials	5 (16.13)	6 (19.35)	6 (13.33)	6 (13.33)	12 (27.91)	12 (27.91)	3 (8.33)	4 (11.11)	5 (29.41)	6 (35.29)
Board of Audit and Inspection Officials	3 (9.68)	4 (12.90)	3 (6.67)	3 (6.67)	6 (13.95)	6 (13.95)	3 (8.33)	3 (8.33)	2 (11.76)	2 (11.76)
Academics	1 (3.23)	1 (3.23)	2 (4.44)	2 (4.44)	5 (11.63)	5 (11.63)	0 (0.00)	0 (0.00)	0 (0.00)	0 (0.00)
Executives in Private Corporations	3 (9.68)	4 (12.90)	9 (20.00)	9 (20.00)	2 (4.65)	2 (4.65)	6 (16.67)	7 (19.44)	3 (17.65)	3 (17.65)
Managers in Private Corporations	1 (3.23)	1 (3.23)	1 (2.22)	3 (6.67)	0 (0.00)	0 (0.00)	4 (11.11)	4 (11.11)	1 (5.88)	1 (5.88)
Military/Police	7 (22.58)	7 (22.58)	0 (0.00)	0 (0.00)	1 (2.33)	2 (4.65)	3 (8.33)	3 (8.33)	0 (0.00)	0 (0.00)
Media	0 (0.00)	0 (0.00)	0 (0.00)	0 (0.00)	0 (0.00)	0 (0.00)	3 (8.33)	3 (8.33)	0 (0.00)	1 (5.88)
Others	2 (6.45)	2 (6.45)	3 (6.67)	6 (13.33)	3 (6.98)	5 (11.63)	0 (0.00)	1 (2.78)	3 (17.65)	3 (17.65)
Total	31 (100.0)		57 (100.0)		27 (100.0)		29 (100.0)		172 (100.0)	

Notes
a) (1) for politicians in the narrow sense, (2) for politicians in the wider sense.
b) The values inside the parentheses are the ratios to the total sum.

Table 7.8 Performance results of standing officers by career[5]

2011–2012

	N	Expertise, Ethicality, Autonomy	Internal Control	Prevention of Sloppy Management	Total Score
Politicians	43	5.37	5.23	4.37	3.48
General Officials	21	5.42	5.71	4.52	3.28
Board of Audit and Inspection Officials	13	5.46	5.3	4.15	3.38
Academics	3	6.00	5.66	5.33	4.33
Executives in Private Corporations	13	5.38	6.00	4.46	3.53
Managers in Private Corporations	6	4.83	5.5	4.33	3.16
Military/Police	9	5.44	5.88	5.22	3.66
Media	4	5.75	6.00	4.75	3.75
Others	4	5.75	5.25	4.00	3.00

2014–2015

	N	Expertise	Ethicality, Autonomy	Internal Control	Internal Audit Performance	Prevention of Sloppy Management	Total Score
Politicians	17	4.64	4.58	4.82	18.63	4.41	1.82
General Officials	10	5.5	5.3	5.50	19.18	5.50	2.00
Board of Audit and Inspection Officials	4	6	6	5.00	19.64	6.00	2.25
Academics	5	6.4	5.4	5.40	20.11	5.40	2.00
Executives in Private Corporations	10	6.2	5.7	5.80	19.38	5.80	2.00
Managers in Private Corporations	1	4.00	4.00	4.00	17.24	4.00	2.00
Military/Police	2	6	6.5	5.50	18.17	5.50	2.00
Media	0	.	.	.	.	.	.
Others	7	5.28	4.28	4.57	18.72	4.57	1.85

Source: Performance Evaluation Team of Public corporations and Quasi-governmental Institutions (2012, 2013, 2015, 2016)

Notes
a) From 2011 to 2012 six-grade (1–6) indicators were used and the indicators from 2014 to 2015 were three grades (1–3).
b) Perfect score for the indicator of internal audit performance is 35 and all other indicators were nine grades (1–9).

from 2011 to 2012 show that standing auditors from academia received 6.0 in the expertise, ethicality and autonomy indicator, which was a relatively higher score than auditors from other career backgrounds. Former managers in private corporations, on the other hand, received 4.83, which was lower than average. In regard to internal control, auditors with management backgrounds received a higher score compared to other types with the score of 6.0, which could be due to the many former managers who have the expertise in finance and accounting and knowledge in relevant industries.

The overall score of standing auditors who were politicians was 5.23, which was lowest among the career types. As was the case in the indicators on expertise, ethicality and autonomy, standing auditors from academia received the highest score in three indicators in average, by earning 5.33 in the indicator on the prevention of sloppy management and by receiving 4.33 in the overall evaluation of standing auditor performance.

There were two most noteworthy characteristics in the results from 2014 to 2015. First, in many indicators, including expertise, former politicians received markedly lower scores in expertise (4.64), ethicality and autonomy (4.58), internal control (4.82), prevention of sloppy management (4.41) and in the total score (1.82).[6] The second trait was that the former officials of the Board of Audit and Inspection and auditors from academia received relatively higher scores in all indicators than the auditors from other career paths. Auditors from academia, in particular, received higher than average scores in expertise (6.4) and internal audit performance (20.11). Standing auditors from the Board of Audit and Inspection, on the other hand, received higher than average scores in ethicality and autonomy (6.0), prevention of sloppy management (6), and in the total score (2.25). 2 auditors who were former military or police officers received the highest score in ethicality and autonomy with 6.5. Both standing auditors have worked at the Incheon International Airport Corporation, and this result is likely due to their expertise, since both auditors worked on managing military supplies as military officers.

The analysis of the performance of standing officers which used the more compartmentalized evaluation indicators of 2014–2015 showed that politicians still received the lowest scores in all indicators, when compared with standing auditors from other career backgrounds. This research posited that this is due to the feature of career itself, that is, because of the influence of expertise. In the next chapter, this study conducted an analysis based on the feature of expertise.

2) Evaluation results in accordance with the standing
   auditor's expertise

In the narrow sense, auditing in the public sector could be defined as inspection on duty and accounting audit. In regard to professional capacity, the expertise of the auditor would depend on the ability to make judicial decisions on whether the accounting records are appropriate or whether the law and regulations have been observed (Sung, 2013). This study reviewed previous studies (Sung, 2013; Ryu and Kim, 2013; Moon and Lee, 2006; Beasley et al., 1999; Klein, 2002;

McMullen and Raghunandan, 1996; Xie et al., 2003) and relevant law (Article 25, Act on the Management of Public Institutions) to produce a typology of the standing auditors' expertise: essential expertise and complementary expertise. Essential expertise included the expertise in law, finance and accounting. Complementary expertise was found in former employees of public institutions or related fields. Although their expertise may not be directly related to auditing, they have the experience and knowledge in the industry, and thus were classified as standing auditors with complementary expertise. This paper also considered the possibility of an individual standing auditor having expertise in various fields. Table 7.9 shows the expertise of standing auditors by career, in accordance with the wider definition of politicians.

Out of 172 standing auditors who were evaluated during the 4 years, 39 auditors had legal expertise (22.67 percent), 50 had expertise in finance and accounting (29.07 percent) and 61 auditors had expertise in the relevant industries (35.47 percent), which made the expertise in relevant industries the most highly rated expertise among standing auditors.

In terms of the wider definition of politicians, standing auditors who were formally politicians with expertise in law and finance/accounting were respectively

Table 7.9 Expertise of standing auditors by career (unit: person)

	N	Essential Expertise		Complementary Expertise
		Law	Finance and Accounting	Relevant industries
Politicians	60	2 (3.33)	3 (5.00)	7 (11.67)
General Officials	31	12 (38.71)	7 (22.58)	15 (48.39)
Board of Audit and Inspection Officials	17	17 (100.0)	17 (100.00)	7 (41.18)
Academics	8	1 (12.50)	3 (37.50)	5 (62.50)
Executives in Private Corporations	23	2 (8.70)	12 (52.17)	10 (43.48)
Managers in Private Corporations	7	1 (14.29)	5 (71.43)	5 (71.43)
Military/Police	11	3 (27.27)	2 (18.18)	4 (36.36)
Media	4	0 (0.00)	0 (0.00)	2 (50.00)
Others	11	1 (9.09)	1 (9.09)	6 (54.55)
Total	172	7)39 (22.6	50 (29.07)	61 (35.47)

Note
a) The values inside the parentheses are the ratios to the total number of auditors (multiple expertise allowed).

two (3.33 percent) and three (5.0 percent) out of 60, the number of which was smaller than the standing auditors from other career paths. In addition, there were no standing auditors with expertise in law or finance and accounting from the media. Five out of seven standing auditors who worked as managers in private corporations had expertise in relevant industries (62.5 percent), marking the highest rate in complementary expertise. In case of former military or police officers, 4 out of 11 had complementary expertise in relevant industries. Former military standing auditors were measured to have knowledge in relevant fields since former air force officers began to work at the Incheon International Airport Corporation as standing auditors.

A categorization of the standing auditors' expertise could be found in Table 7.10. The narrow definition of expertise considered whether the auditors had legal or financial and accounting expertise or not, while the wider definition

Table 7.10 Scores of major indicators in the performance evaluation of standing officers by expertise

2011–2012

Whether Auditor has Expertise		N	Expertise, Ethicality, Autonomy	Internal Control	Prevention of Sloppy Management	Total Score
Narrower Scope	O	39 (33.62)	5.35	5.58	4.33	3.35
	X	77 (66.37)	5.42	5.48	4.54	3.5
Wider Scope	O	56 (48.27)	5.33	5.57	4.32	3.33
	X	60 (51.72)	5.48	5.46	4.61	3.56

2014–2015

Whether Auditor has Expertise		N	Expertise	Ethicality, Autonomy	Internal Control	Internal Audit Performance	Prevention of Sloppy Management	Total Score
Narrower Scope	O	21 (37.5)	5.8	5.42	5.52	19.40	5.52	2.04
	X	35 (62.5)	5.22	4.91	4.94	18.82	4.85	1.88
Wider Scope	O	35 (62.5)	5.68	5.31	5.37	19.19	5.34	2.00
	X	21 (37.5)	5.04	4.76	4.80	18.79	4.71	1.85

Notes
a) The indicator for total score in 2011–2012 used six grades and that during 2014–2015 used the three grades (1–3).
b) The perfect score for internal audit management was 25 and all other indicators used nine grades (1–9).

verified whether the auditors had expertise in law, finance and accounting, or in relevant industries. While the narrow definition was centered on the auditors with essential expertise, the wider definition encompassed the auditors with a wider scope of expertise. The effects of expertise on the results of the standing auditor evaluation were dramatically different in the two periods. In 2011–2012, auditors equipped with the narrower scope of expertise received lower scores in the indicators expertise, ethicality and autonomy (5.38) and prevention of sloppy management (4.33) than the auditors without expertise (5.42 and 4.54 respectively). This also applied to the auditors who had the wider scope of expertise, as they received lower scores than those without expertise in all indicators except the indicator on internal control.

In the evaluation indicators for 2014–2015, on the other hand, expertise and ethicality/ autonomy were separated. The evaluation results from the two years showed that in regard to expertise, auditors with either a narrower scope or wider scope of expertise received the scores of 5.8 and 5.68 respectively, which were about 0.6 higher than auditors without expertise. Auditors with either a narrower or wider scope of expertise also displayed higher results in the indicator on ethicality and autonomy. The fact that auditors with essential expertise in law or finance and accounting, in other words, auditors with a narrower scope of expertise, received higher scores than auditors with a wider scope of expertise, which reflected the influence of the auditors' expertise on the expertise indicator. This study attempted a more detailed analysis by classifying the auditors' performance evaluation by their specific expertise, which could be found in Table 7.11.

This paper examined the relationship between the major indicators for the performance evaluation of standing auditors from 2011 to 2012 and 2014 to 2015. This paper found that in the performance evaluation of standing auditors in 2011–2012, standing auditors with legal expertise received 5.45 in expertise, ethicality and autonomy and 5.54 in internal control, scores which were slightly higher than standing auditors without any legal knowledge. On the other hand, standing auditors with expertise in finance and accounting received lower scores in expertise, ethicality and autonomy by receiving 5.29 and in internal control, by receiving 5.47. This could be traced back to the fact that the indicator of expertise, ethicality and autonomy used in 2011–2012 was a mixture of multiple indicators so that it became difficult to accurately discern the influencing factors. In fact, in 2014–2015, when the expertise indicator was separated, standing auditors with expertise in finance and accounting received noticeably higher scores in both indicators on expertise and on ethicality and autonomy, while auditors with legal expertise scored 0.39 higher than the others who did not have any expertise found in the expertise indicator. Nevertheless, since they have displayed higher scores in the ethicality and autonomy indicator by 0.31, it would be difficult to conclude that this was purely due to the separation of indicators.

The fact that there were relatively more auditors in quasi-governmental institutions and small but strong quasi-governmental institutions in 2011–2012 than in 2014–2015 may serve as a partial explanation to the higher scores of standing auditors without expertise in law and finance and accounting received in the

Table 7.11 Auditors' expertise and the performance evaluation scores

2011–2012

Whether Auditor has Expertise		N	Expertise, Ethicality, Autonomy	Internal Control	Prevention of Sloppy Management	Total Score
Law	O	24 (20.69)	5.45	5.54	4.33	3.29
	X	92 (79.31)	5.4	5.51	4.51	3.5
Finance and Accounting	O	34 (29.31)	5.29	5.47	4.14	3.26
	X	82 (70.69)	5.46	5.53	4.6	3.53
Relevant Industries	O	36 (31.03)	5.41	5.61	4.33	3.27
	X	80 (68.97)	5.41	5.47	4.53	3.53

2014–2015

Whether Auditor has Expertise		N	Expertise	Ethicality, Autonomy	Internal Control	Internal Audit Performance	Prevention of Sloppy Management	Total Score
Law	O	15 (26.79)	5.73	5.33	5.33	19.41	5.46	2.06
	X	41 (73.21)	5.34	5.02	5.09	18.90	4.97	1.90
Finance and Accounting	O	16 (29.57)	6.06	5.60	5.75	19.34	5.68	2.06
	X	40 (71.43)	5.2	4.87	4.93	18.91	4.87	1.90
Relevant Industries	O	25 (44.64)	5.8	5.36	5.52	19.08	5.32	2.00
	X	31 (55.36)	5.16	4.9	4.87	19.00	4.93	1.90

Notes
a) The indicator for total score in 2011–2012 used six grades and in 2014–2015 used three grades (1–3)
b) The perfect score for internal audit management was 25 and all other indicators used nine grades (1–9).
c) The values inside the parentheses are the ratios to the total number of auditors during the period of evaluation.

indicator on the prevention of reckless management. This could be understood as an admission of the selection bias existing in the standing auditor evaluation and that the categorization of institutions itself could have a great influence on the results. The findings showed how the interpretation of results based on simple categorization should remain exploratory.

VI Lessons learned and conclusion

1 Lessons learned

Although this study examined the results of the standing auditor evaluation of public institutions in Korea, its implications are not limited but applicable to other countries, because most countries have similar types of public corporations and quasi-governmental institutions. Although the effective and efficient internal audit system is a key to the transparent management of public enterprises, the standing auditor has been regarded as a political position.

As shown in the analysis, the expertise of the standing auditor is the most critical factor which affects the overall evaluation results. Furthermore, the expertise of standing auditors has significant impacts on and is highly correlated with other evaluation components, including ethicality, autonomy and the prevention of sloppy management.

The evaluation method, i.e. interviews based on reports, may have influenced such results. Since it is difficult to separate the performance of a standing auditor from that of an audit department, report-based evaluation often fails to show the genuine contribution of standing auditors. Intensive interviews with standing auditors are more likely to reveal the level of the auditors' understanding of their roles and the key components of the audit process. Considering that the primary motivation for introducing the standing auditor evaluation system was to increase the level of the auditor's expertise, such results may have positive aspects in terms of reaching the policy goals in part.

The most significant lesson learned from this study is that the expertise of standing auditors does matter in various dimensions of the internal audit process. Thus, increasing the auditor's expertise is critical to the effective management of the audit department and eventually for the overall performance and transparency of public institutions. Considering the fact that auditors' expertise cannot be enhanced in a short period of time, appointing eligible standing auditors with prior job experience in law, finance, accounting and relevant industries, is more important. In that sense, the existence of the standing auditor evaluation system may work against the political consideration and encourage the recruitment of standing auditors with relevant experience.

2 Conclusion

This study categorized the standing auditors' expertise to verify how each factor affects the auditor evaluation conducted by the Ministry of Strategy and

Finance. Although the analysis was conducted on an exploratory level, this study found that the standing auditors' expertise had a distinctive and systematic influence on the results of the standing auditors' performance evaluation, which has considerable implications for the role of standing auditors. The internal control structure and internal audit system have gained greater importance in private corporations, as corporations realized that organized accounting fraud could not be controlled only by external audit. Accordingly, the significance of the role of standing auditors in public institutions is also likely to increase by time. This is why a more in-depth discussion on the role of the auditor as well as an institutional basis for appointing auditors with expertise are pivotal for public institutions, which simultaneously strive for efficiency and public interest.

Notes

1 The term internal audit was used together with self-audit in previous studies conducted in Korea. Relevant legal acts and the Board of Audit and Inspection use the term self-audit (Jin and Oh, 2012). Internal audit and self-audit, however, are clearly different in range, and some studies have pointed out that the range of self-audit is broader than that of internal audit (Heo, and Park, 2009).
2 In case of the overall ratings, six grades (1–6) were used from 2011 to 2012 and three grades (1–3) were used from 2014 to 2015. The perfect score for the internal control indicator was 25 and five grades (1–5) were used for management evaluation of institutions. All other indicators used nine grades (1–9).
3 Article 20 (Committee) of the Act on the Management of Public Institutions states that the market-type public corporation (Type 1 public corporation) and the semi-market-type public corporation (Type 2 public corporation) with the asset size of two trillion won or more are required to have auditing committees within the board of directors. Article 542, Clause 11 of the Commercial Act also obligates a listed company with the asset size of more than two trillion won or more to have an auditing committee.
4 The wider definition of politicians used for analysis
5 The overall score indicator for 2011 and 2012 used six grades (1–6), while the indicator for 2014 and 2015 was composed of three grades (1–3). Moreover, the perfect score for the management performance of internal audit was 25. The indicators of integrity and the internal audit performance used five grades (1–5) and all other indicators used nine grades (1–9).
6 Former managers in private corporations were the standing auditors with the lowest scores in average, but they are excluded from the discussion since the observed value was 1 and lacked representation.

References

Ahn, B. K., and Jeong, S. Y. (2009). Survey on the Condition of Self-Auditing in Public Corporations and Its Political Implications. *Journal of Auditing and Inspection*, *14*(5).

Ahn, Y. H. (2005). Plans for Improving the Auditing System of Local Governments. *Journal of Auditing and Inspection, 10*.

Ahn, Y. H. (2009). *Global Standards-Based Self-Audit for the Central Government*. 2009 Annual KAPAE Conference (June), Seoul, Korea, 3–29.

Ahn, Y. S., and Choi, S. E. (2010). Analysis on the Social Background of Board Members in Korean Local Public Corporations. *The Korean Association for Local Public Corporations*, *6*(2), 19–40.

Baltaci, M., and Yilmaz, S. (2006). *Keeping an Eye on Subnational Government: Internal Control and Audit at Local Levels*. Washington, DC: World Bank Institute.

Beasley, M., Carcello, J., and Hermanson, D. (1999). *Fraudulent Financial Reporting: 1987–1997*. Analysis of U. S. public companies, Committee of Sponsoring Organizations of the Treadway Commission.

Choi, Y. S. (1998). *Improvement Plans for the Auditing System of Local Governments*. Seoul: Korea Institute of Public Administration.

Diamond, J. (2002). *The Role of Audit in Government Financial Management: An International Perspective*. International Monetary Fund Working Paper No. 02/94.

Goolsarran, S. A. (2007). The Evolving Role of Supreme Audit Institutions. *Journal of Government Financial Management*, Fall.

Heo, M. S., and Cha, K. Y. (2010). *Improving Autonomy and Expertise of Self-Auditing Bodies*. Seoul: Audit and Inspection Research Institute.

Heo, M. S., and Park, H. J. (2009). A Comparative Study on the Public Audit System: Focusing on the Internal Audit System. *Korean Journal of Policy Analysis and Evaluation*, *19*(4), 357–380.

Jin, S. K., and Oh, C. H. (2012). A Study of Improving Internal Audit Capabilities in Korean Public Corporations. *International Journal of Policy Evaluation & Management, Korean Journal of Policy Analysis and Evaluation*, *22*(1), 91–125.

Joins People Information. http://people.joins.com

Kim, C. S. (2010). Auditing Methods on Projects Managed by Multiple Departments: With a Focus on Employment Policies. *Journal of Auditing*, *15*, 253–285.

Kim, N. Y. (2012). Audit Trends in Korean Supreme Audit Institution: Comparative Analysis of the Important Problems in Evaluation System and the Operation of Investment Programs by Local Governments with the Audit Recommendations. *Korean Public Management Review*, *26*(2), 33–61.

Kim, N. Y., and Cho, W. H. (2012). The Expertise of Auditors: Survey on Auditors of Board of Audit and Inspection. *Korean Public Personnel Administration Review*, *11*(2), 165–194.

Kim, S. H. (2002). *Plans for Securing the Auditing Effectiveness in Local Governments*. Seoul: Korea Research Institute for Local Administration.

Klein, A. (2002). Audit Committee, Board of Director Characteristics, and Earnings Management. *Journal of Accounting and Economics*, *33*, 375–400.

Ko, H. H. (2015). A Legal Review and Model About Independency of Jeju Special Self-Governing Province Audit and Inspection Commission. *Soongsil University Law Institute*, *34*, 35–39.

Lee, J. H., and Lee, H. Y. (2006). Audit and Performance Evaluation of Government Controlled Companies and Earnings Management. *Yonsei Business Review*, *43*(1), 81–106.

Lee, M. Y., and Lee, Y. B. (2009). A Study of the Evaluation of Informatization Programs Through Linking Evaluation and Audit Results of the Programs. *Korean Journal of Policy Analysis and Evaluation*, *19*(2), 143–176.

Lee, Y. K. (2007). A Study on the Directions of Improving the Independence of Institute of Internal Auditor. *Modern Society and Public Administration*, *17*(2), 109–138.

Lonsdale, J. (2008). Balancing Independence and Responsiveness: A Practitioner Perspective on the Relationships Shaping Performance Audit. *Evaluation*, *14*(2), 227–248.

Marcelo, B. G. (2001). Performance Audit Argument: A Public Management Policy Analysis About Supreme Audit Institutions Role. *Revista Del Clad*, 7.

McMullen, D., and Raghunandan, K. (1996). Enhancing Audit Committee Effectiveness. *Journal of Accountancy*, *182*, 79–81.

Ministry of Strategy and Finance. (2010). *Audit Manual for Public Corporations and Quasi-Governmental Institutions*, Seoul: Ministry of Strategy and Finance.

Moon, S. H., and Lee, H. I. (2006). Corporate Governance and Accrual Estimation Errors. *Management Studies*, *21*, 217–257.

National Law Information Center of Korea. www.law.go.kr

Naver People Search. http://people.search.naver.com/

Oh, S. H., Cho, S. I., and Kim, Y. W. (2009). *Methods for the Employment and Capacity Development of Talented Auditing Human Resources for Improving Expertise in the Board of Audit and Inspection of Korea*. Academic report for the Board of Audit and Inspection of Korea.

Park, H. J. (2010). The Relationship Between Supreme Audit Institutions and Internal Audit Bodies. *Journal of Governance Studies*, *5*(1), 1–29.

Park, H. J. (2013). A Preliminary Study of Public Auditing as an Academic Discipline: The Locus and Focus of Public Auditing. *Korean Public Administration Review*, *47*(1), 351–376.

People Chosun. http://db.chosun.com/people

Performance Evaluation Group of Public corporations and Quasi-governmental institutions. (2016). *2015 Performance Evaluation Report of Standing Auditors and Audit Committee Members*. Ministry of Strategy and Finance.

Performance Evaluation Team of Public corporations and Quasi-governmental Institutions. (2012). *2011 Performance Evaluation Report of Standing Auditors and Audit Committee Members*. Ministry of Strategy and Finance.

Performance Evaluation Team of Public corporations and Quasi-governmental Institutions. (2013). *2012 Performance Evaluation Report of Standing Auditors and Audit Committee Members*. Ministry of Strategy and Finance.

Performance Evaluation Team of Public corporations and Quasi-governmental Institutions. (2015). *2014 Performance Evaluation Report of Standing Auditors and Audit Committee Members*. Ministry of Strategy and Finance.

Public Audit Support Group, Board of Audit and Inspection of Korea. (2016). *Legal Understanding of Public Audit*. Human Culture Arirang Publisher.

Ra, Y. J. (2014). The Relations of Integrity Indices and Auditors Experience of Public Entities. *Korean Corruption Studies Review*, *19*, 19–39.

Ra, Y. J. (2015). *The Auditor System and Operating Status: Analysis of Public Entities*. Korea Institute of Public Finance.

Ryu, S. W., and Kim, N. Y. (2013). *Study on the Capacity and Qualification of Auditors in Public Institutions*. Audit and Inspection Research Institute.

Song, K. K. (2012). *Theory and Practice of Self-Auditing in Public Institutions*. Seoul: Gusang Publisher.

Stapenhurst, R., and Titsworth, J. (2001). *Features and Functions of Supreme Audit Institutions*. Washington, DC: World Bank PREM Note 59.

Sterck, M., and Bouckaert, G. (2006). International Audit Trends in the Public Sector: A Comparison of Internal Audit Functions in the Governments of Six OECD Countries Finds Similarities in Legal Requirements, Organizational Structure, and Future Challenges. *Internal Auditor*, *63*(4), 49–53.

Sung, Y. R. (2013). *A New Understanding of the Public Audit System*. Seoul: Seoktap Publishing.

Xie, B., Davidson III, W., and DaDalt, P. (2003). Earnings Management and Corporate Governance: The Roles of the Board and the Audit Committee. *Journal of Corporate Finance*, *9*, 295–316.

Yoo, S. W. (2009). Corporate Governance and Managerial Performance in Public Enterprises: Focusing on CEOs and Internal Auditors. *KDI Journal of Economic Policy*, *31*(1), 75–103.

Yoon, T. B. (1995). *Local Autonomy and Local Audit System*. Hwaseong: Gyeonggi Development Research Institute.

Yoon, T. B. (2016). *Issues and Improvement Plans for the Control Structure in Public Institutions*, Conference Program, Winter Conference of Seoul Association for Public Administration.

Yu, S. H., and Ahn, C. B. (2011). *Improving Plans for Management and Evaluation of Self-Auditing Bodies*. Audit and Inspection Research Institute.

Yum, C. B. (2010). A Comparative Analysis on Alternatives of Local Government Audit System in Korea. *Korean Policy Studies Review*, *19*(4), 469–503.

8 Industrial relations and the performance evaluation of public institutions

Daesik Choi

I Introduction

The performance evaluation of public institutions (PEPI) is activities related to setting mid- and long-term goals and managing its progress and results. Public institutions are in pursuit of both public interest and profit and unlike private enterprises, provide services to citizens. Because they are used as tools for realizing national policies, therefore, PEPI should be equipped with a certain amount of autonomy for the planning and implementation of projects and should also be responsible for the outcome; ultimately, it should contribute to organization's performance as well as citizen's satisfaction. In this context, PEPI can be understood as a performance management system which encourages public institutions to make genuine efforts in fulfilling their tasks and continue to improve their performance by taking a quality-centered system approach. PEPI takes the PDCA approach to assess *Plan-Do-Check-Act-Feedback*.

Public institutions also run an internal performance management system through which the institutions set targets by department as well as project, and make decisions on performance indicators in order to motivate their employees to accomplish the goals. For the internal performance management system, public institutions use a Logic Model, which provides a logical analysis of the input, activities, output and outcome of programs, and the BSC (balanced scorecard) system,[1] which identifies the strategies for accomplishing the organization's values and which manages performance comprehensively by using a strategic system in which the causation among the strategic components is systemized in the financial, customer, internal business processes, and learning and growth perspectives.

Public institutions use these performance management tools to establish strategic systems which consist of strategic goals, performance goals and performance indicators.[2] The strategies are specified and systemized by setting the strategies for accomplishing the vision or mission, which represents the ultimate values or future of an institution, and then by identifying the critical factors for the institution to accomplish the strategy and selecting the critical performance indicators which could have direct influence on the accomplishment of the goals and could judge whether the goals have actually been accomplished. The most important step is accurately identifying critical success factors and key performance indicators. This step enables the institution to identify its priories for accomplishing strategies with limited resources as well as the performance indicators which are directly linked with the success of the strategies. This is the core step for specifying and systemizing the causation of the value chain.

Industrial relations are used as an indicator for both the aforementioned PEPI and the internal performance management. Labor – management relations in public institutions is assessed by the rational improvement in industrial relations. Rationality, in this context, is *bounded rationality* which is an appropriate behavior for accomplishing goals under the given conditions and limitations. Bounded rationality is further classified as "substantive rationality," which values the most efficient behavior that could maximize utility and "procedural rationality," which emphasizes whether rational steps have been taken to find the best alternative to accomplish the given goals, and evaluates whether the process has been appropriate and whether there has been enough participation from the stakeholders. In PEPI, industrial relations then could be understood as an evaluation of whether the labor-management relations in a public institution has been effectively managed and whether the labor and management have acted rationally to accomplish the given goals.

On that note, indicators for industrial relations should be able to measure labor – management relations in public institutions comprehensively, should be representative as indicators and be appropriate in realizing the strategies of each institution. Considering the influence of industrial relations in PEPI, identifying the causation of the value chain is a very important task. However, research on this topic has been lacking. Thus, this study examines the key factors of industrial relations in public. Based on the literature review, this study examines the current status of industrial relations indicators in PEPI and internal evaluations conducted on public institutions and added suggestions for the development of more comprehensive and representative indicators for industrial relations.

II Characteristics of industrial relations in public institutions and CSF/KPI

1 Characteristics of industrial relations in public institutions and target values

Industrial relations are a concept encompassing the vertical and individual relation between the worker and the employer, the horizontal and collective relation between the labor union and the employer, and the mutual relation between the government, which influences employment and industrial relations. As corporations pursue profit and workers pursue welfare, industrial relations are cooperative and conflicting at the same time. This is a common trait found in the labor and management in public institutions as well as in private corporations. For better industrial relations, both parties should accept their different interests and work on reconciling such differences. That is, both labor and management should make joint effort in producing goods and services efficiently and work together to form an environment in which participation of members is guaranteed in the decision-making process, so that human dignity could be respected and standards and procedure could be observed during the working process. Moreover, both parties should form an environment through which collective bargaining or joint labor-management conferences could be held so that labor and management can discuss not only fair distribution but also topics that could be of interest to both parties.

Industrial relations in public institutions, however, experience relatively stronger interventions from the government, compared to those in the private sector. This is due to the public institutions' characteristic of having their budget and number of employees controlled by the government, and of being used as a policy tool to realize government policies. For this reason, the government is considered as the de facto principal-employer while the public institutions are considered as agents. A public institution's chief manager has limited terms and approaches industrial relations with concerns on political interests rather than economic benefits. Thus, the labor and management in public institutions sometimes collude and focus solely on their own safety rather than following the law and principles. Due to such characteristics, the labor and management in public institutions should put effort in forming and maintaining industrial relations with responsibility and the public interest in mind. Moreover, the labor and management should seek a rational balance in the authorities over human resources, management and collective bargaining with public interest in mind, even in group negotiations. The government, which has been directly and indirectly involved in maintaining the balance in the authorities over human resources, management and collective bargaining, should fulfill its role as a good manager so that the balance could be maintained in the industrial relations in public institutions. Furthermore, when such balance is achieved, the government should find ways to create a collective bargaining structure that provides a certain degree of autonomy to public institutions.

Labor unions in public institutions that are directly involved in industrial relations have certain constraints placed on labor rights. Labor strikes are restricted in public institutions which provide essential public service, for instance, as well as the suspension or termination of services, the suspension of which would jeopardize the everyday lives of citizens. Moreover, labor strikes in public institutions, which provide public service mandated by the national industrial relations act, can be stopped by an emergency adjustment action made by the Ministry of Employment and Labor. Because of such limitations to group actions, labor unions in public institutions focus more on political activities against stakeholders such as the government or the National Assembly, rather than choosing to take industrial actions by going on strikes. It needs to be understood that group actions are restricted due to the missions of public institutions to pursue public interest and since such actions could have great repercussions to the public. Thus, Labor and management in public institutions should put effort in maintaining rational industrial relations within the range of standards and procedures set by the Trade Union and Industrial relations Adjustment Act.

Public institutions provide more secure jobs than private business, and the goods and services provided by public institutions are less affected by market principles. Therefore, employment relationships or human resources are managed rigidly and in a traditional manner, which results in the industrial relations to fail to adjust to the environmental change of the labor market and to be focused only on the permanent workers. The government has been working on securing the flexibility of employment and protecting the disadvantaged, such as temporary employees. However, policies for the numerical flexibility of employment in public agencies, which include the restructuring of permanent workers, the use of temporary workers or part-time workers, and the flexible management of working hours, have yet to take root in public institutions. To address this issue, a long-term and strategic approach is necessary for employment and human resources management in public institutions. Labor and management in public institutions should use a limited number of temporary workers for tasks and flexibility and increase functional flexibility by establishing a high-performance work organization and through upskilling the functions of permanent workers and job rotation (Kim et al., 2004). That is, labor and management in public institutions should improve the flexibility in the labor market and take active actions and practice in improving working conditions of temporary and part-time employees so that good labor norms and order could be instated. The government should also take strong measures to solve the many issues that temporary employees are facing, by reinforcing social insurance, observing the principle of equal pay for equal work, working on improving the discrimination against temporary employees and by investing on human resources for higher productivity.

Considering the increasing roles of public institutions in our society, it is no exaggeration to say that industrial relations in public institutions could set the trend of the relations for the entire country. Accordingly, the government has been implementing the salary peak system, performance-based salary system, and measures to alleviate social polarization in public institutions first and then to spread the trend to private businesses. Such government policies, however, are based upon the premise that the workers of public institutions would concede to give up benefits they had enjoyed, so that they do not seem to be fully implemented despite government intervention, such as through management evaluation. Public institutions have a higher level of social obligation to realize social justice than private businesses, which to some extent also applies to the labor unions in public institutions. This is because the very purpose of labor unions is to realize social and economic justice by creating decent jobs in the entire society. Labor and management in public institutions, therefore, should share social responsibility and practice the responsibility for the sustainable development of the labor community. Effort should be concentrated in monitoring so that employees in supplier firms would not suffer from any discrimination in their working conditions such as in employment and wages, as well as for capacity development of workers in the supplier firms. More effort should also be concentrated on improving the working conditions and job stability of workers from in-house and out-house contractors.

This paper has so far identified the characteristics of industrial relations in public institutions. Then what are the values the labor and management should pursue together? Such characteristics provide meaning for the components of industrial relations in public institutions and provide future guidelines for the labor and management. The primary values that the labor and management of public institutions should pursue are efficiency and equity. Efficiency is a value pursued by the management for the efficient production of goods and services, while equity[3] is valued by the labor so that human dignity and freedom could be realized. Industrial relations in public institutions should reconcile the management's demand for efficient management as well as the labor's demand for human dignity and voice (Budd, 2004). This is because industrial relations in public institutions which fail to find a rational balance between these factors would limit production in both the organization and the individual, which would hinder institutions from achieving high performance. To improve efficiency in management, the labor and management in public institutions should build a cooperative industrial relationship and work hard together to achieve the shared goals. In regards to equity, human resources and labor policies in public agencies should be implemented with the members' consent and all policies on wages, promotion and evaluation should not depend on the employer's sole decision, but should be based on objectively set standards and processes. A decision-making system, which is based on the law on worker participation and cooperation and which reflects the characteristics of the public institution, is needed for better industrial relations. The value on the social responsibility of the labor and management in public institutions should also be emphasized, as both parties are demanded to play their roles and take responsibility in fulfilling the purpose of public institutions, which were established for realizing public interest and social values. The social responsibility of public institutions could be considered to be a normative system of behaviors which demands institutions to solve social and economic problems that arise from their activities so that they could meet the expectations of the stakeholders or the general public. The labor and management in public institutions should contribute to the sustainable development and tend to their stakeholders, observe relevant rules and international codes of conduct so that transparent and ethical behaviors could take place within the organization.

In short, public institutions should strive for the improvement in labor-management partnership for efficient management and make a joint effort to enhance the quality of public service so as to pursue sustainable industrial relations that create value and contribute to social integration and development.

2 Critical Success Factors (CSF) of industrial relations in public institutions

This paper has so far examined the characteristics of industrial relations in public institutions and the values the labor and management should pursue. In this part, this paper analyzes the critical success factors that made up the industrial relations in public institutions through a literature review.

First, this paper finds the necessary factors for effective industrial relations by examining the characteristics of labor-management partnerships[4] or the traits of high-performance work organizations.[5] Through labor-management partnership, the workers and employers can build and maintain a cooperative relationship and create and accomplish a common purpose based on mutual trust and respect. To build such a relationship, both labor and management should respect each other, recognize each as a partner and make the best effort to accomplish the common goals.[6] Research on labor-management partnership has suggested factors that affect industrial relations and organizational performance based on a systemic perspective as follows: the perception and attitude of the top management team, perception and attitude of the labor union and workers, open book management or the level of information sharing, good communication, participation in the decision-making process,[7] as well as the mutual trust and cooperation of the labor and management, interest and participation from the labor union and workers, guarantee of employment flexibility and job stability, a fair compensation system, and investment in educational training (Kochan and Dyer, 1976; Cooke, 1985; Eaton and Voos, 1992; Kochan and Osteman, 1994; Coupar and Stevens, 1998). In addition, labor-management cooperation could be classified into stages of reactive problem solving, anticipatory problem solving and joint future creation. The higher the level of labor-management cooperation, the longer and more strategic the decisions made by the labor and management.[8] In other words, improvement in labor-management partnership is essential to enhance the efficiency of public institutions, which requires a perception and attitude of trust and cooperation from both sides. Successful industrial relations could be achieved when information is shared in various levels, both parties communicate freely with workers participating in the decision-making process while working on continuously developing the capacity of workers.

The analysis on institutional changes in industrial relations, with focus on subjective factors such as the stakeholders' beliefs, values and strategies, has been conducted by using the bargaining theory, which helps analyzing and diagnosing collective bargaining, the key process in industrial relations, as well as the bargaining attitude and behaviors that influence industrial relations. There are two types of collective bargaining: distributive bargaining and integrative bargaining (Walton and McKersie, 1965). Distributive bargaining occurs in a conflicting zero-sum situation when there is a conflict of interest, while integrative bargaining is a situation in which the labor and management can share opinions on issues and enjoy shared benefits. Integrative bargaining is important for the maintenance and development of cooperative industrial relations. Distributive bargaining could be considered to be a consumptive and confrontational bargaining and integrative bargaining a productive bargaining, which is an important factor for the formation of the labor-management partnership (Hur and Choi, 2003; Deery and Iverson, 2005). This is because productive bargaining leads to a swift and peaceful agreement between labor and management and is not only a distributive discussion on how to distribute a limited scarcity value, but also a bargaining of how labor and management can generate profit. Productive industrial relations are necessary also to solve the structural problems found in industrial relations in public institutions, such as the structural weakness of combative labor movements led by labor unions, which could distort work and employment standards, and the institutions' tendency to protect the working conditions of permanent workers (Park, 2015). Integrative collective bargaining or productive bargaining, therefore, is a key component which has positive influences on industrial relations.

On the other hand, the government should have practical discussion with the stakeholders in public institutions so that the bargaining structure could provide autonomy to the employers at public institutions, rather than being overly regulated by the government. A rational balance between bargaining rights and management rights is necessary, due to the characteristics of public institutions. Labor rights should also be recognized in principle but restrictive rules on human resources and management rights, which act as obstacles to higher efficiency, should be reconsidered. The government should also provide policy directions and guidelines on management and human resources management rights by type of institutions, so that the labor and management of public institutions could improve their relations autonomously. Also necessary are policies which could assess such activities fairly and provide incentives, find and promote best practices and provide consultation services through experts in industrial relations (Lee, 2010).

Recently, there have been attempts to approach industrial relations with the social responsibility perspective. Social responsibility, first established as a concept by Bowen (1953) in *Social Responsibility of the Businessman*, was expanded in the business sector through the studies conducted by McGuire and Sethi among others. Social responsibility asks the members of an organization to contribute to the sustainable development of the organization, be considerate to stakeholders and observe related rules and international codes of conducts based on transparent and ethical behavior. Social responsibility can be classified into economic responsibility, legal responsibility, ethical responsibility and philanthropic responsibility (Caroll, 1991). Economical responsibility entails the responsibility to produce products and service, legal responsibility to practice economic activities in a legal manner, ethical responsibility to act ethically so as to meet the social expectations, and philanthropic responsibility to take part in cultural activities, donation and voluntary work, which have no direct connections with business activities.

There are two representative guidelines on social responsibility: the guideline set by the Global Reporting Initiative (GRI) and by the International Organization for Standardization (ISO). United Nation's GRI is an international organization which was launched in 1997, and presents a guideline with the aim to draft an internationally standardized sustainability report. The G4 guideline of GRI has the section on labor practices and decent work, which consists of 8 aspects – employment, labor-management relations, occupational health and safety, training and education, diversity and equal opportunity, equal remuneration for women and men, supplier assessment for labor practices, and labor practices grievance mechanisms (GRI, 2013). The ISO prepared the Guideline on Social Responsibility (ISO 26000) in November 2010 as an international guideline on social responsibility and advised all organizations to follow these principles.[9] The ISO's position on labor-management relations could be found in the parts on human rights and labor practices in the ISO 26000. In regards to human rights, the guideline highlights that there should be no discrimination and that the International Labor Organization's standards on basic labor rights should be observed. For labor practices, the key elements are employment stability and employment relations, working conditions and social protection, social dialog, industrial safety and health, and the development and training of human resources (Rho, 2011). Both guidelines provided by the GRI and ISO 26000 includes principles on guaranteeing basic labor rights and banning discrimination, securing the quantity and quality of employment, as well as acknowledging the importance of industrial safety and health and taking responsibility of the supply chain suppliers and subcontractors. All in all, the guidelines asks corporations to take their social responsibility on the lives of people.

The GRI G4 and the ISO 26000 can also act as catalysts for emphasizing the social responsibility of labor unions and calling for change, as it is the social responsibility of labor unions to pursue human dignity and realize social and economic justice. Labor unions can also be viewed to have the economic responsibility to achieve employment stability, improve working conditions and realize distributive justice, the legal responsibility to take account of the rationality and legality of the national industrial relations act and industrial relations, the ethical responsibility to actively participate in production and to monitor and check ethical activities within the organization, and the philanthropic responsibility to play the role of a cooperative partner to the local community and to be considerate to and take responsibility for the socially disadvantaged, etc. (Lim, 2012). Depending on the labor unions' scope of activity, the primary stakeholders could be considered to be union members and members of the organization, whose activities have a direct influence on the existence and management of the union, the secondary stakeholders as the temporary workers and workers at subcontractors who influence the organization, the tertiary stakeholders as the local community where the members' lives are based on, and the quaternary stakeholder would be classified as the global community (Kim, 2011).

The GRI G4 and ISO 26000 clearly stipulate that the stakeholders from the labor and management are responsible for having social discourse and compromising, with sustainability as their objective, and adjusting their own interest under the paradigm of social responsibility. The labor and management in public institutions are required to share the social responsibility in a higher level, maintain the transparency, efficiency and equity within the organization, and work for more efficient management. The labor and management should also improve the quality of public services so as to improve customer's satisfaction. Both parties should take active interest in creating jobs, mutual growth and in contributing to the society to be socially responsible. More effort from the stakeholders in the labor and management of public institutions is necessary to improve the treatment of workers at subcontractors and to provide them with training opportunities. They should also focus on improving the working conditions and the job stability of indirectly employed workers at subcontractors and service companies. Finally, it is necessary for both parties to make a great effort to alleviate the gap in the working conditions between permanent workers and temporary workers and to strengthen the job stability of temporary workers. The government's role to reach consensus on concerning job stability and flexibility in the society and to act as a balancer for resolving social imbalance and polarization would also be pivotal.

3 The key performance indicator for industrial relations in public institutions

This paper has so far examined the key factors affecting industrial relations in public institutions. Based on such factors, this paper will investigate the key performance indicator for industrial relations in public institutions by studying previous industrial relations evaluation models. Previous research and discussions on the industrial relations in Korea has been centered on labor-management partnership or the high-performance work organization theory (Kim, D. B. et al., 2002; Hur, C. Y. and Choi, D. S., 2003b; Lee, J. M. 2004; Kim, D. O. et al., 2008; Lee, B. H. et al., 2008; Lee, Y. M., 2009 etc.). Among such studies, this paper identified the measurement indicators which could be used in public institutions by using labor-management evaluation models that take efficiency and equity into account.

First of all, Lee (2009) analyzes industrial relations in terms of trust, cooperation, participation and performance. Lee's measurement indicator is divided into labor and management trust and labor and management cooperation and uses the level of procedural fairness as an indicator, which could be used as a reference for public institutions staffs when creating an internal performance index.[10] Lee also stresses that a labor partnership program that fits the level of industrial relations is important and presented the programs that may be of use.

Lee et al. (2008) analyzes industrial relations by using the high-performance work environment theory and by reflecting efficiency and equity. The study set the external environment, such as the market, system and social culture, and the structure of labor and management, the beliefs and values of labor and management, and the strategic choices made by labor and management as the input factors. Labor-management cooperation, motivation, opportunities for participation, and human resource development are set as process factors and the performance of the industrial relations and organizational performance as the output factors. Indicators for equity are motivation and opportunities for participation, both of which are input factors. By fulfilling the workers' various desires and expectations and through fair distribution, the motivation factors help workers trust and be immersed in the organization and influence the organizational performance. Some of indicators for the job security issue could be employee's acceptance,, the rate of transition from temporary to permanent workers and the level of target achievement, effort to overcome discrimination against workers with unlimited contracts and temporary workers, women's ratio in management, the wage level of temporary workers compared to that of permanent workers, the satisfaction level of distribution, opportunity and process in the assessments, and rewards and promotions. Some of indicators for participation could be the management level and effectiveness of proposed policies, satisfaction in job rotation, management level and satisfaction of the joint labor-management conferences, the number of labor-management conferences held every year, the number of joint labor-management committees and the number of meetings held, satisfaction toward the workers' participation system and its effectiveness, proposals made by person and the number of proposals.

Efficient business management and the good quality of the employees' lives, and ultimately the higher performance of the organization could be achieved when the labor and management of public institutions improve their partnership with a balanced perspective on its efficiency and equity. However, there is a limitation to labor-management partnership if both parties focus on realizing their own benefits. Public institutions have a fundamental responsibility to improve the quality of public services. The labor and management of public institutions also have the responsibility to work their very best for the public interest and to improve the quality of work and life of the entire society.

The GRI G4 guidelines and ISO 2600 provide useful information on the components and measurement indicators of the industrial relations' social responsibility for workers in public institutions. The category on "Labor Practices and Decent Work" in the GRI G4 guideline consists of indicators for employment and labor-management relations, training and education, diversity and equal opportunity, gender equality, and the supplier assessment for labor practices.[11] The ISO 26000 categorizes seven core subjects into 37 issues and presented a 5-point scale checklist on the requirements and expectations on the issues. The industrial relations indicator consists of issues on anti-discrimination, basic labor rights, employment stability and employment relationship, working conditions and social protection, social discourse, industrial safety and health, and the development of human resources.[12] The both standards emphasize the effort for abolishing discrimination against temporary workers within the organization, public institutions' effort for the employment stability, including subcontractors and for the lives of the workers. The two guidelines also call for public institutions to take more responsibility in enhancing the stakeholders' quality of life related with labor and employment, by providing safe and healthy working environments. Such indicators can be used as the own performance evaluation criteria for industrial relations: the ratio of subcontractors that work with public institutions that observe the labor standards set by the national industrial relations act, the establishment and management of a governance group based on gender, age, minority and diversity, the number of programs on abolishing discrimination or on social protection and the level of satisfaction toward such programs, the working days lost due to industrial accidents that occurred in public institutions and subcontractors or the number of days the safety and health committee meetings were held, the rate of indirectly employed workers, and the number of workers who have been transitioned from indirect employment to direct employment.[13]

III Current indicators for industrial relations in public institutions and issues

This paper examined the critical success factors and performance indicators for industrial relations in public institutions, under the premise that the labor and management in public institutions should improve efficiency in management and take social responsibility in upholding human dignity and in improving the quality of public services through labor-management partnership. In this chapter, this study will examine indicators for industrial relations that are currently used in the PEPI system as well as in institution's own evaluations system then will suggest ideas for future discussions.

1 Indicators for industrial relations in PEPI

Table 8.1 and Table 8.2 show the changes in indicators for industrial relations through points for consideration, that are listed in the sections for evaluation details and quantitative indicators in the manual for PEPI. Changes in indicators for industrial relations during this period can be largely categorized in two stages: from 2008 to 2010 and from 2011 to 2016.

The indicators from 2008 to 2010, presented in Table 8.1, mostly focused on efforts for and accomplishment in reforming industrial relations. Detailed evaluations have been conducted on whether strategies for reforming industrial relations have been established, efforts in improving the level of labor-management cooperation, and how rational collective agreements have been.

In 2008, there was emphasis on labor partnership or the establishment of industrial relations, based on the high-performance work organization theory. That is, the evaluations were centered on the establishment of labor-management trust by building communication channels, such as joint labor-management conferences, labor-management meetings and management briefing sessions, and on the management of various programs on labor-management cooperation, which could contribute to reforming the labor and management culture. Moreover, the evaluations focused on reforming unreasonable labor practices and forming a productive bargaining culture by assessing the adequacy of the range of labor union membership, whether the support for labor unions has been excessive, whether the number of full-time union officers were appropriate, the balance between collective agreements and management rights, as well as the effectiveness of the collective bargaining process. The indicators, however, significantly changed due to the reform policies implemented by the Lee Myung-bak administration in 2009. Through such changes, indicators on declarations on the harmony of labor and management or joint labor-management declarations were excluded and new indicators on the establishment and accomplishments on rational and legitimate labor-management relations were added. This suggested that the evaluation standards, which had been centered at improving the autonomous partnership between the labor and management, changed its direction to put more emphasis on the

Table 8.1 Changes in indicators for industrial relations in PEPI (2008–2010)

Period	2008	2009–2010
Evaluation Indicator	Rationality in labor-management relations	
Definition	Evaluation on the institutions' efforts to reform industrial relations	
Evaluation Details 1	Has the institution developed strategies for reforming industrial relations? <Points for consideration> • Establishment of strategies for reforming industrial relations • Effort in creating a reformed labor and management culture	
Evaluation Details 2	Has the institution established communication channels for the rational industrial relations? <Points for consideration> • Sharing information through labor and management conferences • Effectiveness of regular discourse • Complaint settlement and level of satisfaction of the labor and management	
Evaluation Details 3	Is the institution operating joint labor-management programs on improving the management system of labor unions, management-related decision-making, problem solving and on training and education for workers? <Points for consideration> • Evaluation on effectiveness of a joint organization on reforming labor-management cooperation and industrial relations • Evaluation on effectiveness of other programs for labor and management cooperation • Review of qualifications for union members • Evaluation on the appropriateness of industrial relations education • Confirmation of the department in charge of personnel management • Current status of support for labor unions • Appropriateness of the number of full-time union officers	
Evaluation Details 4	Is the content of the collective agreement rational and has it been agreed during an appropriate term through an appropriate process? <Points for consideration> • Labor and management agreement and human resources management • Collective bargaining and management rights • Effectiveness of wages and collective bargaining	
Evaluation Details 5	How are the efforts for reforming industrial relations and the accomplishment of the institution's goals related? <Points for consideration> • Efforts for establishing a new culture based on the trust between labor and management within the institution • Evaluation on the effectiveness of declarations on the harmony of labor and management or joint labor-management declarations	<Points for consideration> • Evaluation on establishment of rational and legitimate industrial relations and how well the plans and activities for realizing labor and management cooperation are connected to the goals of the institution

Data: Collected from the manual for the performance evaluation of public institutions and the manual for qualitative evaluations from 2008 to 2010.

management of unions under government control and the observance of standards set by the national industrial relations act and guidelines.

Considering that industrial relations consist of the balance between the values of efficiency, equity and social responsibility, this period had key factors for improving labor-management partnership, such as trust and cooperation between labor and management, sharing management information, communication and training and education, as evaluation factors. Factors related to the establishment of a productive bargaining culture and the balance between bargaining rights and management rights could also be found. Indicators on equity, such as guaranteeing the members' participation in the decision-making process in joint labor-management committees, labor and management meetings, and personnel committees were also included. Nevertheless, the indicator industrial relations for this period were mostly for the evaluation of management efficiency achieved through labor and management cooperation within the group. This marked the beginning of increased government control directly over labor and management collusions which was guided by self-interest rather than by public interest.

On the other hand, the indicators from 2011 until the present have examined the overall content of public institutions management, such as collective agreements and policies on personnel and wages, rather than the improvement of labor-management partnership. The indicators were aimed at improving any unreasonable factors or indications of sloppy management. Government control over industrial relations in public institutions has been reinforced due to the uniform and detailed standards set by the collective agreements analysis table[14] and the sloppy management checklist.[15]

This period could once again be divided into two phases: the first from 2011 to 2013, the second from 2014 until the present time.

The first characteristic of the indicators from 2011 to 2013 was that they were not composed of planning, implementation and accomplishments among the content of the detailed evaluation but that some evaluation indicators were transitioned into the PDCA perspective and the others focused on implementation and accomplishments. The detailed evaluation indicators before 2011 consisted of planning, implementation and accomplishments in consecutive order. On the other hand, the evaluation system after 2011 assessed the planning, implementation and accomplishments for the strategies and practices for reforming industrial relations. The establishment of rational and legitimate industrial relations, however, was changed from being a performance factor to a structuring factor so that the process and outcome could both be considered. Second, evaluation standards of detailed indicators for labor-management cooperation became more comprehensive than in the past. The previous detailed indicators for labor-management cooperation set joint labor-management boards and labor-management cooperation programs as examples, which led public institutions to focus their efforts on the set examples for evaluation. On the other hand, after 2011, the evaluation methods changed to assess the joint efforts and accomplishments made by the labor and management, as well as the institutions' efforts to prevent labor-management conflict, which enabled each public institution to induce

Table 8.2 Changes in indicators for industrial relations in PEPI (2011–2016)

Period	2011–2014	2014–2016
Evaluation Indicator	Labor – management relations	
Definition	Evaluation on the institutions' efforts to improve the rationality in industrial relations	
Evaluation Details 1	Has the institution developed and implemented rational strategies for reforming industrial relations?	
	<Points for consideration> • Development of strategies for reforming industrial relations • Practicing strategies for reforming industrial relations	<Points for consideration> • Development of strategies for reforming industrial relations • Efforts and accomplishments in implementing industrial relations strategies
Evaluation Details 2	Have rational industrial relations been established and labor-management cooperation realized to make concrete progress?	
	<Points for consideration> • Establishment of rational and legal industrial relations • Labor and management cooperation	<Points for consideration> • Establishment and management of rational industrial relations • Labor and management cooperation
Evaluation Details 3	Have there been appropriate effort and progress for communication between labor and management and for reinforcing programs for better industrial relations? <Points for consideration> • Communication between labor and management for forming a consensus • Level of two-way communication • Reinforcement of programs for better industrial relations industrial relations	
Evaluation Details 4–1	[Institution with Labor Unions] Are the collective agreements rational and have there been appropriate effort and progress to improve such agreements?	Have there been appropriate effort and progress from the institution to change collective agreements which violates management rights or the authority over human resources?
	<Points for consideration> • Appropriateness of wages and collective bargaining • Effectiveness of collective bargaining	<Points for consideration> • Evaluation of whether the agenda of the collective agreements are in correspondence with the aims and objectives of related regulations, and whether related regulations on collective bargaining, employment regulations, human resources and on disciplinary action, especially in regards to the adjustment of economic interests and working conditions have been well established

Period	2011–2014	2014–2016
Evaluation Details 4–2	[Institutions without Labor Unions] Have there been appropriate effort and progress for effective management of the joint labor-management conference?	• If rules on management and human resources have been included in existing collective agreements, evaluation is conducted on whether there have been systematic efforts to improve and adjust such agreements. Whether there have been joint labor-management conferences or any other meetings for improving inappropriate clauses and for setting legitimate agendas and whether there have been active discussions on such issues are also evaluated. The process of how unreasonable issues have been reformed is also assessed, based on records of the meetings. • Cases of improving unreasonable clauses on rules on management or human resources considered as accomplishments
	<Points for consideration> • Establishment and management of joint labor-management committees by law • Management of joint labor-management committees • Progress in joint labor-management committees	
Evaluation Details 5	–	[Institutions with Labor Unions] Are the collective agreements rational and the efforts and accomplishments to reform them appropriate? [Institutions without Labor Unions] Have the efforts and accomplishments to manage the joint labor-management committees effectively been appropriate? <Points for consideration>
	–	• Effectiveness of wage and collective bargaining • Appropriateness of collective agreements • Establishment and management of joint labor-management committee by law • Management of joint labor-management committees • Progress in joint labor-management committees

Data: Collected from the manual for performance evaluation of public institutions and the manual for qualitative evaluations from 2011 to 2016.

labor-management cooperation based on their own characteristics.[16] There were also changes in the detailed evaluation standards on communication. The evaluation was centered on the effectiveness of official representative communication channels such as joint labor-management committees and meetings until 2010. However, after 2011, the overall communication system between the labor and management were assessed by considering the existence of communication channels with labor unions and union members so as to create a consensus between labor and management, as well as the targets of communication, the diversity of the content and frequency of communication. Third, the evaluation indicators for institutions with labor unions were differentiated from institutions which do not have labor unions. Public institutions with labor unions had the rationality of collective agreements evaluated while public institutions without any labor unions had the performance of their joint labor-management committees assessed. This was to reflect the fact that important decisions between labor and management representatives in organizations without labor unions are made through joint labor-management committees and to examine whether such committees have implemented the regulations on the promotion of workers' participation and cooperation. However, efforts and progress in managing joint labor-management committees are an important component regardless of the existence of labor unions. This is because the participation criteria and the process for joint labor-management committees are stipulated by law, as the committees are official organizations for worker participation in which labor, management and public benefits could be discussed.

Evaluation indicators from 2014 to the present are related to the public institution normalization policy, implemented by the Park Geun-hye administration. The institutions' efforts to reform collective agreements which violates management rights or the authority over human resources are added as an independent detailed evaluation indicator for the 2014 industrial relations based on the public institution normalization policy. This could be understood as an attempt to reflect the reality of such issues which remain unchanged, despite being repeatedly pointed out as an improvement point in management evaluations and in spite of the suggestions from the National Assembly and the Board of Audit and Inspection. Another change in the indicators are that while all points for consideration in the past had been the same for all detailed evaluation items, which led to confusion, the new indicators provide detailed points for consideration on each item.[17] Points for consideration in evaluating the management capacity of industrial relations, for example, had been limited to checking the plans and performance for education or training sessions on the industrial relations, but after 2011, started education programs on the industrial relations for workers who are involved with the relations. Furthermore, after 2014, evaluations became more specific and comprehensive by evaluating how well connected the labor-management training programs were with the institution's overall HRD system as well as the effectiveness of the programs.

Since the components of industrial relations include efficiency, equity and the balance of social responsibility, key performance factors such as the sharing of management information are excluded from the evaluation criteria, thereby placing emphasis on the efficiency through government control. This becomes possible through the institutions' observance of law and principles, the reinforcement of the authority over human resources and management rights and by stopping sloppy management. Similar to the previous period, there was a lack of evaluation on the social responsibility of the labor and management.

This study has so far examined the changes in labor-management indicators in the PEPI system and their significance. The indicators from 2008 until the present show a continuous reinforcement of government control for the observance of law and principles and in order to rectify unreasonable labor practices in human resources and management. Collective bargaining in public institutions, as a result, turned into a demand on the unilateral concession from the labor union, rather than being a productive and comprehensive bargaining process. Such tendencies could be considered positive in that they achieved a certain balance between bargaining rights and management rights and since the unreasonable factors in the management of public institutions have been considerably improved. However, once the balance between bargaining rights and management rights have been achieved, the labor-management relations should be activated by providing autonomy to the institution. Sharing management information is pivotal for this. The labor and management in public institutions should, of course, work hard not to revert back to the past. Moreover, the management evaluation should also incorporate indicators for the coexistence of labor and management and for the improvement in public services through social responsibility. Labor-management partnership and fairness among workers are pivotal for the coexistence of labor and management in public institutions. More sharing of management information and higher worker participation in the decision-making process should be achieved for the coexistence.

Sharing management information entails sharing information on the corporation's finance and overall management with the workers, labor unions or joint labor-management committees. Opening information on the management of the organization enables the workers to have their questions on the management of the organization answered.[18] Sharing management information helps workers understand the necessity of improving their performance and allow them to understand how their participation in the decision-making process could contribute to the organizational performance. Furthermore, management information helps workers find ways to enhance their performance by educating them on the meanings of their individual tasks. In this regard, sharing management information serves as the basis for the performance pay system, productive bargaining, and decision-making process with the participation from the workers (Hur and Choi, 2003b). For these reasons, details on discussions, decisions and reports have been stipulated as the tasks of joint labor-management committees in related acts[19] so that the labor and management could share management information. Information should be shared for smoother collective bargaining between the labor and management, and for increased worker participation in representative bodies, such as in joint labor-management committees and joint labor-management boards. More necessary information stipulated by law should be shared freely with the labor unions, joint labor-management committees, and the labor representatives.

Since the joint labor-management committee is the official organization where workers could participate in reforming the human resources and labor system or in improving organizational performance by launching joint labor-management boards, this should be reflected in industrial relations indicator for increased equity. For worker participation, the responses toward systemic or environmental change on the strategic level should become more flexible and participation in innovation should increase. For collective bargaining and human resources management, the level of productive bargaining as well as the participation level in innovating employment relationships and human resources management should be enhanced. In the workplace, the level of participation and autonomy in work should be improved.

For the social responsibility of the labor and management in public institutions, which is the pursuit of public interest and social values, the performance evaluation should reflect whether the labor and management have contributed to sustainable development, whether they have been considerate toward stakeholders, whether they have observed related regulations or international codes of conduct, and whether the practices within the organizations have been transparent and ethical. The evaluation should furthermore be conducted in a way to improve such values. The labor and management should pursue numerical flexibility of human resources when utilizing temporary workers but should limit the use of temporary workers in terms of specific tasks and flexibility. Even when utilizing the temporary workforce, continued effort should be put on increasing the functional flexibility of permanent workers. In addition, by managing a consortium with the labor and management of subcontractors, technology should be provided and a standard for coexistence and progress set for employees who are disadvantaged in the labor market. The labor and management in public institutions should strive to take their social responsibility by following the principle of equal pay for equal work and to resolve ongoing discrimination against the disadvantaged workers. The government should actively emphasize the social responsibility of the labor and management in public institutions and devise policies for a win-win and consortiums for coexistence and cooperation.

In short, for the industrial relations in public institutions to improve, we need trust and cooperation between the labor and management, the sharing of management information, good communication, investment in education and training and provision of fair compensation and treatment, and, most of all, the shared effort from the labor and management for improving labor and management partnership. The labor and management of public institutions should also work on establishing a productive bargaining culture and find a rational balance in the authority over human resources and management. Participation of members in the decision-making process should also be ensured for fairness. As for social responsibility, the labor and management should strive to establish peace among stakeholders and in the industry. Such key performance factors should be reflected in the labor-management indicator so that industrial relations in public institutions should contribute to social integration and social development.

2 Indicators for industrial relations in the internal performance evaluation system

This section examines how systematic the labor-management strategies of public institutions have been and how the key performance factors and key performance indicators have been managed, through the labor-management relations indicators listed in management performance reports from 2015 to 2016. I analyze the appropriateness of the key performance factors and indicators within industrial relations in public institutions, in regards to the efficiency, equity and the balance of social responsibility. Moreover, this section examines how the strategies and performance goals and performance goals and performance indicators are connected and provided basis for productive future discussions. Table 8.3 and Table 8.4 are the labor-management strategic maps of each institution, which have served as management systems for labor-management indicators.

The strategic goals in the strategic system for labor-management have set the policy directions for the industrial relations department in each public institution to meet their goals in the medium and long term. These goals reflect the policy directions for the relations in public institutions, which mostly strive to create values and to form the rational, collaborative or productive industrial relations. Strategic goals have been specified as strategies for managing industrial relations, which focus on the development and practice of reforming the relations, the establishment of the relations based on law and principles, the increase in communication between the labor and management, the rationality in bargaining culture and collective agreements, the implementation of government policies on wages and welfare, and the establishment of a labor–management relations culture which accompanies win-win growth.

However, industrial relations strategies in public institutions consisted of items which have been evaluated in PEPI. The outcome of PEPI has great influence on public institutions, which leaves public institutions with no choice but to fully incorporate the items evaluated in PEPI into the internal performance evaluation indicators. To improve the quality of industrial relations, public institutions should diagnose their external environment, internal capacity and the current state of the industrial relations within the institution and devise feasible strategies for industrial relations which would result in high performance. On the other hand, considering that the evaluated items in PEPI have great influence over the strategies and practices of public institutions, increased government effort to reflect the key performance factors of good industrial relations for public institutions in the detailed evaluation items in PEPI is needed.

The performance tasks in the indicator management systems in Table 8.3 and Table 8.4 provide detailed information on the important and prioritized indicators for implementing strategies. These tasks could be understood as the performance goals and critical success factors for each institution. The critical success factors

Table 8.3 Indicators for industrial relations by institution (market-type public corporations)

Institution	Goal Direction	Strategy	CSF	KPI
Incheon International Airport Corporation	Establishment of citizen-friendly industrial relations	Reforming industrial relations	• Reestablishing reform strategies • Practicing and promoting reform strategies	• Number of labor-management disputes
		Rational industrial relations	• Reestablishing rational industrial relations • Enhanced organizational performance through better labor-management cooperation	• growth rate in labor costs • Labor Productivity
		Increasing communication between the labor and management	• Reinforcing labor-management communication channels • Diversifying overall communication channels within organization • Activating joint labor-management committees industrial relations Reinforcing programs for better industrial relations	• Welfare satisfaction • GWP index
		Rational labor-management agreements	• Establishing bargaining strategies • Improving articles on violation of management rights and authority over human resources • Entering rational collective agreements	• Revision of collective agreements • Cancellation of sloppy-management status
Korea Gas Corporation	Reestablishing position as the citizen-centered and trusted public energy corporation	Development and implementation of strategies for reforming industrial relations	• Conducting surveys and interviews on industrial relations • Development and implementation of strategies for reforming industrial relations	• Diagnosis on industrial relations • Establishment of a strategy for labor-management reforms (both short and long terms)

Korea Airports Corporation	Attaining management goals through creative industrial relations	Establishment of a new, fair and responsible labor-management culture	• Labor and management agreement on improving sloppy management • Welfare programs held jointly by the labor and management • Joint labor-management CSR activities	• Running a time-off program • Number of days of labor-management disputes • Joint labor-management CSR activities (mileage)
		Labor-management communication and enhancing personnel management capacity	• Establishment of labor-management communication • Education for enhancing personnel management capacity	• Satisfaction of industrial relations • Rate of labor-management communication • Number of workers who complete personnel management education programs
		Rational collective agreements	• Adding additional rules to collective agreements • Signing pay settlement in 2014 • Implementing reformed human resources and personnel management system	• Reforming collective agreements • Signing pay settlement
		Reforming worker's welfare system	• Continuous improvement of sloppy management • Efforts to create a good workplace • Improving the positions of vulnerable workers	• GWP satisfaction rates • Welfare satisfaction
		Forming a communicative and trusting labor-management culture	• Expansion of two-sides communication channels • Taking lead in practicing social responsibility • Conducting joint research for organizational harmony	• Satisfaction of labor-management communication • complaint settlement rates

(Continued)

Table 8.3 (Continued)

Institution	Goal Direction	Strategy	CSF	KPI
		Industrial relations based on law and principles	• Active implementation of government policies • Improving unreasonable labor-management practices • Reinforcing programs for better labor-management relations	• Labor-management mutual trust • Period for no labor-management dispute
		A leading institution in implementing government policies	• Wage increase in accordance with government guidelines • Establishment of a rational wage system • Implementation of the performance pay system	• Labor productivity by person • Wage growth rate
Korea Expressway Corporation	Industrial relations Creative industrial relations through communication and coexistence	Developing and implementing strategies for reforming industrial relations	• Re-planning reform strategies • Performance analysis and enhancing execution	• Labor-management mutual trust • Reforming industrial relations
		Performance based on coexistence and responsibility	• Establishment and management of rational industrial relations • Executing joint labor-management goals • Labor-management cooperation to prevent conflicts	• Level of satisfaction for joint programs • Execution of social responsibility • Enhancement in the level of labor-management cooperation
		Joint advancement of the labor and management through communication	• Running of various communication channels between the labor and management • Reinforcing programs for better labor-management relations	• Level of satisfaction on communication channels • Improvement in communication and management capabilities
		Realizing rational industrial relations	• Revising unreasonable articles in collective agreements • Conclusion of rational wage agreements and collective agreements	• Running time-off program • Wage growth rate • Rationalization of collective agreements

Company	Strategy	Implementation	Indicators
Korea National Oil Corporation	Crating a rational labor-management culture based on communication and cooperation	Strategic labor-management relations • Systemization of labor-management relations strategies • Checking progress in implementing strategies and strengthening feedback	• Rates of labor-management disputes • Effectiveness of strategies
		Cooperative labor-management relations • Activation of labor-management cooperation programs • Preventing conflicts and disputes	• Labor-management cooperation rates • Joint management accomplishments • Communication rates between the labor and management
		Communication • Realizing a communicative corporate culture • Reinforcing programs for better labor-management relations	• Enhanced communication and personnel management capability
		Rational collective agreements • Conclusion of rational collective agreements • Conclusion of rational wage agreements	• Wage growth rate • Rationality of collective agreements
Korea Water Resources Corporation	Future-oriented industrial relations with fairness	Strategies for industrial relations • Improving industrial relations and establishing strategies for reaching management goals • Complementing strategies for implementing government policies • Implementation of strategies for labor-management reform	Level of satisfaction on industrial relations
		Establishment of rational and legitimate industrial relations • Labor and management culture based on law and principles • Establishment of industrial relations which protect the vulnerable groups and are considerate and understanding • Increased cooperation for attaining goals	Participation rates for social responsibility activities

(Continued)

Table 8.3 (Continued)

Institution	Goal Direction	Strategy	CSF	KPI
		Improving capability and communication between the labor and management	• Encouraging communication among all workers • Increasing participation in management from the labor by running various channels for better understanding between the labor and management • Systematic management of labor-management capacity building programs	Improvement in sloppy management
		Preventing violation of management rights and authority over human resources	• More outreach programs for the rational revision of collective agreements • Establishing the institution's management rights and authority over human resources • Preparation for revising collective agreements as a leading public corporation	Development of human resources
		Rational reform of collective agreements	• Revision of collective agreements to resolve sloppy management • Strengthening consensus between the labor and management • Wages and welfare systems that reflect the public opinion	Wage growth rate

Korea Electric Power Corporation	Establishment of value-creating industrial relations based on coexistence and responsibility	Development of strategies for industrial relations reform Establishment of cooperative industrial relations Activated communication between the labor and management Conclusion of rational collective agreements	• Responses to environmental changes • Performance analysis of strategic tasks and improving implementation • Improving management accomplishments and sloppy management • Joint effort from the labor and management to create good workplaces • Activation of various communication channels • Preventing labor-management conflicts and improving organizational culture • Revising unreasonable articles in collective agreements • Establishing reformed and performance-centered wages system	• Labor productivity • Labor-management disputes • Reforming industrial relations • Resolving sloppy management • Employee satisfaction • Enhanced cooperation • Briefings on management status • Labor and management volunteer work • Communication and management capacity • Running a time-off program • Wage growth rate • Rationalization of collective agreements
Korea District Heating Corporation	Establishment of a management system with a mid- to long-term outlook	Establishment of appropriate industrial relations Activating labor-management cooperation	• Collective agreement based on law and principles • Realization of productive and efficient industrial relations • Establishment of rational and legitimate industrial relations • Forming consensus and preventing conflict • Analysis of stakeholders • Reaching common goal of labor-management cooperation • Management of systematic communication channels • Improving management and cost reduction	• Degree of labor-management cooperation and concessions • Number of labor-management disputes • Advancement of industrial relations • Diagnosis of industrial relations • Establishment of the labor-management cooperation system

(Continued)

Table 8.3 (Continued)

Institution	Goal Direction	Strategy	CSF	KPI
Korea Railroad Corporation	Establishment of peaceful and rational industrial relations for the coexistence of labor and management	Reform strategies for industrial relations	• Reestablishment of short-term strategies for industrial relations • Establishment of a mid- to long-term masterplan for industrial relations • Normalization of industrial relations through implementation of strategic tasks	Labor-management coexistence index
		Rational labor-management relations and labor-management cooperation	• Establishing model for rational industrial relations • Labor-management cooperation: for conflict management and coexistence • Cooperative activities for reaching common targets	Joint labor-management programs
		Activated communication and enhancing capacities	• Institution-wide communication to resolve sloppy management • Two-ways communication to restore trust • Reinforcing customized programs for better industrial relations	Education programs for personnel management capacities
		Strengthening management and human resources right and the conclusion of wages and collective agreements	• Conclusion of rational collective agreements • Preparing improvement plans for collective agreements • Conclusion of wages and collective agreements which observe government guidelines	Improvement tasks for sloppy management

| Korea Land and Housing Corporation | Creating a win-win labor-management culture and normalizing the management to reflect the public opinion | Leading implementation of normalization plans for management | • Implementation of improvement tasks for sloppy management
• Number of years with no disputes
• Setting Time Off limits and observing wage increase rates
• Revising irrational articles in collective agreements |
| | | Creating a win-win labor-management partnership
Realizing a communicative and understanding labor-management culture
Realizing rational industrial relations | •
• Efforts for establishing personnel management network
• Activating joint labor-management programs
• Increased support for increased communication among workers
• Efforts for effective collective bargaining |

listed in Table 8.3 and Table 8.4 included the re-planning of reforming strategies and improving the power of execution, labor-management cooperation for conflict management and coexistence, implementation of the performance pay system, enhancing field-oriented communication, strengthening labor-management capacity, finding and improving articles on violation of management rights and authority over human resources in collective agreements, implementation of government policies, including the salary peak system and the performance pay system, working on creating good workplaces, and practicing joint labor-management social responsibility. Most institutions have endeavored to present critical success factors in accordance with the strategies. However, little connection could be found between the critical success factor of enhancing the industrial relations management capacity and the strategy of enhancing communication, both of which are presented in Table 8.3. More effort from public institutions is necessary to confirm the causation and systemize the prioritized factors for implementing the strategies. On the other hand, the performance tasks in Table 8.3 reflect the institutions' efforts to pursue effectiveness and equity in management by improving labor-management partnership and communication. The Korea Airports Corporation's task to take lead in practicing social responsibility and the Korea Gas Corporation's task of having joint labor-management CSR activities are examples of institutions using social responsibility as a critical success factor. These cases, however, are instances of public institutions using the content presented as points for considerations in the manual for PEPI as a critical success factor, rather than aiming to develop industrial relations by balancing efficiency, equity and social responsibility. This is an obvious result, as institution's strategy for industrial relations is fully based on the points for consideration in the PEPI manual. Considering that the purpose of performance evaluations is to have public institutions faithfully carry out their given tasks and continue to produce outcome, more emphasis should be put on devising customized labor-management strategies and performance tasks which could improve the management quality of each public institution and produce continuous outcome. For instance, if reinforcing labor-management partnership has been set as one strategy, the institution should examine the various factors on labor-management partnership and try to find the factors that are imminent and most important for improving the institution's labor-management partnership. Sharing more management information to build labor and management trust could be an important factor for some institutions, depending on the level of the public institution's industrial relations, while the active participation of the labor union or the workers' in the decision-making process for creating outcome could be important for other institutions.

Performance indicators for public institutions presented in Table 8.3 and Table 8.4 are key indicators for measuring how well the institutions have accomplished their performance tasks during the evaluated year. Public institutions should work on producing representative and appropriate performance indicators to accomplish the critical success factors. Jeju Free International Development Center's performance task of strengthening field-center communication and its indicator, field communication rates, and the Korea Hydro & Nuclear Power Co.,

Ltd.'s performance task of strengthening labor and management relationship as management partners and the indicator, labor unions' trust in the management, found in Table 8.4, are appropriate to check whether the institutions have succeeded in reaching their critical success factors as well as performance tasks. However, the Korea Electric Power Corporation's performance indicator of holding briefings on management status to measure the activation of various performance channels would be only a part of the numerous communication channels which exist among the labor and management stakeholders or members within the institution, and lacks representation as a performance indicator. The Korea Marine Environment Management Corporation's use of flextime usage as a performance indicator for sharing information on management status is also weakly connected to the performance task. In addition, public institutions should also attempt to improve equity by sharing management information and guaranteeing their members with opportunities for participation. To measure these tasks, institutions may use the number of joint labor-management committees, the ratio of labor and management representatives who were present, the satisfaction toward the management of joint labor-management committees, the level of management and satisfaction of the labor and management board meetings on personnel and labor systems, proposed items by person, and the ratio of items adopted compared to items proposed.

To measure the success factor of social responsibility, the Korea Expressway Corporation measures the rate of executing social responsibility, the Korea Gas Corporation the mileages of joint labor-management CSR activities, the Jeju Free International City Development Center the volunteer hours per member, and the Korea Coal Corporation the social responsibility activities, according to Table 8.3 and Table 8.4. However, the performance evaluation reports shows that the social responsibility of the labor and management are mostly limited to volunteer work in the local community or social responsibility activities. Besides, the labor and management in public institutions should also keep in mind that they have the social responsibility to create decent jobs, by putting effort to improve employment stabilities of temporary workers, to alleviate discrimination against indirectly employed workers and develop their capacity, and to prevent industrial accidents in the workplaces of stakeholders, such as subcontractors and actively take such responsibilities. Performance indicators for such responsibilities would include the percentage of temporary workers converted to permanent workers or attainment of the target for the conversion rate, the per capita wage of temporary workers in comparison with permanent workers, elimination of discrimination against temporary workers or workers from subcontractors or their participation rates in education and trainings, and the violations of the national industrial relations act. Other indicators which could be used to measure the relations within public institutions include labor productivity by worker, the decline rate of claims per worker, the employee turnover rate, the average absence rate per month, annual number of quality/service improvements, number of industrial accidents per year, number of collective bargaining or the duration of each bargaining, the implementation level of labor-management agreements, the number of labor-management

Table 8.4 Indicators for industrial relations by institution (quasi-market-type public corporations)

Institution	Goal Direction	Strategy	CSF	KPI
Korea Coal Corporation	Industrial relations with high competitiveness that leads change	Rational development and implementation of reforming strategies for industrial relations	• Reestablishment of mid- to long-term reform strategies for industrial relations • Implementation of reforming strategies for industrial relations	• Reestablishment of strategies • Satisfaction of industrial relations
		Establishment of legitimate industrial relations and realization of labor-management cooperation	• Establishing institution-wide rational industrial relations system • Expanding social responsibility of the labor and management	• Industrial relations index of institution • Improving relationship with subcontractors • Social responsibility activities
		Active communication and strengthening industrial relations capacity	• Improving strategic communication system • Improving industrial relations capacity	• Communication rates • Number of participants in labor education • Training hours of workers in charge of industrial relations
		Rational conclusion and revision of collective agreements	• Wage system for both labor and management • Implementation of the salary peak system • Rational improvement of collective agreements	• Wage increase guideline • Implementation of the salary peak system • Rational collective agreements
Incheon Port Authority	Realization of a meritocratic organizational culture through labor and management cooperation	Establishment of participatory labor-management strategies and improvement in the power of execution	• Improving labor-management strategies by gathering more opinion from members • Promoting labor-management strategies and improving the power of execution	• Degree of strategies accomplishment • Reforming strategic system with reformed industrial relations

Organization	Strategic direction	Initiatives	Performance indicators
	Joint performance by labor and management through cooperation	• Joint effort from labor and management to introduce the salary peak system early • Improving the rate of acceptance of workers on the performance pay system • Creating a happy workplace by spreading the coexistence of work and life balance	• Labor productivity • Reaching joint labor-management goals/ effort for improving cooperation
	Realization of industrial relations based on trust and communication	• Reinforcing complaint settlement system for resolving conflict • Forming consensus for two-way communication channels between labor and management • Strengthening labor-management by holding professional education programs	• Labor-management trust index • Strengthening communication channels and personnel management capacity for improving labor and management trust
	Industrial relations based on law and principles	• Conclusion of collective agreements without disputes • Running legitimate and fruitful joint labor-management committees	• Satisfaction of industrial relations • Conclusion of rational collective agreements through productive bargaining
Jeju Free International City Development Center	Establishment of value-creating labor-management culture through labor-management partnership		
	Leading implementation of government policies	• Implementation of government-recommended policies (implementation of the salary peak system, performance pay for lower level workers) • Rational revision of collective agreements • Reestablishing labor-management strategies	• Change rate of welfare expense per worker • Wage increase • Implementation of government policies • Conclusion of rational collective agreements • Rolling of labor-management strategies in accordance with environmental change

(Continued)

Table 8.4 (Continued)

Institution	Goal Direction	Strategy	CSF	KPI
		Strengthening capacity of industrial relations management	• Strengthening labor-management cooperation • Running field-based labor education programs • Autonomous negotiations without conflicts	• Rates of labor-management cooperation • Rates of labor and management trust • Satisfaction of labor-management education programs • Development effort for JDC-type labor education programs • Effort to prevent labor-management conflicts
		Activating two-way communication	• Strengthening field-centered communication • Running labor-management cooperative programs	• Labor-management communication index • Field communication rates • Activation of joint labor-management programs
		Spreading cooperative, sharing and understanding labor-management culture	• Leading labor-management culture in the Jeju area • Realizing the joint social responsibility of the labor and management	• Hours of volunteer work of labor union members by person • Certificate for company with great labor-management culture
Korea East-West Power Company	Creating stable and productive industrial relations through trust and cooperation	Practicing happy management and labor-management culture	• Leading practices of productive labor-management culture • Establishment of labor-management models for practicing social responsibility	• GWP rates • Satisfaction of human resources policies • Labor-management cooperation rates • Satisfaction of social contribution
		Strengthening labor partnership for higher productivity	• Running joint labor-management organization for improving productivity • Leading implementation of government employment and labor policies	• Improvements made in wages and collective agreements • Difference in gross annual salary • Degree of government policy implementation • Efforts to shorten working hours

Organization	Vision	Strategy	Action	Indicators
Korea Racing Authority	Establishment of future-oriented industrial relations through discourse, trust and toward coexistence	Establishing community with accompanied growth for the labor and managements	• Enhancing personnel management system for strategy implementation • Enhancing capacity development system by class • Creative implementation of joint labor-management programs	• Efforts in enhancing strategic systems • Number of complaints • Satisfaction of welfare and education • Satisfaction of flextime • Implementation of government guidelines
		Realizing of rational bargaining culture	• Signing of rational collective agreements • Establishing bargaining culture with emphasis on principles and efficiency • Application of labor union laws based on law and principles	• Number of burdening laboring practices • Efforts to improve efficiency in collective bargaining
		Establishing a win-win labor-management partnership	• Establishing a labor-management culture which creates outcome • Activating joint labor-management programs • Reinforcing joint labor-management social contributions	• Labor productivity • Awareness of social contribution • Outcome created jointly by the labor and management
		Establishing a mutually trusting organizational culture	• Establishing communicative organizational culture • Encouraging organizational commitment of temporary workers • Establishing a program for balancing work and family	• Satisfaction of industrial relations • Satisfaction of family-friendly P/G • Improving treatment of temporary workers
		Strengthening company-wide labor-management capacity	• Systematic education programs for labor-management capacity • Improving field-oriented industrial relations management capacity • Strengthening relations with related institutions	• Satisfaction of education • Reinforcing personnel management capacity

(Continued)

Table 8.4 (Continued)

Institution	Goal Direction	Strategy	CSF	KPI
Korea Hydro and Nuclear Power Co., Ltd.	Creating a future for the labor and management through respect and harmony	Organizational capacity	• Launching and reinforcing labor-related organizations • Developing organization management capacity of managers • Developing organizational management manual for managers	• Industrial relations index • Labor productivity index • Application of education in field work
		Respect toward workers	• Time Rich movement by all workers • Boosting morale of managers • Reinforcing alternative welfare	• Labor unions' trust in the management • Reforms in collective agreements • Implementation of the salary peak system
		Labor-management communication	• Regularly hosting the K-HNP Festival • Holding joint labor-management workshops • Running the special committee for industrial relations	• Communication and conversation indexes • Social responsibility practices by the labor and management • Reestablishment of reforming strategies
		Human resources capacity	• Strengthening labor education programs, such as programs for certifications for labor attorneys • Expanding the manpower pool for labor experts • Implementation of policies for recovering labor-management leadership	• Labor-management relations index • Labor productivity index • Application of education in field work

Organization	Goal	Sub-strategy	Action items	Indicators
Korea Marine Environment Management Corporation	Establishing creative industrial relations through coexistence and cooperation	Labor-management respect	• Strengthening labor and management relationship as management partners • Enhancing transparency of personnel management system • Establishing a comprehensive system for complaint settlement	• Labor unions' trust in the management • Reforms in collective agreements • Implementation of the salary peak system
		Strategic communication	• Increased exchanges between departments/ occupational groups/ generations • Activating MVs on the department level • Securing and dividing company-wide communication budget	• Communication and conversation indexes • Social responsibility practices by the labor and management • Reestablishment of reforming strategies
		Considerate industrial relations	• Establishing a labor-management culture of trust • Establishing a culture of work and life balance	• Satisfaction of labor-management relations • Implementation of family-friendly policies • Use of Flextime
		Growing industrial relations	• Sharing information on management status • Reinforcing programs for better industrial relations	• Reestablishment of labor-management and mid- to long-term strategies • Number of workers who received labor-management education
		Communicating industrial relations	• Implementation of employee-centered communication channels • Implementation of worker organizations-centered communication channels	• Forming a labor-management cooperative system on pending issues
		Harmonious industrial relations	• Establishing basis for collective bargaining • Establishing rational culture for labor union activities	• Wage growth rate • Conclusion of legitimate collective agreements

communication channels and their communication index, number of complaints raised and settlement of the complaints by person, number of labor-management education sessions and satisfaction rates, the GWP index, and the satisfaction of industrial safety and health.

IV Lessons learned and conclusion

This study examines the directions of managing industrial relations in public institutions and the critical success factors (CSF) and key performance indicators (KPI). Through an analysis of the current indicators used in the PEPI and internal performance evaluation systems, this paper aims to improve strategic performance of industrial relations in public institutions. The findings of this study could be summarized as follows.

First, the labor and management in public institutions should improve labor-management partnership based on the values of efficiency, equity and the balance of social responsibility and enhance the quality of public services. The labor and management in public institutions should take joint responsibility and work together to establish industrial relations which could create sustainable values that contribute to social integration and development.

Second, for the improvement of industrial relations in public institutions, the following factors are necessary: trust and cooperation between the labor and management, sharing of management information, active communication, investment in education and training, fair compensation and treatment, guarantee of worker participation, and the establishment of a productive bargaining culture.

Third, effort from the labor and management to take joint social responsibility, which is one of the critical success factors of industrial relations in public institutions, should be reinforced. The labor and management in public institutions should share the social responsibility and actively take interest and practice creating jobs, and contributing to the society. Labor unions in public institutions should acknowledge their social responsibility for decent work in the entire society as well as realizing social and economic justice, and should serve as leaders in forming desirable work practices and employment order.

Fourth, the labor-management indicators in the PEPI system should be comprehensive in measuring the rationality of industrial relations, and should be improved to enhance management efficiency in public institutions and to contribute to improving public services. Critical success factors, such as the level of sharing management information, worker participation and joint social responsibility of the labor and management, should be incorporated into the indicators. The effectiveness of joint labor-management committees, in particular, should be incorporated as essential items for detailed evaluation regardless of the existence of labor unions in the institutions. Joint labor-management committees should become occasions through which labor unions or representatives of workers share information, and as the official organization for worker participation so as to improve organizational performance.

Fifth, for more effective performance management of internal industrial relations, public institutions should develop customized labor-management strategies linked to organizational performance. Moreover, increased effort should be put on devising representative and appropriate performance indicators, which should be evaluated first in order to execute the strategies. Social responsibility of the labor and management in public institutions should be composed of and managed through more comprehensive and systematic performance indicators which reflect the public interest and social values. For the stable implementation of the internal performance evaluation system in public institutions, active participation from the members and the institution's effort to improve the objectivity and fairness of the internal evaluation system are both necessary.

Finally, the government should assume the responsibility and role as a mediator so that the stakeholders of industrial relations in public institutions could pursue efficient management as well as the normative value of enhancing the quality of work and life.

The critical success factors for industrial relations in public institutions or performance indicators presented in this study would hopefully be of help to workers in each public institution and serve as a starting point for future discussions on strategic performance evaluation of industrial relations in public institutions.

Notes

1 Kaplan and Norton state that since public institutions and nongovernmental organizations is to accomplish their goal of establishment, the accomplishment can be incorporated into the balanced scorecard. Unlike private enterprises, the goal of public institutions in practice is to pursue public interest and accomplishments, and the BSC might be modified for application. For instance, the financial perspective is changed into performance perspective, the customer perspective to external customer and internal customer perspective, the internal business processes as process innovation perspective or activity perspective, and the learning and growth perspective to future perspective. Kaplan and Norton also emphasize that the strategic map, the balanced scorecard, and the establishment, implementation, monitoring, and feedback process should be closely connected (Kaplan et al., 1996; Kaplan and Norton, 2003).

2 Strategic goals are policy priorities which are implemented medium- and long-term, for at least three to five years, in order to accomplish the goals and values of a certain project. Performance goals are sub-concepts of strategic goals and are specific goals for the major programs. Performance goals are more specific than strategic goals and are derived from analyses of tasks or examinations of projects. Performance indicators are tools used to measure whether the performance goals have been accomplished.

3 Whereas equity is related to distributive justice, of maintaining the conditions for a humane life and focuses on the outcome, the right to speak – the voice – is concerned with procedural justice, which finds it just to participate in the decision-making process. This paper used the term equity in the broad sense, which encompasses the right to speak.

4 Dunlop's theory on Industrial Relations System and Kochan, Katz and Mackersie's Three-tier Strategic Choices Model provide frameworks for a systematic analysis of the components of industrial relations and their factors through the Logic Model perspective of input, process and output. These theories also serve as an important theoretical and practical basis for explaining micro level industrial relations including

labor-management partnership and high-performance work organization system, etc. (Dunlop, 1993; Kochan et al., 1994).

5 Unlike traditional organizations which aim to attain organizational efficiency through management control and the compliance of organizational members, high-performance work organizations induce organizational members to commit voluntarily and to actively participate in decision-making and in increasing organizational efficiency, in order to improve the performance of the organization. Kim (2001) emphasizes the importance of cooperative labor-management partnership as a factor which could solve all problems concerning job stability in the process of managing a high-performance work organization (Kim, 2001). Lee (2004) suggests alternative work methods, high immersion human resources management skills and labor-management partnership as key factors of a high-performance work organization. Kim et al. (2008) points out that labor-management cooperation, trust, open book management, educational training and motivation are some of the common factors found in high-performance work organizations and identified labor-management cooperation and trust factors to be the basis of all these factors.

6 The Involvement and Participation Association (IPA) of the United Kingdom, stats that three commitments – joint effort for the success of the enterprise, building trust and greater employee involvement, and recognizing the legitimate role of the partners – should be kept in order to build a labor-management partnership (IPA, 1992).

7 Worker participation concerns the participation and influence of workers or the labor union in all decision-making processes for corporate management. The level of participation of workers based on KKM's strategic choice model could be classified as follows: strategic level of participation as a form of participation of workers or their representatives on long-term policies or decision-making process, functional level of participation as a form of participation through group negotiations or various committees, and the workplace level of participation as the form of participation in everyday activities and the decision-making process which affects the working environment. To increase participation of workers, a participatory working system should be established and managed. Furthermore, worker capacity should be developed systematically and continuously. Finally, effort should be made to strengthen the position and professional capacity of human resources departments within the organizations (Hur. and Choi, 2003a).

8 Reactive problem solving is a stage where the labor and management find the cause and solution together when a problem should arise in the management of the existing system or in the operation of a new system. Anticipatory problem solving occurs when the labor and management participate in the planning stage of a new system or the redesigning of an existing system. The joint future creation is the highest level where the labor and management co-establish strategies to create an ideal future and work together to achieve the goals (Kim et al., 2012).

9 ISO 26000 is an international guideline on social responsibility (SR) set by the International Organization for Standardization, which presented seven core subjects for social responsibility – organizational governance, human rights, labor practices, consumer issues, environment, fair operating practices and community involvement and development – as well as seven key principles consisting of accountability, transparency, ethical behavior, respect for stakeholder interest, respect for the rule of law, respect for international norms of behavior, and respect for human rights (ISO, 2010).

10 Trust between the labor and management is an indicator for how both parties share the objectives and information on the organization and of the stakeholders' behavior and attitude. Labor-management cooperation measures the level of cooperation and each party's willingness to concede for solving a problem. The indicator for the trust dimension includes the level of awareness for the shared objective, the level of mutual recognition of each other as labor-management partners, the level of information sharing between the management and the leaders of the union, the union's rational attitude

towards the management, and the stakeholders' effort to reach a decision in collective bargaining or labor-management councils. For the cooperative dimension, the union's level of understanding of the management, the two parties' level of cooperation, the union's attitude to concede could be used. For participation, the process and method of problem-solving and the availability of communication channels and their levels were considered important. The level of concerted effort for problem-solving, the level of how the union's opinions on environmental change was reflected, the utilization level of grievance procedures and the number of settlements, the average time for settling complaints and the level of satisfaction, the number of labor-management communication channels and its effects, the number of upward communication channels and its effects, the number of joint labor-management conferences and number of passed resolutions, the satisfaction level of the joint labor-management conferences, and the participation rate of the top management team, union representative, and labor representative in the joint conferences could be used as measurement indicators.

11 Indicators for employment is as follows: the creation of new jobs and the rate of employee turnover, the difference in the benefits provided to permanent workers and temporary workers, and the usage of leaves due to family events; indicators for labor-management relations include the labor union and the representative of the workers' participation in the decision-making process and the minimal notification period of changes in important issues such as in processes and restructuring; indicators for industrial safety and health include the ratio of workers managed by industrial safety and health committee, the number of industrial accidents, the number of serious disasters, and the number of absentees; indicators for training and education includes the average hours of education per person by year by type of employment, improvement in employment stability, number or ratio of programs for career development; indicators for diversity and equal opportunities include the establishment of a governance organization for gender, age, minority and diversity; indicators for equal rights for men and women include wage difference by gender, and the ratio of women in management; an indicator for labor practices of suppliers is the ratio of suppliers which follow the labor standards; indicators for complaint settlement include the number of resolved cases compared to the number of cases raised and by the reoccurrence of the nuisances which had been resolved.

12 Indicators for anti-discrimination are concerned with how much employers respect rights for women, the disabled, children and immigrants, regardless of their positions or employment status within the organization; indicators for labor rights are involved with whether the employees have been guaranteed with the rights to organize and have collective bargaining and whether forced labor and child labor has been prohibited were measured; indicators for employment stability and employment relations are related to how the management maintained its responsibility as the employer, as well as the management's effort to avoid using temporary workers and to improve job security, the level of information provided and discussions held on the issues which would likely affect employment, the effort to prohibit arbitrary and discriminatory layoffs, and the maintenance of a win-win employment practice with suppliers and subcontractors; indicators for working conditions and social protection includes the observance of the national industrial relations act or international working standards on wages, working hours and leaves, balance in work and life, the guarantee of living wages, discrimination against workers or layoffs, the management's actions such as reshuffling or outsourcing, which hinder employment stability, the degree of appropriate information available on the management status of the organization and the willingness or effort to take part in social discourse; indicators for industrial safety and health includes the effort to maintain a safe and healthy workplace, effort to analyze and control safety and health hazards, the establishment and management level of a safety and health management system, the participation level of workers in industrial safety and health management, provision of industrial safety and health education, and the effort to manage workplace stress; indicators for the

training and development of human resources includes the equal opportunities for education, effort and implementation for reconciling work and family and the availability of programs against discrimination or on social protection.

13 Bang et al. (2007) present eight categories for measuring the quality of employment in Korea, based on the ILO's People's Security Surveys (PSS), GRI's G3 guidelines, and the ISO 26000 indicators which consist of employment conditions, wages and welfare, training and education, health and safety, equal opportunities in employment, and a fair system for settling disputes and human rights. In the category for job security, Bang et al. (2007). suggest that not only the ratio of temporary workers but also the ratio of indirectly employed workers should be included as a part of the indicator. For industrial safety and health, the study adds whether a joint labor-management committee are held and its accomplishments, the effectiveness of collective bargaining in a fair system for settling disputes and the operation of a labor and management committee and its accomplishments. For human rights, this study considered the number of human rights related trainees and their level of satisfaction.

14 The collective agreements analysis table is created to check whether there have been any irrational labor practices in the collective agreement documents, labor and management agreements and employment regulations. The table is composed of indicators related to the range of application for labor unions, union activities during working hours, the appropriateness of full-time union workers, fairness in appointing union managers, management of labor union management and assistance provided for the union, details on the authority over human resources and management rights, and appropriate level of protection for working conditions and job action.

15 The sloppy management checklist consists of 55 items on eight representative factors of reckless managing such as severance pay, educational costs, childcare expenditure, souvenir expenses, and personal leaves, employment of bereaved families, management rights and authority over human resources.

16 New indicators for preventing labor-management conflict are added but without specific criteria on the evaluation, which might leave the evaluation committee and public institutions in confusion.

17 The points for consideration, such as institution's effort to revise unreasonable collective agreement that could violate management rights and the authority over human resources, remain unchanged and lack details on what exactly would be evaluated.

18 This is also called open-door management or transparent management.

19 Article 20 of the law on worker participation and cooperation stipulates that the labor and management should agree on improving productivity, the performance pay system, hiring, appointing and training workers, improving human resources and personnel management systems, improving the welfare of workers and providing support for balancing work and family life. Article 21 states that issues such as basic planning for employee training and development, installation and management of welfare facilities, launch of internal labor welfare funds, items which have not been passed through the committee for complaint settlement, as well as installing joint labor-management boards should be discussed in joint labor-management committees. Article 22 states that overall management plans and performances, production plans and performance by quarter, and the economic and financial status of corporations should be reported to the joint labor-management committee each quarter.

References

Bang, H. N. et al. (2007). *Employment Quality: Development and Evaluation of Indicators on the Macro, Enterprise and Individual Level*. Korea Labor Institute, 104–105.

Budd, J. W. (2004). *Employment with a Human Face: Balancing Efficiency, Equity, and Voice*. Ithaca, NY and London: Cornell University Press.

Caroll, A. B. (1991). The Pyramid of Corporate Social Responsibility: Toward the Moral Management of Organizational Stakeholders. *Business Horizons*, 39–48.

Choi, D. S. (2016). The Labor Relations and Performance Management in Public Institutions. *Journal of Social Security Law*, *30*, 135–167.

Cooke, W. N. (1985). Toward a General Theory of Industrial Relations. In *Advances in Industrial and Labor Relations* (Vol. 2, 233–252). Greenwich, CT: JAI Press.

Coupar, W., and Stevens, B. (1998). Towards a New Model of Industrial Partnership. In *Human Resource Management: The New Agenda* (145–159). London: Financial Times and Prentice-Hall.

Deery, S., and Iverson, R. (2005). Labor-Management Cooperation: Antecedents and Impact on Organizational Performance. *Industrial and Labor Relations Review*, *58*(4), 588–600.

Dunlop, J. T. (1993). *Industrial Relations Systems* (2nd ed.). Boston, MA: Harvard Business School Press.

Eaton, A. E., and Voos, P. B. (1992). Unionism and Contemporary Innovations in Work Organization, Compensation, and Employee Participation. In *Unions and Economic Competitiveness*. Washington, DC: Economic Policy Institute.

GRI. (2013). Reporting Principles and Standard Disclosures. *G4 Sustainability Reporting Guidelines*, 64–69.

Hur, C. Y., and Choi, D. S. (2003a). *Comprehensive Manual for Labor Management Partnership*. Ministry of Labor.

Hur, C. Y., and Choi, D. S. (2003b). *Improvement in Financial Support for Labor Management Cooperation Programs and the Development of Effect Measurement Tool*. Korea Labor Education Institute.

Hur, C. Y., and Choi, J. I. (2017). *Improving the Wages System in Public Institutions*. Research Paper. Korea Institute of Public Finance.

IPA. (1992). *Towards Industrial Partnership*. The Involvement and Participation Association of the United Kingdom.

ISO. (2010). *Guidance on Social Responsibility (ISO 26000)*. Geneva: ISO.

Jung, T. G. et al. (2013). *Social Responsibility in ISO 26000: Practice the Global Standard*. Hanul, 106–112.

Kaplan, R. S., and Norton, D. P. (1996). *The Balanced Scorecard*. Boston, MA: Harvard Business School Press.

Kaplan, R. S., and Norton, D. P. (2003). *Strategy Maps*. Boston, MA: Harvard Business School Press.

Kim, D. B. et al. (2004). *Agenda for Employment Flexibility and Human Resource Management*. Korea Labor Institute, 214–215.

Kim, D. O. et al. (2008). *Industrial Relations DNA of Top-Ranking Corporations in Korea*. Pakyoungsa, 19–20.

Kim, D. O. et al. (2012). *Comparative Study of Industrial Relations in Korea and OECD Member Countries*. Pakyoungsa, 71.

Kim, Y. G. (2011). *Union Social Responsibility (USR) and Organizational Performance*. Doctoral Dissertation, Seoul School of Integrated Sciences & Technologies, 35–37.

Kim, Y. J. (2001). Perceived Fairness of Layoffs, Severity, and the Survivors' Attitudes. *Journal of Human Resource Management*, *9*(2), 12–14.

Kochan, T. A., and Dyer, L. (1976). A Model of Organizational Change in the Context of Union-Management Relations. *The Journal of Applied Behavioral Science*, *XII*, Spring.

Kochan, T. A., Katz, H. C., and McKersie, R. B. (1994). *The Transformation of American Industrial Relations*. Ithaca, NY: ILR Press.

Kochan, T. A., and Osterman, P. (1994). *The Mutual Gains Enterprise: Forging a Winning Partnership Among Labor, Management, and Government.* Boston, MA: Harvard Business School Press.

Lee, B. H. et al. (2008). *Manual for Industrial Relations Assessment for Participation and Innovation.* Korea Labor Institute.

Lee, H. S. et al. (2013). Research on the Reform of Evaluation Standards for the New Government. *Economics, Humanities and Social Research Council,* 45–50.

Lee, J. M. (2004). *Effective Strategies for Developing High Performance Workplaces.* Academic Report for the Ministry of Labor.

Lee, M. H. (2011). *Analysis on Human Resource Management in Public Institutions in Regards to Industrial Relations,* Research Paper, Korea Institute of Public Administration.

Lee, S. H. (2010). *Rational Coordinating Strategies for Management Rights and Bargaining Rights in the Public-Sector Collective Bargaining System.* Korea Labor Institute, 118–123.

Lee, Y. M. (2009). *Evaluation on the Labor Management Partnership Support Program and Policy Directions.* Korea Labor Institute, 190–191.

Lim, M. S. (2012). *The Impact of Social Responsibility Activities of Corporations and Unions on Workers' Job Satisfaction: The Mediating Effect of Cooperative Labor-Management Relations.* Doctoral Dissertation, Donga University, 25–42.

Ministry of Strategy and Finance. *Handbook on the Performance Evaluation of Public Institutions and the Manual for Quantitative Evaluation (2008–2016).*

Ministry of Strategy and Finance. *Performance Evaluation Reports and Handbooks on Internal Evaluations from Public Corporations (2015–2016).*

Park, G. P. (2015). *A Study of Character Changes of the Korean Labor Policy.* Doctoral Dissertation, Gangwon University, 265–267.

Park, S. A., and Kim, J. K. et al. (2014). *Reforms in Public Institutions.* Pakyoungsa.

Ra, Y. J., and Yoon, T. B. (2010). *Accomplishments and Limitations to the Sustainable Management of Public Institutions.* Korea Institute of Public Finance.

Rho, H. G. (2011). *Social Responsibility Through ISO 26000: Understanding and Practicing the New International Standard.* Pakyoungsa.

Walton, R. E., and McKersie, R. B. (1965). *A Behavioral T of Labor Negotiations.* New York, NY: McGraw-Hill.

Part III
Performance measurement and indicators

9 Target-setting in performance evaluation and public institutions' incentives

Youn Sik Choi

I Introduction

Public institutions are established in accordance with the law. Public institutions use tax as its source of revenue and perform its own functions assigned by law. Public institutions generally serve the public by complementing the market, accomplishing policy goals and realizing public interest. But at the same time, public institutions are entrepreneurial in that they are enterprises which aim to realize public missions in an efficient manner (Korean Society of Public Enterprise, 2003). Since the inefficient management of public institutions could become a burden on the national economy, systematic and efficient management of such institutions is pivotal. The government has therefore implemented the performance management evaluation system as a management tool for public institutions.

However, criticisms of the sloppy management of public institutions and of the performance evaluation itself have been raised lately.

> *The heads of public institutions, which have suffered from net loss during the year, were found to have been paid with a performance pay of over hundreds of millions of won. This was not limited to the heads, as employees also received millions of won as performance pay. Experts point out that moral hazard in public corporations is increasing due to the government's lax performance evaluation on the management of public institutions.*
>
> *(Asia Today, October 13, 2013)*

> *A fundamental operation on the performance evaluation system for public institutions, which was first implemented in 1983, should also be considered. The fact that chronic symptoms recur after thirty years of implementation is a sign that the system itself is problematic.*
>
> *(Editorial, Seoul Shinmun, November 4, 2013)*

This study analyzes the phenomena found in the current performance evaluation of public institutions in Korea with a focus on the quantitative indicators.

This study is a process of finding answers to the following two research questions.

- How is the ratchet principle applied in target-setting?
- What incentives do public institutions have in applying the ratchet principle in target-setting?

To find answers to the aforementioned research questions, this study begins with a theoretical examination of the agency problem that could occur in the target-setting process based on previous studies conducted overseas and introduces the empirical research conducted in Korea. This study further finds implications from each of the findings of the empirical analyses and presents proposals for improving the quality of the evaluation using quantitative indicators.

II Analysis of the current status of the evaluation using quantitative indicators

1 How is the ratchet principle applied in target-setting and what are the consequences?

1 Target-setting based on asymmetric ratcheting

1 THEORETICAL BACKGROUND

The ratchet principle, of using the performance of the past as a basis for future target – setting, is a general method of target-setting commonly found in a number of organizations. Since the agent has personal information on his own capability while the principal is unable to observe the agent's true capability and efforts, information asymmetry between the principal and agent arises in target-setting. The ratchet principle posits that the principal with limited knowledge on the agent's true capabilities will likely consider the agent's past performance as his minimum level (Berliner, 1976; Weitzman, 1980). The principal can alleviate the agency problem by placing appropriate adjustments on the agent's performance and by setting rational targets for the future (Chow et al., 1991).

A number of empirical studies have found that the target setting of the year t + 1 differs when the targets have been met during the year t with the cases in which the targets have not been met. That is, asymmetric ratcheting occurs when the performance of year t exceeded the target, the increase in the target for the time t + 1 was larger than the decrease in the target for the year t +1 when the targets have not been met in year t (Holthausen et al., 1995; Leone and Rock, 2002; Indjejikian and Nanda, 2002; Lee and Plummer, 2007).

The asymmetric ratcheting can be explained with Formula (1).

$$T_{i,t+1} - T_{i,t} = \alpha + \lambda_+(A_{i,t} - T_{i,t}) + \lambda_- D_{i,t}(A_{i,t} - T_{i,t}) + e_{i,t} \tag{1}$$

(In this formula, i stands for an individual evaluation indicator and t for each year. A and T respectively denote the actual performance and target. D is a dummy variable which is 1 when the performance failed to reach the target and 0 when it is not the case.)

According to Formula (1), the target of t + 1 is determined (target change, $T_{i,t+1} - T_{i,t}$) by whether the target has been accomplished during year t (or if not) $(D_{i,t})$, and how much the target has been exceeded (or have not been met) (target variance, $A_{i,t} - T_{i,t}$). λ_+ denotes the target variance of the year t's influence on the target change when the target has been exceeded in year t, and $\lambda_+ + \lambda_-$ stands for the target variance of the year t's influence on the target change when the target in the year t has not been met. The increase or decrease in the target, independent of the actual performance, is signified as α.

By dividing the performance of a certain period into its permanent attributes and transitory attributes, asymmetric ratcheting could help the principal extract the various implicit meanings of performance innovation and use them discriminately. Asymmetric ratcheting is to reflect more of the permanently positive target variance $(\lambda_+ > 0)$ and to reflect less of the transitorily negative target variance $(\lambda_- < 0)$ in future target-setting. In regards to this principle, Leone and Rock (2002) theoretically proved that asymmetric ratcheting provides agents with an incentive to pursue innovative activities, which would lead to permanent improvement in their performance.

2 RESULTS OF EMPIRICAL ANALYSIS[1]

Ahn et al. (2011) conducted an empirical analysis on whether asymmetric ratcheting was applied, based on the data retrieved from the reports on the performance evaluation of public institutions from 1998 to 2008. The study examined 14 institutions, 11 of which have been, as of 2008, defined as public corporations (Type 1) by the Act on the Management of Public Institutions, and three of which were quasi-governmental institutions (Type 1 on industry promotion). All 14 institutions were government-invested institutions in accordance with the Basic Law on Government Investment Management, which was legislated in 1983 and repealed in 2007. The analysis model was set as follows in accordance with previous research.

$$ch\_TARGET_{i,j,t+1} = \alpha_0 \left(1/T_{i,j,t} \right) + \beta_1 \cdot PERFORM_{i,j,t} + \beta_2 \cdot MISS_{i,j,t}$$
$$+ \beta_3 \cdot MISS_{i,j,t} \times PERFORM_{i,j,t} + \Sigma \ \beta \cdot CONTROLS + \varepsilon_{i,j,t} \qquad (2)$$

(i denotes individual public institutions, j individual evaluation indicators and t year.)

$ch\_TARGET_{i,j,t+1}$ and $PERFORM_{i,j,t}$ in Formula (2) each represent the target variance $(T_{t+1} - T_t)$ of year t + 1 and the degree that the performance exceeded the target in year t $(A_t - T_t)$, respectively, and the value was divided by the previous target

(T_t) to unite the units and to alleviate the heteroscedasticity. $MISS_{i,j,t}$ is a dummy variable which is 1 when the performance failed to reach the target ($A_t < T_t$) and 0 when it was not the case ($A_t \geq T_t$). β_1 is the target adjustment factor when the target has been accomplished in year t, $\beta_1+\beta_3$ is the target adjustment factor when the performance was below the target, and β_3 denotes the differential coefficient when the performance was below the target. Symmetric ratcheting occurs when β_1 has a significant and positive value, and β_3 is insignificant. Asymmetrical ratcheting (cost-sticky) occurs when β_1 has a meaningful positive value while β_3 has a meaningful negative value.[2]

The result of the empirical analysis can be found in Table 9.1. The regression coefficients of *PERFORM* were statistically significant at a .01 level of

Table 9.1 Asymmetric target ratcheting

$$ch\_TARGET_{i,j,t+1} = \alpha_0 \cdot (1/T_{i,j,t}) + \beta_1 \cdot PERFORM_{i,j,t} + \beta_2 \cdot MISS_{i,j,t}$$
$$+ \beta_3 \cdot MISS_{i,j,t} \cdot {}^* PERFORM_{i,j,t} + \sum \beta \cdot CONTROLS + \varepsilon_{i,j,t}$$

Independent Variables	Expected Sign	(1)	(2)	(3)	(4)	(5)
Intercept		−0.001***	−0.00***	−0.001***	−0.001***	−0.001***
		(−2.56)	(−2.67)	(−2.77)	(−2.70)	(−2.87)
PERFORM	+	0.154 ***	0.231***	0.231***	0.234***	0.231***
		(3.36)	(4.66)	(4.70)	(4.73)	(4.72)
MISS	−	−0.065 **	−0.057*	−0.057*	−0.055*	−0.055*
		(−2.07)	(−1.85)	(−1.82)	(−1.75)	(−1.74)
MISS*PERFORM	−	−0.131	−0.264	−0.274	−0.273	−0.264
		(−0.43)	(−0.85)	(−0.89)	(−0.88)	(−0.85)
Evaluation Method Control			yes	yes	yes	yes
Evaluation Indicator Control			yes	yes	yes	yes
Financial Characteristics Control				yes		yes
Macroeconomic Control					yes	yes
Year Dummy		yes	yes	yes	yes	yes
Institution Dummy		yes	yes	yes	yes	yes
N		1,440	1,440	1,440	1,440	1,440
Adj-R^2		9.58%	12.66%	13.14%	13.08%	13.66%
F-statistic		5.57***	6.18***	5.66***	5.96***	5.52***

(Source: Ahn et al. (2011), Table 6: 208)

1 The table presents OLS coefficient estimates and (in parentheses) *t*-statistics based on White (1980) standard errors.
2 All variables are winsorized at 1 percent and 99 percent.
3 *, **, *** Significant at 10 percent, 5 percent, and 1 percent two-tailed level, respectively

significance in all models. This shows that the performance in year t was significant in the target-setting of the year t + 1, and indicates that the ratcheting principle was applied in target-setting.[3] However, while the regression coefficients of *MISS*PERFORM* were negative in all models, they were not statistically significant, which suggests that the asymmetric ratcheting principle did not apply to the target-setting process of the evaluated institutions.

3 IMPLICATIONS

Although the *Handbook* suggested various evaluation methods, the common rule is to set the targets of the upcoming year's evaluation indicators based on the performance of the previous year, which clearly shows the application of the ratchet principle. The target ratcheting, therefore, could be predicted in advance.

However, the *Handbook* did not distinguish the cases in which the previous year's performance surpassed the target from the cases in which the performance was below target. Rather, it required institutions to mechanically adjust the performance of the previous years to the targets of the upcoming year by evaluation methods. This was why the asymmetric ratcheting principle has not been applied and the target-setting patterns differed widely by evaluation method.

Theoretically, the asymmetric ratcheting principle should be applied in target-setting for the long-term performance improvement of an organization. Accordingly, the evaluation indicators should be changed to distinguish the cases in which the previous year's performance surpassed the target from the cases in which the performance was below target in the performance evaluation of public institutions so that the results could be reflected discriminately in the targets of the upcoming year.

2 Ratcheting intensity and target achievability

1 THEORETICAL BACKGROUND

Milgrom and Roberts (1992) asserted that when the ratchet principle is applied to the incentive system, the agent displays a tendency to weaken the excellent performance made in year t, since an exceptionally high performance in year t would lead to a higher target in year t + 1, thereby making it difficult for the agent to receive performance pay in year t + 1. Such argument is based on the presupposition that the higher the target is raised, the lower the target achievability becomes despite the same amount of effort.

Formula (1), which was modeled after the asymmetric ratcheting principle, could be made into a graph as presented in Figure 9.1. Two assumptions should be made here. First, the target change $(T_{t+1} - T_t)$ is determined by only the target variance $(A_t - T_t)$. That is, the unknown factors do not affect target change $(\alpha = 0)$. In this case, the x-axis and y-axis each indicate target variance and target change, and zero represents the case in which the performance of year t exactly corresponds with the target but the target of the year t + 1 is at the same level with that

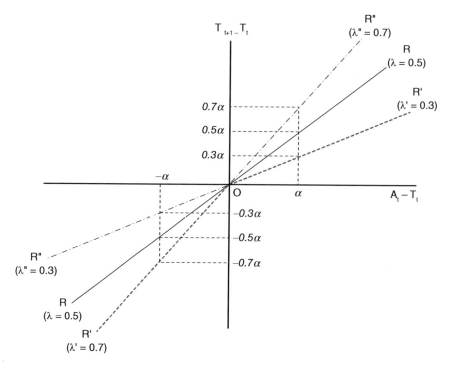

Figure 9.1 Ratcheting intensity

(Source: Choi and Hwang (2012), <Figure 1>: 209.)

of year t. Second, performance (A), with no uncertainty, changes only with the effort by the agent. For instance, if the slope is 0.5 $(\overline{ROR})$, the target of year t + 1 is higher (or lower) than the target of year t by adding (or subtracting) 50 percent of the level of target achievement of year t.

First, consider the rise (or fall) of the ratchet principle slope when the agent over-achieved the target in year t. When the slope falls by $\lambda' = 0.3$ $\left(\overline{OR'}\right)$, the target in year t + 1 will increase by 30 percent of the target variance. On the other hand, if the slope rises by $\lambda'' = 0.7$ $\left(\overline{OR''}\right)$, the target in year t + 1 would increase by reflecting 70% of the target variance. In other words, as the slope rises ($\overline{OR'} \rightarrow \overline{OR} \rightarrow \overline{OR''}$), a relatively stretched target is set (0.3α < 0.5α < 0.7α) despite the target variance (α) during the same year t. That is, if all conditions remain the same, the higher the slope, the more stretched the target and the lower the target achievability. This indicates that the more information on the performance of year t is reflected when setting the target for the year t + 1, (that is, the stronger the ratcheting intensity,) the lower the target achievability becomes in t + 1.

Now, let us consider the rise (or fall) of the ratchet principle slope when the agent performed below the target in year t. The initial slope is $\lambda = 0.5(RO)$. If the slope gets steeper by $\lambda' = 0.7(\overline{R'O})$, the target of t + 1 would decrease by 70 percent of the target variance. On the contrary, if the slope is less steep by $\lambda'' = 0.3(\overline{R''O})$, the target of t + 1 would decrease by reflecting only 30 percent of the target variance. In other words, the less steep the slope $(R'O \rightarrow \overline{RO} \rightarrow \overline{R''O})$, the more challenging the target becomes in t + 1 $(-0.7\alpha < -0.5\alpha < -0.3\alpha)$, in spite of the target variance $(-\alpha)$ during the same year t. If all conditions remain the same, the less steep the slope is, the more challenging the target and the lower the target achievability become. The lower performance information of year t is reflected in the target-setting of t + 1 (that is, the weaker the ratcheting intensity is,) the lower the target achievability in the year t + 1.

2 RESULTS OF EMPIRICAL ANALYSIS[4]

In order to check the effect of ratcheting intensity on target achievability, Choi and Hwang (2012) conducted an empirical study on the performance evaluation reports of 14 public institutions from 1998 to 2008. The analysis model was set as follows.

$$
\begin{aligned}
BEAT_{i,j,t} = \alpha_0 &+ \beta_1 \cdot SLOPE_{i,j,t} + \beta_2 \cdot Prior\_MISS * SLOPE_{i,j,t} \\
&+ \beta_3 \cdot Prior\_MISS_{i,j,t} + \sum \beta \cdot CONTROLS + \varepsilon_{i,j,t}
\end{aligned}
\tag{3}
$$

(i denotes individual public institutions, j individual evaluation indicators and t year.)

The dependent variable *BEAT* in Formula (3) is a dummy variable which becomes 1 when the target has been achieved and 0 when it has not. *SLOPE*, which expresses the intensity of the ratchet principle, is the target change of t divided by the target variance of $t - 1$ $[= (T_{i,j,t} - T_{i,j,t-1}) \div (A_{i,j,t-1} - T_{i,j,t-1})]$. *Prior_MISS* is a dummy variable which is 1 when the target has not been met in $t - 1$ and 0 when it has. *Prior_MISS*SLOPE* was included to reflect the asymmetric ratcheting principle.[5] In case the target had been achieved in $t - 1$, the stronger the intensity of the ratchet principle, the more challenging the target became in t, which led to lower target achievability and the negative regression coefficient of *SLOPE*. On the other hand, if the target was not met in $t - 1$, the target in t becomes easier to achieve as the intensity of the ratchet principle becomes stronger. The regression coefficients of β_1 and $(\beta_1 + \beta_2)$ would likely become negative and positive, respectively.

The results of the empirical analysis could be found in Table 9.2. Model 1 was an analysis which only used the control variables and excluded the predictor variables, and Model 2 was an analysis with additional interest variables. The results of the control variables were extremely alike in all models. As expected, β_1 in Model 2 was negative and $(\beta_1 + \beta_2)$ was positive. This suggests that when the target was achieved (or missed) in t − 1, the target achievability in t decreases (or increases) as the intensity of the ratchet principle increases.

3 IMPLICATIONS

The recent performance evaluations in principle assign the targets (deviation) to have the institutions set challenging targets. This approach seems to be valid compared to other evaluation methods, which calculated the level of targets mechanically since it would enable institutions to set achievable yet challenging targets by reflecting on the volatility of past performances. However, it is uncertain whether the "deviation x multiples" actually intensifies or weakens the ratchet principle. If public institutions could manage the deviation at certain levels favorable to them, the ratchet principle might become the weakest in the target ASSIGN (deviation). In this case, the easiest target, instead of challenging targets, might be set, enabling the target achievability to become higher, implying that targets are under controllable.

3 Serial correlation between the ratcheting intensity and the target achievability

1 THEORETICAL BACKGROUND

There have been many opinions on how much the past performance information should be reflected in target-setting. Milgrom and Roberts (1992), by using the multi-period agent model, proved that a rational principal could gain benefits ex-post by using information on past performances and resetting the agent's target level. However, Laffont and Tirole (1993) used the two-period agent model and argued that setting targets without considering the information on the agent's past performances leads to higher enterprise value. More fundamentally, Weitzman (1980) asserted that past performances should be reflected discriminately in future target-setting, depending on whether the agent met the target during the previous term or not. In the end, the studies showed that whether to entirely or to partially reflect past performances when setting goals depends on the purpose of the evaluation or other circumstances.

On the other hand, Merchant (1985) and Merchant and Manzoni (1989) conducted a survey on listed companies in the United States and found that corporations, with an 80% to 90% probability, set achievable goals when the economy is booming. The low probability of the CEOs to fail to achieve their targets indicated that the various information within the good performance in a term t, such as the agent's capability and external environment variables, had not been adequately reflected in the target of t + 1 (Indjejikian et al., 2014). Indjejikian and Nanda (2002) posited that since the information on past performances cannot be fully reflected in target-setting, the probability of the CEO to receive higher performance pay than expected is not serially independent. In other words, if the past performance information had not been adequately reflected in target-setting, the target achievability would likely be in a positive serial correlation.

2 RESULTS OF EMPIRICAL ANALYSIS[6]

Ahn et al. (2011) examined whether the target achievability of quantitative indicators in the performance evaluation of public institutions displayed serial correlations. An empirical analysis was conducted on the information on the target and performance retrieved from the performance evaluation reports of 14 institutions. The methodology used in Indjejikian and Nanda (2002) was applied, and the study compared the conditional probability of the target achievability in t + 1 being affected by the performance in t, as shown in Formula (4).

$$p = \Pr(A_{i,j,t+1} \geq T_{i,j,t+1} \mid A_{i,j,t} \geq T_{i,j,t}) \, q = \Pr(A_{i,j,t+1} \geq T_{i,j,t+1} \mid A_{i,j,t} < T_{i,j,t}) \tag{4}$$

(In this formula, i stands for individual institutions, j for individual evaluation indicators, t for year, and T and A each represent the target and performance.)

In Formula (4) p denotes the conditional probability of achieving the target in t + 1, after achieving the target in t, q denotes the conditional probability of achieving the target in t + 1 after failing to reach the target in t. If p = q, the probability to achieve the target in t + 1 is independent of whether the target has been achieved in t. On the other hand, when p ≠ q, the probability to achieve the target in t + 1 depends on whether the target has been achieved in t, which shows that the target of t + 1 is affected by the performance in t.

The results of the empirical analysis were as presented in Table 9.3. Panel A was an analysis of the entire sample. While the probability to over-achieve the target in t and to over-achieve the target in t + 1 was 91.24 percent, the probability to fail to achieve the target in t and to overachieve in t + 1 was only 49.75 percent. The results of a non-parametric test on the difference of 2 probabilities showed that the z-statistics were 11.43 and statistically significant at a .01 level of significance. The same analysis was conducted on Panels B to E with different evaluation methods. All results were similar to that of Panel A, aside BETA.

All in all, if the targets have been achieved in t, there is a very high probability that the targets will be achieved in t + 1, and it can be assumed that target achievability displays a positive serial correlation. Moreover, the positive serial correlation was stronger from actual to target (95.51 percent) > TREND (93.12 percent) > (BETA) > ASSIGN (76.47 percent).

3 IMPLICATIONS

This study confirmed that target achievability in the quantitative indicators of the performance evaluation of public institutions displayed positive serial correlations. This may be due to the fact that the various information on the performance in t was not adequately reflected in the target of t + 1. That is, the evaluation method using quantitative indicators has been too standardized to evaluate the public institutions' capacity to improve their performance, which indicates a possibility of the annual targets having being set at a manageable or achievable level. If there is a need to lower the serial correlations found in the target achievability

Table 9.2 Target intensity and target achievability

$$BEAT_{i,j,t} = \alpha_0 + \beta_1 \cdot SLOPE_{i,j,t} + \beta_2 \cdot Prior\_MISS * SLOPE_{i,j,t}$$
$$+\beta_3 \cdot Prior\_MISS_{i,j,t} + \sum \beta \cdot CONTROLS + \varepsilon_{i,j,t} \quad (3)$$

Variable	Predicted Sign	Estimated coefficients	
		Model 1	Model 2
Intercept	?	1.414	1.354
		(0.91)	(0.87)
Slope Variables			
SLOPE	−		−0.703***
			(−3.34)
*Prior_MISS*SLOPE*	+		1.099***
			(3.44)
Performance Measure-level Control Variables		yes	yes
Target-Setting Method-level Control Variables		yes	yes
Firm-level Control Variables		yes	yes
Macro Economy-level Control Variables		yes	yes
Year_Dummy		yes	yes
Institution_Dummy		yes	yes
N		1,130	1,130
Pseudo R^2		24.76%	25.96%
Likelihood ratio, χ^2		247.80***	251.98***

(Source: Choi and Hwang (2012), Table 6: 227)

1 The total sample consists of 1,430 observations between 1999 and 2008 for 14 public institutions.
2 All variables are winsorized at 1 percent and 99 percent.
3 The table presents logit coefficient estimates and Wald $\chi2$ values in parentheses.
4 *,**,*** Statistically significant at the 10 percent, 5 percent, and 1 percent two-tailed level, respectively.

in order to improve the function of the performance evaluation as an annual evaluation of institutional performance, targets should not be mechanically set based on the previous year's performance, but should reflect the performance functions and qualitative factors, such as the level of effort and the influence of external environmental variables.

2 Incentives for public institutions found in the application of the ratchet principle in target-setting

1 Performance management incentives in public institutions

1 THEORETICAL BACKGROUND

There have been many studies in the field of accounting on how CEOs who have the incentive to meet or beat the standard response to targets. According to Murphy (2001), a survey was conducted on 177 listed corporations in

Table 9.3 Frequency distribution of actual vs. target performance in consecutive periods

Panel A. Entire Sample (N = 1,440)

	$A_{t+1} < T_{t+1}$			$A_{t+1} \geq T_{t+1}$			
	N	Frequency	%	N	Frequency	%	z-statistic
$A_t < T_t$	130	% of Total	9.04	129	% of Total	8.96	11.43***
		% of Row	50.25		% of Row	**49.75**	
$A_t \geq T_t$	103	% of Total	7.18	1,078	% of Total	74.82	
		% of Row	8.76		% of Row	**91.24**	

Panel B. TREND (N = 547)

	$A_{t+1} < T_{t+1}$			$A_{t+1} \geq T_{t+1}$			
	N	Frequency	%	N	Frequency	%	z-statistic
$A_t < T_t$	31	% of Total	5.61	36	% of Total	6.50	5.79***
		% of Row	46.30		% of Row	**53.70**	
$A_t \geq T_t$	31	% of Total	5.61	449	% of Total	82.29	
		% of Row	6.38		% of Row	**93.62**	

Panel C. BETA (N = 95)

	$A_{t+1} < T_{t+1}$			$A_{t+1} \geq T_{t+1}$			
	N	Frequency	%	N	Frequency	%	z-statistic
$A_t < T_t$	4	% of Total	3.85	9	% of Total	8.97	1.42
		% of Row	30.00		% of Row	**70.00**	
$A_t \geq T_t$	7	% of Total	7.69	75	% of Total	79.49	
		% of Row	8.82		% of Row	**91.18**	

Panel D. ASSIGN (N = 305)

	$A_{t+1} < T_{t+1}$			$A_{t+1} \geq T_{t+1}$			
	N	Frequency	%	N	Frequency	%	z-statistic
$A_t < T_t$	62	% of Total	20.31	61	% of Total	19.92	4.49***
		% of Row	50.49		% of Row	**49.51**	
$A_t \geq T_t$	43	% of Total	14.06	139	% of Total	45.70	
		% of Row	23.53		% of Row	**76.47**	

Panel E. Actual to Target (N = 493)

	$A_{t+1} < T_{t+1}$			$A_{t+1} \geq T_{t+1}$			
	N	Frequency	%	N	Frequency	%	z-statistic
$A_t < T_t$	31	% of Total	6.32	20	% of Total	4.02	6.90***
		% of Row	61.11		% of Row	**38.89**	
$A_t \geq T_t$	20	% of Total	4.02	422	% of Total	85.63	
		% of Row	4.49		% of Row	**95.51**	

(Source: Ahn et al. (2011), Table 5: 206.)

1 To test whether $\Pr(A_{t+1} \geq T_{t+1} \mid A_t \geq T_t) = \Pr(A_{t+1} \geq T_{t+1} \mid A_t < T_t)$, the difference in proportions was tested (indicated in bold).

2 The sample is 1,440 public institutions' performance measure observations. A_{t+1} is the public institution's actual performance of performance measures for fiscal year t + 1. T_{t+1} is the public institution's target performance of performance measures for fiscal year t + 1. The rows in the table correspond to outcomes for which the public institution's actual performance was less than $(A_t < T_t)$, or greater than or equal to $(A_t \geq T_t)$ its target performance in the previous year. The columns correspond to the same outcomes for the current year, t. N is the number of observations in each cell. For %, the upper number in each cell is a percentage of total observations that are classified in that cell and the lower number of in each cell is the conditional percentage-the percentage of row observations corresponding to that cell.

3 *, **, *** Significant at 10 percent, 5 percent, and 1 percent 2-tailed level, respectively.

the United States to identify the typical pay-performance relation, which is shown in Figure 9.2. The pay-performance relation is essentially an increasing function and, the CEO has the incentive to adjust the performance results for higher performance pay. However, since there usually is a bonus cap to what the CEO could receive, the level of performance the CEO could produce is within the "incentive zone" between the performance threshold and the maximum performance. In other words, the CEO would attempt to achieve the maximum performance so that they could receive the maximum amount of performance pay.

On the other hand, according to the agency theory, the principal, who is less informed of the agent's true capability and efforts, is more likely to set lower performance standards than the maximum performance level the agent is capable of or is manageable by the agent. As a result, if the performance were to be predicted to be slightly lower than the target, the agent could slightly adjust their performance to receive the maximum amount of performance pay. In regards to this phenomenon, a great number of empirical studies have reported cases of avoiding reports on loss, exceeding the previous term's profits and exceeding the profit predicted by financial analysts and the CEOs (Carslaw, 1988; Thomas, 1989; Hayn, 1995; Burgstahler and Dichev, 1997; Kasznik, 1999; Degeorge et al., 1999; Mastumoto, 2002; Abarbanell and Lehavy, 2003; Jacob and Jorgensen, 2007).

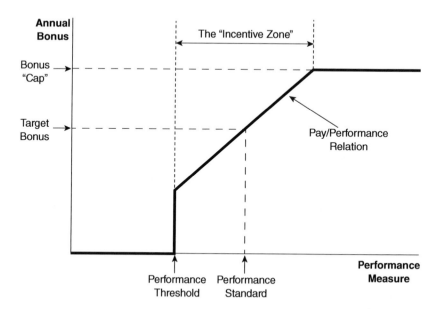

Figure 9.2 Pay-performance relation

(Source: Murphy (2011), <Figure 1>: 251.)

2 RESULTS OF EMPIRICAL ANALYSIS[7]

Specific numbers have been set as targets of the quantitative indicators in the performance evaluation of public institutions in South Korea, which were then compared with the performance. The grades have been calculated in accordance with how well the performance met the target, and the weight has been multiplied by the grades for the final score. If the performance exactly met the target, the institution would be able to receive a score with maximum weight, but if the performance failed to meet the target, only a part of the weight was multiplied to the total score. Additional scores were not provided for exceeding the weight even if the performance exceeded the target. In this sense, the targets in the quantitative indicators in the performance indicators served the same function as the performance maximum, which brought about the maximum bonus in the typical pay-performance relation suggested by Murphy (2001). As a result, public institutions would likely have an incentive to adjust their performance results upwards when the performance was projected to be slightly below the target, so as to get the maximum score in the indicator.

To confirm this hypothesis, Choi et al. (2012) conducted an empirical analysis in accordance with the methodology presented in Burgstahler and Dichev (1997) on the targets and performance data retrieved from the performance evaluation reports of 14 public institutions from 1998 to 2008. Burgstahler and Dichev (1997) insisted that a discontinuity in the earnings distribution occurred when the projected earnings of an firm were slightly below the target earnings and when its CEO decided to increase the earnings. In such situation, if a discontinuity in the earnings distribution occurred with the highest peak in the section where earnings slightly exceed the target earnings, the CEO's earnings management could be suspected. Following Burgstahler and Dichev (1997)'s prediction, if a discontinuity in the performance distribution of quantitative indicators was found near the target, there is a possibility that the public institution managed its performance.

The performance distribution of all 1,413 quantitative indicators is as presented in Figure 9.3 and Table 9.4.[8] Figure 9.3 displays a single-peaked, bell-shaped distribution which is at the apex in the interval in which the performance distribution is slightly higher than the target (0). A comparison between the interval which is slightly lower than the target (0) with the interval that is slightly higher than the target showed that the distribution was not continuous before and after the target (0) and is broken. Moreover, according to Table 9.4, such discontinuity in the performance distribution was statistically significant in most of the intervals.

The study also classified the entire sample (1,413) into the quantitative indicators (516) on business management and the quantitative indicators (897) on main business activities. As shown in Figure 9.4, the performance distribution of quantitative indicators on business management had no specific patterns and was similar to a normal distribution, while the performance distribution of quantitative indicators on main business activities was a single-peaked, bell-shaped distribution which was at the apex in the interval where the performance distribution was

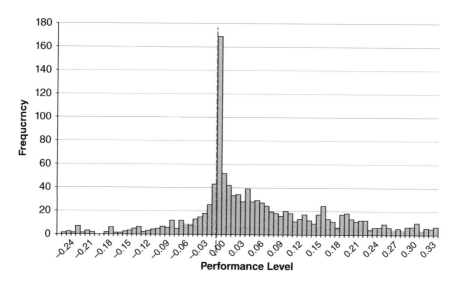

Figure 9.3 Distribution of performance

(Source: Choi et al. (2012), Figure 2: 346.)

slightly higher than the target (0). The difference in the performance distributions was confirmed to be statistically significant.

3 IMPLICATIONS

The discontinuity in the performance distribution of quantitative indicators confirmed the possibility of public institutions adjusting their performance results to get a perfect score when their performances were expected to be slightly below the target. It was further confirmed that public institutions were more likely to adjust their performance results on main business activities, on which the institutions have much more knowledge and information than the evaluators.

The issue of public institutions purposely adjusting their performance in main business activities to their own favor for better results in the performance evaluation has been raised for a long time. In the current situation, under which the targets are not set at the level of the maximum performance potential expected from public institutions, a simple and mechanical comparison between the targets and the performance will likely produce a result quite different from the actual performance. Accordingly, the hidden qualitative factors behind the evaluation results based on quantitative indicators need to be considered.

Since public institutions are exclusive in their industrial fields, they inevitably function as the leading experts. Thus, no matter how much expertise the evaluators may have, there are limitations to their ability to evaluate the institutions' performance in the institutions' main business activities, once the performance results are adjusted. Increased effort to improve the expertise of the evaluators as

Table 9.4 Standardized difference across performance intervals

Interval	Actual Frequency	Estimated Frequency	Ratio	Standardized Difference	Interval	Actual Frequency	Estimated Frequency	Ratio	Standardized Difference
-0.005~0	34	82.5	0.41	-5.81***	0~0.005	147	33.0	4.45	9.39***
-0.01~0	52	104.5	0.50	-5.40***	0~0.01	179	61.0	2.93	8.69***
-0.02~0	82	141.0	0.58	-5.10***	0~0.02	249	86.5	2.88	10.42***
-0.03~0	101	169.0	0.60	-5.41***	0~0.03	296	115.0	2.57	10.78***
-0.04~0	115	194.5	0.59	-5.99***	0~0.04	340	136.0	2.50	11.53***
-0.05~0	127	218.5	0.58	-6.62***	0~0.05	384	143.5	2.68	13.10***
-0.06~0	143	234.5	0.61	-6.36***	0~0.06	425	157.0	2.71	14.16***
-0.07~0	152	255.0	0.60	-6.99***	0~0.07	463	160.0	2.89	15.69***
-0.08~0	164	269.0	0.61	-6.95***	0~0.08	497	164.0	3.03	16.97***
-0.09~0	173	282.0	0.61	-7.09***	0~0.09	524	180.5	2.90	17.24***
-0.10~0	180	289.0	0.62	-7.00***	0~0.10	544	187.0	2.91	17.78***
~0	253				0~	1,160			

(Source: Choi et al. (2012), Table 6: 348.)

1 The total sample consists of 1,413 observations between 1999 and 2007 for 14 public institutions.
2 The actual frequency is the number of observations in a given performance interval (X_i).
3 Estimated frequency is the average observation of actual frequency on each side of the given performance interval ($(X_{i-1} + X_{i+1}) \div 2$).
4 The ratio is calculated by dividing actual frequency by estimated frequency.
5 Standardized difference is "(Actual frequency − Estimated frequency) ÷ standard deviation of $[N \cdot P_i \cdot (1 − P_i) + (1/4) \cdot N \cdot (P_{i-1} + P_{i+1}) \cdot (1 − P_{i-1} − P_{i+1})]$". Here, N is the number of total sample and P_i is the probability that performance goes into a given performance interval.
6 *, **, *** Statistically significant at the 10 percent, 5 percent, and 1 percent 2-tailed level, respectively.

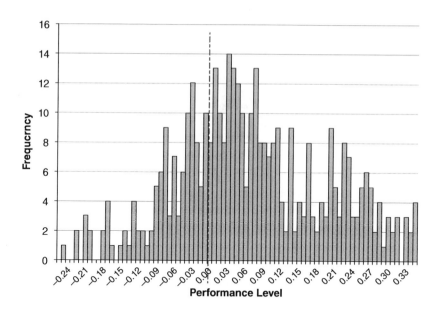

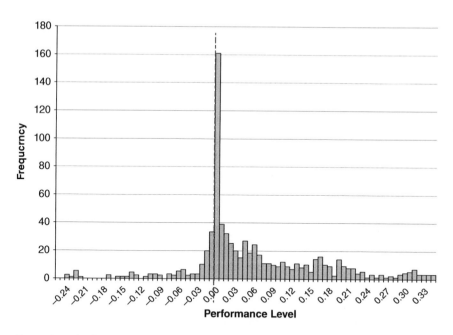

Figure 9.4 Distribution of performance across common (performance management) vs. unique (main business activities) measures

(Source: Choi et al. (2012), <Figure 3>: 349.)

well as the effort to alleviate the information asymmetry between the public institutions and evaluators are necessary. Setting quantitative indicators that incorporate long-term serial performance information is necessary in order to improve the rationality of the target level. Using a set of quantitative indicators for a long period of time or gathering adequate information on the performance levels could be examples of such effort. Accordingly, changing quantitative indicators on main business activities by three years or using only the performance information within five years should also be reconsidered.

2 Effort reduction incentives in public institutions

1 THEORETICAL BACKGROUND

The principal, who wants a long-term maximization of his/her company, expects the agent to multitask and put the appropriate level of effort on all tasks (Fehr and Schmidt, 2004). Contrary to such expectations, the agent tends to strategically spread out their resources and effort across several tasks in order to maximize their own efficiency (Datar et al., 2001; Holmstrom and Milgrom, 1991; Feltham et al., 2006). This is because the agent's performance functions and the pay-performance relation could differ by the characteristics of the tasks.

The agent's incentive to reduce effort is a common agency problem found in the target-setting process. This is especially the case when the ratchet principle is applied in target-setting; the excellent performance in t becomes the basis of the challenging target of t + 1, thus creating an inter-period trade-off between the compensation for t and the compensation for t + 1. That is, an agent who signed a multi-period bonus contract has the incentive to allocate their effort strategically between the periods to maximize the compensation for the entire term. This is especially the case when the typical pay-performance relation proposed by Murphy (2001) is taking place and when the performance of t is expected to easily exceed the target, since the agent would be able to receive the maximum amount of performance pay with less effort. In such cases, the ratchet effect, the tendency to lower the performance of t so that the target of t + 1 would not be too challenging, would take place (Weitzman, 1980; Chow et al., 1991).

2 RESULTS OF EMPIRICAL ANALYSIS[9]

Choi et al. (2015) conducted an empirical analysis on whether the ratchet effect appears in accordance with the incentives to reduce effort in the performance evaluation of public institutions. The samples were drawn from the evaluation results on quantitative indicators from 1991 to 2008 on 14 public institutions. If there were a ratchet effect, the actual performance would be smaller than the expected performance. The ratchet effect could be conceptually measured by Formula (5).

$$RATCHET_{i,j,t} = exPERF_{i,j,t} - PERF_{i,j,} \tag{5}$$

(In this formula, i stands for individual institutions, j for individual evaluation indicators and t for a year.)

Table 9.5 Distribution of ratchet effect

Method of Target-Setting	Observed Numbers	Means	Standard Deviation	Lower 10%	First Quantile	Median	Third Quantile	Upper 10%
TREND	426	−0.094*** (t-value[a] = −7.86)	0.247	−0.430	−0.239	−0.061	0.069	0.193
BETA	63	0.019 (t-value[a] = 0.82)	0.200	−0.144	−0.027	0.036	0.079	0.241
ASSIGN	222	0.023** (t-value[a] = 2.13)	0.257	−0.256	−0.095	0.147	0.388	0.629
Actual to Target	302	0.005** (t-value[a] = 1.97)	0.161	−0.153	−0.066	0.009	0.069	0.164

(Source: Choi et al. (2015), Table 4: 236)

1 Null hypothesis H0: Verifies whether *Ratchet Effect* = 0.
2 The sample for the analysis was the institution-year-indicators of 1,013 institutions with performance values larger than the target values among the institution-year-indicators of 1,294 institutions from 1991 to 2008.
3 *p < .1, **< p.05, ***< p.01

Table 9.6 Characteristics of performance measure and ratchet effect

Variable	Expected Signs	(1)	(2)	(3)
Intercept	?	−0.119	−0.109	−1.869
		(−1.63)	(−1.35)	(−1.56)
CHARACTER	+	0.035*	0.035*	0.037*
		(1.82)	(1.82)	(1.92)
CEO Characteristics Control	±		yes	yes
Financial Characteristics Control	?			yes
Evaluation Method Control	?	yes	yes	yes
Year Dummy		yes	yes	yes
Firm Dummy		yes	yes	yes
N		1,013	1,013	1,013
Adj-R^2		6.00%	6.42%	6.99%
F-Statistic		2.19**	2.24**	2.21**

1 *p < .1, ** < p.05, *** < p.01
2 The sample for the analysis was the institution-year-indicators of 1,013 institutions with performance values larger than the target values among the institution-year-indicators of 1,294 institutions
from 1991 to 2008.
3 All variables are winsorized at the upper and lower 1 percent.
4 The table presents OLS coefficient estimates and *t*-statistics based on White (1980)

exPERF and *PERF* in this formula represent the expected performance and
actual performance, respectively. The difference between the two performances,
RATCHET, is the results of the agent's incentive to decrease effort, which is the
directly measured value of the size of the ratchet effect.[10] If there is a ratchet effect
in the management effort, *RATCHET* would have a statistically positive value.

The results of the empirical analysis were as presented in Table 9.5. *RATCHET*
displayed a statistically significant positive value in ASSIGN and Actual to Target, which suggests that the ratchet effect existed. However, the ratchet effect
did not appear in TREND and BETA. *RATCHET* displayed a negative value in
TREND, in particular, which suggests that the actual performance was larger than
the expected performance.

The results of the analysis on whether the ratchet effect is different depending
on the characteristic of the evaluation indicators could be found in Table 9.6. The
predictor variable *CHARACTER* was 1 for the quantitative indicators of the main
business activities and was a dummy indicator, 0, for quantitative indicators on
business management. The analysis showed that *CHARACTER* in all models had
statistically significant positive regression coefficients that were statistically significant at a .01 level of significance. This proves that the ratchet effect is greater
in main business activities than business management.

3 IMPLICATIONS

The actual performance fell short of the expected performance (ratchet effect) in
the performance evaluation, the size of which differed by evaluation method and

the characteristics of the indicators. First, the sizes of the ratchet effect by evaluation method were larger in the following consecutive order: ASSIGN > Actual to Target > BETA > TREND. The actual performance was below the expected performance in ASSIGN and Actual to Target, which used the performance results from the past three to five years, but in TREND, which used the evaluation results from the past ten years or before, the actual performance exceeded the expected performance. This result showed that rather than being overly dependent on the performance results of the recent years in evaluating the quantitative indicators, observing performance results of a long period and setting the targets at an appropriate level could lead to a better performance.

The ratchet effect was bigger in main business activities than in business management. Because the information asymmetry between public institutions and the evaluators was relatively larger in the evaluation on main business activities, the evaluation team resorted to relying on past performances when setting goals (as found in ASSIGN, etc.). This would lead to a stronger application of the ratchet principle in main business activities, giving the public institutions incentive to be more active in managing the performance of the past year, which led to a larger ratchet effect. Such finding implied that the evaluation team should overcome the lack of information on main business activities and should put various factors, other than the past performances, in consideration for target-setting.

III Lessons and conclusion

1 Lessons learned

This study analyzed the various phenomena present in the quantitative indicator evaluation of the performance evaluation of public institutions. The results of the empirical analysis provide the following answers to the two research questions raised in the introduction of this study.

(RQ1) How is the ratchet principle applied in target-setting?

The analysis showed that the targets in a majority of evaluation methods in the *Handbook* were set in accordance with the ratchet principle. However, asymmetric ratcheting, which is necessary for long-term performance improvements, was not found. The analysis proved that when the target has been met (or has not been met) in t, the target achievability in t + 1 decreases (or increases) as the intensity of the ratchet principle is stronger. The target achievability displayed a positive serial correlation.

(RQ2) What incentives do public institutions have in applying the ratchet principle in target-setting?

The performance distribution of quantitative indicators displayed a single-peaked, bell-shaped distribution with the highest peak slightly higher than the target, with discontinuity found near the target. The discontinuity in the performance distribution was more obvious in main business activities than in business management. Such performance distribution suggested that there is a possibility that the performance results have been adjusted upwards, in cases which the performance was expected to be slightly below the target. The analysis also showed that even in cases which the target has been overachieved, the actual performance was lower than the expected performance. The gap was especially prominent in the evaluation methods with the stronger intensity of the ratchet principle, which implied that the institutions may have purposely lowered the performance of t to prevent the target of t + 1 to become excessively higher, under the influence of the ratchet principle.

2 Conclusion

The results of the empirical analysis conducted in this study had implications in various viewpoints. This study presented the following suggestions for future evaluations on quantitative indicators as follows.

First, the qualitative evaluation should be incorporated into the quantitative analysis, and the qualitative levels should be considered not only in the target-setting stage but also in the final evaluation stage. The current evaluation method on quantitative indicators allows public institutions to set their targets by mechanically adjusting the past performance results. However, the same evaluation method might have targets with different levels of difficulty or achievability, according to the management environment of the institution and the characteristics of the indicators. Thus, the evaluators should consider adopting the asymmetric ratcheting principle or decide on how to set the rate of increase of the targets in the target-setting stage (that is, when the *Handbook* is implemented or revised), in order to increase (or decrease) the mechanically calculated targets. At the evaluation stage, the evaluator could consider adding an stage for giving the final grades by adding (or deducting) points after considering whether the mechanically calculated scores are appropriate in light of the evaluated institution's capacity and effort.

Second, if the quantitative indicators and evaluation method have been deemed to be rational, they should be used for a long period if possible. Public institutions generally have extremely stable management environments and their main business activities tend to be consistent and aligned with their missions. The public institutions, however, tend to revise the quantitative indicators in a two- to three-year-cycle, under the guise of the limitations of performance improvement and the irrationality of the evaluation methods. Nevertheless, it is likely that the public institutions would want to get better evaluation results rather than having critical issues with the evaluation indicators or the evaluation methods. Therefore, the evaluation indicators and methods should be used for a longer period, so that the enactment and revision process of the *Handbook* could be simplified and the evaluation system managed with stability.

Notes

1 This part was based on Ahn et al. (2011).
2 *CONTROLS* in Formula (2) indicates the other factors which could affect target-setting. In this study, the attributes of the evaluation indicators, financial characteristics

of institutions and the macroeconomic environmental factors were set as the control variables. Refer to Ahn et al. (2011) for more details.

3   The regression coefficient of *PERFORM* in Model 5 was 0.231, which could be understood as adding 23.1 percent of the target variance when the performance exceeded the target to the target of year t, in order to set the target of t + 1.

4   This part is based on Choi and Hwang (2012).

5   *CONTROL* in Formula (3) indicates the other factors which could affect target achievement. In this study, the serial correlation of performance, the attributes of the evaluation indicators, financial characteristics of institutions and the macroeconomic environmental factors were set as the control variables. Please refer Choi and Hwang (2012) for more details.

6   This part is based on Ahn et al. (2011).

7   This part is based on Choi et al. (2012).

8   The analysis metrics of the quantitative indicators differed by institutions, varying from kilogram, ton, kilometer, percentage, to million(s) of won. The analysis united the analysis metrics by changing the achievability to $((A_{i,j,t}-T_{i,j,t})\div T_{i,j,t})$.

9   This part is based on Choi et al. (2015).

10 The 2SLS (two-stage least squares) was applied to estimate the ex*PERF* for the actual empirical analysis. Please refer to Choi et al. (2015) for the specific estimation process.

References

Abarbanell, J., and Lehavy, R. (2003). Can Stock Recommendations Predict Earnings Management and Analysts Earnings Forecast Errors? *Journal of Accounting Research*, *41*(1), 1–31.

Ahn, T. S., Choi, Y. S., and Kwon, D. H. (2011). An Examination of Target-Setting: How a Rater Revises a Ratee's Target. *Korean Accounting Review*, *36*(1), 183–223.

Berliner, J. S. (1976). *The Innovation Decision in Soviet Industry*. Cambridge, MA: MIT press.

Burgstahler, D., and Dichev, I. (1997). Earnings Management to Avoid Earnings Decreases and Losses. *Journal of Accounting and Economics*, *24*(1), 99–126.

Carslaw, C. (1988). Anomalies in Income Numbers: Evidence from Goal Oriented Behavior. *The Accounting Review*, *63*(2), 321–327.

Choi, Y. S., and Hwang, I. (2012). Ratchet Principle and Target Achievability: An Empirical Analysis of Objective Performance Measures. *Korean Accounting Review*, *37*(2), 205–235.

Choi, Y. S., Hwang, I., and Song, S. A. (2012). Ratee Incentive and Performance Distribution. *Korean Accounting Review*, *37*(4), 327–361.

Choi, Y. S., Hwang, I., and Yoon, J. C. (2015). The Effect of Target-Setting Uncertainty in Performance Evaluation of Korean SOEs on Effort Reduction Incentive. *Korean Public Affairs Review*, *49*(3), 219–246.

Chow, C. W. (1983). Providing Incentives to Limit Budgetary Slack. *Cost and Management*, *57*, September, 37–41.

Chow, C. W., Cooper, J. C., and Haddad, K. (1991). The Effects of Pay Schemes and Ratchet on Budgetary Slack and Performance: A Multi-Period Experiment. *Accounting Organizations and Society*, *16*(1), 47–60.

Datar, S., Kulp, S. C., and Lambert, R. A. (2001). Balancing Performance Measures. *Journal of Accounting Research*, *39*(1), 75–92.

Degeorge, F., Patel, J., and Zeckhauser, R. (1999). Earnings Management to Exceed Thresholds. *Journal of Business*, *72*, 1–32.

Fehr, E., and Schmidt, K. M. (2004). Fairness and Incentives in a Multi-Task Principal-Agent Model. *Scandinavian Journal of Economics*, *106*(3), 453–474.

Feltham, G., Indjejikian, R., and Nanda, D. (2006). Dynamic Incentives and Dual- Purposes Accounting. *Journal of Accounting and Economics*, *42*, 417–437.

Hayn, C. (1995). The Information Content of Losses. *Journal of Accounting and Economics*, *20*, 125–153.

Holmstrom, B., and Milgrom, P. (1991). Multitask Principal-Agent Analyses: Incentive Contracts, Asset Ownership, and Job Design. *Journal of Law, Economics, and Organization*, *7*, 24–52.

Holthausen, R., Larker, D., and Sloan, R. (1995). Annual Bonus Schemes and the Manipulation of Earnings. *Journal of Accounting and Economics*, *19*(1), 29–74.

Indjejikian, R., Matejka, M., Merchant, K., and Van der Stede, W. (2014). Earnings Targets and Annual Bonus Incentives. *The Accounting Review*, *89*(4), 1227–1258.

Indjejikian, R. J., and Nanda, D. (2002). Executive Target Bonuses and What They Imply About Performance Standards. *The Accounting Review*, *77*(4), 793–819.

Jacob, J., and Jorgensen, B. (2007). Earnings Management and Accounting Income Aggregation. *Journal of Accounting and Economics*, *43*, 369–390.

Kasznik, R. (1999). On the Association Between Voluntary Disclosure and Earnings Management. *Journal of Accounting Research*, *37*(1), 57–82.

Korean Society of Public Enterprise. (2003). *Evaluation on Korea's Management System of Public Enterprises: 20 Years History of Management Evaluation on Government Invested Institutions.* Korean Public Enterprise Association.

Laffont, J. J., and Martimort, D. (2002). *The Theory of Incentives: The Principal Agency Model.* Princeton, NJ: Princeton University Press.

Lee, T. M., and Plummer, E. (2007). Budget Adjustments in Response to Spending Variances: Evidence of Ratcheting of Local Government Expenditures. *Journal of Management Accounting Research*, *19*, 137–167.

Leone, A. J., and Rock, S. (2002). Empirical Tests of Budget Ratcheting and Its Effect on Managers Discretionary Accrual Choices. *Journal of Accounting and Economics*, *33*, 43–67.

Matsumoto, D. (2002). Managements Incentives to Avoid Negative Earnings Surprises. *The Accounting Review*, *77*(3), 483–514.

Merchant, K. A. (1985). Budgeting and the Propensity to Create Budgetary Slack. *Accounting, Organizations and Society*, *2*, 201–210.

Merchant, K. A., and Manzoni, J. F. (1989). The Achievability of Budget Targets in Profit Centers: A Field Study. *The Accounting Review*, *64*(3), 539–558.

Milgrom, P., and Roberts, J. (1992). *Economics, Organizations, and Management.* Englewood Cliffs, NJ: Prentice-Hall.

Ministry of Strategy and Finance. (1985–2015a). *Evaluation Reports on the Performance of Public Institutions.* Ministry of Strategy and Finance.

Ministry of Strategy and Finance. (1985–2015b). *Handbook of the Performance Evaluation of Public Institutions.* Ministry of Strategy and Finance.

Murphy, K. J. (2001). Performance Standards in Incentive Contracts. *Journal of Accounting and Economics*, *30*, December, 245–278.

Rockness, H. O. (1977). Expectancy Theory in a Budgetary Setting: An Experimental Examination. *The Accounting Review*, *52*(4), 893–903.

Stedry, A. C. (1960). *Budget and Control and Cost Behavior.* Englewood Cliffs, NJ: Prentice-Hall.

Stedry, A. C., and Kay, E. (1966). The Effect of Goal Difficulty on Performance: A Field Experiment. *Behavioral Science, 11*(6), 459–470.

Thomas, J. (1989). Unusual Patterns in Reported Earnings. *The Accounting Review, 64*(4), 773–787.

Weitzman, M. (1980). The Ratchet Principle and Performance Incentives. *Bell Journal of Economics, 11*, Spring, 302–308.

10 Issues in quantitative evaluation

Bong Hwan Kim

I Introduction

Public institutions pursue activities in the public interest in various fields of the society. The principal-agent problems in public institutions are more aggravated than those in private corporations, due to the fact that the principals of public institutions are unspecified citizens. The possible increase in the number of free-riders in the monitoring process of institutions adds to the problem. To address this issue and to minimize such problems, most countries conduct external evaluations on public corporations or public institutions which elude market monitoring.

Performance evaluations of public institutions have been conducted in South Korea for more than three decades. Not only have the evaluation methods evolved but also the number of evaluated institutions and the range of evaluated projects have also continued to expand. The performance evaluation has had positive effects on effective cost management by cutting costs and controlling pay raise. However, the evaluation has also led to side-effects, such as failing to prevent excessive debts, increasing the incentives for earnings manipulation, and inducing strategic actions that reduced institutions' efforts (Park, 2006; Chung et al., 2003; Choi et al., 2015).

The purpose of this study is to examine the issues concerning the current performance evaluations on public institutions and to present suggestions by focusing on the business management category, specifically on the evaluation methods for work efficiency. The evaluation of work efficiency is included in the performance evaluation in order to improve the comprehensive work efficiency of public institutions. Indicators of work efficiency are applied most extensively to all institutions regardless of their types. The evaluation of work efficiency accounts for 13.3 percent of the entire quantitative evaluation (based on the 2016 evaluation of public corporations), making the indicator crucial for the evaluation. Examining the issues and suggestions for the work efficiency indicators, which are considered as the most important indicators by nearly all institutions, is important for improving the performance evaluation. Another contribution of this study is to fill the gap in research on performance evaluation of public institutions, where there is a lack of research on specific indicators. While this study reviews issues on all public institutions, it puts particular focus on public corporations.

This study first presents the outline of the performance evaluation on work efficiency, then discusses various work efficiency indicators, and examines changes in the weights on the work efficiency indicators. Next, I raise the issues on the current work efficiency indicators and present suggestions for improvements.

II Outline of the quantitative evaluation on work efficiency

1 Outline of the work efficiency evaluation

The annual performance evaluation of public institutions consists of two categories, business management and major business activities, for a systematic and comprehensive evaluation of the performances of public corporations and quasi-governmental institutions. The business management category is composed of indicators on management strategies and social contribution, human resources and performance management, a performance of financial and budget management and its accomplishment and the management of remuneration and employee welfare benefits (*Handbook on the 2016 Performance Evaluation*). The specific indicators and their weights differ by the types of institutions, but the evaluation of work efficiency applies to all types of public institutions (whether they may be public corporations, quasi-governmental institutions, small but strong quasi-governmental institutions). Work efficiency is also measured through the quantitative evaluation, regardless of the type of institution.

According to the *Handbook on the Performance Evaluation of Public Institutions*, the purpose of the evaluation of work efficiency was to evaluate the improvement in the comprehensive work efficiency. Institutions have been required to choose from indicators such as labor productivity and capital productivity, considering each of their characteristics. Institutions have also been allowed to set detailed indicators other than those presented in the *Handbook* so that the characteristics of each institution could be reflected. The indicators for work efficiency provided in the Handbook were as follows.

- Labor productivity = Value added/Average number of employees
- The Efficiency of project implementation = Net expenditure/Average number of employees
- Capital productivity = Value added/Total assets
- Value Added Ratio = Value added/Sales

According to the *Handbook*, the value added in the indicators above were calculated by adding the net financial expense, rent and the depreciation costs to the income before income taxes from the income statement.

2 Evaluation indicators for work efficiency by public institution

As mentioned above, the *Handbook on the Performance Evaluation of Public Institutions* has provided institutions with the option to choose from various indicators on work efficiency based on their characteristics. However, in reality, most institutions have used similar indicators for the unity among institutions and to enhance the comparability between them. For instance, in the 2016 evaluation, 29 out of 30 public corporations, only excluding the Korea Railroad Corporation, used labor productivity and capital productivity, each with four weights allocated to evaluate work efficiency. The Korea Railroad Corporation used the wages to sales ratio (wages/sales) aside from the labor productivity and capital productivity with three weights on labor productivity and capital productivity and two weights on the wages to sales ratio.

The implicit presupposition of the current work efficiency evaluation is, therefore, that institutions with differing characteristics could have their management efficiency evaluated by using the same indicators, which are labor productivity and capital productivity. Another presupposition is that the comparability between the institutions is more important than characteristics of institutions for the evaluation.

3 Changes in the weights of the work efficiency evaluation by institution type

Since 2011, the evaluation of work efficiency has accounted for 4–10 percent in the entire performance evaluation and has accounted for 6.15 percent to 13.3 percent out of the quantitative evaluation as a whole. Aside fund-management-based quasi-governmental institutions, the evaluation of work efficiency accounted for the lowest ratio in most institutions of all types in 2013. There was a difference in the ratio of the type of public institution; in 2016, the work efficiency indicator had the greatest ratio in public corporations, accounting for 8 percent out of the entire evaluation and 13.3 percent out of the quantitative evaluation, which was followed by 7.69 percent in the entire evaluation and 11.11 percent in the quantitative evaluation in small but strong quasi-governmental institutions. The work efficiency indicator accounted for 6 percent out of the entire evaluation and 10 percent in the quantitative evaluation in commissioned-service-type quasi-governmental institutions and was the lowest in fund-management-based quasi-governmental institutions by accounting for 4 percent out of the entire evaluation and 6.67 percent out of the quantitative evaluation. See Figure 10.1 for the details.

While there were differences by type, the work efficiency indicator has accounted for approximately 6 percent of the entire performance evaluation and weighted 10 to 13 percent in the quantitative evaluation, regardless of the year of evaluation. The work efficiency indicator was particularly important in the performance evaluation or the quantitative evaluation of public corporations. See Figure 10.2 for the details.

III Issues on the current quantitative evaluation on work efficiency

1 Exclusion of institutional characteristics

As mentioned above, the current quantitative evaluation on work efficiency is based on the assumption that different institutions could be evaluated through

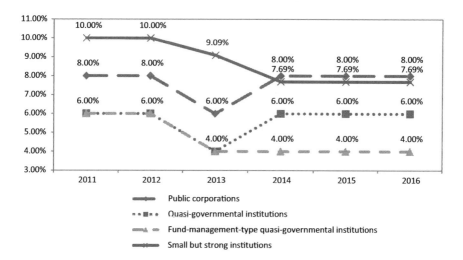

Figure 10.1 Proportion of work efficiency index to total evaluation score (quantitative and qualitative) by institution type

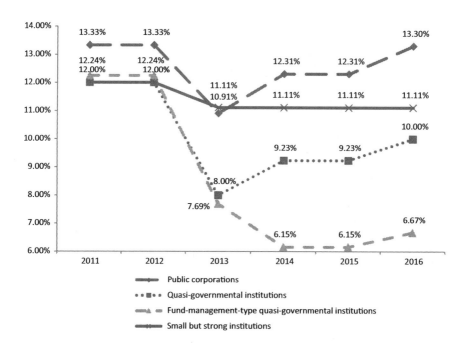

Figure 10.2 Proportion of work efficiency index to total quantitative score by institution type

the same indicators by using the same formula. Public corporations, in particular, have used the same indicators on work efficiency without choosing other indicators or without changing the weight placed on each indicator for at least past three years. Nevertheless, the current evaluation method, of applying the identical indicators to all institutions while disregarding any internal changes within in each institution, would make it difficult to measure the work efficiency that corresponds with the characteristics of each institution.

In the case of public corporations, all institutions that fall into this type have had their work efficiency evaluated by their capital productivity and labor productivity. The productivity, represented by the value added per worker, was measured by labor productivity. The performance rate of the productivity, which was represented by the value added per the invested asset unit, was measured by the capital productivity. This was due to the long-held traditional theory of economics, of land, labor and capital being the three factors of production. Nevertheless, the significance of each productive factor may differ by institution. That is, an asset may be more important for public corporations with larger assets and for corporations that value assets, in which case the capital productivity could be used to measure productivity. On the other hand, labor productivity would be needed for public corporations which place more value on labor. The current system, which applies the same indicators with the same weight on all institutions while disregarding the characteristics of each institution, and fails to consider the best indicators and weights for each institution, is forsaking the efficiency in measuring work efficiency at the cost of uniformity and comparability.

The Busan Port Authority, for instance, has an asset size of more than four trillion and five billion won but only 204 employees. Considering that there was only one new recruit in 2015, measuring the labor productivity of the Busan Port Authority, other than its capital productivity, would not provide ample information for work efficiency evaluation. As pointed out by Parmenter (2012), a larger number of performance measurements do not lead to better performance measurement and in most cases, the opposite is true.

As shown in Table 10.1, although the importance of the average number of employees and total assets vary across institutions, the present evaluation method uniformly evaluates work efficiency without considering the characteristics of each institution.

2 Efficiency and equity of evaluation indicators

There are various ways to define the efficiency of evaluation indicators. Yet if it could be defined as evaluating the subject of the evaluation, that is, the performance, with the smallest number of indicators, the current evaluation indicators for work efficiency are problematic in terms of the efficiency of the performance evaluation as a whole.

Capital productivity has been used as an indicator of work efficiency in the current evaluation, regardless of the types of institutions. Capital productivity is the value added divided by total assets, and as mentioned above, the value added

Table 10.1 Average number of employees and total assets by institutions (2013)

No.	Public Corporations	Average number of employees	Total assets (Unit: 1 million won)
1	Incheon International Airport Corporation	990	7,797,849
2	Korea Gas Corporation	3,215	38,007,896
3	Korea Airports Corporation	1,710	3,689,678
4	Korea Expressway Corporation	5,518	42,677,584
5	Korea National Oil Corporation	1,296	2,880,054
6	Korea Water Resources Corporation	3,916	5,558,652
7	Korea Electric Power Corporation	129	98,862,658
8	Korea District Heating Corporation	1,382	3,955,631
9	Korea Railroad Corporation	28,577	17,914,826
10	Korea Land and Housing Corporation	6,856	105,104,659
11	Korea Coal Corporation	1,703	661,751
12	Busan Port Authority	180	4,569,745
13	Yeosu Gwangyang Port Authority	91	2,096,777
14	Ulsan Port Authority	105	567,823
15	Incheon Port Authority	199	2,175,218
16	Jeju Free International City Development Center	276	717,067
17	Korea Housing and Urban Guarantee Corporation	392	5,699,333
18	Korea Appraisal Board	769	76,043
19	Korea Tourism Organization	916	912,188
20	Korea Resources Corporation	536	2,021,347
21	Korea South-East Power Co., Ltd	1,644	5,800,946
22	Korea Southern Power Co., Ltd	1,692	5,574,022
23	Korea East-West Power Co., Ltd	1,758	5,374,867
24	Korea Racing Authority	3,562	2,490,147
25	Korea Broadcast Advertising Corporation	303	786,847
26	Korea Western Power Co., Ltd	1,504	5,348,973
27	Korea Hydro & Nuclear Power Co, Ltd	7,643	19,212,755
28	Korea Minting, Security, Printing and ID Card Operating Corporation	1,490	355,387
29	Korea Midland Power Co., Ltd	1,831	4,993,560
30	Korea Marine Environment Management Corporation	540	175,532

is calculated by adding several items to the income before the income tax. If the capital productivity were to be simplified and calculated by the profit divided by asset for the sake of the discussion, it could be classified into two parts, of the operating profit ratio (profit/sales) and the asset turnover ratio (sales/asset).

Profit/Asset (Capital productivity) = Profit/Sales (Operating Profit) × Sales/Asset (Asset turnover ratio)

However, the operating profit or asset turnover ratio is evaluated with 1 weight and 3 weights respectively in most public corporations, through the performance evaluation on the management of financial and budget and its accomplishments. The Korea Broadcast Advertising Corporation, in particular, had its operating profit and asset turnover evaluated through the financial and budget performance evaluation (with a total weight of 6). The same indicators have been used in different evaluations on work efficiency and financial and budgeting performance, which has led to lower efficiency of the evaluation itself.

Moreover, since debt reduction through selling assets leads to a decrease in asset size, which in turn has a positive effect on the two indicators of debt reduction and capital productivity, the current evaluation may be unfair, by benefiting institutions that have their debt reduction performances evaluated in the evaluation on the management of finance and budget and its accomplishments (which were 18 out of 30 public corporations in 2015). The weight placed on evaluations and indicators, therefore, should be reconsidered.

3 Lack of institutional autonomy

The current work efficiency evaluation has overlooked the characteristics of each institution and has applied the same indicators set by the evaluation team to various public institutions, failing to reflect the autonomy of the institutions. The lack of institutional autonomy could be problematic for two reasons.

First, it is impossible to use the indicators that reflect the characteristics of each institution. As mentioned above, the current evaluation is less likely to place appropriate weight regarding the relative importance of capital or labor. Moreover, it fails to use accurate work efficiency indicators that reflect the characteristics of each organization, which could make the evaluation more effective. Under the current situation where there is an information asymmetry between the government and the evaluation team on the characteristic work efficiency of each institution, the information on the institutions which have the most information on the appropriate indicators for improving efficiency has not been reflected in the evaluation indicators.

Second, the current evaluation hinders the autonomy the heads of the institutions should have over the management of the institution. The total labor costs (the increase in the total labor costs) and the number of employees (labor productivity) are both controlled, which leaves the heads of institutions with nearly no autonomy over the labor costs. For higher efficiency adequate to each institution's conditions, it would be better to leave the decisions on putting more human resources into projects within the same range of labor costs or on reducing the number of employees to hire more capable employees with higher wages to the heads of the institutions.

4 Excessive weight on profit

The capital productivity and labor productivity used in the work efficiency evaluation have been calculated by dividing the value added by assets or an average number of employees. The value added has been based on the income before the taxes, wages, financial expense, rent and the depreciation costs are deducted. That is, while adjustments can be made, profit is set as the target for improving the productivity of the institutions.

In addition to the work efficiency evaluation, most public corporations have had their performance on the management of financial and budget and its accomplishments evaluated by indicators on profit, including the operating profit ratio, asset turnover ratio and return on equity, with a weight of six at most. Profit accounts for 23 percent of the entire quantitative evaluation. There may be controversy over how to measure the performance and productivity of public institutions which pursue public interest, but the current evaluation has too much emphasis on profit, which needs to be redressed.[1] If profit is not the ex-ante objective of establishing public institutions, it should not be the major factor in the ex-post evaluation on the public institutions (Likierman, 1983; Robson, 1960; Sen, 1975).

5 Increased danger of accounting fraud and the complexity of formulas

The excessive weight placed on profit in the quantitative evaluation increases the incentives for the institutions to manipulate their earnings. Concerns about the increase in accounting fraud after the introduction of the performance evaluation have been raised in various studies. Chung et al. (2013) conducted an empirical analysis on public corporations from 2007 and 2010 and found that as the weight on profit related indicators increased in the performance evaluation, so did the cases of earnings manipulations through accruals. Earnings manipulations were conducted in various ways, such as through abnormal production costs and abnormal discretionary expenses. However, as of current, there are no measures to reduce the probability of committing such accounting fraud and improving the quality of accounting information.

In addition to such earning manipulation, institutions have also employed various irregular classifications of their expenses to improve their evaluation results. To counter this, the formulas for calculating the variables used in the quantitative indicators have become increasingly more complicated. For instance, the number of lines explaining the quantitative management business costs in the *Handbook* increased from 11 lines in 2011 to 31 lines in 2016, showing how the formulas have increased and have become more complex at a fast pace in order to stop expedients. This makes the evaluation methods more elaborate, which may be inevitable to prevent institutions from evading the appropriateness of the evaluation. On the other hand, the overly complex evaluation methodology has led to higher evaluation costs (costs for the evaluation committees to learn the evaluation methods, confirmation costs, and the evaluation costs for institutions) and brought about the vicious cycle of hide-and-seek; of the government amending the evaluation methods and of the evaluated institutions classifying costs in new ways to avoid the evaluations.

Added to the complex formulas are the decisions on revenue creating assets and uncontrollability, which are exceptions to the evaluation. In fact, each institution has attempted to have the revenue creating assets and uncontrollability represent the profits of the institution when publishing annual handbooks on the institution, and such efforts have not been reflected consistently. The decision-making on how to apply such exceptions by the institution has also increased the costs for evaluating groups and hindered many institutions from accepting the evaluation results.

For example, the assets excluded from the calculation of capital productivity have differed by the institution and the sales or profits excluded from the evaluation in accordance with government policies have also been inconsistent. There are cases in which the general asset (inventories) has been excluded, as was the case for the Korea Gas Corporation. There also have been cases when specific assets were excluded, as was the case for the golf course at Gimpo International Airport, which is owned by the Korea Airports Corporation. Furthermore, assets in construction have sometimes been stated or left out, differing by institutions. Some institutions have also expressly excluded foreign exchange-related gains and losses. See Table 10.2 for the details of exceptions.

Although all public institutions may experience changes in their profit or sales due to government policies, there have been institutions which have considered such factors in the calculation, and those which were unable to, because of the

Table 10.2 Exceptions in calculating work efficiency index by institutions of public corporation group I (2016)

Institutions	Work Efficiency	Exceptions
Incheon International Airport Corporation	Labor Productivity	• When calculating value added, the cost of establishing Korea Institute of Aviation Safety Technology can be excluded. • The number of evaluators is calculated based on the current workforce excluding the construction workforce.
	Capital Productivity	• When calculating value added, the cost of establishing Korea Institute of Aviation Safety Technology can be excluded.
Korea Gas Corporation	Capital Productivity	• When calculating value added, added values for M&A related assets not exceeding three years after the acquisition are excluded. • When calculating total assets, exploration blocks for exploitation of oil and gas fields and M&A related assets not exceeding three years after the acquisition are excluded. • Development and production blocks for exploiting oil and gas fields are included in the total assets according to the assets depreciated by the units of production method of the current year. • When calculating total assets, inventories (equivalent to safe inventory) and construction in progress are excluded.

(Continued)

Table 10.2 (Continued)

Institutions	Work Efficiency	Exceptions
Korea Airports Corporation	Labor Productivity	• When calculating average number of employees, workforce required to operate Uljin Flight Training Center is excluded.
	Capital Productivity	• When calculating total assets, construction in progress and the amount of additional asset growth directly related to Uljin Flight Training Center are excluded. The amount of the government's investment in kind of land related to the construction of Gimpo Airport Public Golf Club can be deferred until related revenue is generated.
Korea Expressway Corporation	Labor Productivity	• When calculating value added, sales are calculated by including tolls exempted by laws and government policies as well as ABS* tolls according to the sales on the income statement and by deducting profits from map support project and road maintenance. The cost of goods sold is calculated by excluding expenses of map support project and maintenance of free roads from the cost of goods sold on the income statement. * Asset Backed Securities: the securities issued on the basis of tangible or intangible backed assets.
	Capital Productivity	• Considerations for calculating value added are equal to those of labor productivity index. • When calculating total assets (excluding construction in progress), road accounts for free zone where sales are not realized are deducted and acquisition values of road asset that is deducted due to issuing ABS are included. However, for evaluation, depreciation method for supervisory authority of a toll road follows the straight-line depreciation method.
Korea National Oil Corporation	Capital Productivity	• When calculating value added, revenues related to petroleum reserves as well as M&A related assets not exceeding three years after the acquisition are excluded from the added value. • When calculating total assets, exploration blocks for oil field exploitation, M&A related assets not exceeding three years after the acquisition, petroleum reserves and construction in progress are excluded. Tangible and intangible assets of development and production blocks for oil field exploitation are included in the amount of depreciation of tangible and intangible

Institutions	Work Efficiency	Exceptions
		assets in accordance with units of production method. Investment assets are added to the total assets according to the amount of corresponding depreciation (investment assets × depreciation amount of subsidiary × total amount of depreciated assets of subsidiary).
Korea Water Resources Corporation	Labor Productivity	• Labor productivity can be calculated by excluding "Expansion of Investments in Public Institution (December, 2008)" and expansion of investments and operation management project (e.g., Gyeongin Ara Waterway, 4 Major Rivers Project, etc.) in accordance with the Green New Deal Program. • Labor productivity is evaluated with the exception of water front development business and power generation business (But tidal power generation business is included for evaluation).
	Capital Productivity	• When calculating total assets - Construction in progress is excluded. - New facilities since 1995 that have not reached the normal rate of capacity utilization are included in the capital as much as the capacity utilization for the pertinent year. - Normal rate of capacity utilization can be calculated with the exception of "Expansion of Investments in Public Institution (December, 2008)" and expansion of investments and operation management project (e.g., Gyeongin Ara Waterway, 4 Major Rivers Project, etc.) in accordance with the Green New Deal Program. - Normal rate of capacity utilization can be evaluated by excluding water front development business and power generation business (But tidal power generation is included for evaluation).
Korea District Heating Corporation	Labor Productivity	• When calculating value added, the effect of fuel adjustment mechanism corrects revenue based on accrual basis.
	Capital Productivity	• When calculating value added, the effect of fuel adjustment mechanism corrects revenue based on accrual basis. • When calculating total assets, construction in progress is excluded.

(*Continued*)

Table 10.2 (Continued)

Institutions	Work Efficiency	Exceptions
Korea Railroad Corporation	Labor Productivity	• When calculating value added, disposable profits from land sales of Yongsan station-influenced areas are excluded. • The sales loss due to the opening of SR can be evaluated considering the SR performance since the opening of Suseo KTX.
	Capital Productivity	• When calculating value added, disposable profits from land sales of Yongsan station-influenced areas are excluded. • The sales loss due to the opening of SR can be evaluated considering the SR performance since the opening of Suseo KTX
Korea Land and Housing Corporation	Labor Productivity	• When calculating value added, - The rental amount, which is calculated by multiplying the average of the opening balance and ending balance of security deposit by the exchange rates between monthly rent and security deposit, is included in the added value. - The exchange rates between monthly rent and security deposit refers to the average exchange rates of monthly rent and security deposit of all apartments across the nation, which is announced monthly by the Korea Appraisal Board through the Real Estates Price Information System in accordance with Article 86 of the Housing Act. When calculating the standard value, actual value, and deviation, the same exchange rates for the current year is applied.
	Capital Productivity	• Considerations for calculating value added are equal to those of labor productivity index.

changes within the term or the lack of bargaining power, thereby hindering the consistency of the evaluation.

While the government has promised in words or via documents that there would be no disadvantages to the performance evaluation of public institutions which are working on projects for implementing government policies, there have been cases in which institutions were disadvantaged because such matters have not been reflected in their handbooks or due to the disagreement between the inspecting department and the Ministry of Strategy and Finance. In extreme cases, this led public institutions, which are obligated to implement public projects, to reject such projects out of fear of such disadvantages.

6 Lack of systemic evaluation for sustainable management efficiency

The current indicators of work efficiency in the quantitative evaluation concern the outcome of actions, rather than directly controlling the actions. This way, the indicators serve as Key Result Indicators (KRI) rather than being Key Performance Indicators (KPI) (Parmenter, 2012). Since the work efficiency is measured by the eventual outcome (or profit so to speak) of many stages of actions conducted by individual employees, the current performance evaluation is not clearly connected with what an individual worker in the institution should do every day. In other words, the work efficiency indicators used in the performance evaluation fail to properly manage or control the daily actions of each worker. While it may be difficult for the performance evaluation, which evaluates an institution as a whole, to evaluate the daily activities of all workers working in the institution, the ultimate goal of the performance evaluation should be to have the institutions establish a system that could improve work efficiency by connecting the daily tasks of each employee with the founding purpose of the institution.

This is why the evaluation should be focused on the founding purpose of the institution, the establishment of strategies to fulfill this purpose and the work efficiency that connects the two, which make up the system for improving institutional performance. In case of type 1 public corporations, the improvements in the management of the institution is a sub-indicator of the evaluation indicator on management strategy and social contribution, which is qualitatively evaluated with 3 weights. According to the *Handbook*, there are three specific indicators for the evaluation on management innovation. First, has the institution analyzed and predicted the future and changes in the environment and prepared its responses? Has it adjusted the functions of the institution (by aligning its declining functions and projects), and set its future strategic tasks (by finding new growth engines and new projects) and targets in accordance with its tasks and characteristics? Second, have the institution's efforts and performances been appropriate for the improvement of its ability to react to changes in management environments through efficient management and work process innovation (by simplifying procedures, etc.)? Third, have the institution's effort and performance in enhancing the institution's key work performance by improving nationwide service and alleviating the citizens' burden, be appropriate? Among the three specific indicators, only the second and third indicators evaluate whether the institution has been measuring and has improved the performance of daily tasks, which account for 2 points out of 100. The indicators show how the current evaluation barely touches the issue of how efficient the institution has managed the daily work process.

7 Evaluation of the quality of financial information and improved transparency

High-quality financial information is pivotal to fair and efficient evaluation. Financial information which is of high quality and accurately represents the status of an institution can be obtained through the transparent disclosure of the internal control system and financial information.

One of the most effective ways to obtain high-quality financial information is to strengthen internal control. The internal control system has been evaluated through the evaluation of standing auditors and members of the audit committee. In accordance with Article 36 of the Act on the Management of Public Institutions, the evaluation on the performance of standing auditors and members of the audit committee evaluates whether the auditors' effort and performance have been appropriate and accountable. According to the *Handbook*, the evaluation is conducted by the standing auditors or the members of the audit committee who have worked in public institutions and quasi-governmental institutions during the year of the evaluation. The auditors are, in principle, evaluated once during their terms and the results of the management performance evaluation and the evaluation conducted by the Board of Audit and Inspection, as well as the integrity test conducted by the Anti-Corruption and Civil Rights Commission, could be reflected in the evaluation.

However, the current performance evaluation on standing auditors and members of the audit board is conducted only once during each auditor's term and the evaluation results of the performance evaluation of the public institution are reflected in the evaluation on the auditors. As a result, the incentives of the auditor who should inspect the financial information and the internal system should be aligned with the interests of the institution through the results of the performance evaluation of the institution. The ultimate purpose of the auditor should not be in improving the performance of public institutions but should be in improving their transparency and accountability.

Detailed and transparent disclosure of financial information could also be used to improve the efficiency of an organization. The current evaluation has an indicator on releasing information but the weight is only a lowly 1 and the evaluation of the systematic disclosure of financial information has not been conducted. The OECD considers accountability and transparency to be the most important principles for inspection, evaluation and reporting of the performance of public institutions (OECD, 2016). In spite of the significance of transparent measuring and disclosure of performance for the improved performance of public institutions, the importance of such principles has not been fully reflected in the current performance evaluation.

IV   Improvement plans for the quantitative evaluation of work efficiency

1   Strengthening evaluation of the system for continued improvement in work efficiency

The current evaluation has focused on the financial results rather than evaluating the public institution's effort in devising a system which could continuously improve work or management efficiency. However, as mentioned above, the current method of using the overall results of specific actions as indicators has induced the government and the institutions to play a hide-and-seek game with the costs and induced institutes to manipulate accounts. Not to mention the fact that it is inefficient and costly to have the evaluators control, check and evaluate every little detail in all evaluated indicators. The costs incurred do not only include the evaluation costs but also the opportunity cost of hiding such costs and for reclassifying costs which are not directly related to work efficiency.

To complement this, an evaluation indicator which checks whether the evaluated institution has an appropriate governance system that could minimize the principal-agent problem should be added. Institutions would then be able to continue building a governance system for management efficiency. The OECD (2013) pointed out that the board of directors held the key for the management and performance management of public institutions and called for the board of directors to break free from their traditional and adaptive roles and to focus on the establishment of strategies and the institutions' performances. To realize this, the appointment process of the board of directors should be transparent and the board should have more autonomy over its objectives and priorities. The OECD recommends that the board of directors play specific and appropriate roles in establishing strategies, overseeing the management, and making decisions on the compensation system for the management in order to fulfill the institution's goals. Consequently, for each institution to have systems which could improve management efficiency, continuous evaluation should be conducted on the entire governance system of an institution, including the board of directors.

2 Concretizing the indicators and simplifying the formulas

The current evaluation has measured performance with comprehensive and general indicators, such as profit, without considering specific efficiency goals that correspond with the institution's purpose. Managing performance by using comprehensive performance indicators without using any specific performance targets, however, could lead to unintended results. This was shown in the following case presented by Parmenter (2012).

A hospital in the United Kingdom measured the time it takes for a patient to register in the emergency room and to see a doctor and reflected the duration of time in the performance evaluation to reduce it. According to the analysis of the registration process conducted by the ER workers, it was unlikely that the registration of patients who walked into the ER themselves with mild symptoms or minor injuries was delayed. However, it took a long time for critical patients brought in ambulances to register as they are nursed by the emergency team (the emergency team working in ambulances). Based on this analysis, the workers at the hospital had the patients in ambulances wait in the parking lot for registration until the doctors were ready, in order to meet the performance target by reducing the waiting time after registration and until the patients meet the doctors. Thus, the hospital's parking lot became full with ambulances, and due to the lack of unoccupied ambulances, new emergency patients were unable to be brought to the hospital. A more serious problem was that the critical patients who had been brought in ambulances and have taken priority before the new performance measure had been introduced were now pushed back from the priority list. If the hospital had subdivided the performance measures and focused on the waiting time of critical patients than that of all patients who visit the emergency room, the treatment on critical patients, which should be at the center of focus at the emergency room, could have been expedited. As this example shows, setting and managing goals by using extensive and comprehensive indicators with a vague expectation that all actions of the evaluated subjects could be controlled, could lead to higher incentives to manipulate specific items (behaviors) with the purpose to meet the target. In addition, the more unspecific and expansive the performance measurements are, the more the items which require manipulation. The side-effects of performance evaluations could be minimized by setting the work efficiency the individual public institution wishes to improve and by using specific and simple indicators for evaluation, rather than using comprehensive and common indicators. The formulas also need to be simplified by using the specific items that require management in accordance with government guidelines. By implementing such performance indicators, complicating formulas for preventing the manipulation of the specific items included in the comprehensive indicators would also be unnecessary, thereby reducing the evaluation costs.

3 Emphasis on public interest and the institutions' achievement of goals

The current evaluation method has focused overly on the profit gains of the institution and on cutting the costs by cutting quantitative management costs, rather than concentrating on the achievement of the institution's individual goals. The findings of a study empirically proved that the current evaluation method has contributed to the increase in the institution's expense rather than its growth (Kim, 2015). The current evaluation method is inadequate in encouraging institutions to meet the public interest and establishment goals. For encouraging institutions to improve their goals, for instance, it would be more effective to have the Korea Gas Corporation and the Korea National Oil Corporation focus on securing and supplying resources safely rather than having them use their internal resources to induce cost reduction.

As shown in the case of the ER in the United Kingdom, it is important for the performance measurement to be conducted on important issues within an institution, and also to understand the institution's key success factor beforehand. It is also important to define the purpose of establishment of the public institution, determine the specific key success factors for achieving the purpose of establishment, and to measure the factors necessary for the efficient accomplishment of the purpose. The focus of the evaluation, therefore, should not be on reducing costs in public institutions but should be on the efficient achievement of the institution's goals.

One fast-food chain set its goal as minimizing the amount of wasted chicken, after which the employees started cooking after receiving orders, which lengthened the waiting time and led to a huge drop in the number of customers (Parmenter,

2012). The efficiency of an institution could be improved by focusing more on the ultimate goals rather than reducing costs. The costs saved by a microscopic cost reduction are only minimal, compared to the waste of budget incurred by investments unrelated to the mission of an institution. Minimizing the microscopic cost reduction, which is easily affected by public opinion, and focusing on the specific performance indicators, which correspond to the basic purpose of the institution, would help public institutions achieve its goals. In the case of the Korea Electric Power Corporation, for instance, small-scale cuts on employee welfare benefits would be meaningless if the supply of electric power was unstable and costly. An evaluation which allows the employees to be provided with adequate welfare benefits and induces the institution to serve its true purpose would be much more efficient.

The evaluation, therefore, should put less emphasis on cost reduction and focus more on the institution's goal achievements. Increasing the evaluation weight of major business activities could be a way to achieve this. Although this may lead the comparability between public institutions to fall, increasing the importance of major business activities in the evaluation would help improve the efficiency by reflecting the characteristics of each institution.

4 Strengthening the autonomy of public institutions (and their heads) and weakening the link between performance-related pay and performance evaluation

The current government-led evaluation system has its limits to which the evaluation team could effectively manage and evaluate the various work efficiency in public institutions. One alternative to such issue could be to have the heads of institutions, which have adequate governance systems, to take responsibility for improving management effectiveness. In this case, minimizing the performance evaluation which includes indicators on work efficiency and giving more responsibility to the top management of each public institution, including the head, could be an option. The OECD (2016) has also called for governments to provide public institutions with maximum autonomy for autonomous goal achievement and to minimize interventions on the management of public institutions.

Moreover, the influence of the evaluation on public institutions should be limited to the performance-related pay of the heads of the institution and the top management, and should not be extended to the performance-related pay of junior staffs. This way, there would be fewer incentives for the staffs of public institutions to manipulate costs or accounts for the performance evaluation.

Kim (2015) conducted an empirical analysis on how expanding the autonomy of public corporations by downsizing the performance evaluation and the relation between the performance evaluation results and the performance-related pay affect the profitability and growth of the public corporations. The analysis showed that the profitability and growth of public corporations decreased as the size of the performance evaluation teams grew. Kim (2015) pointed out that as stronger regulations were placed on public corporations, the constraints placed on the management of the enterprise decreased, and that enterprises were unable to make autonomous decisions on how to create profit in the market and on which new project to launch, which had a negative effect on the profitability and growth of public corporations. In addition, the gap in the performance-related pay among institutions was found to have no statistical significance in the enterprises' profitability and growth. After conducting an empirical analysis on a total of 287 public institutions, including public corporations, quasi-governmental institutions and non-classified public institutions from 2006 to 2010, Yoon (2013) found that the larger the amount of performance-related pay became, the frequency of earning adjustments increased as well. If the connection between performance-related pay, which has been considered as the most effective penalty in the performance evaluation, and the result of performance evaluation does not have a positive effect on the result of management but have negative outcomes such as accounting fraud, that connection should certainly be weakened.

Parmenter (2012) argued that the moment the amount of performance-related pay is linked with the KPI, the Key Performance Indicators would turn into Key Political Indicators for higher performance-related pay. Under the current performance evaluation, the results of the performance evaluation are imperative in the amount of performance-related pay for the executives and the staffs at public institutions. Such evaluation method has its merits as it could enable the workers to put maximum effort to achieve their goals. However, it also enables the institutions' goals to be replaced with the results of the performance evaluation or induces the institutions' resources to be overly focused on the evaluation, and is increasing the incentive to manipulate performance indicators for better results. As the link between the performance evaluation and the performance-related pay becomes stronger, and as the proportion of the performance-related pay increases, public institutions are more likely to be lured to manipulate their performance results. The evaluation results, therefore, should either have limited use as reference material for the heads of the institutions' reappointment or for the decision on the performance-related pay of the heads and top management team in public institutions, or should only have limited effect on the amount of performance-related pay.

5 Long-term evaluation

At the moment, the performance evaluation is conducted every year, which makes it difficult for institutions to improve their efficiency by devising new types of projects or by making changes in their organization. New changes will lead to higher volatility of financial indicators, but in the current system under which the evaluation sets the targets (deviation), the increase in volatility would likely result in a bad performance evaluation result. In addition, the government does not wait, even if an institution should fail in its pursuit of new changes or if the changes take time to come to fruition, and instead chooses to conduct immediate evaluations and to place restrictions by means of the performance evaluation. As a result, innovations and risks have become dangerous choices for public institutions.

An evaluation system which encourages safe management by deterring innova-tions and changes and inducing institutions to avoid risks would likely be harmful to the institutions' long-term growth and development. As pointed out by Drucker (1990), organizations which are averse to risks and do not break away from familiar fields to jump into the unknown world cannot survive the 21st century. Drucker pointed out that great accomplishment could not be achieved with the fear of failure. Extending the evaluation cycle would enable institutions to pursue change or to make mistakes, so that they could stop maintaining the status quo or accomplishing minute achievements and accomplish long-term growths.

The annual evaluation is also increasing fatigue among talented human resources and the entire organization in public institutions since one group has to take full charge of the preparation for the annual evaluation. It makes it difficult for institutions to pursue long-term organizational changes and induces them to pursue short-term goals. Rather than conducting annual evaluations, having in-depth evaluations in three to five years and encouraging institutions to become more efficient in the long-term could be an alternative. If the evaluation should be conducted annually, the government could also consider dividing the indicators and evaluating several indicators consecutively.

Long-term evaluations would also enable the manipulated accruals to be reversed over time, which would likely decrease the incentive to manipulate the accruals. Moreover, the influence of errors in the evaluation due to the market situation or by coincidence would be minimized so that the efforts put by institu-tions could be measured more accurately.

6 Strengthening evaluation for improving the quality of information and transparency

As discussed, the precondition for fair and efficient performance evaluation is to secure high-quality financial information. In order to secure such information, the role of the internal control organs, such as the auditors or the audit board, should be strengthened. According to OECD and Korea Institute of Public Finance (2016), auditors in public institutions, especially in the non-classified public insti-tutions, are lacking in their autonomy and expertise. In some institutions, for-mer employees were appointed as auditors, thereby violating the autonomy of the auditor. The same study also found that the integrity of a public institution was improved when its auditor has the expertise, rather than being appointed from related departments. Evaluation of the autonomy and expertise of the auditors or the audit boards should be strengthened to improve the quality of financial infor-mation as well as the transparency of management.

Moreover, the results of the performance evaluation should be excluded from the evaluation of the standing officers or the audit board and more emphasis should be put on the internal control and autonomy of the auditors. Whereas the most important role of the audit board in the United States is to be effective in controlling the production process of the financial report and to verify the reli-ability of the financial statements, the auditors and audit boards in Korea are still focusing on uncovering corruption. In order to provide high-quality financial information and to improve the work efficiency of the institution, there should be a strict evaluation on the auditors' or the audit boards' verification of financial statements. In addition, the appointment process of non-permanent members of the audit board should also be conducted so as to improve the autonomy and expertise of the audit board.

V Lessons learned and conclusion

1 Lessons learned

One-time performance evaluations do not guarantee continuous improvements in public institutions. To bring about continuous improvements, it is a good idea to evaluate the governance system rather than the performance itself. Performance indicators tend to be complicated to prevent any games public institutions might play. Complicated indicators, however, lead to unintended side effects and increase evaluations costs. It is a good idea to keep the indicator formula simple. Excessive evaluation of productivity and profitability blurs publicity and the goals of the institution. It is recommended to reduce the weights on productivity and efficiency and to increase the weights on achieving a main goal of the institution. While a strong connection between performance and performance-related pay encourages the employees in public institutions to work for the performance indicators, it also creates incentives for the manipulation of indicators and results. The connection between the evaluation and performance-related pay needs to be limited to the top management team rather than being applied to all employees.

2 Conclusion

This paper examines issues and suggestions on the current indicators on work efficiency indicators in the annual performance evaluation of public institutions conducted by the government. For years the same indicators on work efficiency have been used in all institutions to increase the comparability. Public corporations, in particular, have used labor productivity and capital productivity as indicators without any exceptions. However, using the same indicator does not reflect unique production factors for each institution and is insufficient for each institution to find their own ways to improve work efficiency. Moreover, the current indicators overlap with the indicators on the management of finance and budget. The indicators also have a risk of encouraging accounting fraud. While complicate formulas have been developed to counter this, the complicated formulas can also lead to higher evaluation costs and lower equity. This study also finds that the current indicators are lacking in evaluating whether the system of each institution ensures continuous work efficiency. This study further points out that the current evaluation is insufficient in improving the quality of the financial information as well as the institution's transparency.

To improve the indicators, I suggest that evaluation should be conducted on the system for continuous improvements on work efficiency and that the evaluation indicators should be more specified and simplified, so that unintended actions from the institutions could be prevented. I further suggest that the weights on the business management indicators should be reduced to put emphasis on the public institutions' pursuit of public interest. The connection between the performance evaluation and the performance-related pay needs to be weakened since the correlation between the performance-related pay and performance improvements are uncertain under the current system. I further suggest that the frequency of the evaluation could be reduced for a long-term and in-depth evaluation. Finally, I propose to establish a system which could improve the quality of financial information and the transparency of the institutions, and could especially improve the evaluation on the auditors and the audit committee.

Note

1 However, as pointed out by Ravi (1987), it is difficult to estimate the social welfare function in reality and profit, which is easier to define and non-controversial, is used as an indicator to evaluate public institutions in a majority of countries.

References

Choi, Y. S., Hwang, I., and Song, S. A. (2015). Effect of target-setting uncertainty in performance evaluation of Korean SOEs on effort reduction incentive. *Korean Public Administration Review*, *49*(3), 219–246.

Chung, J. H., Yoo, J. M., and Yoon, D. H. (2013). The Effect of Performance Measure Characteristic on Earnings Management in Public Enterprises. *Korean Journal of Management Accounting Research*, *13*(1), 1–38.

Drucker, P. F. (1990). *Managing the Non-Profit Organization*. HarperCollins.

Kim, J. Y. (2015). Did the Size of Performance Evaluation Committee and the Incentive Gap Affect the Performances of Public Enterprises? *Korean Journal of Public Finance*, *8*(3), 1–26.

Likierman, A. (1983). The Use of Profitability in Assessing the Performance of Public Enterprises. In V. V. Ramanadham (ed.), *Public Enterprise and the Developing Countries* (pp. 71–86). London: Croom Helm.

Ministry of Strategy and Finance. *Handbook on the Performance Evaluation of Public Institutions (2007–2016)*. Ministry of Strategy and Finance.

Ministry of Strategy and Finance. *Performance Evaluation Report of Public Institutions (2007–2016)*. Ministry of Strategy and Finance.

OECD. (2013). *Boards of Directors of State-Owned Enterprises: An Overview of National Practices, Corporate Governance*. Paris: OECD Publishing. https://doi.org/10.1787/9789264200425-en.

OECD, Korea Institute of Public Finance. (2016). *State-Owned Enterprises in Asia: National Practices for Performance Evaluation and Management*. Paris: OECD Publishing.

Park, S. K. (2006). Performance Management Systems and Organizational Competence in the Public Sector: An Empirical Analysis of 13 Korean State-Owned Enterprises. *Korean Public Administration Review*, *40*(3), 219–244.

Parmenter, D. (2012). *Key Performance Indicators for Government and Non-Profit Agencies: Implementing Winning KPIs.* John Wiley & Sons.

Ra, Y. J. (2015). *Analysis on the Audit System in Public Institutions and Its Current Status.* Korea Institute of Public Finance.

Ramamurti, R. (1987). Performance Evaluation of State-Owned Enterprises in Theory and Practice. *Management Science, 33*(7), 876–893.

Robson, W. (1960). *Nationalized Industry and Public Ownership.* London: George Allen & Unwin.

Sen, A. (1975). *Profit Maximization and the Public Sector.* John Matthai Memorial Lecture, India, Mimeo: Kerala University.

Yoon, S. M. (2013). The Effects of Compensation and Tax Incentive of Public Institutions on Earnings Management for Loss Avoidance. *Korean Accounting Journal, 22*(4), 51–79.

11 Investigation of the theoretical foundation for the quantitative indicator target assignment (deviation) evaluation method in performance evaluation of public institutions

Illoong Kwon

I Introduction

The 2016 Performance Evaluation of Public Institutions classifies public institutions into four broad categories – public corporations, commissioned-service-type quasi-governmental institutions, fund-management-type quasi-governmental institutions and small but strong quasi-governmental institutions. Evaluation criteria can be broadly divided into business management and major projects. Evaluation methods are then further divided into qualitative evaluation and quantitative evaluation. For public corporations, quantitative evaluation is given a higher weight with a 35 percent weight allocated to qualitative evaluation and the remaining 65 percent weight given to quantitative evaluation. The outcome of quantitative evaluation tends to determine the overall rating of an institution given that quantitative evaluation is being given the relatively higher weight and that there is a significant cross-sectional variation among institutions.

For quantitative evaluation, evaluation methods such as target assignment (deviation), target assignment, global performance comparison, mid- to long-term target assignment, target versus performance and trend analysis exist. Among these, target assignment (deviation) evaluation method is most widely used. Target assignment (deviation) evaluation method basically calculates a five-year standard deviation of a given quantitative indicator and grants full score for performance improvement in the excess of one or two standard deviations above last year's performance.

However, neither the theoretical reasoning for such target assignment (deviation) evaluation method nor the objective of such evaluation method has been clearly discussed. Biased evaluation indicator can lead to bias in institutions' behavior. Especially, in the current process in which an institution first proposes the architecture of quantitative performance indicators and the evaluation committee examines it, bias in the design of quantitative performance indicator can occur due to the institution's incentives to first propose indicators that are beneficial for itself. Therefore, it is necessary to clearly evaluate the theoretical foundation for and constructively discuss potential areas for improvements in target assignment (deviation) that is the major evaluation method in current quantitative evaluation.

In approaching the research problem, this research sets a direction in first analyzing circumstances in which target assignment (deviation) can be justified, instead of a direction that first critically points out the problems of target assignment (deviation). The fact that target assignment (deviation) evaluation method has long been used for an extended period of time without a significant problem reflects that the evaluation method has a relatively high acceptability and a low experimental error. However, if there is large gap between the situation justifying the use of current form of target assignment (deviation) evaluation method and realistic environment, appropriate directions for improvement can be discussed.

In searching for the justification of target assignment (deviation) evaluation method, it is necessary to first look at which objectives the evaluation method can achieve. In terms of main objectives of evaluation, objectives such as ex-post evaluating the effort level of the institution and ex-ante providing incentives for efforts by the institution can be considered. Therefore, this research analyzes target assignment (deviation) evaluation method by differentiating the ex-post evaluation perspective from the ex-ante incentive perspective.

II Target assignment (deviation) evaluation method

As explained in detail in the Appendix, target assignment (deviation) evaluation method has the structure of essentially calculating the standard deviation of a performance indicator from previous five years and assigning a perfect score for performance improvement in the excess of one or two standard deviations above last year's performance.

Based the 2016 Evaluation Manual, a closer examination can be made possible using improvement indicators (in other words, indicators increasing in the level of performance) for major businesses. First, a performance benchmark is set as the larger of either last year's performance or average performance in previous three years. However, given the generally increasing trend in performance, last year's performance becomes the performance benchmark in most cases. Under the assumption of absence of extreme values, a score for relevant quantitative performance indicator is determined in the following way.[1]

$$\text{Score} = 20 + 80 \times \frac{Performance - Minimum\ Target}{Maximum\ Target - Minimum\ Target}$$

Minimum target is measured by subtracting two standard deviations of performance in previous five years from the performance benchmark. Also, maximum target is calculated by adding two standard deviations of performance in previous five years to the performance benchmark.[2] Under the assumption that last year's performance is the performance benchmark, the equation can be re-expressed in the following way.

$$\text{Score} = 20 + 80 \times \frac{y_t - (y_{t-1} - 2\sigma)}{(y_{t-1} + 2\sigma) - (y_{t-1} - 2\sigma)}$$

Here, y_t represents quantitative indicator performance/result in the evaluation year and y_{t-1} represents last year's performance. In addition, σ normally represents the standard deviation of quantitative indicator in previous five years. This scoring evaluation method can be re-organized in the following way.

$$\text{Score} = 20 + 80 \times \frac{y_t - (y_{t-1} - 2\sigma)}{(y_{t-1} + 2\sigma) - (y_{t-1} - 2\sigma)}$$

$$= 20 + 80 \times \frac{y_t - y_{t-1} + 2\sigma}{4\sigma}$$

$$= 20 + 80 \times \left(\frac{y_t - y_{t-1}}{4\sigma} + \frac{1}{2} \right)$$

$$= 60 + 40 \times \left(\frac{y_t - y_{t-1}}{2\sigma} \right) \qquad \text{(Equation 1)}$$

However, a perfect score is 100 and any score above 100 is therefore regarded only as 100. That is, as explained earlier, the structure grants a perfect score of 100 if $\frac{y_t - y_{t-1}}{2\sigma} > 1$ or $\frac{y_t - y_{t-1}}{\sigma} > 2$.

III Theoretical foundation for ex-post evaluation

1 Short-term performance

In order to search for the theoretical foundation for the use of target assignment (deviation) evaluation method in ex-post evaluation, it is necessary to make assumptions on how the institution's performance is determined. First, the following way can be considered as the most straightforward, simplest way of performance determination.

$$y_t = k + a_t + e_t \qquad \text{(Equation 2)}$$

Here, y_t represents quantitative indicator performance in the evaluation year, k is the intercept, a_t represents the institution's effort in the evaluation year, and e_t represents exogenous factors that affected performance in the evaluation year. Given that e_t is the exogenous effect uncontrollable by the institution, it can be interpreted as a random variable.

In addition, because effort of the institution (a_t) does not affect future performance (y_{t+1}), it can be simply interpreted as the resulting performance from short-term operation.

Especially, it is assumed that e_t follows a normal distribution with mean of 0 and variance of σ^2. Then, y_t also follows a normal distribution with mean of $k + a_t$ and variance of σ^2. And $y_t - y_{t-1}$, as a factor in target assignment (deviation) evaluation method, follows a normal distribution under the assumption of independence between e_t and e_{t-1}.

$$y_t - y_{t-1} \sim N\left(a_t - a_{t-1}, 2\sigma^2\right)$$

At this point, it is assumed that the purpose of ex-post evaluation is to examine whether effort of the institution increased compared to that of last year. Then, the null hypothesis of such evaluation or verification is as follows.

$$H_0 : a_t - a_{t-1} = 0$$

Under the null hypothesis, $\dfrac{y_t - y_{t-1}}{\sigma\sqrt{2}}$ follows a standard normal distribution.

$$\frac{y_t - y_{t-1}}{\sigma\sqrt{2}} \sim N(0,1)$$

At this point, if σ is unknown ex-ante, it can be estimated using sample standard error. That is, $s^2 = \dfrac{1}{n-1}\Sigma(y_t - \bar{y})^2$ can be used as an estimator of σ^2.[3] Then, as well known $\dfrac{y_t - y_{t-1}}{s\sqrt{2}}$ follows a t-distribution with n − 1 degrees of freedom.

Because target assignment (deviation) uses standard deviation of performance in previous 5 years, the degree of freedom becomes 4 (= 5 − 1). This is known as following.

$$P_r\left(\frac{y_t - y_{t-1}}{s\sqrt{2}} > 1.53\right) = P_r\left(\frac{y_t - y_{t-1}}{2s} > 1.08\right) = 0.1$$

Therefore, if we were to examine whether effort of the institution increased relative to that of previous year with a 10 percent significance, approximately $\dfrac{y_t - y_{t-1}}{2s} > 1$ becomes the standard of judgment. This is consistent with target assignment (deviation) evaluation method for major businesses as summarized earlier.

That is, target assignment (deviation) evaluation method for major businesses can be interpreted as ex-post evaluation process that verifies whether effort of the institution increased relative to that of previous year with a 10 percent statistical significance. In other words, if one is to examine whether effort of the institution increased relative to that of previous year with a 10% significance, current target assignment (deviation) evaluation method can be theoretically justified.

However, it remains unclear whether such evaluation method is appropriate. For example, it can be criticized as an unrealistic evaluation method if last year's performance was achieved with maximum effort, a full score can be granted only with an increase in effort from last year's maximum level.

In particular, if the institution exerts the same best effort in each year, the relevant performance indicator should not exhibit large changes in each year. However, it is easy to find quantitative indicators that doubled since 2010. Therefore, a theoretical criticism can be made that short-term performance determination method proposed in (Equation 2) may not be appropriate.

If short-term performance determination method such as (Equation 2) is appropriate and large annual increases in the relevant performance indicator are intended by evaluation, current evaluation method targets increases in manpower and budget annually allocated to short-term performance and can be interpreted as a way of ex-post evaluating this goal.

2 Long-term performance

If a performance indicator is increasing annually in a consistent manner, another explanation can be considered for determining current year's performance as a function of the institution's effort on top of last year's performance. Stated differently, in case current year's effort not only increases current year's performance, but also enhances future performance, performance can be increasing in each year with the same level of effort by the institution.

Such determination method for long-term performance can be expressed with following equation.

$$y_t = y_{t-1} + a_t + e_t \qquad \text{(Equation 3)}$$

Here, e_t is the exogenous effect uncontrollable by the institution and assumed to follow a normal distribution with mean of 0 and variance of σ^2. Then, it is also assumed that the objective of evaluation is to ex-post verify whether the institution exerted best effort in current year. That is, the null hypothesis of verification is as follows.

$$H_0 : a_t = 0$$

Then, under the null hypothesis, $\dfrac{y_t - y_{t-1}}{\sigma}$ follows a standard normal distribution in the following manner.

$$\frac{y_t - y_{t-1}}{\sigma} \sim N(0,1)$$

At this point, if σ is unknown ex-ante, it can be estimated using sample standard error. That is, under the null hypothesis, $s^2 = \dfrac{1}{n-1}\Sigma(y_t - y_{t-1})^2$ can be used as an estimator of σ^2. Then, as widely acknowledged, $\dfrac{y_t - y_{t-1}}{s}$ follows a t-distribution with n − 1 degrees of freedom.

Because target assignment (deviation) uses standard deviation of performance in previous 5 years, the degree of freedom becomes 4 (= 5 − 1). This is known as following.

$$P_r\left(\frac{y_t - y_{t-1}}{s} > 2.123\right) = P_r\left(\frac{y_t - y_{t-1}}{2s} > 1.061\right) = 0.05$$

Therefore, if we were to examine whether the institution exerted full effort in current year with respect to long-term performance with a 5 percent significance, approximately $\dfrac{y_t - y_{t-1}}{2s} > 1$ becomes the standard of judgment. This is consistent with target assignment (deviation) evaluation method for major businesses as summarized earlier. However, one difference is that the standard deviation of $y_t - y_{t-1}$ is used instead of the standard deviation of y_t in calculating the standard deviation, which differs from current target assignment (deviation) evaluation method.

3 Sub-conclusion

Therefore, there are some aspects supporting that the quantitative indicator evaluation method in the 2016 Public Institution Management Evaluation Manual as an ex-post statistical verification of the institution's effort can be justified with a theoretical foundation. In particular, for short-term performance, current target assignment (deviation) evaluation method for major businesses can be explained as a process of statistically verifying whether the institution's effort increased relative to that of last year.

However, for short-term performance, the institution's performance needs to be maintained at a steady level in the absence of any drastic change in technology or input resource. Therefore, for performance indicators that showed consistent increases in the past, such theoretical foundation may not equally apply.

However, for long-term performance, current target assignment (deviation) evaluation method can be explained as a process of statistically verifying whether the institution's effort in current year exceeded 0. In addition, it can explain the pattern of consistently increasing performance.

However, in this case, it differs from current target assignment (deviation) evaluation method in that the standard deviation of performance increase is used instead of the standard deviation of performance in calculating sample standard error.

Based on the theoretical discussion, improvements for quantitative indicator evaluation method as ex-post evaluation can be considered in the following ways.

First, distinction for whether the evaluation indicator is short-term performance or long-term performance needs to be made. At this point, if the institution's effort in current year affects only current year performance with no direct effect on future performance, its performance can be regarded as short-term. In this case, there should not be a discernable pattern of increase or decrease in performance in the absence of any drastic change in technology or input resource.

Second, for short-term performance, it is necessary to determine whether annually increasing allocated budget and manpower to relevant businesses should be a goal. If so, current target assignment (deviation) evaluation method can be deemed appropriate. However, if the institution is already exerting its best effort and aims to continue its best effort without increasing additional budget and manpower, the benchmark should be the sample average including current year's performance instead of last year's performance. Given that this is partially consistent with the standard of the evaluation manual that reads "benchmark is the larger of last year's performance and average performance in previous three years," current target assignment (deviation) evaluation method can be considered relatively appropriate.

Third, for long-term performance that exhibits consistent annual increases, current target assignment (deviation) evaluation method may be appropriate if the goal of the relevant business is to maintain steady levels of investment. However, the use of the standard deviation of performance increase relative to last year's performance instead of the standard deviation of performance indicator can be theoretically appropriate in calculation of the standard deviation. But, if the relevant business aims to increase investments of more resources and efforts compared to last year for long-term performance, current target assignment (deviation) evaluation method may not be theoretically appropriate.

IV Theoretical foundation for ex-ante incentive system

Previous passage has explored the theoretical foundation for looking at current target assignment (deviation) evaluation method from the perspective of ex-post evaluation of the institution's effort. This passage explores the theoretical foundation for viewing current target assignment (deviation) evaluation method as ex-ante incentive system for the institution's effort.

The theoretical foundation for ex-ante incentive system for effort can be found in the principal-agent theory. In particular, the economics literature has theorized the issue of resolving information asymmetry arising from the principal's inability to observe the agent's effort through compensation structure based on observable performance as hidden action or moral hazard problems.

As for the discussion regarding ex-post evaluation, the discussion on ex-ante incentive can be explained by dividing into short-term performance and long-term performance.

1 Short-term performance

In this research, short-term performance is defined as performance resulting from effort of the institution that affects only current performance, but not future performance. In particular, the process of performance determination for short-term performance is modeled as follows in (Equation 2).

The principal-agent theory implies that when the principal is unable to observe the agent's effort (a_t) in (Equation 2), the moral hazard problem in which the agent does not exert any effort without performance pay occurs. Therefore, a solution in which ex-ante incentives are offered for the agent's effort through the use of performance compensation contract that links observable performance (y_t) to the agent's compensation is proposed.

In particular, optimal performance pay can be derived under the participation constraint in which the agent must voluntarily accept performance pay contract and the incentive constraint in which the agent voluntarily chooses the level of his/her effort with performance pay.[4]

Current target assignment (deviation) evaluation method can be summarized in (Equation 1) and therefore can be interpreted using the following performance pay model.

$$Score = 60 + 40 \times \left(\frac{y_t - y_{t-1}}{2\sigma} \right)$$

$$= c + b \times (y_t - y_{t-1}) \qquad \text{(Equation 4)}$$

That is, performance is estimated by the increase over last year's performance ($y_t - y_{t-1}$) and the score is proportional to the level of the increase. In addition, the slope is inversely proportional to the standard deviation of y_t.

So, this research attempts to confirm whether such evaluation method is consistent with optimal performance pay derived from the principal-agent theory.

In order for this, the agent's expected utility function (E[U]) is first defined as follows.[5]

$$E[U] = E(w) - \frac{r}{2} Var(w) - \frac{1}{2} a^2 \qquad \text{(Equation 5)}$$

Here, $E(w)$ is the expected value of wage, w, and $Var(w)$ is variance of wage w. Also, r represents absolute risk aversion, and $\frac{1}{2} a^2$ can be interpreted as cost of the agent's effort, α. Because expected utility declines with the increase in variance of wage, the agent is considered risk averse.

In addition, it is assumed that the wage function is determined based on (Equation 4).[6]

$$w = c + b(y_t - y_{t-1})$$

When the agent decides on a_t at time t, y_{t-1} is already determined and thus is not a random variable. Therefore, it is assumed that $y_{t-1} = k + a_{t-1}$ for convenience. Then, according to (Equation 2) and (Equation 5), the agent's expected utility function is determined as follows.

$$E[U] = c + b(a_t - a_{t-1}) - \frac{r}{2}b^2\sigma^2 - \frac{1}{2}a_t^2 \qquad \text{(Equation 6)}$$

Then, the condition for the agent's voluntary participation in such performance pay contract relation is as follows.

$$E[U] \geq \bar{U} \qquad \text{(Equation 7)}$$

Here, $\bar{U}$ represents the agent's minimum level of expected utility. That is, the agent wishes to participate in the contract when expected utility from contracting is higher than minimum expected utility, $\bar{U}$.

In addition, the agent's effort is unobservable to the principal and the agent chooses to maximize his/her expected utility. That is, effort level must satisfy the following requirement.

$$a_t = \text{arg}maxE[U] \qquad \text{(Equation 8)}$$

That is, the expected effort level from the agent in compensation contract is the effort level that maximizes the agent's own expected utility.

Let's assume that the principal attaches the value (or weighted value) of p to the performance indicator (y_t). Also, it is assumed that the principal maximizes the expected value of performance, while minimizing wage paid to the agent. If so, the above principal-agent model can be summarized as follows.

$$max\, E[py_t] - E[w_t]$$

Subject to (Equation 7) and (Equation 8)

That is, the principal maximizes expected profit under the condition that both the participation constraint and the incentive constraint are satisfied.

First, by applying (Equation 6) to (Equation 8), the first order condition for the agent's utility-maximizing problem can be calculated as follows.

$$b - a_t = 0 \qquad \text{(Equation 9)}$$

That is, under the performance contract like (Equation 6), the agent chooses the effort level of $a_t = b$ in order to maximize his/her expected utility. Therefore, while the principal is unable to directly observe the agent's effort, he/she can estimate the agent's effort level through the choice of b.

Also, it is assumed for convenience that the principal has the complete bargaining power.[7] Then, the principal no longer has any reason to compensate the agent for more than necessary. That is, the participation constraint (Equation 7) must be satisfied with an equality. Then, by applying (Equation 6) to (Equation 7), the following equation can be derived. The second equality follows from (Equation 9).[8]

$$c = -b\left(a_t - a_{t-1}\right) + \frac{r}{2}b^2\sigma^2 + \frac{1}{2}a_t^2 + \bar{U}$$

$$= -b\left(b - b\right) + \frac{r}{2}b^2\sigma^2 + \frac{1}{2}b^2 + \bar{U} \qquad \text{(Equation 10)}$$

Therefore, by applying the participation constraint (Equation 10) and the incentive constraint (Equation 9) to the principal's expected profit function, the principal's optimization problem can be summarized as follows.

$$max\ p\left(k + a_t\right) - c - b\left(a_t - a_{t-1}\right) = p\left(k + b\right) - \frac{r}{2}b^2\sigma^2 - \frac{1}{2}b^2 - \bar{U}$$

According to the first order condition for optimization of b, optimal slope (b^*) is as follows.

$$b^* = \frac{p}{1 + r\sigma^2} \qquad \text{(Equation 11)}$$

According to (Equation 4), $b = \dfrac{20}{\sigma}$ under current target assignment (deviation) evaluation method. Therefore, there is a difference from optimal slope (that is, score versus performance sensitivity) derived from (Equation 11). However, it has a common characteristic of adjusting the amount of performance increase reflected in score (that is, slope) downward when there is a high standard deviation in performance indicator. In particular, because the optimal performance contract derived earlier has several unique assumptions including the agent's utility function, it is difficult to generally view (Equation 11) as optimal contract condition. Therefore, theoretical reasoning can be found in the direction in which both optimal contract condition and target assignment (deviation) evaluation method reflect the standard error of the performance indicator.

That is, the argument can be supported that current target assignment (deviation) evaluation method finds its theoretical ground as ex-ante incentive system for the institution's effort regarding short-term performance. However, under such theoretical ground, the agent exerts the same amount of effort each year and there should not be a pattern of consistently increases or decreases in performance. However, as pointed out earlier, most of the institutions' quantitative evaluation indicators exhibit an increasing trend each year and thus are not consistent with the theoretical prediction.

Also, the reason why standard deviation exists in the denominator of (Equation 11) is that the agent is risk averse. That is, the agent's wage becomes uncertain when a performance indicator with high uncertainty is used. Therefore, it is in the principal's interest to lower the agent's risk premium by lowering b and, in turn, decrease the fixed pay of c.

However, there can be a room for discussion on whether it is possible to consider large scale public institutions as risk averse. In the theoretical discussion above, it was assumed that the agent's participation constraint is satisfied with an equality. However, given that public institutions' participation in businesses have a compulsory component demanded by law and government, both whether there exists the participation constraint and whether the participation constraint should be satisfied with an equality can be discussed further. In particular, if public institutions are not risk averse (that is, $r = 0$), it is optimal that b be independent of standard deviation. In this case, it is difficult to justify target assignment (deviation) evaluation method as optimal incentive system based on the principal-agent theory discussed above.

2 Long-term performance

If the institution achieves an increasing pattern of performance by exerting the same level of effort each year, it is possible that such performance is long-term performance. That is, if performance is determined according to (Equation 3), performance itself can be increasing each year with the same amount of effort by the agent. Therefore, it is necessary to examine the principal-agent theoretical model in relation to long-term performance in order to explain such a performance indicator.

(Equation 3) can be rearranged in the following way.

$$d_t \equiv y_t - y_{t-1} = a_t + e_t$$

As in the case of short-term performance, it is assumed that the agent's expected utility function follows (Equation 6). Also, it is assumed that wage function follows $w_t = c + bd_t$ and the principal maximizes $E[pd_t] - [w_t]$.[9]

Then, the analysis becomes the same as that for short-term performance above. That is, the slope for optimal wage function is determined in the following way.

$$b^* = \frac{p}{1 + r\sigma^2}$$

However, there is a difference that σ^2 is not the standard deviation of y_t and it is more appropriately estimated by the standard deviation of $(y_t - y_{t-1})$ This is similar to the analysis of theoretical foundation for ex-post evaluation.

Therefore, there is a possibility that dividing the increase in performance relative to last year's performance with standard deviation before reflecting in score can be justified as ex-ante incentive system in the case of long-term performance. In particular, the phenomenon of annually increasing performance with the same level of effort by the agent with respect to long-term performance can be explained.

However, as pointed out in the case of short-term performance, the reason standard deviation is reflected is because the agent was assumed to be risk averse. If public institutions are not necessarily risk averse or the agent's participation constraint becomes meaningless, the principal-agent model discussed above is unable to explain why standard deviation is reflected in quantitative evaluation.

3 Level of difficulty and standard deviation

It is rare to discuss public institutions' risk aversion in discussions about standard deviation in quantitative evaluation. On the other hand, for the reason behind reflection of standard deviation, it is implicitly assumed that "it is difficult to raise performance using an indicator with a small standard deviation." To the contrary, there is an assumption that it is easy to raise performance with effort using an indicator with a large standard deviation. That is, it is shown that standard deviation is utilized as an indicator of the difficulty of work instead of an indicator of risk or uncertainty in the current target assignment (deviation) evaluation method.

If standard deviation in fact represent the difficulty of work, the performance determination process for such a performance indicator can be expressed in the following way.

$$y_t = y_{t-1} + \sigma(a_t + e_t)$$

Here, e_t follows a standard normal distribution with mean of 0 and variance of 1. In this case, the standard deviation of $y_t - y_{t-1}$ becomes σ. When σ becomes larger, the same amount of effort (a_t) brings about a greater increase in performance. That is, it can be interpreted that σ represents both uncertainty of a performance indicator and a coefficient indicative of the indicator's low level of difficulty.

In addition, it is assumed that the agent is now risk neutral. In this case, absolute risk aversion becomes 0 and the agent expected utility function in (Equation 5) becomes the following.

$$E[U] = E(w) - \frac{1}{2}a^2$$

Therefore, if wage function is composed of $w_t = c + b(y_t - y_{t-1})$, the agent's expected utility is determined in the following way.

$$E[U] = c + b(\sigma a_t) - \frac{1}{2}a_t^2 \qquad \text{(Equation 12)}$$

Because the principle is unable to directly observe the agent's effort, a_t, the agent chooses the level of effort that maximizes his/her own expected utility. Therefore, the agent's first order condition for expected utility in (Equation 12) must be satisfied.

$$b\sigma - a_t = 0 \qquad \text{(Equation 13)}$$

Also, if the principal has the complete bargaining power, the agent's expected utility must equal minimum utility level according to the participation constraint. That is, by applying (Equation 13) to (Equation 12), the participation constraint becomes the following equation.

$$c + b(\sigma b\sigma) - \frac{1}{2}(b\sigma)^2 = \bar{U} \qquad \text{(Equation 14)}$$

If the principal's objective function maximizes $E[pd_t] - E[w_t]$, the principal's objective function is the following.

$$E[pd_t] - E[w_t] = p(\sigma a_t) - c - b(\sigma a_t) = p(b\sigma)^2 + \frac{1}{2}(b\sigma)^2 - \bar{U} - b(b\sigma)^2$$

In this case, the principal's first order condition for optimization of expected profit with respect to b becomes the following.

$$b^* = p$$

However, standard deviation is not reflected in b in this case. Therefore, while above model has explicitly considered that standard deviation reflects the difficulty of work, a paradoxical result that optimal performance pay does not reflect standard deviation is achieved.

4 Principle of uniformity

In the economics literature, the principal-agent theory has naturally accepted the assumption that the principal attempts to maximize expected profit. That is, it has been assumed that the principal maximizes expected profit and minimizes wage costs at the same time. However, the Government's objective function for public institutions does not need to be expected profit. In particular, the Government's objective may not be minimization of wage costs in public institutions.

If current target assignment (deviation) evaluation method is the optimal solution to the Government's some objective, the Government's implicit objective function can be inversely inferred from current target assignment (deviation) evaluation method.

That is, current target assignment (deviation) evaluation method grants $b = \dfrac{20}{\sigma}$ in (Equation 1). By applying this to the incentive constraint in (Equation 13), the following equation can be derived.

$$b\sigma - a_t = \left(\frac{20}{\sigma}\right)\sigma - a_t = 0 \rightarrow a_t = 20$$

That is, when the standard deviation determines the difficulty of work at the same time, current target assignment (deviation) evaluation method incentivizes a constant level of effort from the agent regardless of the level of difficulty. That is, if current target assignment (deviation) evaluation method is the optimal solution to the Government's objective, it can be inferred that the Government's objective is for public institutions to invest the same level of effort, regardless of the difficulty.

That is, under the assumption that the Government strives for equality or uniformity with which all public institutions invest the same level of effort instead of pursuing efficiency of achieving maximum performance with minimum costs, current target assignment (deviation) evaluation method seems to be best explained as an ex-ante incentive system.

V Lessons learned and conclusion

1 Lessons learned

This research explores theoretical foundation for target assignment (deviation) evaluation method that is most widely used in quantitative evaluation within the 2016 Public Institution Performance Evaluation.

From the perspective of ex-post evaluation, target assignment (deviation) evaluation method is most consistent with the theory statistically examining whether the institution exerted more effort with respective to short-term performance than last year. However, if it is not possible for the institution to exert more effort each year, this examination may not mean much. In terms of long-term performance, it is consistent with statistical examination of whether the institution exerted effort in current year. However, it is more appropriate to calculate the standard deviation of incremental performance increase rather than the standard deviation of performance.

From the perspective of ex-ante incentive, it was found that target assignment (deviation) evaluation method is consistent the direction of optimal performance contract system under the assumption that the institution is risk averse and the participation constraint is satisfied with an equality. However, it is not consistent with optimal performance contract system when the institution is risk neutral and the participation constraint is meaningless. However, when the standard deviation reflects the difficulty of work and the Government requires all public institutions to exert the same level of effort, the current target assignment (deviation) evaluation method can be explained from the perspective of the ex-ante incentive.

2 Conclusion

Upon actual examination of quantitative indicators of various public institutions, some indicators rarely increase each year, while others significantly increase each year. In addition, while some of the businesses need to be carried out by the institution under laws and policies, some have been pursed voluntarily. And there seem to be large variations in indicators depending on the difficulty of businesses. Despite the large variations, it is shown that a uniform application of target assignment (deviation) evaluation method is not optimal from either the ex-post evaluation perspective or ex-ante evaluation perspective. In addition, it is shown that the evaluation method needs to be altered depending on the objective of evaluation in either ex-post evaluation or ex-ante incentive. Therefore, whether it is targeted for the public institution to exert a constant level of effort each year to given businesses, whether greater amounts of resource and manpower are expected to be invested and whether it is intended for the public institution to maximize performance while minimizing its wage or budget need to be understood and agreed by the evaluator before choosing the evaluation method.

Notes

1 The existence of extreme values is determined by whether the standard deviation of four years without an extreme value is 50 percent smaller than the standard deviation of previous five years and decided by considering processing method and cause of occurrence in previous years. In case of an extreme value, benchmark and standard deviation can be calculated by excluding the extreme value (2016 Public Institution Management Evaluation Manual, p. 32).
2 In case of non-major businesses, maximum target is determined by summing benchmark and standard deviation.
3 As explained in the Appendix, the 2016 Public Institution Management Evaluation Manual uses (n-1) instead of n as the devisor in calculating the standard deviation. While there is a theoretical argument on such difference, it does not cause a material difference and this research decides to ignore such difference.
4 For details, refer to Bolton and Dewatripont (2005).
5 Precise theoretical foundation for expected utility function like (Equation 5) can be found in Holmstrom and Milgrom (1987).
6 Holmstrom and Milgrom (1987) prove that minimum wage contract can take the form of a linear function increasing in performance when the agent's expected utility function takes the form of (Equation 5).
7 It can be shown that there is no effect on optimal b regardless of whether the agent has the complete bargaining power or shares it with the principal in half.
8 It is implicitly assumed that the effort level was determined in time t-1 with the same contract. That is, the focus is on stationary equilibrium.
9 To be precise, in terms of long-term performance, the principal needs to solve the optimization problem by considering not only current year performance, but also expected performance in all foreseeable years. For such case, refer to the theoretical model of Kwon (2006). However, evaluation for public institutions is carried out by considering current year performance without any explicit consideration of future performance.

References

Bolton, P., and Dewatripont, M. (2005). *Contract Theory*. Cambridge, MA: MIT Press.

Holmstrom, B., and Milgrom, P. (1987). Aggregation and Linearity in the Provision of Intertemporal Incentives. *Econometrica: Journal of the Econometric Society*, 303–328.

Kwon, I. (2006). Incentives, Wages, and Promotions: Theory and Evidence. *RAND Journal of Economics*, 100–120.

Appendix

2016 public institution business performance evaluation criteria – target assignment (deviation) evaluation method

- Evaluation method of target assignment indicator is estimated by selecting a score range determined by maximum and minimum targets in consideration of certain benchmarks (normally last year's performance).
- Baseline score for target assignment method is 20 points (out of 100 points total) and score is calculated according to the following. Maximum and minimum scores are 100 and 20 points, respectively, with both binding.

$$20 + 80 \times \frac{Performance - Minimum\ Target}{Maximum\ Target - Minimum\ Target}$$

- Unless specified by the Manual, benchmark for an upward indicator is the larger of either last year's performance and average performance in previous three years. A downward indicator is the minimum value. However, in the absence of prior performance in previous three years according to accounting standard, two years of performance may be used.
- In target assignment (deviation) method, an upward indicator's maximum target is calculated as Benchmark + 1 × Standard Deviation (previous five years), an upward indicator's minimum target as Benchmark −2 × Standard Deviation (previous five years), a downward indicator's maximum target as Benchmark −1 × Standard Deviation (previous five years) and a downward indicator's minimum target as Benchmark + 2 × Standard Deviation (previous five years). However, in the case of major businesses, an upward indicator's maximum target is calculated as Benchmark + 2 × Standard Deviation (previous five years) and a downward indicator's maximum target is computed as Benchmark −2 × Standard Deviation (previous five years). However, in the absence of performance in previous five years under the same accounting standard, the standard deviation of three or four years of performance under the same accounting standard may be used.
- In order to reflect the characteristics of individual indicators, the Manual may decide on maximum and minimum targets.
- In case data for previous five years may not be used due to the discontinuity in data arising from changes in the institution's organizational and business

structures, time period may be shorted and the standard deviation based three or four years may be used. When it is inappropriate to use target assignment (deviation) method due to the discontinuity in data in current year due to change in business structure, normal target assignment methods may be applied.

• Standard deviation used in target assignment (deviation) method is computed in the following way.

$$Standard\ Deviation\ S = \sqrt{\sum_{i=1}^{N} \frac{\left(Y_i - \overline{Y}\right)^2}{n}}$$

$$Y_i = \text{Value of Y in I Year}$$
$$\overline{Y} = \text{Average Value of Y}$$
$$n = \text{Sample Period}$$

12 Empirical analysis of efficiency improvement in public corporations using data envelopment analysis (DEA)

Kilkon Ko

I Introduction

Public corporations have been established and developed under various economic, social and political backgrounds such as the promotion of economic development, solution for lack of private capital, solution for market failure in monopolies, the satisfaction of demand for public services, and domestic and foreign political factors (Kim, 2014: 27–37; Yoo et al., 2011; Hood, 1994; Friedmann, 1954). Under various backgrounds, public corporations not only pursue efficiency as "corporation", but also are called on to serve the public interest as "public" institutions harmoniously. Performance Evaluation System of Public Institutions of the Korean government proposes securing public corporations' management efficiency and public interest as its major rationale for existence. However, public interest and efficiency are "essentially contested concept" (Gallie, 1955). While various evaluation indicators in Performance Evaluation of Public Institutions attempt to reflect the public interest and efficiency, there is a significant gap between what is actually defined and measured and what is proposed by theory. Due to this limitation, while management evaluation of public corporations has been conducted for over 30 years since 1984, it is difficult to find a study that empirically estimates the extent to which public corporations contributed to achieving public interest and efficiency. While hundreds of management evaluation reports are being poured out each year, there is scarce empirical research on a simple question such as whether Korean public corporations' efficiency is improving or deteriorating.

Measuring efficiency is a challenging task. Data envelopment analysis (DEA) (Cooper et al., 2007; Ko, 2016) has been widely used as an effective way of holistically evaluating various input and output factors (Yoo, K.R, 2005; Lee et al., 2012) to calculate the efficiency of public organizations, sensitivity issues according to the choice of input and output variables, assumptions on the direction of changes in input and output variables, and allowance for negative values. Along with evaluation factors, there has been raised concerns about applications of DEA analysis. Hence, instead of developing a DEA model using monolithic assumption, we need to perform an intensive sensitivity analysis. Against this background, I empirically exam how the efficiency of public corporations as "corporation" has changed over years in this chapter. This will help us test whether the public corporations fail to improve their efficiency despite a strong call for their reform. Moreover, if we find heterogeneous trends of efficiency change among public corporations, we can justify more individualized performance management rather than a one-size-fit-all approach.

II Literature review and research question

1 Debate on measuring efficiency of public corporations

Public corporations, the main subject of this research, indicate those public institutions defined in according with "Act on the Management of Public Institutions" The same law classifies public institutions as institutions established by the government (the Act, Article 4, 1st Clause, Item 1), institutions owned 50 percent by the government or 30 percent owned and effectively controlled by the government (the Act, Article 4, 1st Clause, Item 3), institutions 50 percent or 30 percent collectively owned by the government and institutions satisfying one of the above two conditions (the Act, Article 4, 1st Clause, Item 5) and institutions established by institutions satisfying one of the above three conditions (the Act, Article 4, 1st Clause, Item 6). That is, the ratio of government's ownership and effective controllability are the key criterion when the Korean government classifies public organizations as public institutions. Among these public institutions, institutions generating more than half of their sales on their own are classified as public corporations. This research sets the scope of public corporations in accordance with definitions of the above act. Defining public corporations using shares, or ownership, acknowledges that the entrepreneurial nature of public corporations and the analysis of efficiency can be conducted on the basis of the entrepreneurial nature (Boardman and Vining, 2001; Hansman, 2009).

In the analysis of efficiency of public corporations, efficiency and performance are used interchangeably (Majumdar, 1998; Bai et al., 1997). This is the case when the new public management (Pollit and Boukaert, 2011) is applied to public corporations based on the principal-agent theory in the 1990s. Of course, performance and efficiency are not the same concepts because performance is not limited to financial efficiency or economic efficiency and is rather close to "the quality of overall activities in the organization". However, when we raise an issue of poor performance of public corporations compared to the private organizations, the performance generally implies the economic efficiency. To avoid the unnecessary confusion, this paper attempts to measure technical efficiency or economic efficiency of public corporations.

The concept of efficiency itself can be proposed in various ways. Most simply, the ratio of output to input, or highest available level of productivity called technical efficiency in economics, can be used. This is a concept of relative efficiency that evaluates the efficiency of current status relative to the highest level of efficiency called production possibility frontier. When the product is made on the production possibility frontier, we call the production unit achieves the

Pareto-Koopmans efficiency in which there is no feasible efficiency improvement by decreasing inputs or increasing outputs. (Kim, S. M., 2011; Farell, 1957).

In general, the early mainstream discussion of public corporation efficiency was for comparing the efficiency of public corporations with that of private firms which were assumed to be better status. Based on the comparison, public corporations are asked to benchmark the private firms (Savas, 1982; Vining and Boardman, 1992; Majumdar, 1998; Zheng et al., 2003). Such comparison faces, however, a challenge because of fundamental differences between the public corporations due to political interests which want to use the public corporations as a policy tool for delivering universal service. Even though the government privatizes the public corporations, it is not easy to increase market competition due to the economy of scale and monopolistic natures of their service. Hence, instead of comparing public corporations with private firms, we need to evaluate differences in efficiency among more comparable public corporations.

At the same time, time-serial analysis is more relevant than the cross-sectional comparison of efficiency as some public corporations are more vulnerable to time-specific economic and/or political shock. When we adopt the panel analysis of the chance of efficiency within a public corporation, the efficiency analysis generates better production possibility frontier due to more decision-making units and we also infer the efficiency change within a public corporation. [1]

2 Measuring public corporation efficiency

In defining public corporation efficiency, this research follows the concept of Pareto-Koopmans efficiency from the theoretical perspective. This is basically a perspective of using multiple inputs and outputs to construct production possibility set (Cooper et al., 2007). The most widely used method to transform the multiple inputs and outputs into an efficiency score is data envelopment analysis (DEA) model introduced by Charnes et al. (1978). In measuring the effect of the program, this model employs a linear programming method using linear combinations of inputs and outputs and maximizes the ratio of outputs to inputs under constraints. This approach began to be widely used in measuring the efficiency of various programs and activities within the public sector where estimating the market value is difficult (Charnes et al., 1981; Smith and Mayston, 1986; Ruggiero, 1994; Afonso et al., 2010).

In Korea, DEA has been widely used for efficiency of the local public corporations (Moon, 2011), city development corporations owned by each local government (Kim and Lee, 2005; Yoo, K. R., 2008), subway corporations owned by each local government (Yoo and Kim, 2012), and local water and sewage corporations (Yoo, S. W., 2014; Kim, S. M., 2011; Yoo, K. R., 2016). Various DEA models are also used such as: the slack-based dynamic DEA model (Moon, 2011), the nonradial DEA model (Yoo, K. R., 2008), the directional distance function model (Yoo, K. R.2012), and the negative value DEA model (Yoo, K. R. 2005, 2016).

There are also several studies using the panel data such as Lee (2010), Moon (2011), Kim, S. M. (2011) and Yoo, K. R. (2015). First, because invested capital is a semi-fixed variable in short-run, Moon (2011) applies the slack-based dynamic model that reflects this characteristic. According to the analysis result, static models tend to overestimate inefficiency compared to dynamic models. Research utilizing this model has various advantages, but also has the disadvantage of having difficulty with the interpretation of negative-valued inputs.

Lee (2010) analyzes the public corporation efficiency across time. Utilizing CCR model that assumes constant returns to scale for 12 major government-invested institutions from 1990 to 2007, he uses wage and capital as input variables and sales and operating income as output variables. This research also compares efficiency score of DEA with the performance evaluation of public evaluation score. However, it does not adopt techniques such as Malmquist efficiency analysis, window analysis, and meta frontier efficiency analysis specialized for the panel data. At the same time, there was no discussion about how to deal with the negative inputs and outputs.

Kim, S. M. (2011) uses Fare et al.'s (1994) model that applies Malmquist Productivity Index in order to analyze the efficiency of water supply corporations across time. Malmquist analysis is a methodology that estimates change due to the change of production frontiers due to technology advance and technological efficiency. However, as in the case of Moon's (2011) research, there is no consideration about negative-valued inputs.

A noteworthy debate in estimating public corporation efficiency is on the selection of inputs and outputs. As discussed above, both local and foreign research use various input and output variables in estimating efficiency. Focusing on the efficiency of manufacturing-type public corporations, Zalm and Taskin (1997) use the number of workers in the industry, raw materials, current value of fuel and electricity and capacity size measured in horsepower as input variables and use current value of total sales as output variable. While total capacity size is a proxy for invested capital, the proxy is used given that the characteristic of capital may be different in different industries.

Surely, industry-specific variables may be used when analyzing certain sectors of the public sector such as electricity and airports. For example, the number of transferring passengers and the number of airport users can be dependent variables and output variables for airports and electricity generation per plant as output variable for electricity companies (Gillen and Lall, 1997; Foreman-Peck and Waterson, 1985). While not using DEA in estimating public corporation efficiency, Vining and Boardman (1992) that analyzes a change in productivity following privatization proposes total sales per person, total sales per assets per person, return on total assets, net profit margin and net income as dependent variables for technological productivity in the regression model. When using DEA in general, most commonly used variables are the labor force and capital as input variables and total sales-related variables as output variables (Ko, 2016).

3 Research question

From the literature review, we derive an exploratory research question on the trend of public corporations' efficiency. Because of the emphasis on serving public interests, academic research hesitates to measure to the efficiency of public corporations. In addition, there is skepticism on the relevant method for estimating efficiency. Although DEA is a well-established method, many scholars who are accustomed to using linear regression have an antipathy using DEA for measuring efficiency. However, the argument that "efficiency of public corporations is low" is repeated without evidence when the government considers privatization of public corporations. Without the systematic analysis of the trend of public corporations, it is impossible to rationalize the performance management of public corporations. Therefore, this paper raises a research question: Have efficiency of public corporations decreased over the years?

III Methodology and data

1 Variable and model selection

In the estimation of public corporation efficiency, we might consider using the regression model or stochastic frontier analysis. The regression model, however, is difficult to deal with multiple outputs and inputs at the same time. In contrast, while the stochastic frontier analysis can build a model using multiple inputs and outputs, it uses too many assumptions on the production function and distribution of an error term. However, DEA uses fewer assumptions about production function, and has an advantage of a nonparametric approach. In order to conduct more thorough analysis through a structured process, a flowchart for research is proposed as in Figure 12.1.

First, we select outputs and input variables using the survey on practitioners. We asked 178 central and local public institutions and other public service organizations to suggest three inputs and outputs usable for calculating their organization's efficiency.[2] Through this survey, we identify average personnel, asset, capital, sales and general administrative costs as inputs, and total sales, net income, liability and value-added are proposed as outputs. In addition, the same question was asked to 30 personnel in charge of performance management evaluation at public corporations and similar answers on major inputs and outputs were obtained. Based on this, we finally selected the number of workers, asset size, capital size and the amount of operating costs (cost of goods sold + selling and administrative expenses) as inputs, and operating income, total sales and net income as outputs.

Second, we need to choose relevant DEA models which differ according to the choice between input and output orientation, the assumption about returns to scale, the treatment of negative values and the decision on the time windows of the panel data. This paper adopts the input-oriented variant returns to scale(VRS) model. When we run the input-oriented and output-oriented models, we found

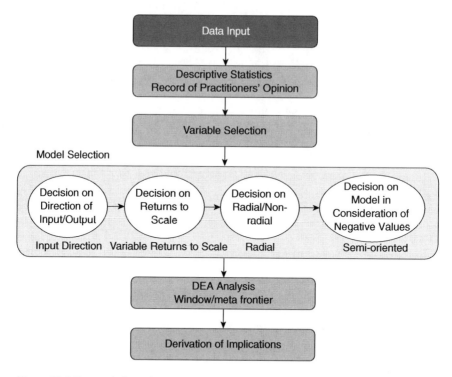

Figure 12.1 Research flow chart

that the output-oriented model fails to distinguish differences in efficiency among public corporations. Hence, we decided to use input-oriented model. Regarding the assumption of return to scale, as public corporations consist of different sizes and their efficiency can vary according to size, we adopt the variant return to scale model.

Next, we adopt semi-oriented radial measure (SORM) model to deal with negative values. Many models have been proposed to deal with negative values such as directional distance function model (RDS) developed by Portela et al. (2004), slack-based measure model (SBM, MSBM) developed by Sharp et al. (2006) and semi-oriented radial measure (SORM) developed by Emrouznejad et al. (2010). RDS model treats negative values as the distance between maximum and minimum values, MSBM also uses a distance concept, and SORM model treats a negative value by dividing it into two. Each methodology has its pros and cos. RDS model has the advantage of being able to derive values showing little difference from those under the basic methodology of DEA but has the problem of violating scale invariance, as does MSBM. SORM model has the advantage of generalizing the radial model by adjusting scores downward for negative values, but has a problem of having an excessive number of variables.

This research chooses SROM model. The problem of SORM is that the number of input variables additionally increases for each increase in the number of negative values. This research uses a total of four input variables, three input variables and three variables containing negative value, resulting in a total of ten input variables. We performed the sensitivity test by comparing the result of traditional variant return to scale model with that of SORM and found that their correlation coefficient of efficiency score is 0.95.

SORM model partly adjusts inputs and outputs that have a mix of positive and negative values with respect to k DMU before using them in the calculation of efficiency score. Let's denote the number of columns of output having purely positive values among m number of input variables X as p and those having a mix of positive and negative values as l. The number of columns of output having purely positive values among r number of output variables Y as w and those having a mix of positive and negative values as e. While those variables consisting of purely positive values need not be adjusted, the following adjustments are made for l and w.

$$X_{lj}^1 = \begin{cases} X_{lj} \ if \ X_{lj} \geq 0 \\ 0 \ if \ X_{lj} < 0 \end{cases}, X_{lj}^2 = \begin{cases} 0 \ if \ X_{lj} \geq 0 \\ -X_{lj} \ if \ X_{lj} < 0 \end{cases}$$

$$Y_{ej}^1 = \begin{cases} Y_{ej} \ if \ Y_{ej} \geq 0 \\ 0 \ if \ Y_{ej} < 0 \end{cases}, Y_{ej}^2 = \begin{cases} 0 \ if \ Y_{ej} \geq 0 \\ -Y_{ej} \ if \ Y_{ej} < 0 \end{cases}$$

Adjusted variables are calculated according to the following input direction SORM-VRS model.

$$Min \, h$$

$$s.t. \sum_{j=1}^{n} x_{ij}\lambda_j s_i^- = h \times x_{ik} \, (For, i = 1, \ldots, m)$$

$$\sum_{j=1}^{n} x_{lj}^1 \lambda_j + s_{l1}^- = h \times x_{lk}^1, \sum_{j=1}^{n} x_{lj}^2 \lambda_j - s_{l2}^- = h \times x_{lk}^2$$

$$\sum_{j=1}^{n} y_{rj}\lambda_j - s_r^+ = y_{rk} \, (For, r = 1, \ldots, s)$$

$$\sum_{j=1}^{n} y_{ej}^1 \lambda_j - s_{r1}^+ = y_{ek}^1, \sum_{j=1}^{n} y_{ej}^2 \lambda_j + s_{r2}^+ = y_{ek}^2$$

$$s_i^- \geq 0, s_r^+ \geq 0, \lambda_j \geq 0, t \geq 0$$

$$\sum_{j=1}^{n} \lambda_j = 1$$

Here, h implies radial efficiency of public corporation k x is an input of public corporation and becomes a two-variable, x^1 is the positive part of x, x^2 is the negative part of x, and the same is true for y, y^1 and y^2. If both x and y take on positive values, this model is equivalent to radial variant return to scale input direction model. Subscripts i and r denote variables having all positive values, while l and j denote variables consisting of both positive and negative values and transformed into a two-variable. s implies the slack portion of each variable. That is, S_{l1} and S_{l2} denote slacks of transformed input variables using values of positive and negative input values, while S_{r1} and S_{r2} denote slacks of transformed output variables using values of positive and negative output values. λ is a sort of shadow price and implies weight applied to an inefficient firm's input and output factors relative to those of an efficient firm. $\sum_{j=1}^{n} \lambda_j = 1$ is the assumption on variable returns to scale and the omission of this assumption leads to a constant return to scale SORM model.

2 Analysis of efficiency across time: window analysis and meta frontier analysis

Window analysis is a technique used in the dynamic situation. Developed by Klopp (1985), this methodology targets estimation of time-dependent efficiency score in the presence of panel data (Cooper et al., 2007).

A basic idea of window analysis is based on treating inputs and outputs estimated across multiple time of the same DMU independently. In this case, for k points for n decision-making units(DMUs), the p point is additionally assumed. p can't be larger than k. This is defined as window. That is, by repeating windows smaller than total estimation period, efficiency score for the same DMU is estimated. Through numerical and geometric averages, efficiency score at each observational point is derived. Then, by analyzing the trend of this score, change in efficiency score for each DMU is estimated. The number of calculations is given in Table 12.1.

In line with Yoo's (2015) research, estimating meta frontier efficiency results in the same result as estimating all DMUs in a single window. However, window analysis estimates change in production in each window by altering its size. In this case, the same DMU is treated differently in each window and the number of DMUs is greater than that of DMU used in single meta frontier analysis by ΔDMU.

There is no clear guideline on whether window analysis that tracks efficiency change across time using panel data is technically superior to meta frontier analysis.

Table 12.1 Formulas for analytical subjects in window analysis

Classification	Formula
Number of Window	$w = k - p + 1$
Number of DMU in Each Window	$np / 2$
Total Number of DMU Treated Differently	npw
ΔDMU	$n(p-1)(k-p)$

Meta frontier analysis is used the all-time periods as a size of a window(Cooper et al., 2007). When efficiency scores of DMU at various points move rather stable, the trend of change in efficiency can be calculated using meta frontier analysis.

Another advantage of using meta frontier analysis is its ability to be applied to the unbalanced panel. Missing values in the panel data can cause the vulnerability of window model especially when we use a short-period data. Meta frontier analysis allows constructing more robust efficiency frontier in such a case.

We performed both window and meta frontier analysis and found several drawbacks of the window model. First, due to the characteristic of window analysis in calculating moving averages by averaging several data points, first and last year have different efficiency scores from those of other years. At the same time, efficiency scores tend to be high. 47 DMUs out of 177 total DMUs (27 percent) showed an efficiency score of 1. That is, when one window is comprised of three periods using SORM-VRS model, the number of cases where inefficient firms are identified as efficient was quite large. In contrast, meta frontier analysis showed 21 percent of DMUs are efficient. Therefore, we adopted the meta frontier model in this chapter.

3 Data

This research collected data by requesting each public corporation. We provided a detailed guideline to public corporation managers. First, we asked them to provide financial variables measured by K-IFRS (international financial reporting standard), not K-GAAP (generally accepted accounting principle). As the Korean government changed the public corporations' accounting principle from K-GAAP to K-IFRS in 2011, some public corporations make a financial statement using both K-GAAP and K-IFRS. To avoid confusion, we asked the public corporation managers to report financial variables measured by K-IFRS. Also, we requested them a standalone financial statement instead of consolidated financial statements to avoid, including subsidiaries.

Second, we asked to report the average number of employees following the Korean government's management evaluation manual as public corporations differently count the regular and irregular employees.

Third, given the difference between real price and nominal price, data in nominal price was requested and converted using GDP deflator. In each year, data for some of the public corporations was omitted for analysis, but existed.

Accordingly, 302 observations from 29 public corporations were obtained for the 17-year period from 1999 to 2015. After data cleaning, however, 225 observations for 27 public corporations from the period 2007–2015 were finally used.

IV Results

1 Descriptive statistics

Yearly descriptive statistics for variables used in the analysis are provided in Table 12.2. Looking at input variables, the minimum value of average personnel

Table 12.2 Yearly descriptive statistics for input and output variables used in analysis (unit: person, billion Korean won)

Class		Input Variable				Output Variable			
Year	N	Variable	Mean	Standard Deviation	Minimum	Variable	Mean	Standard Deviation	Minimum
2007	19	Average Personnel	4079.65	8003.60	125.80	Sales	3653.1	7799.94	68.47
		Capital	6268.22	11639.4	−575.20	Net Income	138.45	326.84	−705.35
		Total Assets	9785.56	18088.0	245.94	Operating Income	171.58	390.22	−102.15
		Operating Costs	3513.87	7681.24	62.63				
2008	21	Average Personnel	4164.93	7631.05	127.30	Sales	4184.7	8447.60	83.40
		Capital	6844.38	10799.9	−613.47	Net Income	−28.44	958.14	−3908.61
		Total Assets	16553.8	33074.7	321.80	Operating Income	−24.38	737.95	−3153.71
		Operating Costs	4315.83	9328.61	48.71				
2009	21	Average Personnel	4024.29	7351.42	139.70	Sales	4078.4	8362.17	75.29
		Capital	6842.70	10574.1	−587.32	Net Income	143.91	390.99	−707.76
		Total Assets	16786.3	32310.6	386.36	Operating Income	104.00	277.92	−755.40
		Operating Costs	3929.45	8428.00	50.22				
2010	21	Average Personnel	3911.31	7118.40	152.60	Sales	4880.7	9676.83	73.98
		Capital	7517.37	11882.7	−708.11	Net Income	115.59	504.81	−1579.00
		Total Assets	18854.8	36713.1	372.93	Operating Income	51.99	385.13	−1478.23
		Operating Costs	4771.18	9881.26	43.12				
2011	27	Average Personnel	3533.09	6171.36	152.20	Sales	5301.8	9442.53	74.22
		Capital	7117.70	10378.8	−744.18	Net Income	148.46	785.48	−3243.79
		Total Assets	17873.4	34361.5	107.86	Operating Income	16.28	722.94	−3459.30
		Operating Costs	5141.71	9857.01	58.04				

Year	N							
2012	27	Average Personnel	3530.72	151.80	Sales	6020.2	10943.24	83.93
		Capital	7037.49	−776.34	Net Income	177.42	683.49	−2623.46
		Total Assets	18540.9	238.96	Operating Income	−63.84	875.73	−3143.45
		Operating Costs	5845.94	50.58				
2013	27	Average Personnel	3555.26	170.70	Sales	6211.8	11740.98	88.30
		Capital	7141.89	−796.69	Net Income	245.80	332.85	−36.53
		Total Assets	19252.9	291.42	Operating Income	−52.08	871.50	−4315.27
		Operating Costs	5967.70	57.64				
2014	27	Average Personnel	3622.48	171.80	Sales	6428.7	12270.35	97.99
		Capital	7340.23	−801.58	Net Income	402.16	576.60	−82.59
		Total Assets	19529.8	213.08	Operating Income	106.21	647.94	−2593.48
		Operating Costs	6022.49	65.55				
2015	25	Average Personnel	3727.62	174.50	Sales	6163.3	11929.84	111.76
		Capital	6842.82	−807.90	Net Income	570.14	1124.56	−1552.18
		Total Assets	18583.9	219.24	Operating Income	204.26	2516.49	−5453.05
		Operating Costs	5594.91	76.47				

is 3530.72 (person) in 2012 and maximum of 4164.93 (person) in 2008. Capital peaked at 7517.37 (billion Korean won) in 2010 and was lowest at 6268.22 (billion Korean won) in 2007. Total assets and operating costs showed steady increases up to 2014 but declined slightly in 2015. In terms of output variables, average sales were highest at 6428.7 (billion Korean won) in 2014 and lowest at 3653.2 (billion Korean won) in 2007. Sales showed a steady pattern of increase and are similar to the trend of total assets and operating costs. Net income showed negative average values in 2008, 2012 and 2013. Net income was lowest at −28.44 (billion Korean won) in 2008 and highest at 570.14 (billion Korean won) in 2015. Operating income was lowest at −63.84 (billion Korean won) in 2012 and highest at 204.26 (billion Korean won) in 2015.

2 Comparative analysis of meta frontier analysis and window model

Next, the efficiency numbers are estimated as results of the relative efficiency of 27 public corporations in each year. Looking first at estimated results from meta frontier analysis in Table 12.3 and Figure 12.2, 2015 and 2011 were high, while 2008 and 2009 were relatively low. As evident in above descriptive statistics, the reason for the high value in 2015 was due to high net income and operating income relative to personnel and asset size.

Meta frontier analysis results are provided in Table 12.4. Examining overall averages, Jeju Free International City Development Center, Korea Gas Corporation, Korea Appraisal Board, Korea Racing Authority and Korea Coal Corporation were relatively more efficient. In the case of Korea Coal Corporation, its efficiency score is pretty high, while it suffers from deficits of net profits. The high efficiency score is because of the nature of DEA. DEA derives efficiency using the ratio of outputs to inputs. When inputs or outputs simply have a negative value, DEA does not impose a penalty in calculating efficiency. Hence, caution is necessary when we interpret efficiency of such public corporations.

Table 12.3 Meta frontier analysis: annual efficiency trend

Year	N	Mean	Standard Deviation	Minimum	Maximum
2007	19	0.85	0.16	0.45	1
2008	21	0.83	0.15	0.48	1
2009	21	0.84	0.15	0.50	1
2010	21	0.86	0.14	0.56	1
2011	27	0.87	0.12	0.62	1
2012	27	0.86	0.16	0.37	1
2013	27	0.85	0.15	0.41	1
2014	27	0.87	0.16	0.42	1
2015	25	0.90	0.13	0.54	1

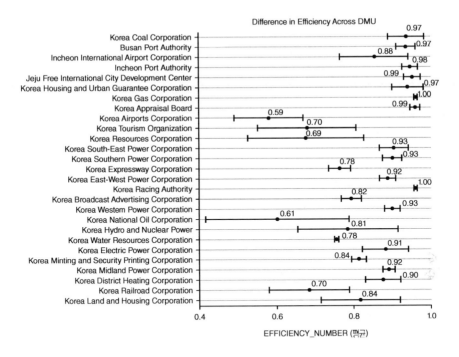

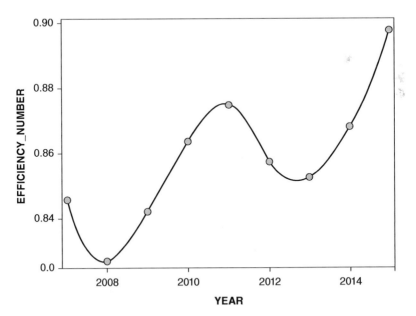

Figure 12.2 Meta frontier analysis: yearly and firm-specific trends

Table 12.4 Meta frontier analysis: annual efficiency trend by firm

Firm Name	Year								
	2007	*2008*	*2009*	*2010*	*2011*	*2012*	*2013*	*2014*	*2015*
Korea Coal Corporation	0.91	0.86	1	1	0.97	1	1	1	1
Busan Port Authority	0.95	0.98	0.94	1	1	0.97	0.93	0.95	1
Incheon International Airport Corporation	0.8	0.71	0.81	0.85	0.92	0.95	0.93	0.97	1
Incheon Port Authority	1	1	0.98	0.99	1	0.99	0.95	0.95	0.95
Jeju Free International City Development Center	1	1	1	1	0.99	0.94	0.95	1	1
Korea Housing and Urban Guarantee Corporation	.	1	1	1	0.9	0.99	0.9	1	1
Korea Gas Corporation	1	1	1	0.99	0.99	1	1	1	0.98
Korea Appraisal Board	1	1	1	1	1	1	1	0.99	0.96
Korea Airports Corporation	0.45	0.48	0.5	0.56	0.62	0.66	0.63	0.7	0.71
Korea Tourism Organization	0.83	0.66	0.69	1	0.65	0.62	0.65	0.62	0.54
Korea Resources Corporation	1	0.74	0.8	0.71	0.68	0.56	0.56	0.44	0.73
Korea South-East Power Corporation	.	.	.	.	0.93	0.92	0.88	0.94	1
Korea Southern Power Corporation	.	.	.	.	0.94	0.96	0.94	0.91	0.89
Korea Expressway Corporation	0.73	0.75	0.77	0.8	0.8	0.82	0.8	0.81	.
Korea East-West Power Corporation	.	.	.	.	0.92	0.95	0.9	0.89	0.92
Korea Racing Authority	0.99	1	1	1	1	0.99	0.99	0.99	0.99
Korea Broadcast Advertising Corporation	0.86	0.81	0.77	0.79	0.8	0.84	0.84	0.83	.
Korea Western Power Corporation	.	.	.	.	0.94	0.96	0.92	0.9	0.92
Korea National Oil Corporation	0.61	0.75	0.72	0.64	1	0.37	0.41	0.42	0.58
Korea Hydro and Nuclear Power		.	.	.	0.76	0.7	0.67	0.9	1
Korea Water Resources Corporation	0.77	0.79	0.77	0.78	0.78	0.76	0.78	0.77	0.78
Korea Electric Power Corporation	0.91	0.82	0.9	0.87	0.85	0.89	0.97	1	1
Korea Minting and Security Printing Corporation	0.85	0.83	0.81	0.85	0.82	0.8	0.85	0.85	0.87
Korea Midland Power Corporation	.	.	.	.	0.93	0.94	0.92	0.91	0.9
Korea District Heating Corporation	0.81	0.9	0.98	0.87	0.89	0.95	0.94	0.89	0.9
Korea Railroad Corporation	0.62	0.6	0.58	0.62	0.64	0.72	0.8	0.87	0.85
Korea Land and Housing Corporation	.	0.68	0.67	0.82	0.89	0.92	0.89	0.92	0.95

Figure 12.3 categorizes public corporations according to the trends of change in efficiency. First, there are nine public corporations in the upward trend including Korea Coal Corporation, Busan Port Authority, Incheon International Airport Corporation, Korea Airports Corporation, Korea Expressway Corporation, Korea Hydro and Nuclear Power, Korea Electric Power Corporation, Korea Railroad Corporation, and Korea Land and Housing Corporation with significant regression coefficients. The public corporations with the most significant improvement efficiency are Korea Hydro and Nuclear Power, followed by Korea Land and Housing Corporation, Korea Railroad Corporation, Korea Airports Corporation, Incheon International Airport Corporation, and Korea Electric Power Corporation.

Next, firms have a trend of change in efficiency results in u-shaped trend can be seen in Figure 12.3. There were 14 public corporations showing a visually declining or an inverse U-shaped trend. Among them, there were eight firms with statistically significant time-series slopes including Korea Appraisal Board, Korea Racing Authority, Korea Broadcast Advertising Corporation, Korea Midland Power Corporation, Incheon Port Authority, Korea Southern Power Corporation, Korea Tourism Organization, and Korea Resources Corporation. Notable is Korea District Heating Corporation's inverse U-shape trend, rising and then falling. Those with a declining trend are Korea Resources Corporation, Korea Tourism Organization, Incheon Port Authority, and Korea Midland Power Corporation. The declining trend, or the regression coefficient, is 0.01–0.03 and is smaller than that of the upward trend of 0.1–0.6.

V Lessons learned and conclusion

1 Lessons learned

"Have public corporations improved their efficiency over the years?" is an important question not only in Korea, but also in other countries. In this chapter, based on DEA analysis of time-series data for 27 public corporations from 2007 to 2015, we provide evidence on the heterogeneous patterns of efficiency change among public corporations. This result provides 3 important lessons for countries that wish to systematically manage their public corporations.

First, we need to emphasize the importance of the database measuring monitoring financial and administrative activities of public corporations. The Korean government has annually implemented the performance evaluation of public institutions since 1984 and requested them to publicize their financial and administrative data. At the beginning, many public corporations complained that the burden of data collection was too heavy. However, the standardized data format and systematic data collection methods have reduced the burden over the years. Also, the Korean government improves the comparability and reliability of the publicized data by reexamining the data. Due to the availability of high-quality data, DEA as well as other performance evaluation can be done with small costs. Therefore, countries who are interested in measuring efficiency of public institutes make an effort to construct a high-quality database.

Second, the government needs to develop a relevant model to evaluate the efficiency change of public institutions. Instead of making a commonsensical argument that public institutions are inefficient, the government should be aware that efficiency of public institutions is pretty heterogeneous. In the Korean case, nine public corporations are in the upward trend, four in the U-shaped trend, 13 in the downward trend and one public corporation in the inverse U-shaped trend, as shown in Table 12.3. Without the such evidence of efficiency, we may make a mistake using a one-size-fit-all management strategy to all public institutions. By integrating the efficiency analysis model into the database of public institutions, the government can use develop individualized performance management strategy with less cost.

Finally, the evidence-driven performance management should be emphasized. We admit that measuring performance or efficiency is not an easy task given the complexity of public institutions. However, we can produce better evidence by emphasizing to find more relevant methods using our data. For instance, in terms of methodology, we found that meta frontier analysis is considered to be more appropriate than the window model given the issues of over calculation of efficiency score. More application of systematic methods allows for a higher quality of evidence. Were it not for such an effort, performance management remains in the realm of a black box or arbitrary intuitions.

2 Conclusion

Despite the skeptics on measuring the efficiency of public corporation, our DEA model shows the possibility of systematic analysis of efficiency change of each public corporations. Some public corporations showing the continuous improvement of efficiency over the years can be a benchmark to other public corporations. If other public corporations show the consistent decrease of efficiency, the government needs to analyze why they fail to improve their efficiency. As such, instead of management evaluation based on a cross-sectional evaluation, the government focuses more on time-serial change of efficiency. Given that annual performance evaluation usually limits its evaluation to year-to-year change, the future performance evaluation should introduce performance measures reflecting longitudinal changes.

We can derive some methodological implications. Due to the negative values of inputs and outputs, SORM model turns out more relevant. At the same time, if we consider different sizes of public corporations and the variant return to scale, the variant return to scale model is preferred to the constant return to scale model. Finally, the window model is less effective in distinguishing differences in efficiency among public corporation than meta frontier model. In future research, if we are able to accumulate more data covering longer periods, we can improve our understanding of public corporations' efficiency.

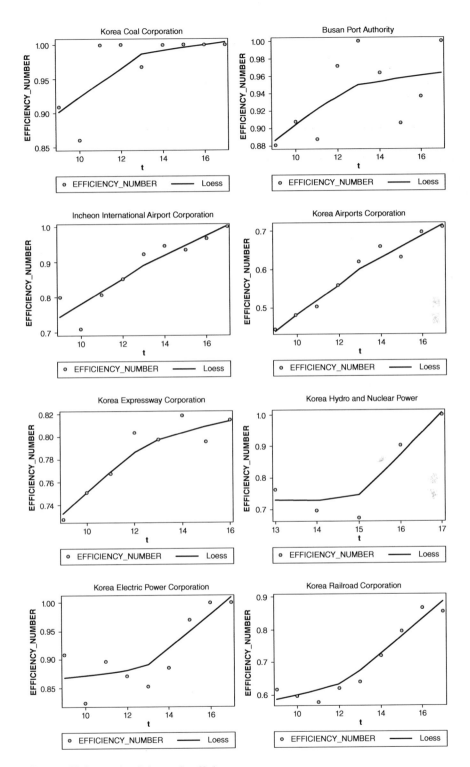

Figure 12.3 Trends of change in efficiency

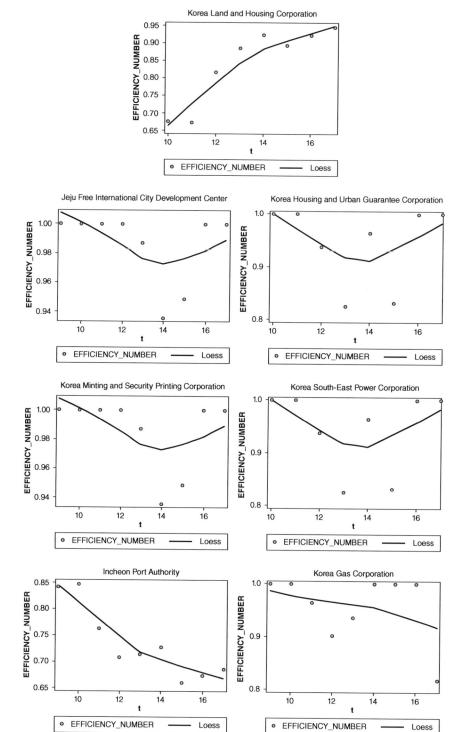

Figure 12.3 (Continued)

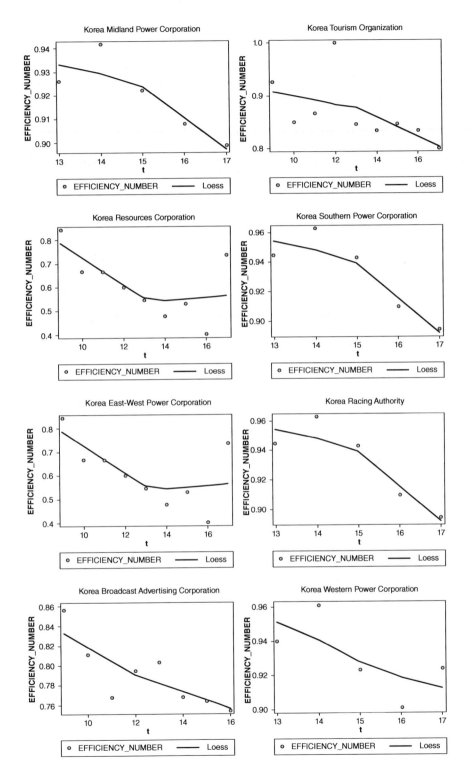

Figure 12.3 (Continued)

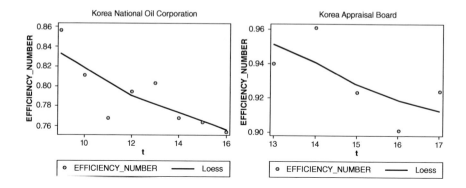

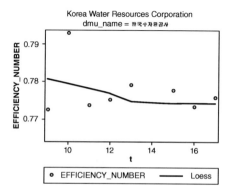

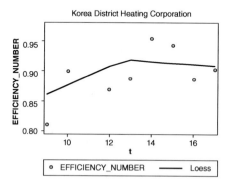

Figure 12.3 (Continued)

Notes

1 It is advantageous to control for the effects of cross-sectional differences across firms or time invariant factors using panel data analysis.
2 This data has been secured through a survey from the Research Center for Organization Assessment at the Graduate School of Public Administration of Seoul National University.

References

Afonso, A., Schuknecht, L., and Tanzi, V. (2010). Public Sector Efficiency: Evidence for New EU Member States and Emerging Markets. *Applied Economics*, *42*(17), 2147–2164.

Anwandter, L., and Teofi lo, O., Jr. (2002). Can Public Sector Reforms Improve the Efficiency of Public Water Utilities? *Environment and Development Economics*, *7*, 687–700.

Bai, C., Li, D. D., and Wang, Y. (1997). Enterprise Productivity and Efficiency: When Is Up Really Down? *Journal of Comparative Economics*, *24*(3), 265–280.

Chang, J. I., Kwak, C. K., Shin, W. S., and Oh, C. H. (2013). *Research on Changes Over Time in Management Evaluation of Public Institutions (II)*. Korea Institute of Public Finance.

Charnes, A., Cooper, W. W., and Rhodes, E. (1978). Measuring the Efficiency of Decision Making Units. *European Journal of Operational Research*, *2*(6), 429–444.

Charnes, A., Cooper, W. W., and Rhodes, E. (1981). Evaluating Program and Managerial Efficiency: An Application of Data Envelopment Analysis to Program Follow Through. *Management Science*, *27*(6), 668–697.

Cooper, W. W., Seiford, L. M., and Tone, K. (2007). *Data Envelopment Analysis: A Comprehensive Text with Models, Applications, References and DEA-Solver Software* (2nd ed.). New York, NY: Springer.

Dunleavy, P., and Hood, C. (1994). From Old Public Administration to New Public Management. *Public Money & Management*, *14*(3), 9–16.

Emrouznejad, A., and Amin, G. R. (2007). DEA Models for Ratio Data: Convexity Consideration. *Applied Mathematical Modelling*, *33*(1), 486–498.

Emrouznejad, A., Anounze, A. L., and Thanassoulis, E. (2010). A Semi-Oriented Radial Measure for Measuring the Efficiency of Decision Making Units with Negative Data, Using DEA. *European Journal of Operational Research*, *200*, 297–304.

Farell, M. J. (1957). The Measurement of Productive Efficiency. *Journal of the Royal Statistical Society*, *120*(3), 253–290.

Foreman-Peck, J., and Waterson, M. (1985). The Comparative Efficiency of Public and Private Enterprise in Britain: Electricity Generation Between the World Wars. *The Economic Journal*, *95*, 83–95.

Friedmann, W. (1954). *The Public Corporation: A Comparative Symposium*. Toronto: Carewell Co.

Gallie, W. G. (1955). Essentially Contested Concepts. *Proceedings of the Aristotelian Society*, *56*(1), 167–198.

Gillen, D., and Lall, A. (1997). Developing Measures of Airport Productivity and Performance: An Application of Data Envelopment Analysis. *Transportation Research Part E: Logistics and Transportation Review*, *33*(4), 261–273.

Hansmann, H. (2009). *The Ownership of Enterprise*. Cambridge: The Belknap Press of Harvard University Press.

Joo, K. T., and Yoon, S. S. (2006). Research on Effectiveness of Public Corporation Privatization. *Korean Journal of Public Administration, 44*(3), 67–92.

Kang, J. S., and Ryu, S. W. (2007). Analysis of Customer Service and Management Evaluation Results Depending on the Characteristics of Government-owned Institutions. *Korean Public Administration, 16*(4), 3–30.

Kim, D. G. (2011). *Cost-Benefit Analysis* (3rd ed.). Seoul: Park Young Sa.

Kim, H. J., and Lee, H. Y. (2005). Analysis of City Development Corporations Using Data Envelopment Analysis. *The Korea Spatial Planning Review, 47,* 77–88.

Kim, H. S. (2007). Empirical Analysis of the Effect of Public corporation Privatization on Management Performance. *The Korean Journal of Public Finance, 22*(1), 35–60.

Kim, J. K. (2014). *Public Corporation Policy.* Seoul: Moon Woo Sa.

Kim, S. M. (2011). Evaluation of Regional Water Supply Productivity Using Malmquist Index. *Journal of Water, Policy and Economy, 16,* 127–136.

Klopp, G. (1985). *The Analysis of the Efficiency of Production System with Multiple Inputs and Outputs.* Chicago, IL: University of Illinois.

Ko, K. K. (2016). *Development of Analytical Model for Estimating Public Corporation Efficiency.* National Assembly Budget Office Research Report.

Lee, J. D., and Oh, D. H. (2012). *Analytical Theory on Efficiency.* Seoul: Jipil Media.

Lee, S. Y. (2010). Estimation of Public Corporation Efficiency Using DEA (Data Envelopment Analysis). *Korean Public Management Review, 24*(4), 51–71.

Majumdar, S. K. (1998). Slack in the State-Owned Enterprise: An Evaluation of the Impact of Soft-Budget Constraints. *International Journal of Industrial Organization, 16,* 377–394.

Ministry of Strategy and Finance. (2016). *2016 Public Corporation and Quasi-Government Entity Management Evaluation Manual.*

Moon, K. M. (2011). Invested Capital and Efficiency of Regional Public Corporation: Application of Slack-Based Dynamic Data Envelopment Analysis Model. *The Korea Association for Policy Analysis and Evaluation Letter, 21*(2), 219–246.

Park, S. R. (2002). Analysis of Productivity of Public Corporations and Private Firms. *Regulation Research, 11*(2), 9–67.

Park, Y. S., and Nam, H. W. (2011). Analysis of Effect of External Characteristic of Public Institutions on Management Evaluation Result. *The Korea Association for Policy Analysis and Evaluation Letter, 21*(1), 79–100.

Yoo, H., Lee, W. H., and Bae, Y. S. (2011). *Public Corporation Theory.* Seoul: Beopmunsa.

Yoo, J. Y. (2014). Research on the Effect of Out-Tasking by Regional Water and Sewer Public Corporations on Cost Efficiency. *The Korean Journal of Local Finance, 19*(2), 101–130.

Yoo, K. R. (2005). Treatment and Application of Negative-Valued Data in Input and Output Factors in Evaluation of Efficiency Using Data Envelopment Analysis. *The Korea Association for Policy Analysis and Evaluation Letter, 15*(4), 173–197.

Yoo, K. R. (2008). Analysis of Factors in Public Sector Efficiency: Focus on City Development Corporations. *Korean Public Administration Review, 42*(3), 79–109.

Yoo, K. R. (2012). Evaluation of Productivity and Technological Development of Regional Water and Sewer Public Corporations. *Korean Public Administration Review, 46*(1), 157–180.

Yoo, K. R. (2015). Evaluation of Technological Gap in Operating Efficiency of Regional Public Institutions: Focus on Public Institutions in Jeonrabuk Province. *The Korea Local Administration Review, 29*(4), 265–294.

Yoo, K. R. (2016). Evaluation of Public Corporation Efficiency Using Semi-Oriented Non-Radial Measure Model. *The Korea Association for Policy Analysis and Evaluation Letter*, *25*(1), 61–89.

Yoo, K. S., and Kim, S. J. (2012). Research on Analysis of City Railway Management Efficiency Using DEA. *Seoul Studies*, *13*(4), 237–246.

Yoo, S. H. (2010). Analysis of Reliability and Validity of Management Evaluation of Public Institutions: Focus on 2008 Results. *The Korea Association for Policy Analysis and Evaluation Letter*, *20*(4), 171–202.

Yoo, S. W. (2014). Research on Factors in Public Institution Management Evaluation: Focus on Political Connection and Conflicts of Executive Officers of Public corporations. *Korean Public Administration Review*, *48*(1), 339–368.

13 Collaboration and performance evaluation

Context and indicators

Taehyon Choi

I Introduction

"Commissioned-service-type quasi-governmental institutions" (QGIs) in South Korea assume the important function of implementing a number of public policies in areas that include industry, employment, public health, safety and environment. They have been functioning as a linkage between government and civil society through various forms of policy tools including regulation, assistance and service. By establishing QGIs, the government has been creating social values through flexible and efficient implementation of public policy without having to expand the apparent size of government.

At a time of increasing importance of collaboration in public administration, it is necessary to investigate the institutional status of QGIs pertaining to collaboration. Among public institutions in South Korea, QGIs function at the core of public collaboration. These kinds of institutions need to cooperate with relevant governmental bodies, local governments, private organizations, and other public institutions to achieve performance. As relatively autonomous agencies, QGIs are situated at a very important crossroads from the perspective of public collaboration.

In this chapter, we analyze the historical context of QGIs and the current performance indicators they use to suggest ways to facilitate collaboration initiated by QGIs and measure their efforts appropriately. Research on QGIs is relatively rare compared to research on public corporations. From the perspective of collaboration, QGIs are located in a more important position than public corporations, in that QGIs are more public in nature than public corporations; QGIs perform direct delivery of services such as regulation or support and connect with diverse public and private actors, making them an ideal subject for research on public collaboration.

In the following, we first review the legal status and institutionalization process of QGIs and discuss why collaboration is required in this era. The discussion is intended to provide a macro institutional background on which to analyze the quality of performance indicators. Next, at the micro level, quantitative performance indicators used by QGIs are analyzed from the perspective of collaboration; that is, whether and how much they reflect the nature of collaboration. For this purpose, indicators are categorized according to the characteristics of activities reflected in those indicators, the average scores of the indicators for each category are analyzed, and general patterns in using the indicators are discussed. Based on the analysis, we discuss the practical issues of designing indicators and a performance evaluation system to create social values through collaboration.

II Collaboration structure for policy implementation in South Korea

1 Institutionalization of the public sector in South Korea

1 Structure of the public sector and QGIs

A key characteristic of the process of institutionalization of the public sector in South Korea is the variety of quasi-governmental organizations, quasi-non-governmental organizations and private organizations in close contact with the government that have been functioning around the small central government (Chung et al., 2014; Kim, 2002). While scholars have not agreed on a definition, QGIs are usually referred to as "intermediate organizations," "organizations under government," "the third sector," or "mediating organizations." These organizations have assumed a significant role in actually implementing the government policies (Chung et al., 2014; Kim, 2002; Yoon, 1997). Chung and Han (2005) formalized organizations existing in between the public and private sectors on the continuum of publicness. According to them, the "public sector" can be divided into the "government sector" and "public institutions." The government sector can further be divided into "government ministries" and "executive agencies." Public institutions can be placed in the gray area between public and private, while QGIs are more public than public corporations (Chung and Han, 2005). Such intermediate agencies have been assuming the function of enforcing the policy direction of the government on civil society and mobilizing the human and financial resources of civil society. These quasi-governmental organizations disguise the true size of the Korean government; when considering only the size of the central government, Korea has never had a large government. However, when quasi-governmental organizations are included, the size of the Korean government would be identified as large.[1]

Among the many types of quasi-governmental organizations including QGIs and public corporations, this chapter targets 18 QGIs. These are the institutions identified as intermediate agencies with a relatively high level of publicness. They can be viewed simply as part of government. However, they are established separately under respective special laws because it is more desirable for them to function independently from the government in terms of size and budget management. As the term "commissioned-service-type" implies, these institutions are entrusted with numerous tasks of the government and implement them as their main function. Entrusted tasks broadly include regulation, support and direct delivery of service. As Table 13.1 indicates, the official objectives of QGIs are similar to those of the government in area and language.

2 Institutionalization of QGIs

The history of the institutionalization of public institutions in South Korea can be divided into several steps. First, Kim et al. (2008) divided the institutionalization of Korean public institutions into five stages. Park (2014), following the Ministry of Strategy and Finance (2011), divided it into four stages (Figure 13.1). The two models are quite similar, and we use the classification of the Ministry of Strategy and Finance (2011) and Park (2014), while focusing on the institutionalization of QGIs at each stage.

The first period is characterized by the establishment and direct government control of public corporations (1962–1984). This period corresponds to the age of fast economic development since the Third Republic, during which the public sector became actively institutionalized. During this period, social overhead capital and strategic public corporations such as POSCO were newly established by

Table 13.1 Organizational goals of QGIs

Name of Institution	Organizational Goal
Road Traffic Authority	Conduct businesses for prevention of traffic accidents, aim for greater efficiency in transportation safety management and contribute to protection of citizens' life and property
National Health Insurance Service	Contribute to improvement in national health and social welfare through insurance payments for prevention, diagnosis and treatment of citizens' disease and injury, birth and death and health improvement, and aim for health improvement and stabilization of life for the elderly by providing medical care expenses for physical activity and housekeeping activity
Korea Trade-Investment Promotion Agency	Contribute to the economy through promotion of trade and support for cooperation in investment and industrial technology between domestic and overseas corporations, support for inviting overseas professionals and related businesses for intergovernmental trade agreements
Korea Agro-Fisheries and Food Trade Corporation	Improve income of citizens in agro-fishery businesses and contribute to the balanced growth of the economy by stabilizing demand and supply of agro-fishery products through price stabilization and enhancement of distribution system and promoting food product industries
Korea Environment Corporation	Contribute to the environmental-friendly growth of the economy by promoting prevention of environmental damage, improvement in environment, promotion of recycling of resources and greenhouse gas-related business in preparation for climate change

Data: Reconstructed by the author based on each institution's webpage, founding laws and the open system for management information of public institutions (alio.go.kr)

the economic development plan (Kim et al., 2008: 411). Figure 13.1 shows several QGIs whose foundations were formed during this period. Except for the Road Traffic Authority, which was formed earlier, most of the QGIs were established during this period.[2] Due to the mergers of organizations and changes in name as indicated in Figure 13.1, the legal status of many QGIs changed after this period. Nevertheless, the key point is that the public sector in South Korea was largely institutionalized during this period and the values and cultures of the period were imprinted on the structure and process of QGIs.

The second period covers the Chun Doo-hwan, Roh Tae-woo, Kim Young-sam, and early Kim Dae-jung administrations with the legal foundation of the Framework Act on the Management of Government-Invested Institutions (1984–1999). In addition, the Public Institution Performance Evaluation System was introduced (1984). At the same time, the government certification system of personnel management and budget to regulate QGIs was abolished, so they gained autonomy to some degree (Kim et al., 2008: 411). Also, this period is when the basis was prepared for privatization and public sector reform that began after the financial crisis of the late 1997. QGIs established during this period include the Korea National Park Service, the Korea Occupational Safety and Health Agency and the Korea Employment Agency for the Disabled. In short, this period was characterized by institutional alignment following the establishment of various new institutions during the previous period.

During the third period (1999–2007), radical privatization and restructuring of public institutions were carried out as part of the four major public sector reforms right after the financial crisis. Both the Framework Act on the Management of Government-Invested Institutions and the Framework Act on the Management of Government-Affiliated Institutions (2003) were enacted during this period.

The Framework Act on the Management of Government-Affiliated Institutions provided the legal foundation for the management system of affiliated institutions including performance evaluation, open application system of CEOs and customer service surveys (Lee and Park, 2004; quote from Kim et al., 2008: 411). As shown in Figure 13.1, no new QGI was established during this period, except for the Korea Rail Network Authority that was founded in 2004. Instead, during this period many QGIs changed their institutional status. In particular, the Health Insurance Review and Assessment Service and the National Health Insurance Service were organized in their current forms in 2000. In addition, the current Korea Rural Community Corporation was formed as a merger of the Farmland Improvement Association, the Federation of Farmland Improvement Associations and the Rural Development Corporation. Also, the Korea Veterans Health Service gained its current name. In short, this period was characterized by reorganization of existing institutions.

The fourth period covers from 2007 to the present (as of 2017), during which the ownership of public institutions that previously had been scattered across relevant government bodies was concentrated within the Ministry of Strategy and Finance and the Public Institution Management Committee, according to the Act on the Management of Public Institutions that was enacted in 2007. According to

Legislation	Act on Budget and Accounting of Government-Invested Institutions / Act on the Management of Government-Invested Institutions (73)	Framework Act on the Management of Government-Invested Institutions	Framework Act on the Management of Government-Invested Institutions	Framework Act on the Management of Government-Affiliated Institutions	Act on the Management of Public Agencies
Year	1962	1984	1999	2003	2007 Present
Kim et al. (2008)	1st Period	2nd Period	3rd Period	4th Period	5th Period
Park (2014)	1st Period	2nd Period	3rd Period	3rd Period	4th Period
	Korea Trade-Investment Promotion Agency (62) Postal Insurance Welfare Associations (80)	Postal Service Promotion Associations (87)			Postal Logistics Agency (12)
	Land Improvement Association (62) Agricultural Development Corporation (70)	Rural Development Corporation (70) Federation of Farmland Improvement Associations (95)	Korea Agricultural and Rural Infrastructure Corporation (00)		Korea Rural Community Corporation (08)
	Rural Community Development Corporation (67) Korea Intellectual Corporation (77)			Korea Rail Network Authority (04)	Korea Agro-Fisheries & Food Trade Corporation (12) Land and Geospatial Informatrix Corporation (15)

Korea Transportation Safety Promotion Authority (81)	Korea Transportation Safety Authority (95) Korea National Park Service (87)	Road Traffic Safety Management Authority (99)		Road Traffic Authority (08)
Korea Traffic Safety Association (54)				Korea Employment Agency for the Disabled (10)
Korea Vocational Training Management Authority (82)	Human Resources Development Service of Korea (98) Korea Employment Promotion Agency for the Disabled (90)			
Korea Resources Recovery and Reutilization Corporation (80)	Environmental Management Corporation (87)		Korea Environment and Resources Corporation (04)	Korea Environment Corporation (10)
Health Insurance Management Service (78) National Health Insurance Associations (77)	National Health Insurance Management Service (98) Health Insurance Associations (88)	National Health Insurance Service (00) Health Insurance Review & Assessment Service (00)		
Korea Gas Safety Corporation (74) Korea Electrical Safety Corporation (74) Korea Support Welfare Corporation (81)	Korea Veterans Welfare Corporation (85) Korea Occupational Safety Agency (87)	Korea Veterans Health Service (00)		Korea Occupational Safety & Health Agency (09)

Figure 13.1 Institutional origin of QGIs in Korea

the Act, a new comprehensive management system encompassing the scope and classification of public institutions, and corporate governance reform was established (Ministry of Strategy and Finance, 2011; Park, 2012; Park, 2014). There was no significant change for QGIs during this period. In 2010, the Korea Environment Corporation was formed from the merger of the Environment Management Service and the Korea Environment Resource Corporation. Although not significant, not a few QGIs changed their name as a signal of reformation.

In summary, QGIs changed in line with the periods of institutional changes for public institutions in general. These institutions were established mainly during the developmental era in the 1960s to 1980s and have continued to implement policies in the areas of industrial development, employment, public health, safety and environment. Some institutions experienced mergers as a part of the restructuring process for the public sector after the 1997 financial crisis. The subsequent period demonstrated a relatively stable operation and partial expansion, indicating stabilization in the institutionalization process.

2 Theoretical background of policy implementation and collaboration

1 QGIs and collaboration

The major theoretical concern of new governance in the earlier period of the 1990s was the change in the mode of public service delivery from direct to indirect (Milward and Provan, 2000; Rhodes, 1994). Scholars at that time focused on policy implementation networks involving both for-profit and non-profit organizations in addition to governmental actors (Milward and Provan, 2000). As the idea prevailed that New Public Management would increase the efficiency of government by adopting market mechanisms into the public sector, various modes of market governance were attempted (Peters, 1997).

Since the 2000s, collaboration has been brought into the core of governance in addition to a market-oriented perspective. As democratic values, not merely efficiency, regained their importance in delivering public goods, emphasis has been placed on collaboration among public managers, stakeholders and citizens in producing and delivering public goods and service (Denhardt and Denhardt, 2000). Concepts such as participatory governance, collaborative governance, collaborative public management and new public service reflect this recognition (O'Leary and Bingham, 2009). Procedural aspects of public policy decisions and implementation incorporating public deliberation and social learning have also been emphasized (Bell and Hindmoor, 2009; Chambers, 2003).

The concept of collaboration mentioned in this chapter can be understood in this context, where it refers to mutual activities by various stakeholders with different interests to achieve shared public goals (Choi, 2014). An important issue regarding collaboration in academic discussions is whether non-governmental actors are given actual decision-making power (Ansell and Gash, 2008; Choi, 2014).

However, the academic use of the term is different from the practical use of the term among government entities in South Korea, which focuses more on coordinated implementation of policy than on deliberative and participatory governance. While the true nature of collaborative governance lies in democratic decision-making through dialogs instead of votes (Chambers, 2003), another important aspect is whether collaboration among stakeholders can lead to improvement in performance. Accordingly, for the purpose of this chapter that focuses on QGIs, collaboration refers to broad forms of multi-party activities initiated by QGIs to improve the performance of policy implementation. This means more a functionalistic understanding of collaboration than a democratic one.

Because this chapter aims to understand collaboration around QGIs, it is useful to distinguish the concept of collaboration from concepts indicating other similar multi-party activities performed by QGIs. First, collaboration is different from regulation. For example, in the case of safety regulations implemented by various QGIs (industrial safety, gas and electric safety, traffic safety), ensuring conformity from regulated entities is necessary to improve performance. Therefore, regulatory institutions strive to garner conformity from regulated entities, not just through legal enforcement, but also though attraction, education and advertisement.[3] During this process, cooperation occurs with other specialized institutions for legal enforcement, attraction and education. However, most of these regulations differ from collaboration in that there is no process for consensus building on the goals of the activities.

Collaboration is also different from unilateral support for civic entities, which is the very goal of some institutions. For example, performance of institutions related to industrial development (Korea Trade-Investment Promotion Agency, Korea Agro-Fisheries and Food Trade Corporation, etc.) is conditional on the performance of their clients (corporations and farmers/fishermen) who received support from the institutions. This is basically a 1:1 unidirectional relationship based on the intention of the receiver who enjoys service to raise their profit and the goal of the institution to boost national economy. By contrast, collaboration implies that multiple actors share resources and knowledge to achieve shared goals.

To summarize, collaboration can be characterized by goals that are difficult to achieve with only an institution's own resources, but can be achieved by sharing such goals with other actors, collaborative effort beyond a 1:1 relationship, and improvement in collective performance of related entities from the perspective of the pertinent QGI. Figure 13.2 graphically displays the collaborative structure of QGIs. First, a single institution prepares the implementation of policy with relevant government bodies; this may affect policy decisions through policy information gathered during this process. Second, the institution implements the policy by sharing goals with related institutions and target groups. Third, performance of the institution stems not only from direct activities of the institution, but also from common activities with collaborative partners. Finally, performance is subject to the influence of the general policy environment, which is out of control of any involved actors.

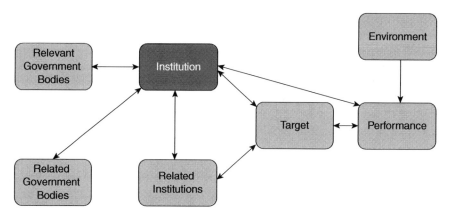

Figure 13.2 Collaborative structure of QGIs

2 Current collaboration evaluation system for QGIs

During 2016, there was an evaluation system for collaborative activities to pro-mote collaboration between QGIs and other public institutions. The Ministry of Strategy and Finance initiated the evaluation system in 2013 (Ministry of Strat-egy and Finance, 2016). In 2015, 23 projects were selected and six exemplary collaborative projects were awarded (Ministry of Strategy and Finance 2016). Although the evaluation of these collaborative projects was carried separately from the major public institution performance evaluation system, awarded institutions earned an additional one point in their annual performance evalua-tion and collaborating institutions earned a maximum of 0.3 points depending on the degree of the contribution (Ministry of Strategy and Finance, 2016: 2). Table 13.2 is a summary of the exemplary collaborative projects selected in 2015. Among QGIs, the National Health Insurance Service and the Korea Trade-Investment Promotion Agency received awards (shaded areas in Table 13.2). Note that this system indicates a limited understanding of collaboration in gov-ernment compared to the usual meaning of it among scholars; that is, this case shows government focuses on improving public service through collaboration between public institutions rather than on active participation by civic actors. In addition, it is notable that the evaluation was done not in a quantitative but in a qualitative way.

Likewise, collaboration is an important qualitative evaluation factor in the annual public institution performance evaluation. In particular, while the above evaluation of collaborative projects considers only collaboration between pub-lic institutions, the annual performance evaluations, especially in the qualitative section, put much emphasis on partnership and participation by various actors. Accordingly, the general tendency is to encourage collaboration in designing new projects and revising/improving current projects.

Table 13.2 Exemplary collaborative tasks of public institutions in 2015

Project Name	Related Institution	Content
Promotion of Expressway EX-Hub	Korea Expressway Corporation	Enhancement of transfer for public transportation such as subway and inner-city bus near expressways around Gacheon Station and Dongcheon Station
Technological and Business Development of Recycling Cinders	Korea East-West Power Corporation	Production of high-quality and low-price building materials made out of recycled cinders -> Reduction in building cost (30 percent) and resolution of between-floor noise in apartments (6db)
Customized Health Examination Information Service	National Health Insurance Service	Computerization of health examination reports originally on paper -> confirmation through necessary institutions such as daycare center; no further requirement for parent's submission
Total Care Service for Small and Medium Businesses in Water Business Going Abroad	Korea Water Resources Corporation	Provide one-stop service for overseas expansion from technology development to sales route
Overseas Expansion of Large and Small and Medium Businesses Together and Sharing of Buyer Information	Korea Trade-Investment Promotion Agency	Expansion of contact with high-quality buyers for small and medium businesses exposed to low-quality buyers
Creation of Social Jobs at Incheon International Airport	Incheon International Airport Corporation	Creation of 54 new jobs that are not infringing on incumbent business areas within Incheon International Airport

Note: Shaded are QGIs

Data: Press release of Ministry of Strategy and Finance (2016: 1)

Nevertheless, arguments continue on whether public institution performance evaluation is an appropriate system to evaluate collaboration. In his study of collaboration between public institutions, Park (2013) identified several issues in public institution managers' perceptions of the evaluation mechanism of collaboration. First, public institution performance evaluation is conducted every year despite that performance improvement by collaboration usually takes time to be realized. Second, it is impossible to avoid the possibility of unnecessary or cursory collaboration for the purpose of evaluation. Finally, it is difficult to quantify the contribution and performance of each actor in collaboration. Such concerns need to be considered in the design of the evaluation system, as will be discussed in the following sections.

3 *Increasing importance of collaboration*

Although collaboration is generally emphasized in today's public administration, for QGIs, collaboration is related to some unique values. First, it has been argued that the policy environment is becoming more and more complex, so to solve current policy problems we need collaborative activities (Cleveland, 2000; Weber and Khademian, 2008). QGIs were established during the industrial era when organizations could improve their performance by focusing on their internal capacity and legal authority. In the current post-industrial society, it is both difficult and undesirable for QGIs to improve performance solely based on their past capacities. The difficulty comes from the cost of information and lack of expertise. An organization adapting to a complex environment pays higher information costs than one in a stable environment. It must also acquire expertise, which is costly and sometimes difficult to even recognize. The undesirability exists because even when collaboration is required for QGIs to achieve higher performance, they are likely to choose an easy way: performance indicators that reflect only the organization's own activities are easier to control than collaboration indicators. Biased indicators for an organization's own activities may produce an appearance of good performance, but they ignore potential social values that can be created by collaboration.

Second, as policy implementation agencies, QGIs assume an ideal position to initiate collaboration in the policy implementation network. While they work with relevant government bodies for policy implementation, they also interact with various interest groups, other public organizations, private firms, and citizens. QGIs can play a pivotal role in producing public values that civil society cannot produce because of its lack of collaborative culture (Choi, 2014). Unlike the public service network perspective, supply contracting of public services in South Korea is more a kind of rent-seeking than a form of collaboration. The capabilities of civic organizations to lead collaboration have not yet achieved a sufficient level. By contrast, QGIs manage resources to initiate and facilitate collaboration among stakeholders within the scope of their organizational goals.

Third, QGIs can function as motivators to enhance their partners' capacity through collaboration. As shown in Table 13.1 and Figure 13.2, QGIs have been given roles to serve the public interest when civil society was not mature enough to generate public values. However, the ability of government constantly has been questioned since the 1990s (Kettl, 2000), and particularly since the financial crisis in South Korea in 1997 (Choi and Choi, 2017). Since then, the basis of the management of public institutions in South Korea has been moving toward privatization of public institutions (public corporations in particular) with recognition of the increased capacity of the civic sector as a result of democratization and economic development (Kim, 2015). Collaboration between QGIs and other civic partners offers an opportunity to share the QGIs' knowledge with their partners.

Finally, financial challenges in the public sector require collaboration. Severe social problems and the emergence of a pluralistic society in South Korea have led to an increase in demand for QGIs' projects, but resources available to QGIs have not increased proportionately. The central government's policy framework has aimed for a smaller government since the late 1990s and the government is facing the pressure of a fiscal deficit that has never been an issue in the last few decades. In addition, the expansion of public institutions was viewed negatively in the Park Gyeun-hye administration under the framework of "normalization of the abnormal." Amid this context, it is difficult to secure appropriate public resources for QGIs to meet the increase in demand. It is vital that QGIs collaborate with civic actors to mobilize resources to solve common policy problems. With the government's lack of financial resources, QGIs require collaboration to overcome their lack of resources. Collaboration now has become a necessity rather than a choice for them.

III Analysis of performance indicators for main business activities

In this section, we analyze quantitative performance indicators for main business activities from the perspective of collaboration, and then discuss the limitations of the current evaluation system and ways for improvement. The focus is on how the conceptual elements of collaboration discussed in the previous section are reflected in the current performance evaluation system. As we described, the performance of collaboration is qualitative, time-lagging, and it is difficult to attribute the result to a specific actor. In the following sections, we provide a typology of the performance indicators, and analyze the characteristics of collaboration-related indicators. Indicators for analysis include 87 indicators for the main business activities of 18 QGIs in 2015 (2016 Public Institution Performance Evaluation Manual). Then we discuss limitations and future directions for a better performance indicator system for collaboration.

1 Characteristics of performance indicators

1 Classification of indicators

87 performance indicators were classified according to two criteria.[4] One is the characteristic of the activity reflected in an indicator. The other is based on the beneficiary of the activity.

1 CLASSIFICATION BY ACTIVITY

Depending on the characteristic of the activity reflected in an indicator, we categorized the 87 performance indicators into eight types. First are indicators designed around activities using the institution's own resources and minimizing collaboration with external institutions. These are labeled "refinement indicators." The refinement indicators do not reflect social outcomes brought by activities of the institution, but rather reflect improvement in internal activities, error reduction, and productivity. For example, indicators such as the Korea Postal Logistics

Agency's "quality improvement in logistics,"[5] and the Land and Geospatial Informatrix Corporation's "reduction in processing time of survey"[6] depend entirely on the institution's own resources and reflect the result of refinement of knowledge and skill.[7]

Second are indicators that simply measure the volume of internal activities done within the institution. These are labeled "internal product indicators." For example, an indicator used by the Land and Geospatial Informatrix Corporation, "increase in digitized land and geospatial informatrix,"[8] measures the volume of internal products of the institution.

Third, contrary to those indicators focusing on internal activities, are some indicators defined not by internal activities but by external outcomes. These are labeled "outcome indicators." These are close to ideal outcome indicators and composed of indices reflecting a desirable status of the society that is expected to be reached through comprehensive activities of the institution. For example, indicators such as the Korea Rural Community Corporation's "enhancement in agricultural productivity"[9] and "increase in income of farm villages"[10] do not reflect input factors of the institution and are composed of elements reflecting social benefits that might be created by successful operations of the institution.

The other indicators are, to some extent, related to collaboration; however, these indicators can be categorized in different ways depending on the view of collaboration. Actual classification may depend on how an indicator is defined and calculated as well as the nature of the activity. Note that indicators that directly measure collaborative activities were rarely found in the analysis; collaboration was inferred from the definition and elements of an indicator and the institution's explanation provided during the annual performance evaluation.

Fourth, indicators classified as "official collaboration indicators" include those that are designated as "collaboration indicator" in the Public Institution Performance Evaluation Manual. These indicators reflect a desirable status of the society expected from shared activities between two or more institutions. Despite the official naming of these as "collaboration" indicators, whether they reflect substantive collaborative activities between multiple institutions is in question.

Fifth, although not ideal, some indicators can be classified as "collaboration indicators," which include performance elements that are difficult to improve by using only the institution's own resources, so require collaboration with other entities (government, other public institutions, civil society, or individuals). In this sense, these indicators are closest to the academic concept of collaboration. For example, indicators such as the Korea Employment Agency for the Disabled's "employment for the disabled in businesses through overall support service"[11] reflect activities whose performance can be improved only through collaboration with other institutions. These indicators reflect more substantive collaboration than official collaboration indicators that target collaboration only between public institutions.

Sixth, we need to distinguish collaboration indicators from three similar types of indicators that strongly reflect relationships with private actors; these are "regulation indicators," "support indicators," and "service indicators." Unlike the refinement or internal product indicators, these indicators do not depend purely on activities of an institution and are determined by the reactions of service recipients. These indicators measure the extent to which desirable output or outcome is achieved through citizens' compliance with regulation (regulation indicators), through citizens' productive activities that are facilitated by the support of the pertinent institution (support indicators), and through the number of participants who enjoy the services provided by the institution (service indicators). The substance of the activities of these indicators differs from the core concept of collaboration. For example, performance improvement in regulation indicators does not necessarily require that the target people agree with the goals of the institution. Service indicators only need the general public to enjoy the service provided by an institution at will or by law, and do not require them to be aware of the goal of such service. While support indicators seem quite similar to collaboration indicators, there are notable differences. In support indicators, the goal of the supporting institution and beneficiaries are compatible with each other, just like in the case of usual collaboration. However, collaboration in this case is not necessarily voluntary on the part of the supporting institution to achieve a better outcome; the support itself is a delegated job of the institution by law. In addition, support indicators are composed of one-to-one activities between beneficiaries and the institution instead of involving multiple actors. With regard to collaboration indicators, collaboration is desirable or even required in order to improve performance; it requires close communications and coordination, and conflict management. Unlike collaboration indicators, the nature of activities reflected in support indicators is fundamentally a part of client service. There is rarely any concern about conflict or jurisdiction issues in support indicators.

2 CLASSIFICATION BY SUBJECT

Benefits of an institution's activity can be attributed to different subjects. Although academics are interested in distinction between input, throughput, output and outcome, from a practical viewpoint such as that of public institutions that design and propose their own performance indicators, what is important is the targets of the activity reflected in an indicator. As shown in the following section, more than a few indicators were given a title that appears to be an outcome indicator; however, the elements of the indicators are inputs or throughputs, which reflect the institutions' systematic bias in presenting their indicators. This discrepancy between face and substance is interesting, perhaps reflecting a response to the normative requirement of outcome measures. It is also likely that the institutions have developed a cognitive logic model based on the internal activities and social outcomes from their past experience.

In this chapter, we took a practical viewpoint and categorized indicators according to the subject to which the effect of an institution's activity is attributed. First, some indicators measure performance of an institution using the desirable change of the institution, other institutions or contractors, all of which are basically service providers. That is, the indicators reflect whether the capacity of the subject is enhanced through the institution's activities, whether the error rate of the institution has declined or whether the delivery of service has improved. We label these as "provider indicators." Most refinement indicators and internal product indicators may fall into this category.

Second, some indicators measure performance of an institution by the benefit given to clients of the institution. We label these as "client indicators." This type of indicator is related to regulation (e.g., clients of the safety regulation institutions), support (e.g., clients of industrial institutions), and service delivery (e.g., recipients of veterans' medical service). Performance reflected in these types of indicators include the positive reaction of the customer, a change in clients' behavior and an increase of the benefit to them.

Third, some indicators measure the performance of the institution by the benefit given to the public. We label these as "social indicators." These indicators usually concern the change in the perception of citizens regarding safety or increased income of the general public. The Korea Rural Community Corporation used social indicators that measure the benefit created for the general farming industry beyond its client farmers.

2 Scores of indicators by type

In this section, we analyze the scores of the 87 indicators according to their types. A summary of the scores based on the record in the 2016 Public Institution Performance Evaluation Report is presented in Table 13.3.[12]

First, indicators were not homogeneously dispersed across categories. Regulation, service and support were all client indicators. In addition, refinement or internal product indicators that put emphasis on the enhancement of the institution's activities were all provider indicators. Indicators reflecting collaboration and outcome indicators that are highly related to collaboration were composed mostly of client and social indicators.

Second, regarding the number of indicators, there were 17 regulation indicators, 15 collaboration indicators, 14 refinement indicators, 12 support indicators, and 12 outcome indicators. Since each indicator was given an official weight, we can analyze the importance of each type by the sum of its weights. According to the weight, the outcome indicators were most important (8.67 on average), followed by the refinement indicators (8.36 on average). As for the outcome indicators, although their proportion according to the number was 13.79 percent, their proportion according to the weight was 16.30 percent, which is compatible with the perspective that outcome measures are desirable. It is noticeable that the refinement indicators, which would not be viewed as desirable because they focus only on internal activities and ignore those activities' social consequences, were the second largest (17.24 percent by number and 14.58 percent by weight). In spite of their inferiority as an indicator from a scholarly viewpoint, it seems that QGIs preferred this type of indicator with the belief that improvement in the quality of internal activities would ultimately improve social conditions. In addition, and maybe more important to QGIs, outcome is not as measurable as input.

Table 13.3 Results of management evaluation by indicator type (2015 business)

Indicator Type	Number of Indicators	Sum of Weighted Value	Average of Weighted Value	Average of Difficulty Level	Average of Raw Score	Average of Adjusted Score
Refinement	14 (16.09)	117 (18.34)	8.36	0.9500	87.35	82.87
Provider	14	117	8.36	0.9500	87.35	82.87
Internal Product	9 (10.34)	61 (9.56)	6.78	0.9222	90.05	83.13
Provider	9	61	6.78	0.9222	90.05	83.13
Outcome	12 (13.79)	104 (16.30)	8.67	0.9500	80.86	76.83
Client	1	5	5.00	0.9000	74.36	66.92
Social	11	99	9.00	0.9545	81.45	77.73
Official Collaboration	3 (3.45)	20 (3.13)	6.67	0.9000	87.51	78.76
Client	1	4	4.00	0.9000	100	90
Social	2	16	8.00	0.9000	81.26	73.13
Collaboration	15 (17.24)	93 (14.58)	6.20	0.9200	87.28	79.98
Provider	1	10	10.00	1.0000	100	100
Client	8	49	6.13	0.9250	83.97	76.99
Social	6	34	5.67	0.9000	89.58	80.62
Regulation	17 (19.54)	130 (20.38)	7.65	0.9353	82.73	77.37
Client	17	130	7.65	0.9353	82.73	77.37
Support	12 (13.79)	84 (13.17)	7.00	0.9250	90.75	83.97
Client	12	84	7.00	0.9250	90.75	83.97
Service	5 (5.75)	29 (4.55)	5.80	0.9400	84.62	79.01
Client	5	29	5.80	0.9400	84.62	79.01
Sum/Average	87 (100)	638 (100)	7.33	0.9333	86.14	80.28

Note: Values inside brackets are percentiles

Data: Reconstructed based on Public Institution Performance Evaluation Committee Report (2016)

Third, the support indicators recorded the best performance of all (90.75 on average); however, because the coefficient of the level of difficulty[13] assigned to each indicator was relatively low (.9250 on average), the adjusted average score was 83.97, which is still the highest but closer to the following types such as the refinement indicators. The collaboration indicators scored 87.28 on average, which is similar to the score of the refinement indicators (87.35), internal product indicators (90.05) and official collaboration indicators (87.51). Somewhat surprisingly, the average coefficient of the level of difficulty for the collaboration indicators was only 0.9200, which was similar to that of the simple internal product indicators, which, in theory, are expected to be easier to control than collaboration indicators. The outcome indicators that reflect the performance of the overall activities of an institution, including collaboration, scored the lowest (80.86 on average). However, they recorded a high average difficulty coefficient of .9500, so showed smaller differences from other indicator types in terms of the adjusted average score.

Fourth, when focusing on the subject criterion, there were 44 client indicators, 24 provider indicators and 19 social indicators. In terms of the average weight, social indicators (7.84) and provider indicators (7.83) recorded similar weights, with client indicators having the lowest average weight (6.84). Scores earned by each indicator type were in the order of provider indicators (83.69), client indicators (79.34) and social indicators (78.16), which is consistent with the theoretical expectation that outcome measures are more difficult to control and achieve than input or throughput measures. From this scholarly perspective, however, the fact that the provider indicators recorded the highest average difficulty coefficient (0.9417) is open to question.

3 Analysis of results by indicator type

1 OFFICIAL COLLABORATION INDICATORS

Table 13.4 summarizes the official collaboration indicators defined in the Public Institution Performance Evaluation Manual. There were only two official collaboration indicators related to QGIs. One is "reduction in the number of casualties per 10,000 vehicles"[14] applied by both the Korea Transportation Safety Authority and the Road Traffic Authority, and the other is "performance in providing safety service in trains"[15] applied by both the Korea Transportation Safety Authority and the Korea Railroad Corporation. In the case of "reduction in the number of casualties per 10,000 vehicles," even though the Korea Transportation Safety Authority allocated a weight of ten points to the shared indicator, the Road Traffic Authority allocated a weight of six points. For "performance in providing safety service in trains," the Korea Transportation Safety Authority allocated a weight of four points and the Korea Railroad Corporation allocated a weight of 11 points. Given that the weight reflects the importance of the indicator to the institution, it is noticeable that the same official collaboration indicator

Table 13.4 Official collaboration indicators

Institution Name	Indicator Name	Weight	Difficulty Level
Korea Transportation Safety Authority	Reduction in the number of deaths per 10,000 cars	10	Normal
	Offering of safe railway transportation service	4	Normal
Road Traffic Authority	Reduction in the number of deaths per 10,000 cars	6	Normal

Data: Reconstructed based on Public Institution Performance Evaluation Committee (2016)

has different weights in related institutions. This calls for additional research on the effect of this difference on the quality of collaboration between pertinent institutions.

The official collaboration indicator of the Korea Transportation Safety Authority and the Road Traffic Authority is a social indicator. One resulting question is how measuring collaboration between them by a social indicator would affect their collaboration. Although a social indicator is desirable in general, it is questionable how much effort each institution would devote to co-manage the collaborative goal and evaluate each partner's contribution. In order to facilitate the use of official collaboration indicators, empirical research is warranted on how collaboration between institutions was conducted in terms of managing these official collaboration indicators.

As shown in Table 13.3, the official collaboration indicators recorded the third highest average raw score, but were sixth in terms of the average adjusted score due to having the lowest difficulty coefficient. The low difficulty coefficient implies that the indicators were perceived not to reflect as much actual collaboration as they did a certain type of simple division of labor. The low performance may not be because it is difficult to achieve collaboration but because the indicators are social and client indicators, for which it is relatively difficult to earn a high score.

2 COLLABORATION INDICATORS

Table 13.5 summarizes the 15 collaboration indicators. These 15 indicators represented 17.24 percent of the total 87 indicators and 14.58 percent of the total weights (Table 13.3). These indicators were used mostly by the Health Insurance Review & Assessment Service, the Korea National Park Service, the Korea Agro-Fisheries and Food Trade Corporation, and the Human Resources Development Service of Korea. As collaboration takes diverse forms, indicators in this category covered a wide range of activities, from those simply reflecting voluntary participation of customers such as the Korea National Park Service's "green point participation rate"[16] and "green point garbage collection rate"[17] to those requiring political group decision making such as the Health Insurance Review & Assessment Service's "expansion of health insurance coverage"[18] and "performance in health insurance policy development."[19] Some indicators reflected activities that regulate citizens' behavior, but require collaboration with other actors, including the Health Insurance Review & Assessment Service's "performance in developing levy sources for health insurance and comprehensive collection of social insurance,"[20] which required collaboration with investigation agencies and local governments. Other indicators reflected supportive activities, as found in the Korea Agro-Fisheries & Food Trade Corporation's "promotion of direct trade of agricultural and marine products."[21] That is, in practice, a collaboration indicator would reflect different forms of activities as well as pure collaboration, although collaborative activities are at the core of a project that includes a wide range of activities.

Table 13.5 Collaboration indicators

Institution Name	Indicator Name	Weight	Difficulty Level
Health Insurance Review and Assessment Service	Expansion of Health Insurance Coverage	5	Normal
	Performance in Policy Development for Health Insurance	3	Normal
Korea National Park Service	Improvement Rate in Environment Health Index	12	Normal
	Participation Rate in Green Point	4	Normal
	Collection Rate for Green Point Garbage	4	Normal
National Health Insurance Service	Performance in Development of New Tax Resources for Health Insurance and Collective Collection of Social Insurance	10	High
Korea Agro-Fisheries & Food Trade Corporation	Promotion of Direct Trade of Agro-Fishery Products	5	Normal
	Promotion of Wholesale Markets for Agro-Fishery Products	4	Normal
Korea Veterans Health Service	Improvement Level in Coverage of Veteran Health Service	4	Normal
Human Resources Development Service of Korea	Participation Rate in Job Development and Training of Small and Medium Corporations	7	High
	Performance in Support for Youth Employment	7	High
	Improvement Performance in Entry Time of Foreign Workers	6	Normal
Korea Employment Agency for the Disabled	Performance in Enhancement of Employment Rate of the Disabled	7	Normal
	Creation of Employment for the Disabled at Businesses by Providing Overall Support Service	5	Normal
Korea Environment Corporation	Performance in Resource Recycling	10	Normal

Data: Reconstructed based on Public Institution Performance Evaluation Committee (2016)

The Human Resources Development Service of Korea's "performance in improving entry period of foreign workers" [22] provides an insight on collaboration indicators. Entry period of foreign workers was defined as the "sum of the number of days elapsed between issuance of a work permit for individual workers and entry into Korea" (Public Institution Performance Evaluation Committee, 2016: 604). Although this indicator is used by the Human Resources Development Service of Korea, much of the process was under the jurisdiction of other government organizations including the Ministry of Justice, the Ministry of Employment and Labor, and employers. This means that the performance of the activity the indicator reflected was not under control of the institution, and it would be difficult for it to earn a good score of the indicator without collaboration. From the perspective of collaboration and benefit to the public, a shortened entry period of foreign workers benefits not only the workers, but also those corporations that intend to hire them, and serves the goal of each government agency involved. In this sense, this indicator is illustrative; the Human Resources Development Service of Korea dared to depend on collaboration with other agencies even though it was able to define the indicator as reflecting only the section of the whole entry period it covered. How much the institution was actually collaborating with other relevant departments, however, is a practical question and an issue of qualitative evaluation. A similar challenge is faced by QGIs such as the Human Resources Development Service of Korea and the Korea Employment Agency for the Disabled, which need to collaborate with relevant government bodies and private businesses to help their clients find a job.

In short, we found some interesting characteristics of collaboration indicators used by QGIs. First, these indicators normally involved multiple government agencies. This finding provides empirical evidence of the importance of QGIs for collaboration in the public sector because of their location in the network of collaborators. As discussed above, QGIs function as a medium for collaboration in the area of complex policy implementation networks. Second, QGIs may not grasp entire control of the performance of the activities reflected in the indicators. As shown in Figure 13.2 and by the example of the Human Resources Development Service of Korea, many different actors were involved as well as processes under other agencies' jurisdiction. As shown in Table 13.3, the average score of the indicators in this category was only among the middle, implying that it is difficult to earn a high score. Third, ironically, collaboration indicators and official collaboration indicators were given the lowest difficulty coefficient (0.9200). This irony implies the need for a mutual understanding between scholars and practitioners regarding how to evaluate the difficulty level of collaboration activities and their performance indicators.[23]

3 REGULATION, SERVICE AND SUPPORT INDICATORS

Table 13.6 summarizes the regulation, service and support indicators. 34 indicators were categorized into these types, representing 39.08 percent of the total 87 indicators, and 38.09 percent of the total weights (Table13.3). Regulation indicators were heavily used by QGIs, especially by those responsible for safety such as the Korea Transportation Safety Authority, the Korea Occupational Safety and Health Agency and the Korea Environment Corporation. Service indicators simply reflected the number of recipients of programs provided by pertinent QGIs. Support indicators were utilized mainly by institutions related to the creation of economic values such as the Korea Trade-Investment Promotion Agency, the Korea Agro-Fisheries and Food Trade Corporation and the Human Resources Development Service of Korea. Although the performance of support activities heavily depends not only on the quality of support by pertinent institutions but also on the performance of their clients, support indicators earned the highest average raw and adjusted scores. The variance, however, tells a different story. Support indicators above the average score were those used mostly by QGIs such

Table 13.6 Regulation, service and support indicators

Type	Institution Name	Indicator Name	Weight	Difficulty Level
Regulation	Health Insurance Review and Assessment Service	Improvement in Medical Practice	12	Normal
		Improvement in the Quality of Medical Service	10	High
	Korea Transportation Safety Authority	Performance in Enhancement of Safety Level for Business Vehicle	10	High
		Performance in Improvement of the Quality of Personnel in Transportation Business	6	Normal
		Performance in Improvement of Vehicle Safety	5	Normal
	Korea National Park Service	Reduction Rate of Safety Accidents of Visitors	8	Normal
	Road Traffic Authority	Recompletion Rate of Traffic Education	4	Normal
	Korea Gas Safety Corporation	Improvement Rate in Inappropriate Facility	4	Normal
	Korea Occupational Safety & Health Agency	Reduction in Accidents at Focused Management Businesses for Accident and Death Prevention	14	High
		Reduction in Accidents at Support Businesses for Construction of Safety and Welfare	7	Normal
	Korea Electrical Safety Corporation	Reduction in Fire Accidents at Electric Facilities for Required Examination	7	Normal
		Reduction in Fire Accidents at Residential Units	7	Normal
		Reduction in Fire Accidents at Vulnerable Facilities	3	Normal
		Reduction in Accidents at Electric Facilities	8	High
	Korea Environment Corporation	Performance in Management of Program for Reduction in Green House Gas	6	High
		Performance in Reduction of Nitrogen Oxide Output	6	Normal
		Performance in Reduction of Water Pollution	13	High
Service	Korea National Park Service	Participation Rate in Exploratory Programs	7	Normal
	National Health Insurance Service	Enhancement of Checkup Inspection Rate and Timely Management of Patients with Issues	9	High

Type	Institution Name	Indicator Name	Weight	Difficulty Level
	Korea Trade-Investment Promotion Agency	Development of Promising Overseas Projects and Participation Rate	2	Normal
	Korea Veterans Health Service	Enhancement of Veteran Health Service	8	High
		Increase in Coverage of Brand Programs of Veteran Health Facilities	3	Normal
Support	Korea Trade-Investment Promotion Agency	Performance in Support for Development of Domestic Corporations Exporting Overseas and New Market Expansion	7	High
		Performance in Support of Tailored Service for Promising Exporting Corporations	7	High
		Performance in Expansion of Importing Buyers	7	Normal
	Korea Gas Safety Corporation	Performance in Support for Corporations	6	Normal
	Land and Geospatial Informatrix Corporation	Business Budget for Private Corporations	5	Normal
	Korea Agro-Fisheries & Food Trade Corporation	Global Competitiveness for Exports of Agro-Fishery Products	10	Normal
		Performance in Construction of Foundation for Food Product Industry	8	Normal
	Korea Rural Community Corporation	Enhancement of Production Rate of Rice-only Farms	9	Normal
	Human Resources Development Service of Korea	Performance in Customer-centered Support of Overseas Employment	4	Normal
		Prevention of Exit of Skilled Professionals Working in the Same Function	3	Normal
	Korea Employment Agency for the Disabled	Performance in Employment of the Disabled Listed for Different Life Stages	6	High
		Performance in Passing Rate for National Technical Certifications of Graduating Students from Vocational Development Training and Maintenance of Their Employment	12	Normal

Data: Reconstructed based on Public Institution Performance Evaluation Committee (2016)

as the Korea Trade-Investment Promotion Agency and the Korea Agro-Fisheries and Food Trade Corporation, which have been supporting exporting firms since the developmental era. Although they are among the top performing institutions in the group of QGIs in the past five years, there was a practical concern that the high scores of the support indicators may be due partly to a selection effect; that is, relatively promising clients would more likely to be selected as partners. This concern often was expressed in the annual performance evaluation reports.

2 Limitations and recommendations

In this section, we discuss limitations of the indicators used by QGIs from the perspective of reflecting collaboration and recommendations for improvement of the evaluation system.

1 Paucity of quantitative indicators reflecting collaborative activities

The empirical analysis of the 87 quantitative indicators reveals that not enough indicators have been developed and are being used to reflect the performance of collaborative activities. As discussed in the second section, although many of the business goals of QGIs require collaboration in theory, collaborative activities were underrepresented in the system of performance indicators; instead large weights were given to input or throughput measures such as refinement and internal product indicators. These indicators were often defined by the institutions in a way that allowed the institutions to improve the score simply by inputting more financial and human resources. It is not surprising that some institutions prefer these indicators to collaboration indicators because they can measure and control the activities reflected in the refinement and internal product indicators more easily than collaborative activities and their performance. Note that the refinement and internal product indicators earned the highest average scores of all (82.87 and 83.13 respectively) except for the support indicators (83.97). Although these indicators deliver information about the institutions' effort to achieve their goals, they do not show what social benefits were created by the activity. Furthermore, these indicators are rooted in a mechanical perspective of public administration that prevailed in the industrial era. The traditional perspective is good at dealing with issues and pursuing efficiency in a relatively simple policy environment. Conversely, a collaborative management model emphasizes the adaptability of an organization in a complex environment and its contribution to the upper system (Robertson and Choi, 2010). Although this perspective is gaining more attention, as shown in the use of official collaboration indicators and collaboration indicators, given the nature of policy implementation these days, collaborative activities are not properly captured by the performance evaluation system.

2 Collaboration to help capacity building of the civil society

Collaboration can provide an opportunity for participants to build their capacity by sharing their knowledge and experience as well as improve their performance.

To take advantage of this benefit of collaboration, the performance evaluation system needs to encourage institutions to use indicators that measure the degree of capacity building of clients through collaboration. For example, in the case of the Korea Employment Agency for the Disabled's "performance in enhancement of employment of the disabled," [24] an appropriate evaluation would consider the extent to which collaboration among employees, employers and the institution enhances the managerial capacity of the employers to take care of disabled employees and create values through it. That is, rather than focusing on counting the number of disabled employees, the performance of the activity should be evaluated in terms of effort to improve employers' own capacity to manage disabled employees. Capacity building is also crucial for support indicators. For example, the Korea Trade-Investment Promotion Agency's "performance in expanding deal making for buyers of Korean exports"[25] considered only whether the institution's support helped small businesses to make a deal with foreign importers. However, more appropriate evaluation of the service would consider whether the institution's service helped the firms improve their own capacity to search, negotiate and reach a deal in the future. By enhancing the capacity of clients, the Korea Trade-Investment Promotion Agency would be able to expand its service to other clients while keeping the growth of the former clients sustainable.

This raises another issue regarding the quality of support indicators, which has implications for the design of collaboration indicators. The performance improvement in support indicators basically depends on the performance of those who receive support; whether private firms increase the amount of export, and whether young job seekers eventually get a job. For a more accurate evaluation of support indicators for the Korea Trade-Investment Promotion Agency, we need to analyze the net effect of the Agency's support on the expansion of the clients' business. In reality, the causal relationship between support and outcome is murky. In the cases of the Korea Trade-Investment Promotion Agency's "performance in support for tailored service for promising exporting firms"[26] and the Korea Agro-Fisheries and Food Trade Corporation's "performance in structuring foundation for the food industry,"[27] simply counting numbers of clients and their revenues doesn't tell much about the real contribution of the supporting activities. Finally, as mentioned above, when support is delivered exclusively to registered clients (even to relatively strong ones), it introduces the issues of selection bias and service equality. The same issues of selection bias and service equality can be raised in designing collaboration indicators when QGIs that initiate collaboration have multiple choices on with whom to collaborate. Inclusiveness is key to the quality and success of collaboration.

3 Facilitating use of collaboration indicators between public institutions

The analysis of the indicators revealed that few collaboration indicators were used between QGIs, other than some cases in which a couple of QGIs might enhance public interest through collaboration. For example, the Korea Trade-Investment Promotion Agency and the Korea Agro-Fisheries and Food Trade Corporation are responsible for supporting export-related businesses; the Korea Agro-Fisheries and Food Trade Corporation and the Korea Rural Community Corporation are responsible for promoting income of agro-fisheries; and the Health Insurance Review and Assessment Service and the National Health Insurance Service are responsible for national health insurance. Nevertheless, the analysis showed that they did not use any official collaboration indicator. It is even likely that they perceive other institutions more as competitors than as collaborators. Legal enforcement of the use of official collaboration indicators would be a way to facilitate collaboration among them. More radically, reorganization such as a merger can be considered instead of collaboration when the functions of 2 institutions (e.g., the Health Insurance Review and Assessment Service and the National Health Insurance Service) should be tied together.

On the other hand, a case can be made that collaboration between public institutions may not always be desirable. According to the New Public Management idea, efficiency is ensured when there is competition between institutions. In addition, sometimes checks and balances between public institutions may create democratic value beyond simple efficiency. Collaboration is not a panacea; the context in which competition, checks and balances, or reorganization can serve public interest better than collaboration should be considered.

4 Limitations inherent in collaboration indicators

Although outcome measures would usually be considered ideal for measuring the result of collaboration, it is necessary to take QGIs' perspective into account in designing collaboration indicators. Since the collaboration process is a black box to outsiders, outcome measures would be preferred. However, because outcome measures often are out of the control of institutions, they are less preferable to those institutions. Given that institutions possess the right to define and suggest indicators for their annual performance evaluations, we need a practical approach. If so, one important factor is how to motivate institutions to be involved in collaboration that leads to high scores, even by using collaboration indicators in the form of "shared" throughput measures. A more fundamental question is whether it is appropriate to measure the result of collaboration by quantitative indicators. The performance evaluation system has changed every year with regard to the balance between quantitative and qualitative scores. Accordingly, collaboration has usually been evaluated in a qualitative way. Therefore, another viable way would be to sophisticate the qualitative evaluation system as well as strengthen the quantitative approach.

5 When to measure performance of collaboration

Collaboration, if measured by outcome, needs time to reap the benefit. It takes time to prepare the conditions for collaboration; it takes time to realize any social effect such as capacity building. Logically, if collaboration is regarded as the best option, it means that the pertinent problem requires a complex and long-term approach rather than a traditional bureaucratic approach. From this perspective, a question can be raised whether it is appropriate to use collaboration indicators for an annual evaluation. There are a few counterarguments against this perspective. First, many programs other than collaborative ones are suitable for longer-term evaluation, so collaboration is not an exception. Second, most of the evaluation focuses on annual marginal improvement compared to the previous years. Evaluation of the performance of collaboration also can be performed in that way. Particularly, the current evaluation system adopts a long-term trend measure, which can appropriately be used for collaboration indicators.

IV Lessons learned and conclusion

1 Lessons learned

QGIs form a unique state apparatus that has been institutionalized during the developmental era of South Korea. They exist in the gray realm between the public and the private sectors and take on the public responsibility of policy implementation. Due to their unique institutional status, they assume an important position to facilitate collaboration among different public, private and civic actors. In addition, having accumulated knowledge and resources in the areas of safety, trade, employment, industry and public insurance, they can help private partners to build their own capacity through collaboration.

Although collaboration is key to a new paradigm in public administration, it is not easy to encourage collaborative policy implementation, partly due to the current annual performance evaluation system. To earn higher scores, QGIs usually prefer indicators that measure internal activities such as refinement and internal production. However, we found several exemplary collaboration indicators. They were neither very useful in earning a high score nor evaluated as difficult to achieve. There is much room for further development of collaboration indicators.

In addition to developing new quantitative indicators that reflect collaborative activities and performance, we argued that a qualitative approach is necessary to consider the long-term effects and invisible aspects of collaboration such as internal coordination processes and other positive by-products, including long-term capacity building of collaborating partners.

2 Conclusion

In this chapter, we first analyzed at the macro level the institutionalization of QGIs in South Korea, showing how they are well-suited to facilitate collaboration in public policy implementation. Then we analyzed at the micro level the currently used performance indicators of QGIs from the perspective of collaboration. Finally, we discussed limitations of current indicators and future directions to develop appropriate collaboration indicators to encourage collaborative activities by QGIs. Key lessons from the analysis were summarized above.

Given the importance of collaboration to effective and efficient policy implementation, it is necessary to design an indicator system that can fairly reflect the challenges and performance of collaboration. It is not easy for QGIs to select collaboration as a way to implement their programs because their history of institutionalization is rooted in the strong developmental state model. Efficiency, speed, and command and control have ruled their behavior. In this sense, QGIs are eminent examples of the paradigm shift in public administration. How they implement policy will tell us whether a paradigm shift in public administration in South Korea is a real trend or just rhetoric.

QGIs' effort to facilitate collaboration, therefore, should be appreciated properly. It may not be fair to compel them to use collaborative modes of policy implementation by using the performance evaluation system as leverage. Instead, the performance evaluation system needs to be designed to send a signal that if QGIs increase collaborative efforts, then their effort will be compensated through getting legitimate appreciation. As discussed above, it is difficult to design appropriate collaboration indicators. Instead of focusing excessively on developing quantitative indicators, the performance evaluation system reform needs to focus on the big picture that can balance quantitative and qualitative methods and trigger a virtuous circle between collaborative efforts and evaluation.

Notes

1 The calculation of the size of public debt is one of the most important practical issues related to the quasi-governmental organizations.
2 When we consider the organizational legacy before the establishment of the Republic of Korea, the foundation of some institutions responsible for agriculture, land registration, railway, and postal service can surely be traced back to the late Chosun Dynasty.
3 For example, those responsible for safety including Korea Transportation Safety Authority, Road Traffic Authority, Korea Gas Safety Corporation, Korea Electrical Safety Corporation, and Korea Occupational Safety and Health Agency are running education and public relationship programs as their major businesses (Public Institution Performance Evaluation Committee, 2016).
4 It should be noted that we frequently found a discrepancy between the name of a certain indicator and its substantive activity reflected in the calculation of the indicator. Such discrepancy is normally found in many indicators so that they look more like outcome indicators or collaboration indicators when they are biased toward input or throughput activities. In this chapter, classification was conducted on the basis of the substantive activity implied in the pertinent indicator.
5 This indicator was calculated by summing the weighted average of 1) the number of acceptances for industrial accidents per 200,000 work hours at the Korea Workers' Compensation and Welfare Service; 2) the number of processed car insurance claims per 100,000 driving hours (collisions); and 3) on-time rate at the Daejeon Exchange Center (Public Institution Performance Evaluation Committee, 2016: 546).
6 This indicator is calculated as "(survey processing days/number of surveys processed)/survey benchmark date" (Public Institution Performance Evaluation Committee, 2016; 563).
7 In this chapter, we did not use the abbreviated names of the institutions because they are not all well-known to the public.

8 This indicator was calculated as "(number of lots digitized in current year – number of lots digitized in last year)/number of lots digitized in last year" (Public Institution Performance Evaluation Committee, 2016: 563).

9 This indicator was calculated as "nationwide average farming income/nationwide average farming hours" (Public Institution Performance Evaluation Committee, 2016: 579).

10 This indicator was calculated as "nationwide average non-farming income/nationwide average farming income" (Public Institution Performance Evaluation Committee, 2016: 580).

11 This indicator was calculated as "increase in the number of workplaces for the disabled after providing service" (Public Institution Performance Evaluation Committee, 2016: 612).

12 Note that the average scores of the indicators in certain categories can be sensitive to small changes in categorization due to the small sample size. For example, the score for the Human Resources Development Service of Korea's "performance for supporting youth employment," which was categorized as a collaboration indicator, was 55.59, an outlier in the category (the overall average score of the indicators in the category was 86.14).

13 The Public Institution Performance Evaluation Committee assigned either 1 (high) or 0.9 (normal) to each indicator to reflect the perceived level of difficulty in achieving its goal.

14 This indicator was calculated as "number of casualties per 10,000 vehicles" (Public Institution Performance Evaluation Committee, 2016: 502).

15 This indicator was calculated as "incidences of customer damage/distance of railway travelled" (Public Institution Performance Evaluation Committee, 2016: 504).

16 This indicator was calculated as "number of participants in green point" (Public Institution Performance Evaluation Committee, 2016: 511).

17 This indicator was calculated as "collected volume of green point garbage/total garbage collected" (Public Institution Performance Evaluation Committee, 2016: 511).

18 This indicator was calculated as "medical fees supported by expansion of health insurance coverage" (Public Institution Performance Evaluation Committee, 2016: 496).

19 This indicator was calculated as "number of cases for improvement in health insurance payment" (Public Institution Performance Evaluation Committee, 2016: 497).

20 This indicator was calculated as the weighted sum of "(collection rate of health insurance premium in current year x additional amount of health insurance levy source)/health insurance premium charged" and "national pension, employment and industrial accident insurance premium collected/premium charged" (Public Institution Performance Evaluation Committee, 2016: 520).

21 This indicator was calculated as "amount of trade in cyber exchange" (Public Institution Performance Evaluation Committee, 2016: 570).

22 This indicator was calculated as "sum of entry period for foreign workers/number of foreign workers entered" (Public Institution Performance Evaluation Committee, 2016: 604).

23 Eventually, the difficulty coefficient system was abolished in 2017.

24 This indicator was calculated as "number of disabled workers in businesses required to hire disabled workers/number of workers in those businesses" (Public Institution Performance Evaluation Committee, 2016: 611).

25 This indicator was calculated as "number of buyers (number of companies) who completed deal making in the current year based on service provided by the institution" (Public Institution Performance Evaluation Committee, 2016: 529).

26 This indicator was calculated as "exports of small and medium size firms using customized service/nationwide exports of small and medium size firms" (Public Institution Performance Evaluation Committee, 2016: 529).

27 This indicator was calculated as "sum of marginal increase rate in annual sales of consulted firms /number of firms" (Public Institution Performance Evaluation Committee, 2016: 572).

References

Ansell, C., and Gash, A. (2008). Collaborative Governance in Theory and Practice. *Journal of Public Administration Research and Theory*, *18*(4), 543–571.

Bell, S., and Hindmoor, A. (2009). *Rethinking Governance: The Centrality of the State in Modern Society*. Cambridge: Cambridge University Press.

Chambers, S. (2003). Deliberative Democratic Theory. *Annual Review of Political Science*, *6*(1), 307–326.

Choi, T. (2014). Revisiting the Relevance of Collaborative Governance to Korean Public Administration. *The Korean Journal of Policy Studies*, *29*(2), 21–41.

Choi, J., and Choi, T. (2017). The Changes of Political Environment of Public Policy. In J. Choi, H. Kwon, and M. G. Koo (eds.), *The Korean Government and Public Policies in a Development Nexus: Sustaining Development and Tackling Policy Changes* (pp. 9–29). Springer.

Chung, M. K., and Han, S. I. (2005). *Research on Size and Characteristics of the Quasi-Governmental Sector in Korea: Focus on Quasi-Governmental Agencies*. The Korean Association for Public Administration Conference Proceedings, April, 1–26.

Chung, Y. D. et al. (2014). *Public Administration in a Modern Country* (2nd ed.). Paju: Beopmunsa.

Cleveland, H. (2000). The Future Is Uncentralized. *Public Administration Review*, *60*(4), 293–297.

Denhardt, R. B., and Denhardt, J. V. (2000). The New Public Service: Serving Rather than Steering. *Public Administration Review*, *60*(6), 549–559.

Kettl, D. F. (2000). The Transformation of Governance: Globalization, Devolution, and the Role of Government. *Public Administration Review*, *60*(6), 488–497.

Kim, J. K. (2002). *Research on the Relation Between Organization/Association and Government: Focus on Business Organizations Under the Ministry of Commerce Industry and Energy*. The Korean Association for Public Administration Conference Proceedings, December, 709–729.

Kim, N. C. (2015). Research on Legal Limitation of the Role of Public Institutions According to Principle and Standards of Functional Reorganization of Public Institutions. *Public Law Review*, *44*, 287–314.

Kim, P. S., Hong, G. P., and Kim, W. H. (2008). Public Institution Governance, Performance of Innovation in Management Systems and Future Tasks. *Korean Public Administration Quarterly*, *20*(2), 406–437.

Lee, S. C., and Park, B. S. (2004). Plan for Efficient Implementation of the Performance Evaluation System of Government Agencies. *Korean Society and Public Administration*, *15*(1), 27–49.

Milward, H. B., and Provan, K. G. (2000). Governing the Hollow State. *Journal of Public Administration Research and Theory*, *10*(2), 359–380.

Ministry of Strategy and Finance. (2011). *2008–2010 Advancement of Public Corporations White Paper*.

Ministry of Strategy and Finance. (2016). *Collaboration Among Public Institutions Improves the Daily Life of the Public: Selection of Exemplary Tasks of Collaboration Among Public Institutions in 2015*, Press Release 2016. 2. 23.

O'Leary, R., and Bingham, L. B. (eds.) (2009). *The Collaborative Public Manager: New Ideas for the Twenty-First Century*. Georgetown University Press.

Park, G. K. (2013). *Research on Promoting Public Institution Collaboration*. Ministry of Strategy and Finance Research Project.

Park, S. H. (2012). *Comparison and Implications of Managing Agencies for Public Institutions in Major Countries*. The Korean Association for Public Administration Conference Proceedings, December, 1632–1655.

Park, S. H. (2014). History and Evolution of Public Corporations: Focus on Public Interest. In S. Park and J. K. Kim (eds.), *Innovation in Public Corporations: Issues and Cases* (pp. 3–27). Seoul: Park Young Sa.

Public Institution Performance Evaluation Committee. (2016). *Public Institution Performance Evaluation Manual*.

Peters, B. G. (1997). *The Future of Governing*. University Press of Kansas.

Rhodes, R. A. W. (1994). The Hollowing Out of the State: The Changing Nature of the Pservice in Britain. *The Political Quarterly*, *65*(2), 138–151.

Robertson, P. J., and Choi, T. (2010). Ecological Governance: Organizing Principles for an Emerging Era. *Public Administration Review*, *70*(s1), s89–s99.

Weber, E. P., and Khademian, A. M. (2008). Wicked Problems, Knowledge Challenges, and Collaborative Capacity Builders in Network Settings. *Public Administration Review*, *68*(2), 334–349.

14 Public utility performance indicators under price regulation

Sounman Hong

I Introduction

Management evaluation systems for South Korean public institutions experienced a significant change due to the 2007 "the Act on the Management of Public Institutions" (hereafter, "the Act"), which is conducted every year to enhance the efficiency and transparency of public institution management. As of 2016, 119 institutions have been designated as public corporations or quasi-governmental institutions. They are evaluated according to the Act by means of a public institution management evaluation committee under the ministry of strategy and finance. That management evaluation system is considered to have significantly contributed to improvement of transparency, efficiency and performance in the main business activities of public institutions. However, despite such positive contributions, there has been some criticism that the system does not sufficiently reflect the characteristics of public institutions.

This research focuses on public institutions regulating public utility rates, in order to contemplate the managerial implications of the evaluation system and its performance indicators. For some public institutions coming under the Act, public utility rates imposed on the public are subject to rate-of-return regulation. That is, the price (i.e., utility rate) is regulated at the level of the service's "overall cost." Overall cost is calculated by adding "appropriate profit" (i.e., appropriate investment return) to the accounting cost incurred by the institution. The government regulates public utility rates charged by large public corporations, including Korea Electric Power, K-Water, Korea Railway, Korea Expressway and Korea Gas, fixing them to the overall cost level. As the Act mainly regulates large-scale public corporations among other public institutions, it is important to understand the effect of governmental rate regulation on the decision-making of the institution.

When public utility rates are maintained near overall cost, regulated public institutions might overinvest in fixed capacity. Among items comprising overall cost, the appropriate profit is calculated as a certain fraction of capital expenditures of the public institution. This formula treats higher capital expenditures as the institution incurring higher opportunity costs, thus allowing higher appropriate profits. Under that system, regulated institutions can be compensated with higher public utility rates for investments in fixed capacity and thus may overinvest in fixed capital. Therefore, government regulation may distort the investment decisions of regulated utilities. Consequently, it is necessary to consider the potential bias when designing a management evaluation system for regulated public institutions and selecting performance indicators.

This study briefly explores regulation of public utility rates in South Korea and theoretically shows that such regulation can bias investment decisions made by of public institutions. Then, the effect of regulating public utility rates on management performance is further examined through the case of the dam and water business of K-Water. Lastly, attributes of management performance indicators to be attained by public institutions under rate regulation are explored and implications for public policy are drawn.

II Understanding public utility rate regulation

1 The legal system underlying public utility rate regulation in South Korea

Public utility rate regulation managed by the central government is conducted on the basis of the "Act on Price Stabilization." Article 4 (5th Clause) of the Act leaves the principle of calculation, period of calculation and method of calculation subject to presidential decree, while Article 6 (its enforcement provision) requires public utility rates to conform to the overall cost level. The provision calculates overall cost by summing the "appropriate cost" and "appropriate investment return" and leaves details on the standards of calculation to the Minister of Strategy and Finance.

Figure 14.1 summarizes the legal system for the regulation of public utility rates as managed by the central government in South Korea. As Figure 14.1 shows, the Minister of Strategy and Finance is entrusted with the Price Stabilization Act and related enforcement regulations pronounces the "Calculation Standard for Public Utility Rates" as a Ministry directive to regulate public utility rates. According to that standard, a responsible ministry may specify calculation standards for individual public utility rates that reflect the characteristics of individual business (e.g., calculation standards for electricity, running water, railway fares, etc.), but must adhere to the principle that public utility rates must be set at the level of overall cost (refer to the "Basic Principle of Calculation of Public Utility Rate in Calculation Standard for Public Utility Rate").

2 Calculation of overall cost

Calculation Standards for public utility rates is defined by a calculation equation for overall cost in a detailed way. Decomposition of the overall cost defined in the calculation standard for public utility rates is briefly summarized in Figure 14.2. The overall cost is calculated by adding the appropriate investment return that is in the spirit of opportunity costs to the appropriate cost shown on the actual income statement. The appropriate investment return is, in turn, calculated as the

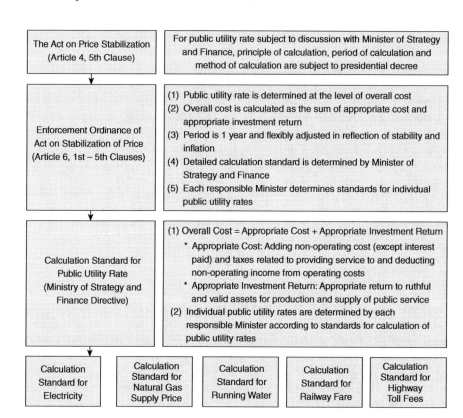

Figure 14.1 Legal system related to calculation of central public utility rate

product of the cost base and the appropriate investment rate of return calculated for each public utility.

The actual calculation of the cost base and appropriate investment rate of return comprising that component of overall cost can be quite complex, but its concept is relatively simple. The cost base is the amount of assets invested by the institution to engage in a regulated business, and appropriate investment rate of return is the institution's weighted average cost of capital (WACC)

III Theoretical discussion

1 Averch and Johnson effect

The argument has been around since the 1960s that says that the choice of regulated institution may be biased when a public utility rate is regulated using overall cost. A representative study is the research of Averch and Johnson (1962), which assumes a situation in which a regulated institution uses labor (L) and capital (K)

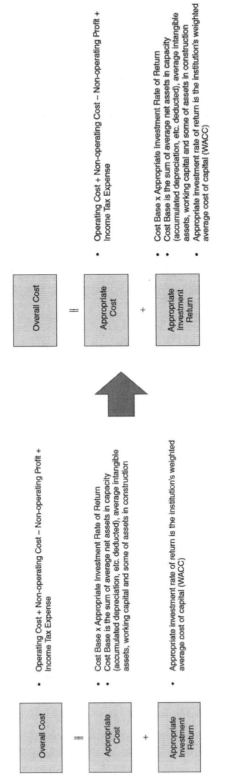

Figure 14.2 Overall cost as defined in the calculation standard for public utility rates

as factors of production and produces public service of Q. Then, Q is sold at price of P per unit. This P is assumed to be a function of Q in a monopolistic market. At that moment, the institution attempts to maximize its profit π by minimizing hiring of (or investment in) labor and capital (but, w and r represent the price of labor and capital, respectively, in the ensuing Equation (1)).

$$(1) \quad \max_{L,K} \quad \underbrace{\pi}_{\text{Profit}} = \underbrace{P(Q) \times Q(L,K)}_{\text{Total Revenue}} - \underbrace{wL}_{\substack{\text{Labor} \\ \text{Cost}}} - \underbrace{rK}_{\substack{\text{Capital} \\ \text{Cost}}}$$

Assuming that the public utility rates of this institution are regulated and set to correspond to overall cost, the following restriction is derived. Comparing Equation (2) and Equation (1), the assumption about capital cost in Averch and Johnson (1962) is different when used for calculating profit and applying regulation. While the profit of this institution appearing in Equation (1) uses capital cost of r, regulation of overall cost uses capital cost of s that is higher than r. That is, Averch and Johnson (1962) assume that the regulator uses an appropriate investment rate of return that is higher than the actual capital cost of the institution at r in regulating the public utility's costs at the overall cost level (assuming s > r).

$$(2) \quad P(Q) \times Q(L,K) = \underbrace{wL}_{\substack{\text{Appropriate} \\ \text{Cost}}} + \underbrace{sK}_{\substack{\text{Appropriate} \\ \text{Investment Return}}}$$

Equation (2) can be explained by comparing it with the overall cost used in calculation of a public utility in South Korea, as explained in Figure 14.2. In Equation (2), cost related to labor, i.e., wages (wL), is a concept that corresponds to the appropriate cost in the Calculation Standard for Public Utility Rate. Nevertheless, the cost related to capital, sK, is the amount related to the aforementioned appropriate investment return.[1]

Averch and Johnson (1962) derives the maximization condition for the economic profit of Equation (1) using Kuhn-Tucker conditions under the restriction of Equation (2). For ease of interpretation, the amounts of labor and capital (or investment) to maximize profits are determined for cases in which the public institution is not affected by regulation of the public utility rates (Case 1) and the case in which a public institution is affected by regulation of public utility rates (Case 2).

In Table 14.1, MP denotes marginal product and represents the incremental amount of public service when each unit of production factors, capital (K) and labor (L), are applied. That is, in the absence of regulation of public utility rates

Table 14.1 Analysis of result in Averch and Johnson (1962)

	(Case 1) No regulation on public utility rate	(Case 2) Regulation on public utility rate (but, s > r assumed)
Profit Maximizing Condition	$\dfrac{MP_K}{MP_L} = \dfrac{r}{w}$	$\dfrac{MP_K}{MP_L} = \dfrac{r - \Delta(s-r)}{w}$ but $\Delta > 0$

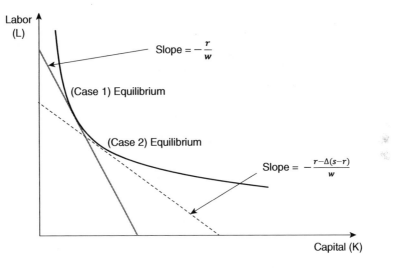

Figure 14.3 Analysis of result in Averch and Johnson (1962)

(Case 1), the institution applies labor and capital to the point where the ratio of value created by production factors equals the ratio of the costs of production factors. However, according to Averch and Johnson (1962), the cost of capital becomes lower and decision-making of the institution becomes biased when a public utility rate is regulated based on overall cost (Case 2). For ease of interpretation, profit-maximizing conditions for (Case 1) and (Case 2) summarized in Table 14.1 and are graphed in Figure 14.3.

The conclusion of Averch and Johnson (1962) can be summarized as follows. They assume that the regulating authority guarantees appropriate investment rate of return(s) that are higher than the actual cost of capital (r) with respect to capital (the assumption of s > r). Under the assumption, the situation in which the regulated public institution maximizes economic profit by applying production factors is assumed. In this case, the institution acts as if the cost of capital falls compared to non-regulated scenarios and thus overinvests in capital.

2 Actual applicability of the Averch and Johnson Model

Averch and Johnson (1962) explains why the regulated institution overinvests in fixed capacity when the government regulates public utility rates using overall cost. However, applying this theory to the case of domestic public corporations can be difficult. While Averch and Johnson (1962) assumes that the regulating authority guarantees the appropriate investment rate of return(s) that are higher than actual cost of capital (r). Likewise, the calculation standard for public utility rates in South Korea defines the appropriate investment rate of return as the actual cost of capital when calculating overall cost (i.e., s = r according to the calculation standard for public utility rates). Thus, because the assumption of Averch and Johnson (1962) does not hold, its results cannot be applied.

However, this study suggests that overinvestment of capital occurs according to current domestic regulation when the appropriate investment rate of return is set to the actual cost of capital. Why? The appropriate investment rate of return is determined by calculating weighted average of cost of debt (loans, etc.) and equity capital (government ownership, etc.). At that moment, the cost of debt is, in general, significantly higher than the cost of equity (Myers, 1984). That is, Myers' (1984) pecking-order theory of financing implies that a firm in need of capital first uses retained earnings, then external capital such as debt and finally internal capital such as equity issuance in the presence of information asymmetries. In other words, retained earnings provides the lowest cost of capital, with external capital next, and then internal capital has the highest cost (Myers, 1994; Shyam-Sunder and Myers, 1999).

The fact that the cost of external capital is significantly higher than the cost of internal capital is akin to the assumption that the government's guaranteed level of the appropriate investment rate of return (s) is higher than the actual cost of capital (r) in Averch and Johnson (1962). That is, the appropriate investment rate of return is determined by the weighted average of external and internal capital costs. However, public institutions make their investment decisions based on the cost of external capital (i.e., debt) as opposed to WACC. To aid one's understanding of this fact, the appropriate investment rate of return (WACC) as the weighted average of costs of external capital and internal capital can be expressed as follows.

$$
\text{(3)} \qquad \text{WACC} = \alpha \times \underbrace{r_{debt}}_{\text{Cost of Debt}} + (1 - \alpha) \times \underbrace{r_{equity}}_{\text{Cost of Equity}}
$$

The weighted average cost of capital (WACC) here is the appropriate investment rate of return(s) that appears in the Averch and Johnson (1962) model. However, the model's cost of capital (r) should be viewed as cost of external capital. The following two cases help to explain why:

- First, assume that the institution needs to raise new capital to invest in greater fixed capacity. At that time, the institution uses external capital to finance the project since it is relatively cheaper than internal capital to do so, such that the cost of capital for the institution becomes the cost of external capital.

- Second, assume that the institution has enough retained earnings to invest in greater fixed capacity and, at the same time, debt can be retired using retained earnings. In this case, even if the retained earnings are used, the cost of capital is still the cost of debt because the retained earnings are not used to repay the debt. In other words, the proper opportunity cost is the cost of debt, in this case.

Discussion so far can be summarized as in Figure 14.4. In both cases, the assumption of Averch and Johnson (1962) that the appropriate investment rate of return should be greater than the cost of capital (r) holds. For ease of interpretation, the argument so far may be summarized as follows. Assume that the institution with regulated public utility rates set according to the firm's overall cost chooses to invest in capacity with no economic value using external capital. Even if the investment does not produce any economic value, it benefits the institution. The debt's principal is included in the appropriate overall cost as capacity is depreciated, and interest on debt will be returned via the public utility rates charged as reflected in the appropriate investment return of overall cost. Here, appropriate investment rate of return used in the calculation of appropriate investment return becomes greater than the cost of external capital and such

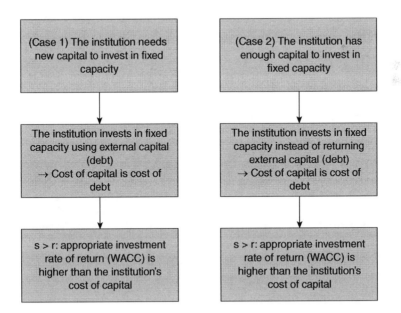

Figure 14.4 The case in which the cost of debt is lower than the cost of equity

Type	Institution's Decision-Making
Case of No Regulation of Public Utility Rate	Invest when future economic value generated by invested capacity exceeds the value of debt (if not, repayment of debt is not possible)
Case of Regulation of Public Utility Rate	Beneficial to invest even when by invested capacity does not produce future economic value • Principal of debt is repaid through public utility rate as part of "appropriate cost" of overall cost in the form of depreciation (repayment of principal possible) • Interest of debt is returned through "appropriate investment return" of overall cost (beneficial even when interest payment is made above interest expense) • If invested capacity generates any economic value, the benefit of overinvestment becomes even greater

Figure 14.5 Regulation of public utility rates and its impact on investment decision making

decision-making benefits the institution. Figure 14.5 explains how regulation of public utility rates based on overall cost influences decision-making of the regulated institution.

IV Case study: multi-regional water supply system and dam water businesses utilizing South Korean water resources

So far, it has been explained that a regulated institution has an incentive to over-invest in capacity that may be factored in the calculation of a public utility's rates, when such rates are regulated under rate-of-return (i.e., the price is set at overall cost). While this argument is theoretically accepted in academia, empirical investigation entails much greater difficulty. For example, using public corporations in South Korea, services for which overall cost regulation is applied such as electricity, running water, gas and railway tends to be a monopolistic market. Empirical analysis requires finding comparable institutions at (but not under) the overall cost regulation, and such cases are hard to find.

Consequently, this study was unable to provide an empirical analysis as to whether the investment decision-making of a public institution is biased (i.e., whether an overinvestment in fixed capital was made). Alternatively, this research shows that public institutions under such overall cost regulation earn sizable profits in regulated businesses, and such high profitability can serve as suggestive, albeit not compelling, evidence of the regulated utilities' overinvestment in fixed capital. Specifically, this study explores data from the multi-regional water supply system and dam water businesses of K-Water.

1 Does the rate level fall short of costs?

On September 19th, 2016, the South Korean Ministry of Land, Infrastructure and Transport announced that the rates or price of the multi-regional water supply system and dam water would be increased by 4.8 percent from September 23rd. The reason given for the hike, the government explained, was that step-wise realization of cost is necessary. The argument of the government is quoted in the following.

> Price level increased by 27.5% over the last 10 years with a 30.7% increase in the price of various raw materials, while cost of multi-regional water system and dam water only had a one-time increase (4.9% in January 2013) over the last 10 years with the price remaining at 84% of production cost. This increase raises cost relative production cost (rate of cost realization) from 84.3% to 88.3% for multi-regional water system and from 82.7% to 86.7% for dam water.
>
> *Source: Press Release of the Ministry of Land,*
> *Infrastructure and Transport, 2016.9.19*

That is, the government argued that the current cost of the multi-regional water system and dam water was falling far short of overall operating costs. Yet, looking at disclosed information on the web page of K-Water, the rate of cost realization for running water has continued to fall: from 86.2 percent in 2004 to 77.8 percent in 2013. It may be due to a lack of increase in the utility's price while production costs for running water was constantly increasing.

Looking at the argument and disclosed data of K-Water, one may expect that K-Water, the institution responsible for multi-regional water system and dam water businesses, has suffered accounting losses. To confirm the argument of the government, income statements for main business activities of K-Water in 2014 is summarized in Table 14.2. This information is profit/loss for 2014 and thus precedes the realization of the cost increase.

As can be seen in Table 14.2, all of the regulated businesses of K-Water made profit in 2014. Among them, multi-regional water system business and dam water business earned about 22.5 billion South Korean won and 78 billion South Korean won, respectively, of net income. Apart from the amount of net income, the profitability level is even more surprising. In particular, the dam water business achieved a 42 percent operating income margin in 2014. However, the performance of the unregulated businesses is rather poor. By contrast, the 4 Major River business incurred a large loss, while Gyungin Ara Waterway and development business earned relatively low operating income margins.

Table 14.2 Profit/loss of main business activities of K-Water

Type	Regulated Business				Unregulated Business		
	Running Water System		Dam		4 Major River Business	Gyungin Ara Waterway	Development Business
	Multi-regional	Local Outsourcing	Dam Water	Management			
Income (Sales)	1,130,748	177,306	264,029	247,665	25,914	320,403	763,387
Cost of Goods Sold	1,024,504	138,417	142,394	156,506	29,818	291,861	714,105
SGA	57,409	13,243	10,643	15,923	–	7,906	15,968
Operating Income	48,835	25,646	110,992	75,236	(3,904)	20,636	33,314
Net Income	22,528	19,109	78,001	55,504	(2,777)	15,682	26,035
Operating Income Margin	4%	14%	42%	30%	−15%	6%	4%

Note: in millions of Korean won; data are for profit/loss in 2014

In conclusion, the government's argument that the rates of multi-regional water system and dam water are much below production cost needs further investigation. When the government announces that the utility rate is far below cost, government is mentioning the "overall cost" by "cost". That is, the rate-of-return regulation is a system that guarantees the realization of accounting profits for the regulated utility. The guaranteed accounting profits become even more pronounced if the public institution carries out investment in fixed capacity.

K-Water plans sizable investments in capacity over the next few years. In the 2016 Parliamentary Inspection, K-Water disclosed that "While current realization rate is 84%, capital for reinvestment is limited" and "the Company expects reinvestment of 3.5 trillion Korean won on replacement of old pipe and dualization of pipe." Such large-scale investments will act as a rationale for increases in public utility rates under the rate-of-return regulation. While improving the quality of public service through reinvestment in outdated capacity is necessary, it is necessary to prevent bias in investment decision-making of public institutions under the overall cost regulation scheme.

2 Comparison of metropolitan water and dam water businesses

Comparing the multi-regional water system and dam water businesses under the overall cost regulation scheme (Table 14.2), the profitability of a dam water business is much higher. Analyzing the cause for the difference in profitability of these two businesses is beyond the scope of this research. However, this study shows that the rate-of-return regulation affecting public utility rates may partly explain the difference in profitability of the two businesses. That is, while multi-regional water system business earned a 4 percent operating income margin, the dam water business achieved 42 percent, as seen in Table 14.2. However, looking at the weight of appropriate investment returns included in overall cost, that figure for a dam water business is significantly higher. Figure 14.6 shows data modified by differentiating appropriate cost from appropriate investment return in the status of overall costs for multi-regional water systems and the dam water businesses. While the appropriate investment return of multi-regional water system business is 13 percent of overall cost, the appropriate investment return of dam water business is 34 percent of overall cost.

By looking at the case of K-Water, this research shows that the company earns sizable profits from both businesses even if the rates of multi-regional water system and dam water businesses fall short of cost. In addition, the profitability of a dam water business is higher than that of multi-regional water system business. One potential cause of the difference is proposed to be the weight of appropriate investment return in overall cost. That is, the weight of appropriate investment return is set much higher for a dam water business, allowing for much higher profitability.

Annual Production Cost and Rate of Running Water

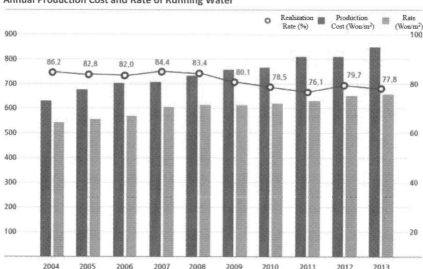

Figure 14.6 Rate of cost realization for running water

Data: based on country-wide average rate of running water; sourced from K-Water homepage (www.kwater.or.kr/info/sub01/sub04/pipe15 Page.do?s_mid = 91)

V Regulation of overall cost and public corporation performance indicators

1 Criteria for performance indicators

Under the situation where rates are subject to rate-of-return regulation, the institution may make overinvestment in capacity and thus inflate its performance. The possibility of such biased investment decision-making can be mitigated by an appropriate design of performance indicators. That is, performance indicators may play a role in mitigating the unintended consequences of rate-of-return regulatory schemes.

Figure 14.7 summarizes the items subject to high likelihood of bias when the Averch and Johnson effect takes place. With an overall cost regulation scheme, there is a possibility that investment in fixed capacity might be inflated and income (total sales) might be overvalued due to an increase in public utility rates. Also, because interest rate on debt is lower than appropriate investment rates of return under an overall cost regulation scheme, excess financing using external capital might be possible. Under such a situation, the following four items need to be taken into account when designing performance indicators.

- **Evaluation of Efficiency:** First, evaluation of efficiency related to the effect relative to a limited resource rather than performance relative to a simple

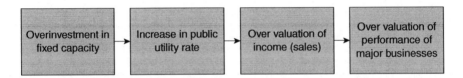

Figure 14.7 Items subject to bias under an overall cost regulation scheme

effect is needed. Here, "a limited resource" implies the amount of investment in fixed capacity.

- **Evaluation of Cost Reduction:** Second, an evaluation of cost reduction instead of improvement in profit is needed. As shown in Figure 14.7, there is the possibility of overvaluation of income (total sales) due to an increase in public utility rates. In that case, the institution's profit does not correctly represent its performance. However, an evaluation of cost reduction efforts (excluding depreciation) is less susceptible to bias and can fairly evaluate the efforts of the institution. Evaluation of cost per output in public service may be considered, too.

- **Evaluation of Debt Ratio:** Third, overinvestment in fixed capacity will be financed by external capital and, therefore, it is necessary to examine the ratio of internal capital to external capital.

- **Evaluation of Inducing Low Rate Level:** Fourth, it is necessary to induce lower levels of rates by evaluating a rate level on the basis of comparison with exogenous variables such as an increase in consumer prices.

2 Evaluation of indicators for business management and main business activities of K-Water

For public institutions that are subject to rate-of-return regulation, caution is warranted in designing performance indicators. If so, let's examine whether current management performance indicators used by the Ministry of Strategy and Finance meet these criteria. Table 14.3 provides a list of K-Water's performance indicators in 2015 taken from the *2015 Public Institution Management Evaluation Manual.* Only quantitative indicators pertaining to business management and main business activities are considered. On the right most side of Table 14.3, results from examining whether K-Water's performance indicators satisfy the four criteria noted above are indicated.

Upon examination, management performance indicators of public institutions in 2015 generally satisfy the criteria necessary to prevent biased investment decisions made by the institution. First, the capital productivity indicator meets the requirement of strengthening the "evaluation on efficiency." That is, by evaluating value added relative to total assets of the institution, investment in fixed capacity that does not create enough value added is penalized in the evaluation. In addition, achievement rates for debt reduction and medium-to-long term financial

Table 14.3 Analysis of characteristics of indicators for business management of K-Water

Type	Indicator	Equation	Achievement of the 4 Criteria of Performance Indicator
Evaluation Area: Business Management			
Operating efficiency	Labor productivity	$$\frac{Value\ Added}{Average\ Personnel}$$	
	Capital productivity	$$\frac{Value\ Added}{Total\ assets}$$	Evaluation of efficiency
Financial budget management and performance	Operating income to sales before deducting depreciation	$$\frac{Operating\ income\ before\ deducting\ depreciation}{Total\ sales}$$	
	Achievement rate of debt reduction	$$\frac{Actual\ debt\ reduction}{Planned\ debt\ reduction} x100$$	Evaluation of debt ratio
	Medium-to-long term financial management plan achievement	$$\frac{Debt}{Equity}$$	Evaluation of debt ratio
Operating cost for quantitative management	Operating cost for quantitative management	$$\frac{SGA}{Total\ sales}$$	Evaluation on cost efficiency
Evaluation Area: Main Business Activities			
Securing safe and ample water resources	Reduction efforts for dam tidal current	$Annual\ average\ Chl - a$ $concentration\ x$ $reservoir\ capacity$	
	Reduction efforts for flood damage	$$\frac{Flood\ Damaged\ Area}{Precipitation\ During\ Flood}$$	
Supplying clean and safe running water	Preventive efforts for loss of running water	$$\frac{Cut\ off\ Time\ for\ local\ reservoir}{Pipe\ extension\left(km\right)}$$ $$+\frac{\sum Cutoff\ population\ x\ cutoff\ time}{Population\ receiving\ water}$$	
	Enhancing efforts for safety and quality of drinking water	$$\frac{Number\ of\ Times\ Global\ Drinking\ Water\ Index\ is\ Achieved}{Number\ of\ Times\ of\ Water\ Examination}$$	
	Efficiency in water supply	$$\frac{Water\ flow}{Water\ Production}$$	

Source: 2015 Public Institution Management Evaluation

management plan achievement both, respectively, reduce incentives for investment in fixed capacity through external financing by inducing a reduction in debt. Lastly, operating costs for quantitative management is consistent with the "evaluation on cost efficiency" and the evaluation of sales and general administrative costs relative to total sales penalizes any attempt at over-booking income (i.e., total sales).

In conclusion, current management evaluation indicators are deemed to have been constructed to mitigate negative side effects of rate-of-return regulation. Among the aforementioned four criteria, while there is no quantitative evaluation indicator for inducing low rates, evaluation of efficiency/cost reduction/debt reduction is conducted in its place. Therefore, the management evaluation system has, to some extent, the effect of mitigating negative side effects of the rate-of-return regulation of a public utility. However, contrary to the confidence of scholars covering the area of business management, quantitative indicators for main business activities do not seem to have been designed to consider the possibility of biased investment decision-making by public institutions. Therefore, it is necessary to check whether public institutions are making unnecessary and non-essential investments in facilities through a quantitative evaluation covering the areas of their main business activities that might reflect evaluation results.

VI Lessons learned and conclusion

1 Lessons learned

This research focuses on public institutions that are subject to rate-of-return regulation and examines necessary attributes for performance indicators used in evaluating these institutions. According to the Stabilization of Price Law and its enforcement regulations, rates for services provided by large public corporations such as electricity, railway, gas and running water are subject to rate-of-return regulation. It was explained that public institutions under such regulation over-invest in capacity to maximize profit and public utility rates may thus increase as a result. This research shows that a centralized performance management system may mitigate this unintended consequence of government regulation by evaluating the performance of these regulated utilities with proper indicators.

2 Conclusion

This study examined the financial performance of each business of K-Water. Despite the government's claim that cost realization of the utility rate nears 80%, K-Water earns sizable profits from regulated businesses and this tendency is more pronounced for businesses with a higher ratio of capital expenditure to overall cost. Furthermore, attributes to be attained by performance indicators for regulated public institutions are explored and four criteria including 1) evaluation of efficiency, 2) evaluation of cost reduction, 3) evaluation of debt reduction, and 4) evaluation of inducing low public utility rates are proposed. Lastly, upon the evaluation of K-Water's quantitative indicators from the 2015 Public Institution Management Evaluation, we found that they are generally in line with the four criteria. In sum, we conclude that the current management evaluation system may partly contribute to mitigating negative side effects of rate-of-return regulation as highlighted by Averch and Johnson (1962).

Note

1 For information, Averch and Johnson (1962) does not consider depreciation cost for ease of analysis (p. 1054).

References

Averch, H., and Johnson, L. L. (1962). Behavior of the Firm Under Regulatory Constraint. *The American Economic Review*, 1052–1069.

Myers, S. C. (1984). The Capital Structure Puzzle. *Journal of Finance, 39*, 575–592.

Shyam-Sunder, L., and Myers, S. C. (1999). Testing Static Tradeoff Against Pecking Order Models of Capital Structure. *Journal of Financial Economics, 51*, 219–244.

15 Plan for constructing performance governance of public corporations

Gu Hwan Won

I Introduction

While many scholars emphasize the importance of performance management, their discussion are mostly about conceptual definition on target (Pollitt, 2001) phased processes (Grindle, 1980: 11; Lasswell, 1975: 2). Of course, performance management is usually interested in mission and vision of organization and achievement of target. However, performance management is a holistic practice deriving strategic priority that can contribute to the achievement of mid-to-long term targets of the organization; constructing commensurate performance target and indicators for individuals and groups; and successfully implementing and confirming achievement of the organization's targets.

In relation to performance management, it is first necessary to imprint the reasons for existence and the establishment of the organization. Then, a repeated learning process of determining which efforts to be performed to satisfy the mission of the organization is necessary. The mission identification and its implementation should be directed to serves public interest. As the misplaced mission of public institutions and failure of serving public interests will cause social costs paid by citizens, meticulously constructing mission, vision, strategic goal and performance target by the public sector are the most elementary concept that can secure the public's trust and validity of the organization's existence.

In performance evaluation as a part of performance management, it is vital to construct performance indicators capable of fulfilling mission, vision, strategic goal and performance target in performance management of the public sector. Performance indicators can be referred to as the medium that harmonizes efforts to achieve the organization's reason for establishment and activities of public institutions. To do so, performance indicators are to be specific, measurable, attainable, realistic, relevant and timely.

Under such recognition, this chapter discusses the construction of performance governance model for public corporations using a case of power generation public corporation, Korea Electric Power Corporation (KEPCO).

II Theoretical discussion on performance management

Facing the call for promoting performance management for the public institutions, we firstly need to consider how to define the structure of performance management. While performance management for private firms revolves around clear indicators such as profit, there are various subjects and entities that public institutions consider. In other words, there are various stakeholders and conflicting entities with different opinions that what should be counted as performance of public institutions. Therefore, the problem of how to structure the performance management system in the public institutions start from the clarification of various interests to be reflected in the performance management system (Zarnmuto, 1988: 105). As such, performance management system covers a wide range of definition. It includes various perspectives such as a citizen-centered perspective on the outcome (Brudney and England, 1982: 132; Freeman and Sherwood, 1970: 8).

Performance management system is also for organization's success by focusing on the achievement of its operations and goals (Pollitt, 2001). The emphasis on the citizen-centric approach does not ignore the whole activity of planning, checking, evaluating and circulating in order to improve, enhance and increase performance perceived by organizations. Hence, performance management needs to be connected to major activities justifying the existence of public institutions (Gumm, 1989: 15; Bouckaert, 1992: 30; Hood, 1991: 3–19). In this regard, public institutions seek for autonomous responsibility as well as for improving their managerial efficiency.

Bouckaert and Halligan (2006) define conceptual factors of performance management by differentiating depth and span of performance. That is, the depth of performance is understood as the process of selecting the framework of performance analysis, measuring and analyzing data, incorporating processed data and using integrated data for performance improvement, while the span of performance is understood as input, process, output and result of performance management system. They also divide performance management model into four groups based the depth and span of performance: performance administration in which the focus is on performance measurement while lacking data integration and connection to application; management of performances in which individual performance management is satisfied, but not linked to management of entire system; performance management that links individual performance management to entire performance management system; and performance governance that applies the concept of social governance to performance management models. Figure 15.1 shows the performance management system proposed by Bouckaert and Halligan (2006) is multidimensional entity.

This paper focuses on three aspects of performance management of public corporation. First, scholarly opinions on the span of performance can be classified into horizontal and vertical approaches. That is, the horizontal approach takes the stance of understanding input, process, output and result of policy cycle as the span of performance measurement, while the vertical approach differentiates micro, meso and macro level (Bouckaert and Halligan, 2006). The Article 2 of

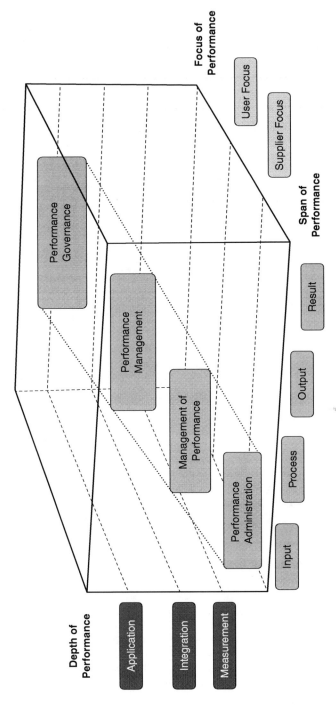

Figure 15.1 Conceptual factors for understanding of performance management system

Source: Reworked Using Concepts of Bouckaert and Halligan (2006) by the Author

Act on Evaluation of Government Work of the Korean government adopts the horizontal approach adopting as input, process, output and result.

Next, the analysis will be conducted with a focus on measurement, integration and application by adopting Bouckaert and Halligan's (2006) view of the depth of performance. It is crucial to see whether performance management system is limited to simple measurement of performance indicators including selection and data collection, whether appropriate compensation management system is structured through the integration of estimated performance indicators and whether integrated performance information is utilized in performance improvement and guarantee of responsibility.

Lastly, it will be analyzed whether performance management system is managed from the user-centered perspective away from the supplier-centered perspective. Also, it will be examined whether social system of value-sharing is structured by moving from a within-organization and input-centered relation model to a performance-centered and outside-organization paradigm. In particular, it is to be tested whether performance management system in administrative institutions is improved through performance governance. That is, one of the key administrative changes is the change in the entity. With rising demand for the quality and quantity of public service from the public and limited capacity of the government, quality management is sought after by any entity (Kolderie, 1983: 45). Therefore, autonomous change for performance management boils down to the participation of various interested parties by moving away from extant government-centric view. That is, in order to secure creativity and dynamics of various and complex modern society, various entities need to be able to participate in the process of performance management (Stoker, 1998: 39). As for free competition in the market, cooperative or collective participation by individual acting entities in the public sector is even understood as the legitimacy of the system (Curtis, 1999: 157). In particular, while the most inherently important factor in running performance management is cooperation with public officials (Wang and Gianakis, 1999), civil participation in performance management can be the driver that motivates politicians and political elite to focus on social goals with long-term vision by going beyond short-term performance management (Swindell and Kelly, 2000) and empowers the public with the spirit of participation (Burke, 1968: 288–294).

III Plan for constructing performance governance of public corporation

1 Case selection for constructing performance governance of public corporation

In order to analyze cases of construction of performance governance of public corporations, public corporations involved in power generation will be analyzed. Electric power public corporations are among the largest public corporations in Korea and greatly affect the economy.

Power generation business in Korea began by a deputy of the Emperor in 1989 as Han Sung Electric Corporation and was conducted by three power generation companies (Cho-Sun Electric, Kyeong-Sung Electric, Nam-Sun Electric) under the Japanese rule. That is, generation and transmission business is conducted by Cho-Sun Electric, while distribution business is carried out by Kyeong-Sung Electric and Nam-Sun Electric. Following the independence of Korea from Japan on August 15th, 1945, electric power business in Korea was operated by the three companies and later by merging them into Korea Electric Power Corporation (KEPCO) in July 1961. Afterwards, shares held by the public were acquired by the government and the company was designated as a national public corporation in December 1981. However, in order to resolve the organizational rigidity and enhance management efficiency resulting from the large size, KEPCO was selected to be privatized in 1987, and its power generation business was divested into six subsidiaries on April 2nd, 2001.

The number of participants in the electric power market is 1,222 as of the end of 2016. Among them, there are six public corporations including Korea Hydro & Nuclear Power, Korea South-East Power Corporation, Korea Midland Power Corporation, Korea Western Power Corporation, Korea Southern Power Corporation and Korea East-West Power Corporation. The market share of power generation by the six public corporations is 75.4 percent with the remaining 24.6 percent by private firms. Among the six public corporations in the power generation market, the share of generation capacity is 27.4 percent for Korea Hydro and Nuclear Power, followed by 10.3 percent for Korea East-West Power Corporation, 10.1 percent for Korea South-East Power Corporation, 9.8 percent for Korea Western Power Corporation, 9.3 percent for Korea Southern Power Corporation and 8.5 percent for Korea Midland Power Corporation (Korea Power Exchange, (2016: 6.), Electricity Market Statistics).

2 Plan for construction of performance governance with respect to performance span

1) From input orientation to result orientation

While performance management is understood to be a process of collaboratively promoting improvements in individual performance, performance management is recognized as the core system for eliminating inefficiency in the public sector and managing the integration of individuals and organization in achieving organizational goals at the macroscopic level (Behn, 2002; Pollitt, 2001). Therefore, performance management is a process of selecting strategic goals in line with the organization's mission and vision, constructing/evaluating performance goals and indicators and circulating the organization's mission and vision.

The important thing about the span of performance management is the need for change in perspective from output-oriented to result-oriented. The output is the objective side of measuring the efficiency with which to achieve certain goals, but result focuses on equity and responsiveness by measuring the subjective response of interested parties to output (Brudney and England, 1982: 127). For example, building generator through cutting costs is not an objective itself, but an intermediate step before reaching the final outcome. Even if the generator was cost-efficiently built with low costs, it is difficult to conclude that ultimate objective of building the generator was achieved.

Result-oriented performance management can contribute to turning input-oriented and organization-oriented perspective into external-oriented and responsibly business management practice, and promote proactive business with goal-oriented initiatives. In particular, it has the advantage of being able to eliminate unnecessary functions within the organization, to promote organizational restructuring around core capacities, and to strengthen actual realization of public interest externally through operation centered around responsibility about performance.

2 Plan for construction of performance governance within span

1 STATUS

Upon examination of missions and significant power strategies generation public corporations, most emphasize the role as a global leader, environment and

Table 15.1 Vision and major strategy of power generation public corporations

Institution	Vision and Major Strategy
Korea South-East Power Corporation	Clean and Smart Energy Leader – Strategy: Future Growth, Reinforcement of Power Generation Business
Korea Southern Power Corporation	Global Top Ten Power Company – Strategy: Enhancement of Competitiveness of Power Generation, Future Growth Engine, Strengthening of Core Capacity, Sustainable Management
Korea Western Power Corporation	Beyond Energy, Create Happiness – Strategy: Creation of Public Interest, Environment-Friendly Management, Enhancement of Internal Capacity, Strengthening of Business Competitiveness
Korea Midland Power Corporation	Global Top Class Energy Company – Strategy: Strengthening of Business Competitiveness, Future Growth Engine, Strategic Core Capacity, Sustainable Management
Korea East-West Power Corporation	Most Valuable Power Company – Strategy: Enhancement of Competitiveness of Power Generation, Future Growth Business, Core Capacity, Sustainable Management
Korea Hydro and Nuclear Power	Trusted Global Energy Lead – Strategy: Safety First Management, Internalization of Management Innovation, Restoration of Trust, Strengthening of Foundation for Future Growth

Source: Reconstructed from each institution's webpage

happiness of the public with Korea Hydro & Nuclear Power putting safety first management as its strategic goal.

However, there are several problems upon examination of performance indicators for major businesses of power generation companies.

First, while there is a strong tendency for a transition from input-oriented to result-oriented in terms of qualitative performance indicators, quantitative performance indicators are not closely linked to the institution's vision and strategic goals because they are limited to management of generation capacity and contracting of fuel.

Second, in terms of quantitative performance indicators for power generation public corporations, quantitative performance indicators are focused on operating indicators such as stoppages and purchases of fuel and thus do not include construction of generators related to medium-term power generation plan (procurement of power generation capacity, cost-cutting, prevention of accidents, etc.) and new business development (new businesses home and abroad, new regeneration energy, R&D business, etc.).

Third, in the case of Korea Hydro and Nuclear Power, nuclear power generation and facility safety business are measured by contribution to electric capacity and competitiveness of unplanned loss rate, but actual performance indicators are limited to reduction in unplanned loss and cross-country comparison. In particular, there is a lack of consideration of performance goal in relation to strategy on nuclear strategy and much focus is devoted to moderating stoppage.

Fourth, in order to realize each generator's vision and strategy, there is a need for a systematic linkage between performance goals and performance indicators, but there is a lack of performance goals and performance indicators that can help promoting future growth and becoming a global leader as they are limited to operations and fuel supply. In particular, while all power generation firms are proposing goals related to future growth, performance goals and performance indicators related to future growth are currently missing.

Fifth, while power generation firms' contribution to the daily life of the public is very important, performance indicators related to the environment are insignificant. Although much emphasis is placed on environment in vision and strategy, performance indicators related to environment-friendly factors are assigned a weight of only 2.

2 PLAN FOR IMPROVEMENT

The following items need to be considered to strengthen performance management system within the span of power generation public corporations.

First, in order to constructively tackle performance management for major businesses of power generation public corporations, the business scope must be clearly defined as well as corresponding performance indicators. Major businesses pursued by the institutions need to be selected in line with performance goals of each business in the reflection of the needs of market and customers based on founding charter and strategic standards.

Table 15.2 Current performance indicators for major business of power generation public corporations

Institution	Major Business and Performance Indicators	Formula
Five Power Generation Firms	1 Generation Capacity Operations (34)	
	(1) Reduction in Unplanned Loss (13)	$\dfrac{Unplanned\ Loss}{Standard\ Capacity} \times 100$
	(2) Global Competitiveness of Stoppage Rate (9)	$Formula = \dfrac{Stoppage\ Time}{Total\ Time}$ $Performance = \dfrac{Institution's\ Stoppage\ Rate}{NERC\ Stoppage\ Rate}$
	(3) Generation Capacity Operations (Qualitative) (12)	Plan-Do-Check-Act (Nine-Grade Qualitative Evaluation)
	2 Contracting Operation of Fuel (16)	
	(1) Enhancement of Competitiveness of Bituminous Coal Raw Price (10)	(Improvement in Internal Improvement) x 0.8 + (Enhancement of Global Competitiveness) x 0.2
	(2) Contracting Operation of Fuel (Qualitative) (6)	Plan-Do-Check-Act (Nine-Grade Qualitative Evaluation)
Korea Hydro and Nuclear Power	1 Nuclear Power Generation and Capacity Safety Business (21)	
	(1) Contribution of Nuclear Power Generation to National Electric Supply (7)	$\dfrac{Benchmark\ Capacity - Planned\ Loss - Unplanned\ loss}{Benchmark\ Capacity}$
	(2) Competitiveness of Unplanned Loss Rate Among Development 7 Nations (7)	$\dfrac{KHNP\ Unplanned\ Loss\ Rate}{Global\ No.1\ Unplanned\ Loss\ Rate}$
	(3) Nuclear Power Generation and Capacity Safety Business (Qualitative) (7)	Plan-Do-Check-Act (Nine-Grade Qualitative Evaluation)
	2 Nuclear Safety Management Business (29)	
	(1) Safety Management Index of Nuclear Plant (9)	$\dfrac{Riskiness\ of\ Power\ Plant - Riskiness\ Benchmark}{Riskiness\ Benchmark}$
	(2) Operating Index of Overall Safety of Nuclear Facility (9)	$\dfrac{Sum\ of\ Overall\ Safety\ Indices\ for\ Operating\ Nuclear\ Plants}{Number\ of\ Operating\ Plants}$
	(2) Nuclear Safety Management Business (Qualitative) (11)	Plan-Do-Check-Act (Nine-Grade Qualitative Evaluation)

Source: Modified the Ministry of Strategy and Finance (2016), Public Institution Management Evaluation Manual

* () denotes the weight of evaluation indicator

Second, while the supply of fuel and efficient management of generation capacity are important indicators, these need to be linked values to be achieved such as satisfaction and happiness of the public. While securing economics of fuel purchases, prevention of generation capacity and improvement and enhancement of facility are necessary from the perspective of the supplier side of power generation, their ultimate performance goals (e.g. electric welfare) need to be linked.

Third, development of new businesses and expansion of performance indicators are needed. When most of the fuels are comprised of fire power from coal and nuclear, the public's anxiety over power generation has intensified. Therefore, there is a need for conversion to result-oriented performance indicators and expansion of performance indicators regarding new regeneration energy business such as new business development and R&D to carry out citizen-oriented business. In particular, environment-related performance indicators need to be considered for sustainable management.

Fourth, indicators need to be differentiated into safety, efficiency and future growth because the interest in safety of nuclear energy is most important. While keeping performance indicators on the safety management index and overall nuclear facility safety index in place, performance indicators such as earthquake and other disasters need to be reflected. As recent earthquakes near the sites of

Table 15.3 Types of performance bias

Researcher	Type	Content
Smith (1995)	Tunnel vision	Tendency to select performance indicators among various other indicators that are easy to measure
	Suboptimization	Tendency to focus on partial output instead of entire performance
	Myopia	Focus on short-term performance unrelated to achievement of long-term goal
	Measure fixation	Tendency to focus on measured indicators themselves instead of desirable results
	Misrepresentation	Tendency to report wrong or biased performance to disguise performance
	Misinterpretation	Tendency to misinterpret measured results in favor of themselves
	Ossification	Tendency to maintain performance indicators lacking effectiveness as indicators
	Gaming	Intended behavior to preempt strategic advantage besides proposed information above
Hood (2006, 2007)	Ratchet effect	Lowering target to facility target achievement and reduce the burden on selecting maximum target in the next measurement period
	Threshold effect	Tendency to achieve as low performance above the threshold as possible rather than overachieve
	Output distortion	Tendency to focus on work measured work and pay less attention to unmeasured work

Data: Reworked from Yoo and Kim (2016)

nuclear power plants heightened anxiety of the public, performance indicators related to earthquakes and other disasters need to be included. In addition, while efforts to reduce unplanned loss need to continue from the perspective of efficiency, indicators related to efficient management of generation capacity need to be strengthened.

Fifth, global perspectives related to power generation from coal, water and nuclear need to be strengthened. In particular, the possibility of medium-to-long term supply of fuel needs to be analyzed from a global perspective and strategic mind toward generation facility needs to be in place. Current performance indicators take the form of simply comparing with overseas generation facility and status and make it difficult to derive conclusive meaning. Construction of performance indicators from global perspective needs to be linked to performance indicators suggestive of the direction of future change, instead of simple comparison.

Sixth, environmental factors related to power generation need to be reflected. Current performance indicators lack indicators related to power generation and instead focus on securing power generation capacity and supply from the institution-centered view. By preventing factors negatively affecting the environment due to power generation, it is necessary to construct performance indicators that safeguard the stable life of the public. In particular, the institution in responsible of power generation must act proactively in preventing damage near power plant including fine dust and nuclear radiation.

3 Plan for construction of performance governance with respect to performance depth

1 From measurement orientation to application orientation

While measurement and evaluation of performance constitute an important part of performance management, it is undesirable to recognize the result of performance measurement as a tool for offering a reward to individuals or departments. Performance management should not be limited to the level of simple measurement and the ability to apply performance information needs to be cultivated in order to utilize measured performance information for improvement of the organization (Martocchio, 2009; Selden, 2008).

In order to enhance the depth of performance management, the concept and definition of performance management that are in line with performance goals need to be made clear, the methodology for performance measurement needs to be decided, the step of measuring and analyzing collected data takes place first, measured performance information is to be combined with the organization's vision and strategic goals, and plans for applying performance information for sustainable growth and development of the organization must be prepared (Van Dooren et al., 2010: 55).

Measured performance information becomes a tool for examining the overall operational process of the organization and rechecking basic data for incentive payment and vision and strategic goals of the organization. Therefore, performance indicators unrelated to strategic goals can be constructed in the selection process and the paradoxical incident can happen when flawed data exists in the measurement itself (Adcroft and Willis, 2005; Bohte and Meier, 2000). Also, it is important to secure reliability of data measurement because measured performance data is used in all aspects of performance management (Barrett and Greene, 2000).

Application of performance information can be the ultimate factor of performance management and is the medium that strengthens an internal and external responsibilities of the organization. Types of application of performance information can be categorized as hard use and soft use with hard use implying application as internal control tool for organizational and human resource management and incentive and soft use implying application as a tool for prioritization of strategic goals (Van Dooren et al., 2010).

2 Plan for construction of performance governance within span

1 STATUS

Performance management of power generation companies in relation to measurement, integration and application of performance indicators has the following limitations.

First, both internal and external integration and application of performance indicators are unsatisfactory because the suitability of performance goal, performance indicator and performance measurement is conducted by the external institution.

Second, there is lack of performance indicators on future growth businesses related to vision and strategic goals of power generation public corporations, methods for performance measurement are institution-oriented, and integration and application of performance among power generation public corporations are less than satisfactory.

Third, the work stoppage is included in two indicators such as reduction in unplanned loss (weight of 13 points) and global competitiveness of stoppage rate (weight of nine points), which are quantitative performance indicators for power generation public corporations. Therefore, when a stoppage occurs, both performance indicators of power generation firms will be affected and performance score declines. Even if power generation public corporations achieve good performance in other indicators, work stoppage lowers overall performance score.

Fourth, in the case of Korea Hydro and Nuclear Power, there is an issue of reliability in methodology and data of performance measurement regarding performance indicators from a global perspective. That is, while the management evaluation manual directs compliance with WANO standard, it differs from the standard of IAEA and differs in the measurement of unplanned loss. There are ambiguous cases in comparison from the global perspective. For example, an operator of German nuclear power plant owns and operates nuclear power plants in Sweden and the standard of comparison differs depending on whether the Swedish nuclear power plant will be understood from ownership and operation or whether it will be understood from the perspective of local areas. It is difficult to draw implications from cross-country comparison due to the problem of performance measurement itself.

Fifth, error in performance measurement hinders integration and application of performance. When there is error in performance measurement, the probability of integration and application becomes lower. It is important to secure accuracy and reliability of performance measurement.

2 PLAN FOR IMPROVEMENT

In order to strengthen performance management system in terms of the depth for power generation public corporations, the following items need to be considered.

First, it is necessary to examine whether performance indicators related to the founding charter and strategic objectives of the organization are in place, whether the selection of objective for performance indicators, and whether performance measurement is being conducted reasonably need to be continuously checked.

Second, in the case of power generation public corporations, indicators for effort on the improvement of air quality are newly added (expected to be applied in management evaluation from 2018), and target assignment method is used for

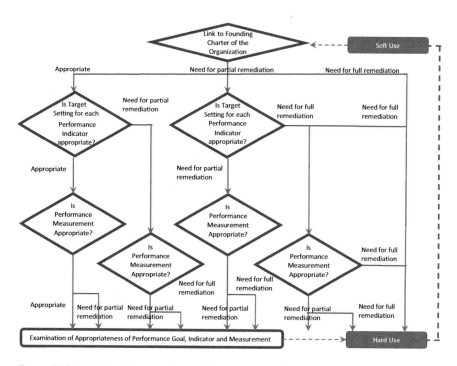

Figure 15.2 Analysis of appropriate performance target, indicator and measurement

performance measurement. That is, Ministry of Trade, Industry and Energy conducts evaluation of target assignment method for improvement in environment, but there is no mean in measurement if an easily achievable target from the perspective of the institution is proposed. In particular, targets for improvement in the environment must be proposed in a challenging way from the perspective of the standard of international community and promotion of business innovation in power generation.

Third, plans for separating an indicator for a stoppage from indices of reduction in unplanned loss and global competitiveness index for stoppage rate and lowering its current weight must be considered.

Fourth, when measuring global indices for Korea Hydro and Nuclear Power, standards for cross-country comparison must be maintained the same and assume benchmarking of best cases for comparison.

Fifth, in order for performance measurement, integration and application to be organically linked, continuous improvement in the method for performance measurement and reliability in data must be secured. In addition, data from performance measurement must be utilized in not only hard uses such as organizational and human resource management and incentives, but also in connection with vision and strategic goals.

4 Plan for construction of performance governance with respect to focus on performance

1 From supplier orientation to user orientation

There are many stakeholders in the public sector and it is difficult to define targets demanded by various stakeholders that often conflict with one another. In particular, arbitration of stakeholders is often decided in the political context. Due to the highly complex nature of interests, the public sector tends to cater the focus of performance on the institution-oriented thinking and neglects the perspective of the public who is the user.

In our case, while operated by six power generation firms according to Power Industry Structure Reorganization, the monopolistic structure of operations is still maintained. Monopoly in supply of service makes elasticity of price to demand difficult and limits the choice of the user. Also, the exclusive tendency of decision-making process for the supply of service restricts a participative the decision-making. That is, they are recognized as the sole provider of power and there is lack of a circulating system of reflecting opinion in decision from the perspective of the user. Therefore, efforts to amend the institution's vision and strategy through user-oriented thinking are needed.

From the supplier-oriented perspective, the institution must focus on the value to the public. Instead of simply generating and supplying power, the institution must focus on value creation and consider the quality of service and timeliness of supply in performance management.

Table 15.4 Scope of new regeneration energy accepted by countries

Country	Solar Heat	Solar Panel	Wind	Water	Geothermal Volcanic	Geothermal Deep Heat	Geothermal Shallow Heat	Bio Mass	Waste	Landfill Gas	Hydrogen	Fuel Cell	Coal Gasification	Vacuum Residue
IEA	O	O	O	O	O	O	O	O	△		O			
EU	O	O	O	O	O	O	O	O	△	O	O			
USA	O	O	O	△	O		O	O	△	△	△			
Japan	O	O	O	O	O	O	O	O	△	O	△			
Korea	O	O	O	O	O	O	O	O	O	O	O	O	O	O

Source: National Assembly Research Service of Korea (2016: 9), *Plan for Improvement of Supply and Development of New Regeneration Energy*

2 Plan for construction of performance governance within focus

1 STATUS

Upon examination of performance management of power generation public institutions through the user-oriented perspective, there are following limitations.

First, current performance indicators for power generation public institutions are derived from the institution-oriented thinking. As work stoppage and reduction in unplanned loss are recognized as important indicators by all power generation firms, there is a tendency to manage reduction in unplanned loss from the perspective of the institution. Performance indicators are merely treated as a tool for achieving high score and consideration of the user's perspective is becoming rare. That is, myopia in which short-term performance is pursued instead of achievement of long-term goals and measure fixation in which focus is on performance indicators themselves instead of desirable outcome are happening.

Second, while environmental problems due to coal power and nuclear power generation need to be considered, environmental problems as performance indicators are not sufficiently selected from the user-oriented perspective. In addition, there is no clear system of performance goal and indicators that can respond to earthquakes occurring near nuclear power plants.

Third, current performance indicators lack a system of indicators on new regeneration energy and R&D as future growth engine when there is a strong preference for environmentally friendly regeneration energy instead of coal power and nuclear power from the perspective of the user. Current system of indicators includes coal power as part of future growth industry and therefore is not consistent with the image of new industry. In particular, the scope of new regeneration energy business is too broad compared to that of other countries.

Fourth, while benchmarking is being conducted for various analyses in relation to the construction of performance indicators at institutions, there are unsatisfactory cases showing lack of participation by the user. Participation of the user has the drawback of higher decision-making costs, time, lack of concerted decision and lack of expertise, but decision-making through participation of the user may be consistent with ultimate objective pursued by performance indicator.

1 PLAN FOR IMPROVEMENT

In order to strengthen performance management system from the perspective of focus of power generation public institutions, the following items need to be considered.

First, it seems necessary to redefine the scope of unplanned loss from the perspective of the user instead of the perspective of the institution with respect to unplanned loss among current performance indicators. In particular, measuring unplanned loss by separating peak period from non-peak period can help understand the perspective of the user. In addition, while various alternatives are being explored to secure economies of fuel supply, plan to stably supply fuel in an

Table 15.5 Rate of mandatory supply for new regeneration energy

Year	2015	2016	2017	2018	2019	2020	2021	2022	2023	2024–
Rate (%)	3.0	3.5	4.0	4.5	5.0	6.0	7.0	8.0	9.0	10.0

Source: Act on Vitalization of Development, Use and Dissemination of New Energy and Regeneration Energy, Enforcement Ordinance Schedule 3

environmentally friendly manner from the perspective of the user needs to be contemplated.

Second, there is need to consider environmental factors of coal power and nuclear power plants from the perspective of the user. In order to achieve environmental welfare of the public, indicators for environment management need to be selected and administered in the medium-to-long term. In addition, while power generation public corporations propose indicators for environmental evaluation such as green product purchase rate, CO_2 output, SOx output, NOx output, Dust output, coal ash recycling rate, desulfurized plaster recycling rate and industrial water recycling rate, they need to be transformed into a system of performance indicator with legal force and let the society propose goals.

Third, consideration of new regeneration energy as future growth business needs to be made. While current performance indicator partly includes coal power as future growth business, coal power needs to be excluded from future growth business. In particular, Article 12–5 of Act on New Regeneration Energy defines RPS system and Schedule 3 of the same Act defines the rate of mandatory supply.

Act on Vitalization of Development, Use and Dissemination of New Energy and Regeneration Energy defines "Areas turning existing fossil fuel into use and converting re-useable energy such as sunlight, water, geothermal heat, rain, biomass into use including solar energy, bio energy, wind, water, fuel, coal liquefaction and gasification, vacuum residue gasification, oceanic energy, water energy, geothermal energy and hydrogen energy, etc." as new regeneration energy. While new regeneration energy lacks economics due to high initial investments and low-price competitiveness, its importance and need for development is increasing as a solution to depletion of fossil fuels and environment problems.

Fourth, as a way of converting performance management system of power generation public institutions into user-oriented, plans to assure the participation of the user with legislative tool need to be considered. Regularization of participation of civil associations and strengthening of disclosure of indicators are needed.

V Lessons learned and conclusion

1 Lessons learned

Power generation business in Korea began by a deputy of the Emperor in 1989 as Han Sung Electric Corporation and was conducted by three power generation companies under the Japanese rule. Following the independence of Korea from Japan on August 15th, 1945, electric power business in Korea was operated by the three companies and later by the merged Korea Electric Power Corporation (KEPCO) established in July 1961. However, as the large monopolistic public corporation with its size exceeding that of entire Korean economy under the government control, KEPCO reached its limit in terms of management efficiency. Therefore, the Korean government sold a part of the government-owned shares in KEPCO to the market in 1998 to enhance efficiency of KEPCO and pursued the policy of dividing its power generation business into six subsidiaries on April 2nd, 2001. The market share of power generation by the 6 public corporations is 75 percent with the remaining 25 percent by private firms.

In order to efficiently manage performance of power generation business, the focus on input indicator needs to be changed to a focus on result indicator with the need for consideration of electric welfare in addition to indicators such as fuel supply, efficient management of power generation capacity and continuous expansion of performance indicator on new regeneration energy and R&D. Second, in order to organically link performance measurement, integration and application, ratchet effect needs to be eliminated by using medium-to-long-term target assignment, and performance integration and application from the perspective of users, such as contribution to supply and demand of electricity is needed instead of performance measurement centered around total revenue. Also, in addition to inflexible application such as organizational human resource management and incentive based on data from performance measurement, flexible application by linking to vision and strategy is needed. Third, in order to transform performance management system of power generation public corporations into customer-centered, legislative guarantee of customer participation and environmentally friendly factors of coal power and nuclear power plants need to be considered.

2 Conclusion

Performance management is understood as an important institutional tool for structurally achieving strategic goals in accordance with mission and vision of the organization. In particular, while there has been a lack of interest in performance management due to the monopolistic position of the public sector as opposed to the private sector, performance-oriented management technique is becoming a managerial system to bestow responsibility both internally and externally and contribute to the strengthening of internal capability. Therefore, performance management of power generation public institutions enjoying monopolistic positions needs to be systematically introduced and administered in order to enhance their status as public institutions.

In order to enhance performance management, efforts to integrate performance management from various perspectives such as the scope, depth and focus of performance need to be strengthened. That is, there is a need for the transition from input orientation to result in orientation, and integration and application of measured data in performance improvement must be assumed. Furthermore, institution-oriented performance management needs to transform into user-oriented performance management. That is, individual performance management needs to be converted into performance governance model system by applying the concept of social governance to performance management model that is linked to an overall performance management system.

References

Adcroft, A., and Willis, R. (2005). The (Un)intended Outcome of Public Sector Performance Measurement. *International Journal of Public Sector Management*, *18*(5), 386–400.

Barrett, K., and Greene, R. (2000). Truth in Measurement. *Governing*, *13*, 86–88.

Behn, R. D. (2002). The Psychological Barriers to Performance Management. *Public Performance & Management Review*, *26*(1), 5–25.

Board of Audit and Inspection of Korea. (2005). *The Manual for Policy Accomplishment Evaluation*. Board of Audit and Inspection of Korea.

Bohte, J., and Meier, K. J. (2000). Goal Displacement: Assessing the Motivation for Organizational Cheating. *Public Administration Review*, *60*(2), 173–182.

Bouckaert, G. (1992). Public Productivity in Retrospective. In M. Holzer (ed.), *Public Productivity Handbook*. New York, NY: Marcel Decker.

Bouckaert, G., and Halligan, J. (2006). Performance and Performance Management. In B. Peters Guy and J. Pierre (eds.), *Handbook of Public Policy* (pp. 443–459). London: Sage.

Brudney, J. L., and England, R. E. (1982). Urban Policy Making and Subjective Service Evaluation: Are They Compatible? *Public Administration Review*, *42*(2), 125–143.

Burke, E. M. (1968). Citizen Participation Strategies. *Journal of the American Institute of Planner*, *34*(4), 288–294.

Curtis, D. (1999). Institutional Options for Local Governance or Community Self- Management. *Local Governance*, *25*(3), 153–166.

Freeman, H. F., and Sherwood, C. (1970). *Social Research and Social Policy*. Englewood Cliffs, NJ: Prentice-Hall.

Gawthrop, L. C. (1984). *Public Sector Management: Systems and Ethics*. Bloomington: University of Indiana Press.

Grindle, M. S. (1980). Policy Content and Context in Implementation. In M. S. Grindle (ed.), *Politics and Policy Implementation in the Third World*. Princeton, NJ: Princeton University Press.

Gumm, L. (1989). A Public Management Approach to the NHS. *Health Services Management Research*, *2*(1), 12–35.

Hood, C. V. (1991). A Public Management for All Seasons. *Public Administration*, *69*(1), 3–19.

Hood, C. V. (2006). Gaming in the Target World: The Targets Approach to Managing British Public Services. *Public Administration Review*, *66*(4), 127–153.

Hood, C. V. (2007). Public Service Management by Numbers: Why Does It Vary? Where Has It Come From/ What Are the Gaps and the Puzzles? *Public Money and Management*, *27*(2), 53–78.

Im, D. J. (2009). The Effect of Reflux Factors on Reflux Activity and Work Performance. *Korean Government Research*, *18*(2), 225–251.

Jo, C. H. (2002). *Restructuring and Privatization of Electricity Business*. Seoul: Korea institute of industrial economies.

Kang, H. S. (2004). Redesigning Organizational Performance Measurement System: From the Perspective of Organizational Learning Theory. *Korea Policy Institute*, *13*(2), 117–142.

Kettl, D., and Kelman, S. (2007). *Reflections on 21st Century Government Management*. Washington, DC: IBM Center for the Business of Government.

Kim, B. C. (2006). *A Case Study of Auditor's Performance Audit: Focusing on National R&D Projects*. Doctoral Thesis, Sungkyunkwan University.

Kolderie, T. (1983). Rethinking Public Service Delivery. In B. H. Moore and ICMA staff (eds.), *The Entrepreneur in Local Government*. New York, NY: The International City Management Association.

Kong, B. C. (2004). Linking Evaluation and Budget Management to Performance Management. *Korea Policy Institute*, *13*(2), 67–89.

Korea Power Exchange. (2016). *Electricity Market Statistics*, June. Korea Power Exchange.

Kum, J. D., and Lee, S. D. (2009). An Empirical Study on the Negative Effects of Performance Management System. *Korean Society and Administration Research, Korea Policy Institute*, *20*(25), 347–377.

Lasswell, H. D. (1975). Research in Policy Analysis: The Intelligence and Appraisal Functions. In F. Green and N. Polsby (eds.), *Handbook of Political Science*, Vol. 6. Reading, MA: Addison-Wesley Publishing Co.

Lee, G. H. (2010). *Issues and Policy Direction of Budget Management by Local Government. E-KRILA FOCUS*. Seoul: Korea institute of local public administration.

Lee, G. H., and Im, D. J. (2009). *Analysis of the Actual Condition of Satisfaction Index in Performance Management Plan and Improvement Plan*. Seoul: Korea Institute of Public Administration.

Lee, S. H. (2008). A Study on the Successful Management Plan of the Public Sector BSC. *Korean Government Scholarship*, *42*(1), 253–272.

Lee, S. H., and Jo, J. Y. (2008). *A Study on Factors Affection the Acceptance of Performance Evaluation System*. Korea public administration summer presentation.

Martocchio, J. J. (2009). *Strategic Compensation: Human Resource Management Approach*. Prentice-Hall.

McCoy, E. (1992). The Management of Public Provision. *Australian Journal of Public Administration*, *51*(4), 420–439.

MOCIE. (1999). *Basic Plan of Electricity Business Restructuring*. Republic of Korea: Ministry of Trade, Industry and Energy.

MOCIE. (2002). *Second National Energy Basic Plan (2002–2011)*. Republic of Korea: Ministry of Trade, Industry and Energy.

Moon, Y. S. (2001). Meta-Evaluation by the Framework Act on Government Business Evaluation. *Korea Society for Policy Analysis and Evaluation*, *11*(1), 151–151.

Park, H. B., and Choi, S. M. (2009). Factors Affecting the Effectiveness of Self-Evaluation of Government Services. *Policy Analysis*, *19*(4), 181–208.

Park, H. Y., and Joo, J. B. (2009). *Analysis of Actual Condition and Effectiveness of Performance Management of Local Governments*. Seoul: Korea Institute of Local Administration.

Pollitt, C. (2001). Integrating Financial Management and Performance Management. *OECD Journal on Budgeting*, *1*(2), 7–37.

Rho, H. J. (2007). Public Value Creation and policy Competence. *National Assembly of Budget Office*, 9, 86–97.

Selden, S. C. (2008). *Human Capital: Tools and Strategies for the Public Sector*. CQ Press.

Shin, S. H. (2009). Government Performance Management and Auditor's Role. *Audit*, *101*, 72–80.

Smith, P. (1995). On the Unintended Consequences of Publishing Performance Data in the Public Sector. *International Journal of Public Administration, 18*(2), 79–94.

Song, S. G., and Baek, J. K. (2009). The Effect of Performance Management System Perceived Fairness on BSC Organizational Performance. *Industrial Economics Research, 22*(5), 2313–2330.

Stoker, G. (1998). Public-Private Partnerships and Urban Governance. In J. Pierre (ed.), *Partnerships in Urban Governance* (pp. 34–51). London: Macmillan Press.

Swindell, D., and Kelly, J. (2000). Liking Citizen Satisfaction Data to Performance Measures. *Public Productivity and Management Review, 24*(1), 30–52.

Van Dooren, W., Bouckaert, G., and Halligan, J. (2010). *Performance Management in the Public Sector.* Oxon: Routledge.

Wang, X., and Gianakis, G. A. (1999). Public Official's Attitudes Toward Subjective Performance Measures. *Public Productivity and Management Review, 22*(4), 537–553.

Won, G. H. (2007). Electric Power Industry Restructuring and ROE: The Case of Korea Electric Power Corporation. *Energy Policy, 35*(10), 5080–5090.

Won, G. H. (2010). Plan for Efficiency of Performance Management System for Local Governments. In *Social Science Studies.* Chungnam University, Research Center for Social Science, *21*(4), 23–48.

Yoo, S. H., and Kim, J. H. (2016). *Plan for Enhancement of Effectiveness of Management System of Financial Performance Goal.* Board of Audit and Inspection, Audit and Inspection Research Institute.

Yoon, S. J., and Jo, T. J. (2010). Analysis of the Influence Factors on the Organizational Commitment and Job Satisfaction of the Central Government Performance Management System. *Government Research, 16*(2), 48–72.

Yoon, S. J., Lee, G. H., and Hong, J. H. (2008). *Comparison Analysis of Overseas Case on Performance Management System.* Seoul: Korea Institute of Public Administration.

Zarnmuto, R. F. (1988). Organizational Adaption: Some Implication of Organizational Ecology for Strategic Choice. *Journal of Management Studies, 25,* 105–120.

Index

Note: Page numbers in *italic* indicate a figure and page numbers in **bold** indicate a table on the corresponding page.